*The Politics of Identity in
Greek Sicily and Southern Italy*

GREEKS OVERSEAS
Series Editors
Carla Antonaccio and Nino Luraghi

This series presents a forum for new interpretations of Greek settlement in the ancient Mediterranean in its cultural and political aspects. Focusing on the period from the Iron Age until the advent of Alexander, it seeks to undermine the divide between colonial and metropolitan Greeks. It welcomes new scholarly work from archaeological, historical, and literary perspectives, and invites interventions on the history of scholarship about the Greeks in the Mediterranean.

The Politics
of Identity in
Greek Sicily and
Southern Italy

MARK R. THATCHER

OXFORD
UNIVERSITY PRESS

OXFORD

UNIVERSITY PRESS

Oxford University Press is a department of the University of Oxford. It furthers
the University's objective of excellence in research, scholarship, and education
by publishing worldwide. Oxford is a registered trade mark of Oxford University
Press in the UK and certain other countries.

Published in the United States of America by Oxford University Press
198 Madison Avenue, New York, NY 10016, United States of America.

Library of Congress Control Number: 2021940309

ISBN 978-0-19-758644-0

DOI: 10.1093/oso/9780197586440.001.0001

1 3 5 7 9 8 6 4 2

Printed by Integrated Books International, United States of America

To my grandfather, Curt Roy, whose passion for history taught me to be a lifelong learner, to always be curious, and to keep wanting to learn more.

Contents

List of Figures

Maps

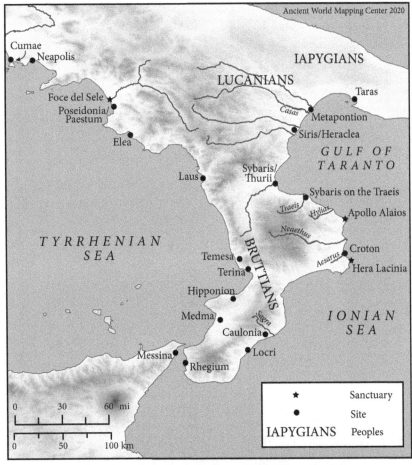

FIG. 0.1 Map of southern Italy. By the Ancient World Mapping Center.

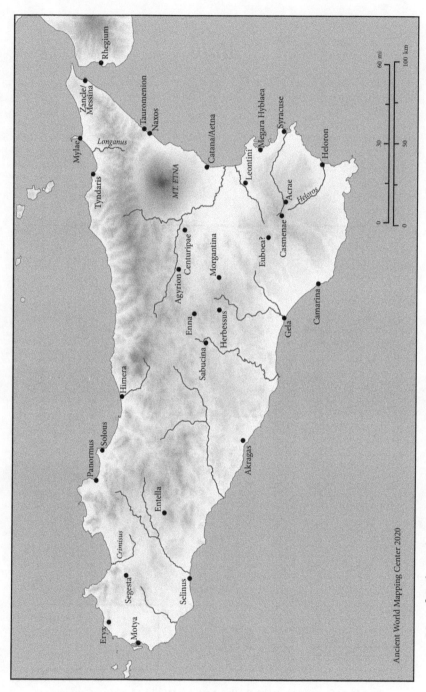

FIG. 0.2 Map of Sicily. By the Ancient World Mapping Center.

Ancient World Mapping Center 2020

Acknowledgments

THIS BOOK HAS been shaped by innumerable teachers, colleagues, and friends over the last two decades, beginning with my first teachers: my parents, Cathy and Steve Thatcher, and my grandfather, Curt Roy. My interest in Sicily was first piqued by my trip with the Intercollegiate Center for Classical Studies in Rome in the fall of 2002; one view of the lights of Messina across the Straits from Reggio, and I never looked back. This project began as a dissertation at Brown University, and I am grateful to my committee members, Sue Alcock and David Konstan; Chris Witmore also gave helpful advice on archaeological matters. Thanks are due above all to my adviser and mentor, Kurt Raaflaub, whose generous willingness to read drafts, provide expertise, and offer advice was critical both during the dissertation process and ever since. The dissertation became a book only through the support of Carla Antonaccio, who believed in this book even before I did, and Stefan Vranka at Oxford University Press, who was willing to wait for it. Both of them gave much-needed assistance and advice over the years. I am grateful also to the anonymous readers for the press, whose critical eyes vastly improved the final product.

Writing is a lonely endeavor, and so the conversation, companionship, and support of my colleagues in the Boston College Department of Classical Studies, especially Kendra Eshleman, Gail Hoffman, and Chris Polt, were and are particularly important. I similarly benefited from the warm encouragement of past colleagues and friends at the University of Arizona, Creighton University, The Ohio State University, and Brown University. The twice-annual meeting of junior faculty in New England known as MACTe has been a source of friendship and advice; several chapters were workshopped with this group and emerged better for it.

On the other hand, writing is also a collaborative process. I am grateful to Carla Antonaccio, Radcliffe Edmonds, Virginia Lewis, Dominic Machado, Brian McConnell, Kathryn Morgan, Nigel Nicholson, Kurt Raaflaub, and Carrie Sulosky Weaver, who have all been valuable interlocutors over the years and whose comments on various parts of the project at different stages were useful. Hanne Eisenfeld also read virtually every word of this book, often many times, and always with helpful suggestions. Needless to say, all remaining errors are my own. Brian McConnell was kind enough to welcome me onto his excavation team at Palikè, Sicily, in 2017, an experience from which I learned a lot, and to assist in many other ways. Finally, I owe a considerable debt to my teachers, especially Charles Fornara, Jinny Jensen, and Robert Wallace, who were not involved in this project but have nevertheless deeply influenced my approach to the ancient world.

Generous support for this project was given by the Dean's Office of the Morrissey College of Arts and Sciences at Boston College and by the Behrakis Endowment for Hellenic Studies. I particularly thank Mary Crane for her un-canny ability to find untapped pots of money, and both Kendra Eshleman and Gail Rider for further assistance in this area. A Tytus summer fellowship at the University of Cincinnati supported early progress. Two separate stays at the Fondation Hardt in Vandoeuvres, Switzerland, one of which was funded by a bursary, vastly accelerated the revisions to the manuscript, and a semester of leave from teaching through BC's Faculty Fellowship program enabled its completion.

Critical assistance in securing the images was given by Gioconda Lamagna, Laura Maniscalco, Brian McConnell, Antonella Pautasso, Chris Strauber, and Carrie Sulosky Weaver. Lindsay Holman and her team at the Ancient World Mapping Center drafted the area maps, and Daniel Weiss drew the city plans. Although I have drawn on the relevant Loeb volumes and other widely used translations, especially Verity 2008 and Hammond 2009, all translations are my own unless otherwise noted. Portions of chapter 3 previously appeared in somewhat different form in the *Bulletin of the Institute of Classical Studies*, as Thatcher 2012.

Special thanks are due to Gail Rider, administrator extraordinaire, who makes the thorniest practical problems easy, and to the Interlibrary Loan Department at the Boston College Libraries, whose staff never failed to find the most obscure books and articles. This book was completed during the COVID-19 pandemic, and I want to thank the Boston College staff members in particular for their valiant work in keeping the libraries open and academic work continuing under these most difficult circumstances.

My deepest thanks are due to my family. Our beloved cat, Isabel, sustained me with her warm and fuzzy presence during the writing process; while she did not live to curl up on the final product, she contributed greatly to its progress. Above all, Hanne Eisenfeld, my partner in life and in work, gave constant companionship and support during the entire gestation of this project. It is a cliché to say this in acknowledgments but true nonetheless: I couldn't have done it without you.

List of Abbreviations

THE ABBREVIATIONS OF ancient authors and works follow the *Oxford Classical Dictionary*. The abbreviations for journals follow the conventions of *L'Année Philologique*.

BNJ   Worthington, I., ed. 2007. *Brill's New Jacoby*. Leiden: Brill
               Online.

*CAH*² IV   Boardman, J., N. G. L. Hammond, D. M. Lewis, and
               M. Ostwald, eds. 1988. *Cambridge Ancient History*, Vol. 4: *Persia,
               Greece, and the Western Mediterranean, c. 525–479 BC*. 2nd ed.
               Cambridge: Cambridge University Press.

*CAH*² V   Lewis, D. M., J. Boardman, J. K. Davies, and M. Ostwald, eds.
               1992. *Cambridge Ancient History*, Vol. 5: *The Fifth Century BC*.
               2nd ed. Cambridge: Cambridge University Press.

*CAH*² VI   Lewis, D. M., J. Boardman, S. Hornblower, and M. Ostwald,
               eds. 1994. *Cambridge Ancient History*, Vol. 6: *The Fourth Century
               BC*. 2nd ed. Cambridge: Cambridge University Press.

*CAH*² VII.1   Walbank, F. W., A. E. Astin, M. W. Frederiksen, and
               R. M. Ogilvie, eds. 1984. *Cambridge Ancient History*, Vol. 7,
               Part 1: *The Hellenistic Age*. 2nd ed. Cambridge: Cambridge
               University Press.

*CAH*² VII.2   Walbank, F. W., A. E. Astin, M. W. Frederiksen, and R. M.
               Ogilvie, eds. 1990. *Cambridge Ancient History*, Vol. 7, Part 2: *The
               Rise of Rome to 220 BC*. 2nd ed. Cambridge: Cambridge
               University Press.

CT   Hornblower, Simon. 1990–2008. *A Commentary on Thucydides*.
               3 vols. Oxford: Clarendon Press.

DK   Diels, H., and W. Kranz. 1952. *Fragmente der Vorsokratiker*. 6th
               ed. Berlin: Weidmann.

FGE   Page, D. L., ed. 1981. *Further Greek Epigrams.*
           Cambridge: Cambridge University Press.
FGrH   Jacoby, F., ed. 1923–1958. *Die Fragmente der griechischen
           Historiker.* 3 vols. Berlin: Weidmann.
HCT   Gomme, A. W., A. Andrewes, and K. J. Dover. 1945–
           1981. *A Historical Commentary on Thucydides.* 5 vols.
           Oxford: Clarendon Press.
IACP   Hansen, M. H., and T. H. Nielsen, eds. 2004. *An Inventory of
           Archaic and Classical Poleis.* Oxford: Oxford University Press.
IG   *Inscriptiones Graecae.* 1873–. Berlin: De Gruyter.
ISic.   Prag, J., ed. *Inscriptiones Siciliae.* http://sicily.classics.ox.ac.uk/.
IvO   Dittenberger, W., and K. Purgold, eds. 1896. *Die Inschriften von
           Olympia.* Berlin: A. Asher.
ML   Meiggs, R., and D. Lewis. 1988. *A Selection of Greek Historical
           Inscriptions to the End of the Fifth Century BC.* Rev. ed.
           Oxford: Clarendon Press.
PEG   Bernabé Pajares, A., ed. 1988. *Poetae Epici Graeci.* Berlin: De
           Gruyter.
PMG   Page, D. L., ed. 1962. *Poetae Melici Graeci.*
           Oxford: Clarendon Press.
SEG   *Supplementum Epigraphicum Graecum.* 1923–. Leiden: Brill.
Syll.[3]   Dittenberger, W. 1915–1924. *Sylloge inscriptionum Graecarum.*
           4 vols. 3rd ed. Leipzig: S. Herzel.
TrGF I   Snell, B., ed. 1986. *Tragicorum Graecorum Fragmenta*, Vol.
           1. Göttingen: Vandenhoek & Ruprecht.
TrGF V   Kannicht, R., ed. 2004. *Tragicorum Graecorum Fragmenta*, Vol.
           5. Göttingen: Vandenhoek & Ruprecht.
West   West, M. 1989–1992. *Iambi et Elegi Graeci.* 2nd ed.
           Oxford: Oxford University Press.

I

Introduction

IDENTITY IS EVERYWHERE in the twenty-first century. From the halls of
Congress to small towns and major cities, identities are a driving force of
political polarization. Bitter debates about what it means to be an American
have become commonplace. Identity has been used as a tool of oppression; it
has also been a force for change, when protesters take to the streets as a way
of taking pride in their identities and empowering their communities. In an
age of globalization, the desire to promote local cultures in many countries—
Scottish in the United Kingdom, Basque in Spain, or indigenous peoples in
Mexico—is fueled by a sense of separate identities. Hollywood films such as
Black Panther and *Crazy Rich Asians* (both released in 2018) center the experience of underrepresented groups and enable artists and audiences alike to
take pride in the particularities of their own identities. We all know what identity is, though it is rather hard to pin down, and it seems an inherent feature
of the modern world. It was also central to the experience and the politics of
ancient Greeks, including, as this study will demonstrate, those who lived in
Sicily and southern Italy.

Some scholars have even gone so far as to suggest that the modern preoc-
cupation with identity is just that—modern—and that ancient peoples were
not very concerned with the allegedly anachronistic concept of identity.[1] It has
long been observed, for example, that the Greek language lacks vocabulary
that would translate as "identity," "ethnicity," or even "ethnic group" (though

1. E.g., Will 1956; Just 1998; Purcell 2005; Boardman 2006; Gruen 2011.

The Politics of Identity in Greek Sicily and Southern Italy. Mark R. Thatcher, Oxford University Press. © Oxford University
Press 2021. DOI: 10.1093/oso/9780197586440.003.0001

ethnos sometimes comes close to the last).[2] But in reality, identities mattered to people in antiquity just as much as they do today and deeply affected their outlook on the world. Although ethnicity and identity are concepts developed and defined by modern scholars, they nevertheless correspond to an essential aspect of the lives of ancient Greeks. While Greeks did not analyze these concepts abstractly, they did discuss them in more concrete terms, by asking what it meant to be Athenian or Greek or Dorian. In other words, rather than developing abstract theories of ethnicity or identity, they articulated, communicated, and debated the particular factors that made up their identities.

A close look at Syracuse, the largest and most powerful Greek city in Sicily, reveals some of the various identities that were relevant there. In the aftermath of their victory over Carthage at Himera in 480 BCE, Syracusans emphasized that they were Greeks, victorious over the barbarian invaders. Pindar's *Pythian* 1, for instance, celebrates Himera in specifically Hellenic terms, declaring that the battle had "rescued Greece from harsh slavery" (75), rhetoric reminiscent of contemporary recollections of the Persian Wars. The poem thus encourages its audiences to privilege their identities as Greeks over other possible self-perceptions. The prominence of Hellenic identity did not emerge naturally, moreover, but rather was promoted from the top. The tyrants of the Deinomenid family—first Gelon (485–478) and then Hieron (478–467)—found Greekness a useful tool for shoring up their support and creating legitimacy for their regime.[3] Later kings and tyrants, such as Dionysius I (405–367) and Hieron II (269–215), did something similar.

But like all Greek colonies, Syracuse was also an independent *polis*, separate from all other Greeks, and Syracusans emphasized a number of factors that made it distinctive. For example, two unique topographical features of the city—its island citadel Ortygia and its spring of Arethusa—appear in several passages of Pindar and are reflected figuratively on its coinage.[4] No other city could boast these features. Its people were fiercely proud of being Syracusan and guarded their *polis* identity closely. The Syracusans also claimed to be Dorian, because of their origin as a Corinthian colony and their claim to a legacy that went back to the mythical Dorian Invasion. One of Thucydides's speakers, a Syracusan statesman named Hermocrates, expressed his pride in those Dorian and Peloponnesian origins (6.77.1), and centuries later, a Syracusan character in Theocritus did the same (*Id.* 15.89–93). Pindar, too,

2. Hall 1997, 34–36; cf. Renfrew 1998; McInerney 2001; Morgan 2003, 9–10.

3. The Deinomenids made use of other identities as well; see chapters 3 and 4.

4. Pind. *Ol.* 6.92–94; *Pyth.* 2.5–7; *Pyth.* 3.68–70; *Nem.* 1.1–6; for the coins, see Kraay 1976, 210.

celebrates the *eunomia* and social order that this Dorian heritage supposedly bestowed (*Pyth.* 1.60–66). Because of its focus on shared origins and kinship with other Dorians, this identity should properly be understood as a form of ethnicity.

During the Peloponnesian War, however, a different way of thinking came to prominence: regional identity. In 424, nearly all of the Sicilian *poleis* were at war with one another, and Athens had sent the so-called First Sicilian Expedition to intervene. At a peace conference that year, the same Hermocrates spoke successfully in favor of uniting against the Athenians. "We are all of us neighbors," he said, "fellow dwellers in one land, in the midst of the sea, all called by the single name of Sikeliotai" (Thuc. 4.64.3). This idea of a pan-Sicilian regional identity that brought together all inhabitants of the island was not new—half a century earlier, Pindar had described the whole island of Sicily as Zeus's gift to Persephone, suggesting a conception of Sicily as a unity (*Nem.* 1.13–18)—but Hermocrates's appeal brought it to new prominence, and it was this sense of shared identity that caused the Syracusans, along with other Sicilian Greeks, to change their policies, make peace with one another, and force out the Athenians. Thus, the Syracusans identified themselves variously as Syracusan, Dorian, Sicilian, and Greek. These four types of identity are all part of the complex and multilayered idea of what it meant to be Syracusan.

The coexistence of these multiple collective identities, adopted by a single community, raises a number of questions. How did these identities relate to one another in the minds of the Syracusans? Were they seen as totally separate or as overlapping in various ways? What are the differences between various identities, and how should each be defined? How did each sense of identity develop originally, and how did they change over time? The evidence presented so far makes it clear that there was no chronological progression from one identity to another; rather, all of these identities were constantly available, ready to be deployed as desired. So what factors led the Syracusans to emphasize one in one situation and another in a different context? What mechanisms and media did they use to articulate and proclaim these identities, and what sources can we use to recover and understand them? In the short outline above, I cited epinician poetry, historiography, myths, and coinage, but many others were available, such as inscriptions, material culture, religious practices, and visual evidence. How did each contribute to the complex world of identity in the Greek West?

Moreover, these multiple identities clearly made a significant impact on Syracusan politics. How did various tyrants and leaders use identities for political gain? A great many Sicilian leaders, from the Deinomenids to the tyrant

Dionysius I in the fourth century and King Hieron II in the third, derived some of their legitimacy from the rhetoric of identity. What techniques were involved, and were different identities susceptible to different uses? Did the claims of political elites affect how ordinary people viewed their own identities? Events in the realm of politics certainly were able to shape and reshape identities; a familiar example is the drastic remodeling of Hellenic identity at Athens in the decades following the Persian Wars. But the reverse also happened: political decision-making was often informed and conditioned by multiple identities. Politics and identities thus shaped and reshaped each other in a reciprocal cycle that has the potential to substantially affect our understanding of Greek political history.

This study explores the intersection of politics and identity in Greek Sicily and southern Italy. It advances two main arguments. First, the multiple identities claimed by the western Greeks cannot be understood individually or separately; instead, they are deeply intertwined, full of overlapping strands that must be untangled and analyzed together. Each of these strands is important in itself (which makes it worthwhile to distinguish them clearly), but their interactions make the whole far more complex, in ways that have not been fully understood. Second, identity played a far greater role in Greek politics than is usually recognized. Identity was often created through conflict and was reshaped as political conditions changed; it created legitimacy for kings and tyrants and contributed to the decision-making processes of *poleis*. Identity and politics among the western Greeks were deeply entangled.

Three examples, drawn from the case studies that make up this volume, will help to set out these rather broad propositions in more detail. The first concerns Croton in southern Italy, where Achaean ethnicity was intertwined with *polis* identity in a more complex manner than previously appreciated (see chapter 2). Croton's foundation myths, a key tool for articulating identity, traced the city's origins to the northern Peloponnese via the founder Myscellus and thereby defined it as ethnically Achaean. But the stories of Myscellus were not shared by other Achaean cities such as Metapontion and Sybaris. Rather, they also served to define Croton's *polis* identity by articulating elements that make Croton distinctive, such as its local landscape and its great success in athletics. Other mechanisms for constructing identity, such as coins, myths of heroes, and the major cult of Hera Lacinia, display a similar pattern. Thus, Croton's expressions of Achaean ethnicity were also at the same time expressions of its *polis* identity, and neither type of identity can be fully understood without the other. Further, these entangled identities arose out of political conflicts, especially in the sixth and fifth centuries. Croton and other Achaean cities fought a series of wars against their non-Achaean (but Greek) neighbors, including

Locri, Siris, and Taras, which collectively led to the articulation of Achaean ethnicity defined in contrast to those Others. Political competition was thus central to the creation of Achaean identity.

Next, a strategy frequently used by Sicilian kings and tyrants to create legitimacy for their rule was mobilizing their subjects' sense of Greekness. We have already seen the Deinomenids' use of the memory of the Battle of Himera in 480 for this purpose. Almost a century later, in 397, Dionysius I of Syracuse launched another war against Carthage, calling on Sicilian Greeks to defend the Greekness of their island, in order to shore up his power (chapter 3). Even in the Hellenistic period, the man who became King Hieron II secured power in the 270s by trumpeting his victories over the Mamertines, a group of non-Greek Campanian mercenaries who had seized Messina (chapter 6). These are all classic cases of the creation of unity within a group through contrast with an Other, deployed for political purposes, and this strategy remained prominent over more than two centuries. Yet it is also clear that Greekness was not always at the forefront of Sicilian thinking. These same leaders fought numerous wars against other Greeks, as did those Sicilians and Italian Greeks not ruled by tyrants. Conversely, they often enjoyed friendly relations with their non-Greek neighbors, and under the right circumstances, the native inhabitants of Sicily could be considered Sikeliotai alongside the Greeks (chapter 4). Thus, appreciating the real significance of Greekness in the West requires a carefully calibrated approach that takes other identities into account as well.

Finally, during the Peloponnesian War, not only Syracuse but a number of Sicilian *poleis* made momentous decisions of war and peace that were informed by their identities (chapter 5). In the early 420s, most of the Sicilian *poleis* aligned into two ethnic blocs—the Dorians were fighting the Chalcidians (a Sicilian term for Ionian)—and it appears that a strong preference for siding with members of one's own ethnic group guided these decisions. Only one city, Camarina, failed to follow these ethnic boundaries, siding with the Chalcidians despite being Dorian. I argue that it acted on the basis of its unique conception of its *polis* identity, which had been shaped by centuries of hostility from its mother city, Syracuse. The war concluded, as we have already seen, with peace among the Sikeliotai on the basis of regional identity (chapter 4). In each of these phases of the war, the protagonists were not forced by identity into any particular decision, nor was identity their only consideration; nevertheless, identity was a key lens through which they viewed their options. Moreover, across the island, politicians were guided by a whole series of different identities and moved from one to another quickly and easily. Analyzing the role of ethnicity alone, or of separate *polis* identities, would not give a complete picture of these political dynamics.

Scope of Research

As these examples suggest, this study will range widely. Nevertheless, identity is far too large a topic to cover comprehensively in a single monograph, and I therefore limit my discussion in several ways. I focus on four types of identity:

- a separate civic or *polis* identity for each *polis*;
- sub-Hellenic ethnicities (such as the Dorians, Ionians, and Achaeans) that brought some cities together while separating them from others;
- regional identities, particularly the Sikeliotai or Greeks of Sicily; and
- an overarching sense of Greekness.

Ethnicity and *polis* identity are not the same thing, nor are Hellenic and regional identities. Instead, each of these types of identity was defined in different ways (I discuss these definitions at length below), and they all had significant but qualitatively different impacts on the communities that adopted them.

These were not, of course, the only identities available to western Greeks. The networks among Corinthian, Spartan, and Phocaean colonies analyzed by Irad Malkin and others, for instance, were important sources of identities for those cities.[5] Various intra-*polis* communities may also have been quite important, such as the deme, *genos* (clan), and *phyle* (tribe, or subdivision of the citizen body) identities that were prominent at Athens.[6] But in the West, much less is known about such smaller groups,[7] and instead my investigation will focus on the various identities available to any *polis* as a whole. Moreover, this is a study of communities, not individuals, and of collective identity rather than personal identity. Communities are, of course, made up of individuals, and—notwithstanding my blithe use of generalizations like "the Syracusans"—it is clear that not all members of a community thought in lockstep. But the sources for the Greek West are rarely fine-grained enough to investigate the attitudes of individuals or of dissident groups within a community. Instead,

---

5. Malkin 1994; Malkin 2011; Dominguez 2004.

6. On the Attic demes, see Osborne 1985, 72–74; Whitehead 1986, 223–234; Kellogg 2013; cf. the idea of small-scale "community identity" discussed by Mac Sweeney 2011. On *phylai* outside Athens, see Grote 2016.

7. The evidence is collected by De Angelis 2016, 136–141.

I will explore the ways in which entire communities formed themselves and articulated their identities.

Furthermore, this study focuses on the substantial diversity among the western Greeks themselves. They had arrived from many parts of Greece, and they had established many separate *poleis* across wide swaths of territory.[8] Only rarely did they think of themselves primarily as Greeks. Much important work has been done in recent decades on the varied relationships between Greeks and non-Greeks in the West and on the strategies of opposition and accommodation that created the region's diverse ethnic landscape.[9] This study focuses instead on relationships, accommodations, and contrasts between Greeks and other Greeks.

Apart from these limitations, however, the scope of this study is quite broad: two large and populous regions and a period of some four hundred years, c. 600–200 BCE. This lengthy chronological range does not match the standard scholarly division of Greek history into Archaic, Classical, and Hellenistic periods. Instead, this study attempts to bridge the gulf between Archaic and Hellenistic historians and between Hellenists and Romanists. The Greek West often falls through the cracks as neither a geographically nor chronologically central part of Greek history (especially in the fourth and third centuries) nor an essential component of Roman history.[10] But in Sicily and southern Italy, the same cities and the same regions remain players across the whole chronological spectrum, and there is much continuity between different periods. Taking the long view allows us to observe what changes and what stays the same over a lengthy period. I do not begin with colonial foundations in the eighth and seventh centuries but rather with the moment when their identities began to take recognizable forms (due especially to the state of the evidence; see further in chapter 2). At the other extreme, Hannibal's invasion of Italy gave the Greeks of Italy the opportunity to express their identities through independent political action for, as it turned out, the last time. While the Greeks of Italy under the later Roman Republic and Empire continued to express their identities,[11] the context of that expression was sufficiently different from that of earlier times that I have chosen to close my study there.

---

8. For general accounts, see Dunbabin 1948; Boardman 1999; Dominguez 2006a; Tsetskhladze 2006-2008; Lyons, Bennett, and Marconi 2013; Lomas forthcoming.

9. See, e.g., Purcell 1994; Malkin 1998; Cordano and Di Salvatore 2002; Hall 2002, 90–124; Antonaccio 2003; Antonaccio 2004; Giangiulio 2010; Shepherd 2011; Shepherd 2014; Frasca 2015.

10. Cf. Lomas 2000, 167–168; Dench 2003, 295–297.

11. E.g., Lomas 2015.

This study also casts a wide net geographically, drawing examples and evidence from both Sicily and southern Italy in order to broaden the scope of comparison and contrast. In antiquity as today, the two regions were sometimes considered a single unit and sometimes not. The very term *Magna Graecia* varied in its valence, referring sometimes to Italy alone and sometimes to both regions.[12] In recent decades, a standard handbook has been T. J. Dunbabin's *The Western Greeks* (1948), which covers both Italy and Sicily in the Archaic period; the forthcoming *The World of the Western Greeks* (edited by K. Lomas) will do the same over a longer period. On the other hand, both the *Atti* of the Taranto Convegni on Magna Graecia and the journal *Kokalos*, published in Palermo, focus almost exclusively on Italy and Sicily, respectively. But the two regions have much in common (even as they also differ in some ways), and bringing them together gives us a larger body of evidence; this in turn enables larger conclusions about the dynamics of identity that will, it is hoped, be applicable to the Greek world more generally.

Thinking about that broader view, beyond Sicily and southern Italy, invites the question of whether or to what extent the region I have chosen was typical of the Greek world at large or whether it was unique. This is a complicated issue. On one level, the dynamics of identity politics that I lay out in this introduction and explore throughout the book can, I think, be found throughout the Greek world. Greeks anywhere had multiple identities to choose from, and these identities often influenced their political behavior; as I will argue below, this is an understudied topic and an important new conclusion. Yet might the colonial context of the Greek West, for instance, have produced different social dynamics and thereby a different set of identities, or different ways of articulating them, from those that were available elsewhere? Certainly, the relationship of a colony toward its mother city, for example, would be mostly irrelevant back in the mainland, apart from scattered exceptions, whereas Syracuse and Corinth retained tight ties for centuries. Similarly, the close proximity of non-Greeks (whether actually living in Greek *poleis* or in nearby communities) might lead to different conceptions of Greekness from those in mainland Greece.

Yet the uniqueness of Sicily and southern Italy must not be overstated; surely similar dynamics would occur in, for instance, Cyrenaica or the Black Sea (not to mention Ionia and Caria). Conversely, proximity to non-Greeks might lead to easy familiarity with them (as at Megara Hyblaea and Camarina)

---

12. Smith 2003, 2–7; Simon 2012, 161–181; cf. Musti 1988. Strabo 6.1.2 includes Sicily (cf. Liv. 7.26.15), while most sources do not (e.g., Polyb. 2.39.1; Liv. 31.7.11).

or to hostility (at Syracuse and Taras), thereby producing plural conceptions of Greekness. The question is not only whether western Greece differed from the rest of the Greek world in this regard but also whether it was uniform within itself, and it is clear that there was great diversity within the West. The colonial context was by no means the only relevant factor; it must be acknowledged but should not be overplayed. In light of these factors, my analysis of the Greek West constitutes an extended case study of a region that has some distinctive features but is not defined by them. My methods and conclusions can, I argue, be applied elsewhere (see the book's conclusion for some discussion of this), but my analysis does not exhaust the dynamics of identity among the Greeks.

Theorizing Identity

If the Greeks had no definition of identity, modern scholars have not done much better. The concept of identity is notoriously slippery. Florian Coulmas, for instance, refuses to "parade a couple of dozen definitions of 'identity'" and ultimately punts, expressing only the hope that the concept of identity will become clearer over the course of his book.[13] More helpfully, Kwame Appiah quotes the mid-twentieth-century sociologist Alvin Gouldner, who posits that "the process by which an individual is classified by others in his group, in terms of culturally prescribed categories, can be called the assignment of a 'social identity.'"[14] Richard Jenkins, too, emphasizes that identity "is a process—*identification*—not a 'thing'; it is not something that one can *have*, or not, it is something that one *does*."[15] Identity is produced through social interactions, which enable people to identify themselves and others. Yet Jenkins offers only a very broad designation of identity as the process through which "we know *who's who* and *what's what*."[16]

While all of these definitions have useful elements, the very breadth of the field has led to a fundamental conceptual difficulty. If identities (plural) come in so many varieties, how can we conceptualize all of them within a single framework? A narrow, precise definition may exclude some forms of self-presentation that we would instinctively want to classify as identity. But if we take a broad and open-ended approach, we risk opening the floodgates

---

13. Coulmas 2019, 4–5.

14. Appiah 2018, 4–5, citing Gouldner 1957, 282–283.

15. Jenkins 2014, 6; cf. Melucci 1996, 68–86.

16. Jenkins 2014, 14.

so wide that we lose all analytical precision. If everything is a form of identity, then nothing is—the concept becomes meaningless. Some scholars, in fact, have proposed doing away with the term altogether, for precisely this reason.[17]

We should not throw out the baby with the bathwater, however, and the framework of multiple identities proposed here is a useful way forward. It allows us to examine a wide range of different types of identity, defining each of them in a precise and specific way, while taking a larger view of the umbrella concept of identity. Within this large umbrella, I include all the subjective and internally defined self-perceptions of communities, which worked together to define who counted as a member of the community and what it meant to be a member.

This definition emerges from a number of firmly established elements.[18] Scholars now universally agree, first and foremost, that identities are *constructed* and *subjective*. Social groups do not simply exist but instead emerge from the interactions among individuals, defined and continuously redefined through a process of social negotiation. They are created and articulated according to the needs and perceptions of the community itself (although the perceptions of nonmembers also play a role).[19] Moreover, identities are *flexible* and constantly changing as those needs and perceptions change. New identities emerge, old ones are redefined, and some eventually cease to be relevant. Not everyone will agree on the definitions as they are negotiated, and so identities are often *contested*. While objectively observable elements typically factor into identities in some way, identities have no objective reality. They exist only in the minds of group members and in the interactions between them (and between members and others). This should not indicate that identities are unimportant; in fact, identities have a social reality, in the sense that group members believe they exist and act accordingly, that leads them to play

---

17. Brubaker and Cooper 2000, who prefer "identification"; cf. Hall 1996; Malešević 2006, 13–36; with the cogent response by Jenkins 2014, 7–16. I follow Jenkins and others in retaining "identity." Other scholars identify a similar problem of definitional vagueness but with less drastic prescriptions; e.g., Gleason 1983; Hall 1996; Tilly 2003; McCoskey 2003. Brubaker and Cooper and others also warn of the risk of reification inherent in discussing identity "groups," but I will continue to refer to groups such as "the Syracusans," because, although the definition and membership of this community did change over time, there was always a group called "the Syracusans."

18. For clear overviews of the elements summarized here, see Jenkins 2014; Appiah 2018, 3–32; cf. also Eisenstadt and Giesen 1995; Cerulo 1997; Ashmore, Deaux, and McLaughlin-Volpe 2004. Many of these insights came originally from work on ethnicity, beginning with Barth 1969; cf. Jenkins 2008; Eriksen 2010.

19. On the role of nonmembers, see Jenkins 2014, 104–114.

a central role in human social interaction. And finally, identity is also *multiple* and *situational*: everyone has many identities that become more or less relevant in different contexts. This is familiar in the modern world, where someone may be Bavarian, German, and European in different contexts or an American, a New Yorker, and a Brooklynite; it is no less true in antiquity.

This framework of multiple identities helps us toward an essential goal in the study of ancient identities: understanding how ancient Greeks saw themselves. Because identity is so subjective, the study of identity in antiquity should aim to get inside the heads of the ancient Greeks, to find out what was important to them. This means focusing on the ways in which identity is defined by internal, emic perceptions, rather than applying modern analytical categories. This approach allows us to avoid artificially prioritizing any one identity according to modern preconceptions—for example, deciding that ethnicity is the only identity we are interested in—but rather to follow the data wherever they lead.

Since the seminal work of the Norwegian anthropologist Fredrik Barth (1969), scholars have focused on how communities define themselves in opposition to other groups. Identity is thus articulated at the notional boundaries between communities, where the factors that distinguish one group from another are most readily apparent. Within the boundary of a community are those who share certain characteristics; outside the community are those who differ in those respects.[20] Thus, the basis of any identity consists of *meaningful sets of similarities and differences* or what are often called the *criteria* of identity.[21] Although Barth (and many subsequent scholars) focused on ethnicity, the insight actually applies to all forms of identity: the Sikeliotai, for instance, defined themselves in opposition to Athens, using the natural boundary of the sea as its criterion.

Following Barth, most scholars have focused primarily on difference as the key determinant of identity. But in reality, similarity and difference are opposite sides of the same coin. Constructing a meaningful difference between Greeks and Persians, for instance, requires a sense of similarity among Greeks. In actual practice, what the sources show varies: sometimes the difference between two groups is highlighted, but in other cases the similarity among group members comes to the forefront while difference recedes into

---

20. Barth 1969. His work has influenced virtually all subsequent work on ethnicity; on his legacy, see Vermeulen and Govers 2000; Jenkins 2008; Eriksen 2010.

21. Originally, Horowitz 1975; cf. Hall 1997, 19–26.

the background. This variation is an inherent part of identity, and attention must be paid to both similarity and difference.[22]

Clearly, many such criteria are possible (a nearly infinite range, in fact), but not all will actually be meaningful most of the time. Hence, the concept of *salience*—the extent to which community members feel that a particular characteristic is relevant or important to their identity—is critical.[23] Some possible criteria matter greatly, while others are ignored. Moreover, salience changes situationally and over time; it is extremely flexible and often subject to debate. Which criteria are salient at which times cannot be determined based on external, objective facts, since salience is subjectively constructed, just as much as identity itself. This is another reason the study of identity must begin from ancient attitudes, not modern frameworks. Salience is what makes identity matter to people: an identity that is highly salient in a certain situation is deeply important to community members, so much so that it can cause them to act. In this way, identity becomes entangled with politics.

Identity and Politics

Identity politics is sometimes portrayed in modern political discourse as a new phenomenon: beginning in the postwar period with decolonization and the civil rights movement in the United States, spreading as a reaction to globalization, and bursting forth to dominate politics in the early twenty-first century.[24] In reality, however, identity and politics have been linked for as long as both have existed. The most common instantiation of identity politics today consists of an identity group mobilizing to protect its interests, whether that involves get-out-the-vote campaigns and the election of new leaders or rioting, violence, and civil war.[25] There are certainly examples from Sicily and southern

22. Jenkins 2014, 134–150.

23. Stryker 1968; Stryker 1980, 60–61, 81–84; Ashmore, Deaux, and McLaughlin-Volpe 2004, 87–89; Jenkins 2008, esp. 42–53; other scholars use similar concepts without the term: Sen 2006, 26–28; Eriksen 2010, 38–39.

24. Such a view is usually presented with an agenda; e.g., David Brooks, "Identity Politics Run Amok," *New York Times*, September 2, 2016; Mark Lilla, "The End of Identity Liberalism," *New York Times*, November 18, 2016; cf., from opposite sides of the political spectrum, Caldwell 2020; Klein 2020. But some scholars have argued that identity only became historically significant at varying points between the early modern period and the nineteenth century; e.g., Gellner 1983; Nash 1989, 1–4; Howard 2000, 367–368; *contra*, Smith 1986; Jenkins 2014, 31–36.

25. Cf. Sen 2006. There is a voluminous literature on the mobilization of identity in social movements; e.g., Johnston and Klandermans 1995; Stryker, Owens, and White 2000.

Italy that fit this pattern, such as the *stasis* that broke out in Syracuse in 466, after the fall of the Deinomenids, over whether new citizens imported by the former tyrants would retain their citizenship and the privileges that came with it (see chapter 3). But this is only one form of a much broader relationship between identity and politics that pervades the history of the Greek West.

Identity has often been overlooked by Greek historians, especially those who write "traditional" political-military history. Earlier scholars tended to take the sources' ethnic claims at face value, thereby both reifying the ethnic groups in ahistorical and problematic ways and obscuring identity's dynamics and nuances.[26] More recently, many historians have denied the validity of identity as a historical factor at all, relegating the topic to the softer field of social history. Major recent syntheses of Greek history by eminent scholars such as Malcolm Errington and P. J. Rhodes, as well as classic works such as those of Donald Kagan on the Peloponnesian War, mainly ignore identity.[27] There are certainly important exceptions to this trend, especially in the work of Simon Hornblower, and the Archaic period has generally been better served than later times.[28] Comparative work is also helpful. Phoenician identities have recently begun to receive more attention, showing that they display many of the same dynamics discussed here.[29] Within Sicily and southern Italy, numerous articles (cited throughout this book) analyze individual episodes, but this important issue within ancient history deserves fuller and more sustained examination.

Politics is a wide-ranging field, not easily reducible to a single concise definition.[30] Internally, politics includes the issues of how polities are governed, how policy is made, how leaders are chosen (or choose themselves), and popular attitudes toward all of these things. Externally, politics includes more than war, peace, and diplomacy, the traditional arenas of foreign policy. It also encompasses more broadly what a polity sees as its place in the world and its

---

26. E.g., Mitford 1835, 284–285, 293–294; Grote 1859, 173–177; Glotz and Cohen 1929, 605; Bury and Meiggs 1975, 292; see also the history of scholarship in Hall 1997, 4–16.

27. Errington 2008; Rhodes 2010; for a firm rejection of identity, see Kagan 1969, 347. Cf. also Will 1956; Sealey 1976; Hammond 1986; Lewis 1992; Pomeroy et al. 2018.

28. Esp. Hornblower 2011; cf. also Alty 1982; Shipley 2000; Funke and Luraghi 2009. On the Archaic period, see Osborne 2009; Hall 2014.

29. Above all Quinn 2018; cf. Quinn and Vella 2014. See also Farney 2007 on ethnic identity in Roman Republican politics.

30. For some attempts, see Lasswell 1950; Goodin 2011, 4–5; Pyrcz 2011, 8–10; Roskin, Cord, Medeiros, and Jones 2014.

more informal relationships with others—for example, hostility, friendship, or kinship. Identity is deeply implicated in all of these.[31]

Many approaches to the politics of identity take as their starting point the model of ethnicity known as instrumentalism. In brief, instrumentalism holds that ethnic groups (or, I would add, other types of collectivities) are essentially interest groups—people bound together by shared interests, usually economic—that begin to articulate a shared identity as a tool for furthering those interests. In other words, ethnicity only develops as a means to a political end.[32] A number of episodes from antiquity can best be understood through an instrumentalist lens, such as the emergence of the Sikeliotai as a politicized regional group in 424. All the *poleis* of Sicily felt threatened by Athenian incursions and saw their shared interest in ending that threat; they therefore lined up under a single banner and acted politically to achieve their goal. Once this identity had served its purpose, Sicilians went back to fighting one another only two years later (Thuc. 5.4–5).

Yet by placing economic interests ahead of subjective self-identification, the instrumentalist model underplays the extent to which identities often pre-exist their politicization. As we will see in chapter 4, for example, a much looser sense of Sicilian regional identity can be traced as far back as the very different context of the Deinomenid period. Moreover, this line of thinking suggests that identities were profoundly meaningful to the people who held them, since identities could not affect policy choices or attitudes toward leaders if they were not deeply rooted. Instrumentalist approaches, by contrast, tend to be rather cynical, seeing identity only as a means to an end rather than as a deeply felt belief.[33] By underestimating the experience of identity from the inside, these theorists fail to appreciate that identities feel very real to members of the group in question, even as those identities are being deployed for political ends. Moreover, by reducing identity to a set of shared interests, instrumentalism tends to flatten all collectivities into the same thing: groups of people pursuing their economic interests. I prefer instead to draw attention to the many nuances and peculiarities of any individual identity group and how these shape and are shaped by the political contexts in which they are embedded. These reciprocal influences between identity and politics follow three broad patterns.

31. For modern examples, see Sen 2006; Appiah 2018.

32. Early exponents of this approach include Cohen 1969; Glazer and Moynihan 1970; cf. Hall 1997, 17–19; Jenkins 2008, 46–50.

33. Cf. Amartya Sen's concept of "identity disregard"; Sen 2006, 20–23.

First, new identities were often created and existing ones reshaped through political conflict and competition. This is not a new idea; it is essentially a more pointed version of the idea of the creation of identity through an opposition between Self and Other. The Persian Wars are a classic example: under the experience of foreign invasion, Greek identity, which had previously been rather loose and frequently irrelevant, drastically increased in salience and was reshaped around a new Greek/barbarian antithesis.[34] In the West, repeated wars with Carthage did something similar throughout the fifth and fourth centuries; in Italy, Taras emphasized its Greekness in the context of conflict with Italic peoples, including Rome.[35] Similar processes can be seen for other types of identity as well. The small Sicilian city of Camarina developed a distinctive *polis* identity through conflict with its mother city, Syracuse, while war with Athens drastically increased the salience of Sikeliote identity, and we will see many more examples throughout this book.

Second, identities had the potential to shape political decision-making. This is an especially critical point, because from Thucydides onward, Greek politics, especially interstate relations, have traditionally been analyzed in terms of realist calculations of self-interest, with no role for identity. Considerations of identity were certainly not determinative; beliefs about identity did not force any polity to make any particular decision, but they did tend to shape debates and condition attitudes toward various policy options. The Sicilian war of the 420s, which resulted in the Athenian intervention described above, is a good example. At first, most Sicilian *poleis* aligned with one another according to ethnicity, either Dorian or Chalcidian, and Athens intervened because of kinship (*syngeneia*) with the Chalcidians. While doubtless numerous other factors went into all of these decisions, ethnicity played a key role. The expectation of practical gain worked hand in hand with a moral belief that it was right to help one's kinsmen. Later, Hermocrates's speech in 424 led Sicilians to rethink their political interests in line with a different identity; now thinking of themselves as Sikeliotai, rather than Dorians or Chalcidians, encouraged them to pursue an anti-Athenian policy. Identity was not the only or necessarily even the most important factor in most decisions, but it was part of the mix and could even be decisive.

Third, kings, tyrants, and political leaders relied on identity as a way of creating legitimacy—essentially, the acceptability of a ruler to his people and a moral sense that a leader or policy is right—for themselves and their

---

34. Hall 1989; Hall 2002, 172–205; Mitchell 2007.

35. For Carthage, see chapter 3; for Taras, see chapter 6.

policies.[36] Recent work on Greek tyranny has emphasized how successful tyrants engaged in self-representation and dialogue with their people, developing ideologies that presented themselves as legitimate rulers.[37] The Deinomenids, for instance, inscribed themselves within preexisting identities, presenting themselves sometimes as Syracusan, sometimes as Dorian, and sometimes as Greek in order to mobilize support for their regime. Moreover, their actions shaped what their people thought about these identities, as the tyrants promoted versions of them that would be helpful to the regime's legitimacy. These examples cannot be dismissed as mere propaganda, a term that suggests one-way control of a passive target population by tyrants or politicians, since they required a receptive audience.[38] Such rhetoric could only be successful if it appealed to genuine and widespread preexisting beliefs, encouraging people actively to accept the arguments offered to them. For leaders of all kinds, whether rulers trying to stay in power or orators hoping their proposals would be adopted, identity was a key weapon in their arsenal of persuasion.

Taking these three patterns together demonstrates the wide range of influence between identity and politics. Neither concept should be prioritized, by focusing only on the impact of identity on politics or vice versa. Rather, their linkage is best understood as reciprocal: influence flowed in both directions. Historians of Greek politics must grapple with identity in a sensitive and up-to-date way, taking into account its multiplicity, flexibility, situationality, and capacity to affect the course of events, or risk missing out on a significant element of Greek history.

A Typology of Identities

As pointed out above, there were innumerable possible criteria for identity. Some collectivities might define themselves through kinship, some through residence in a region or a particular village, some through religious participation or legal rights, and others through something else entirely.[39] The four types of identity discussed in this book—polis, regional, ethnic, and Greek— should thus be carefully distinguished. Each was articulated in antiquity

---

36. Barker 1990; Beetham 1991; Pyrcz 2011, 9–10.

37. Lewis 2009; Luraghi 2013b; Mitchell 2013; Morgan 2015; Nicholson 2015.

38. Jowett and O'Donnell 2015; for antiquity, see Enenkel and Pfeijffer 2005.

39. On the multiplicity of identities, see Sen 2006, 23–32; Appiah 2018; in Classics, see, e.g., Mac Sweeney 2009; Giangiulio 2010; Malkin 2014; Shepherd 2014; Gruen 2016; Quinn 2018.

according to different criteria. While Greek ethnic groups, such as the Dorians and Ionians, probably defined themselves through belief in their respective common ancestry (on this point, see further below), the Sikeliotai did not. Instead, the latter predicated their identity on an entirely different criterion: residence on the island of Sicily. Citizenship in a particular *polis* was a defining criterion for yet another type of identity, while Greekness was defined in many ways over time but always returned to the collective name "Hellenes." Much flexibility remained in demarcating specific communities; for instance, Athens and Syracuse did not necessarily define their *polis* identities in exactly the same way. But both were still *poleis*, and no one would mistake either of them for a regional collectivity. Each of the four types took on unique characteristics and had the potential to function in different ways. After all, being someone's neighbor is a different relationship from being their fellow citizen or being their blood relative. Highlighting each of those different criteria creates a qualitatively different kind of community, and it is on this qualitative level that we must distinguish them.[40]

Polis Identity

The fundamental unit of political organization among the western Greeks was the *polis*. It is striking that the *ethnos*, such an important form of state in mainland Greece, did not exist there, and while small territorial empires such as that of the Deinomenids did play a role, the *polis* continued to dominate Sicilian politics. Civic or *polis* identity was always centered around an individual *polis*, and its defining criterion was citizenship, or membership in the citizen body. *Polis* identity thus distinguished Syracusans from Akragantines but also separated Syracusan citizens from the enslaved population, a sort of "internal" Other, and from other noncitizens.[41] Those noncitizens, of course, participated in the daily life of the city and could sometimes be treated as part of the broader community, though usually a subordinate part. At Athens, for instance, metics fought alongside citizens, and not only metics but even slaves had a role in the Panathenaic procession.[42] Still, they could never straightforwardly be considered "Athenians" (οἱ Ἀθηναῖοι).

---

40. Cf. Eisenstadt and Giesen 1995, 77–84.

41. Cartledge 2002, 133–166; Lape 2010, 45–46.

42. Shapiro 1996, 221; Maurizio 1998; Parker 2005, 258–263; Wijma 2014, 37–64; cf. Beck 2020, esp. 3–4, on "identities of place" that can transcend these divisions.

Scholars in recent decades have rightly moved away from a focus on a sharp, legally defined boundary between citizen and noncitizen that changes only through legislation and toward a social paradigm of citizenship, in which membership in a community is defined instead through social practice.[43] Such a definition develops through an informal process of negotiation between community members to arrive at a consensus of who is in and who is out. Myths of belonging, ranging from colonial foundation myths to Athenian autochthony to many other types, played a key role in this process. So, too, did religious rituals: the *polis* can be defined in religious terms, as a community of cult, and participating in the city's cults, such as (at Athens) the Apatouria for men and the Brauronia for women, was one marker of community membership.[44] All of this sounds very much like the concept of identity outlined above, and in fact, much that has been said about citizenship describes *polis* identity well.

Yet there is far more to the discourse of civic identity than a simple declaration of affiliation with a certain *polis*. We can frequently identify a much more subtle set of self-perceptions, encompassing characteristics that citizens believe define their *polis* and its people. These similarities bind the *polis* together as a community. At Athens, for instance, both autochthony and Ionian ethnicity were deeply entwined with Athenian civic identity.[45] Neither of those characteristics was unique, of course; many *poleis* claimed to be Ionian, and other peoples, such as the Arcadians, claimed to be autochthonous.[46] Nevertheless, the Athenians developed a sense that these widely shared characteristics, in fact, were salient for their identity as Athenians. The Syracusans did something similar with their Dorian origins, and there was a similarly tangled relationship between Achaean ethnicity and *polis* identity in Croton and Metapontion.[47]

Of course, all *poleis* were not identical. The work of the Copenhagen Polis Center over the last few decades has shown enormous variation from one *polis*

---

43. Davies 1977; Manville 1990; Manville 1994; Connor 1994; Lape 2010; Wijma 2014, 13–27; Blok 2017; Cecchet and Busetto 2017.

44. It goes too far, however, to call the *polis* the fundamental unit of Greek religion, as has been claimed by Sourvinou-Inwood 1988, Sourvinou-Inwood 1990, and others; cf. the critiques of Parker 2011, 57–61; Kindt 2012; Mili 2015, 6–12; and see further in chapter 2.

45. Rosivach 1987; Connor 1993; Shapiro 1998; Pelling 2009; Forsdyke 2012; Fragoulaki 2013, 210–220.

46. Nielsen 2002, 70–72; Roy 2014.

47. Syracuse: chapters 3 and 6; Croton and Metapontion, chapter 2.

to another, and we cannot assume that *poleis* of Magna Graecia had much in common with Athens, by far the best-attested *polis*.[48] In Athens from the fifth century onward, citizenship was extremely tightly regulated, but in Sicily and southern Italy, attitudes were generally much more flexible, and it was relatively easy for people to come and go from the citizen body.[49] Since much previous work on civic identity in the Greek world has focused on Athens, a fresh view from a different part of the Greek world will provide an important new perspective.[50]

Regional Identity

Regional identity, on the other hand, is predicated on geographic proximity within limited physical boundaries and opens up a different set of issues altogether. Relatively limited attention has been devoted to regional collectivities per se (with the partial exception of some Aegean islands), but work on *ethnē*, many of which combined geographic and ethnic identities, helps fill the gap.[51] Mere physical proximity alone was not enough to produce a clearly articulated regional identity. In Italy, for instance, the Greeks settled only the southern portions of the peninsula, and its boundaries were therefore much more fluid and contested. In the fifth century, Antiochus of Syracuse advocated for a definition of Italy that included only the southernmost part of the toe. While the concept soon became more expansive, debate remained as to whether Taras, located where the heel of Italy meets the instep, was part of Italy or rather in a separate region, Iapygia.[52] Italiote identity was weak and rarely salient.[53]

---

48. See, e.g., Lomas 2000; Rutter 2000b; cf. Redfield 2003, 1, on Locri as a "third type [other than Athens and Sparta]; a different way of being Greek."

49. Lomas 2006; see chapter 3.

50. On *polis* identity in Athens, see Loraux 1986; Connor 1993; Connor 1994; Cohen 2000; Anderson 2003; Lape 2010; elsewhere, see Dougherty 1994; Pretzler 1999; Nielsen 2005.

51. Islands: Reger 1997; Constantakopoulou 2005; Kowalzig 2007, 224–266; Malkin 2011, 65–118; Kouremenos 2018; cf. Vlassopoulos 2007 on the Peloponnese. Regional *ethnē*: McInerney 1999; Nielsen 1999; Morgan 2003; Larson 2007; Greaves 2010; Mackil 2013.

52. Antiochus F3 (= Strabo 6.1.4), and cf. F2. On ancient definitions of Italy, see Prontera 1992; Lombardo 2002; Simon 2012, 66–72; Luraghi 2013a on Antiochus F2–3, with further references there.

53. But at Thuc. 6.44.3, the people of Rhegium say that they will do "whatever seems right to the other Italiotes" (ὅτι ἂν καὶ τοῖς ἄλλοις Ἰταλιώταις ξυνδοκῇ). The Italiote League came to prominence mainly in the fourth century: Wonder 2012; Fronda 2013; Fronda 2015.

In Sicily, however, the sharp natural boundary of the sea made the island an ideal site for the development of a regional identity based on geographical boundaries. In its most developed fifth-century form, this collectivity, the Sikeliotai, was thought to encompass all who lived on the island. In theory, this would include the Phoenicians in western Sicily as well as the three native groups, the Sikels, the Sikanians, and the Elymians, though in practice it referred mainly to Greeks. Crucially, however, this regional identity cut across other groups, since it included both Dorians and Chalcidians in Sicily while excluding Dorians and Ionians living elsewhere; moreover, it was constructed in part through opposition to other Greeks, the Athenians. Thus, Sicilian identity intersected with Greek ethnic categories in a manner far more complex than has been previously recognized.

Greekness

The Greeks themselves were unable to agree on a definition of Greekness.[54] The so-called Hellenic Genealogy in the pseudo-Hesiodic *Catalogue of Women* traces the common descent of all Greeks from the mythical Hellen, thus staking out the boundaries of Greekness through kinship.[55] From the time of the Persian Wars, by contrast, Greeks could be defined through opposition to Persia and others who were lumped together as barbarians.[56] Ethnographic knowledge and interaction with foreign peoples sometimes contributed to that sense of opposition and difference, but in other cases blurred those boundaries.[57] Isocrates in the fourth century described the Greeks as a people defined by shared culture, rather than blood.[58] Language may or may not have been a key marker of Greekness.[59] Herodotus's often-cited definition of τὸ Ἑλληνικόν as being based on shared blood, language, temples, and customs

---

54. On Greekness generally, see Hall 1989; Cartledge 2002; Georges 1994; Asheri 1997; Cassola 1997; Hall 2002; Hall 2004; Sourvinou-Inwood 2005, 24–63; Dominguez 2006b; Mitchell 2007; Mitchell 2015; Hornblower 2008; Morris 2012; Vlassopoulos 2013.

55. Ps.-Hes. *Cat.* F9–10a Merkelbach-West; cf. Hdt. 1.56.3. See West 1985, 50–60; Hall 1997, 36, 41–49; Hall 2002, 25–29; Konstan 1997; Fowler 1998; Robertson 2002, 7–11; Ormand 2014, 42–51; but see also Gehrke 2005 on genealogical connections across cultural boundaries.

56. Hall 1989; Mitchell 2007; Harrison 2020.

57. Skinner 2012; Vlassopoulos 2013.

58. Isoc. *Paneg.* 50; Said 2001; Hall 2002, 172–228.

59. Hall 1995 argues strongly against the salience of language; *contra*, Figueira 2020; on Sicily, cf. Willi 2008, esp. 1–4.

(8.144) is clearly only the most prominent of many voices.[60] Moreover, the Greeks came to no agreement as to whether certain marginal peoples, such as the Macedonians and the Epirotes, were Greek or not.[61] All of these factors should give us pause in seeking a single definition of Greekness, for it was clearly many things and changed over time. Scholars, too, have difficulty agreeing on whether to analyze the Greeks as an ethnic or cultural group.[62] For this reason, I avoid using the term *ethnicity* to describe Greekness, since it was only sometimes conceptualized using ethnic criteria (under the definition of ethnicity adopted below), and I instead reserve that term for the so-called sub-Hellenic ethnic groups, particularly Dorians, Ionians, and Achaeans.[63]

Nonetheless, Greekness remained a discursive category that many Greeks, over many centuries, found useful, even as its definition changed drastically from the Archaic period through the Hellenistic age (and beyond). In fact, Greeks across the Mediterranean actively debated and contested what it meant to be Greek, including in highly charged rhetorical contexts. Herodotus's definition, for instance, is placed in the mouth of an Athenian orator addressing the Spartans to explain why Athens would never side with Persia. This passage should be read against claims that the fifth-century Athenian *archē* was actually enslaving other Greeks, much as the Persians had attempted. The Athenian claims are self-serving in the context of contemporary politics and represent not a neutral definition but rather a sharply contested one. In some situations, Greekness overshadowed and even undercut other forms of identity, such as *polis* identity or regional collectivities; at other times, the reverse occurred, and *polis* identity, for instance, was stronger than Greekness. Because of these shifting relationships, it is useful to think of Greekness as a separate type of identity.

In Sicily and southern Italy, scholars have often focused particular attention on early colonization as a catalyst for the initial development of a sense of Greekness.[64] On this model, contact with indigenous peoples in newly settled

---

60. On this justly famous passage, see Thomas 2001, 213–217; Hall 2002, 189–194; Zacharia 2008b.

61. Epirus: Malkin 2001b. Macedonia: Hall 2001; Asirvatham 2008.

62. Ethnic: Konstan 2001; Hall 2002, esp. 125–171. Cultural: Hall 1989; Cartledge 2002; Hall 2002, 172–228.

63. In doing so, I follow the approach of Hall 1997; Hall 2002; Malkin 2001c; Robertson 2002; Luraghi 2008.

64. E.g., Dunbabin 1948, 90; Fowler 1998, 15; Malkin 2005b; Dominguez 2006b; Porciani 2015; *contra*, Hall 2004; Skinner 2012, 175–211.

lands would have spurred the Greek colonists to recognize what they shared among themselves and how they differed from the natives, leading to a bipolar dichotomy between Greeks and "barbarian" natives. Such a model assumes a relative cultural unity among Greeks and a strong cultural contrast between the Greeks and the indigenous peoples, as well as a constant state of tension, if not outright conflict, between Greeks and natives. This is surely part of the story of Greekness, and a growing sense of cultural unity may well have been assisted by the growth of networks that linked the western Greeks to Greeks on the mainland and throughout the Mediterranean.[65] Nevertheless, this picture is too simple: relationships between Greek settlers and their indigenous neighbors sometimes led to conflict but equally often to cooperation; meanwhile, conflict and cultural differentiation among Greeks were just as significant.[66] As a result, the Greekness of the western Greeks should be seen as multivalent and flexible, only one of many forms of identity that were relevant there and partaking of all the definitions described above.

Ethnicity

Ethnicity has provoked by far the most controversy of these types of identity. Anthropologists have proposed a wide range of definitions, but they tend to cluster around two aspects of ethnic groups: either a belief in common ancestry or a shared culture.[67] Focusing on culture seems logical at first; most ethnic groups do seem to share a common culture, and archaeologists have drawn attention to material culture as a form of ethnic signaling that was shared broadly across whole societies.[68] Some scholars, in fact, have argued in favor of an extremely broad concept of ethnicity focusing on shared cultural features; they consider kinship too narrow a criterion to be meaningful, especially since our knowledge of ancient perceptions of kinship derives primarily from written sources produced by elites. Kinship, these scholars argue, can

---

65. Malkin 2005b; Malkin 2011. Of course, similar networks also linked Greeks to non-Greeks, especially the one mediated by Heracles-Melqart in western Sicily: Malkin 2005a; Miles 2010, 96–111; Quinn 2018, 113–131; cf. Gehrke 2005; Vlassopoulos 2013.

66. See, e.g., Di Stefano 1988; Shepherd 1995; Shepherd 2005; Albanese Procelli 1996; Leighton 1999, 219–268; Anello 2002a; Morel 2002; De Angelis 2003; Hall 2004; Sammartano 2015.

67. For balanced treatments of these issues, see Jenkins 2008; Eriksen 2010. See also broadly Roosens 1989; Banks 1996; Hutchinson and Smith 1996; Emberling 1997; Levine 1999.

68. On the archaeology of ethnicity, see esp. Jones 1997; Morgan 1999a; Morgan 2009; Antonaccio 2010; see further below.

hardly serve as a criterion for ethnic identities known and felt to be relevant by all.[69] This critique, I suggest, understates the extent to which the written evidence available to us is merely the tip of an iceberg of oral discourse. But more important, although shared culture plays an important role in articulating ethnicity and identity in many ways (as we will see throughout this book), in fact, such a definition is far too broad to stand.

The modern world offers numerous examples of cultural groups that do not claim common ethnicity. Fans of the Boston Red Sox demonstrate intense pride in membership, maintain a common historical memory, and deploy a shared material culture in the form of hats and jerseys to signal their loyalty. No one, though, would say that the Red Sox Nation is an ethnic group.[70] Such examples could easily be multiplied: all four types of identity discussed in this book are associated with specific cultural features. Conversely, despite the importance of shared cultural elements in many constructions of identity, culture is not the same as identity. Rather, a particular cultural pattern or practice becomes salient for identity only when people think it is. Not all elements of their culture will matter to a given community as part of its shared self-image, and we cannot objectively decide which ones did. From our scholarly perspective, observing from outside the culture in question and thousands of years later, determining which cultural features were salient, and whether they were salient for ethnicity or some other type of identity, is very tricky. A group with an observable shared culture may or may not be an ethnic group, and hence a more focused concept of ethnicity is needed.

Thus, I will define ethnicity as a form of identity predicated on a perception of kinship or shared ancestry among group members. This notion of common descent or origins is usually fictive, a constructed myth that can sometimes be objectively disproved by scholars, but (like identity as a whole) it typically has a social reality, since group members find it highly meaningful. Among classicists, this definition is closely associated with the work of Jonathan Hall,[71] but it has a long pedigree in anthropology and other disciplines as well. Even anthropologists whose definitions of ethnicity begin with culture often include a group's belief in kinship among its members as an element of that shared

---

69. E.g., Konstan 1997; Morris 1998; Jones 1998; Malkin 2001c; Antonaccio 2001; Antonaccio 2010; Sourvinou-Inwood 2005, 26–28; Boardman 2006; Dominguez 2006b; Mitchell 2006; Shepherd 2006; Ruby 2006; Snodgrass 2006; Vlassopoulos 2015; Gruen 2020, 1–7.

70. For similar arguments, see Hall 2002, 13, 24.

71. Hall 1997; Hall 2002; more recently, see Vlassopoulos 2015, with Hall 2015. For various approaches to ethnicity in Classics, see Parker 1998; Malkin 2001c; McInerney 2001; Siapkas 2003; Luraghi 2008, 6–12; Mac Sweeney 2009, 101–102; McInerney 2014b; Luraghi 2014.

culture.[72] This definition is usefully precise, allowing ethnic groups to be distinguished analytically from other types of collectivity and compared with other ethnicities elsewhere. While there was a wide range of ethnic groups in Greece, including Boeotians, Thessalians, Arcadians, and many more, this book will mainly be concerned with the Dorians, Ionians, and Achaeans.

Kinship is visible in the ancient sources in several ways. A number of Greek ethnic groups developed genealogical myths that delineated their descent from an eponymous ancestor, such as Dorus for the Dorians.[73] A process of aggregation then brought these groups together, culminating in the Hellenic Genealogy of the late sixth century, mentioned above, in which Dorus, Aeolus, Ion, and Achaeus appear as sons or grandsons of Hellen. The myth thus articulates both the separateness of those four ethnic groups and also their unification into a single larger group, the Greeks, who are here defined ethnically. The existence of these myths is difficult to explain without ascribing ethnic significance to them, since the mythical figures have few independent stories attached to them; they seem to exist solely to explain relationships between ethnic groups in the present. Moreover, kinship terminology was used from at least the fifth century and probably earlier to describe relations between *poleis*; thus, the relationship between Athens and Leontini (both Ionian communities) is described as kinship or *syngeneia*.[74] Similarly, kinship terms were sometimes used to qualify descriptions of ethnic groups; for instance, Phayllus of Croton is "Achaean by *genos*" in Herodotus (8.47). Both genealogical discourse and these statements of kinship in the present strongly support the definition of ethnicity based on common ancestry that I have proposed and that it was sometimes a salient way for communities to relate to one another.

Interactions

Each of these four types of identity was articulated according to different criteria, and as a result, it is crucial to distinguish them. But we must also observe how different identities work together. Although classicists have made great

---

72. E.g., Horowitz 1985, 55–64; Smith 1986, 22–31; Nash 1989, 5–6; Jenkins 2008, 10–14; Eriksen 2010, 12–13. However, some anthropologists do place a heavy emphasis on purely cultural definitions (e.g., De Vos 1975; Patterson 1975), as do many archaeologists (e.g., Morgan 2009, 18–22; Antonaccio 2010).

73. For the role of myth in ethnogenesis, see also Malkin 1994; Malkin 1998; Luraghi 2008.

74. E.g., Thuc. 3.86.3; cf. Jones 1999; Patterson 2010. See further in chapter 5.

strides in studying identities in ancient Greece, the various types have usually been treated one at a time. Landmark works such as Edith Hall's *Inventing the Barbarian* (1989) and Jonathan Hall's *Ethnic Identity in Greek Antiquity* (1997), for instance, explored only Greekness and ethnicity, respectively. Despite the progress made by each of these studies, they give the impression that only their one type of identity matters. Conversely, others have argued for the un-importance of certain kinds of identity. Erich Gruen, for example, has recently argued that ethnicity (in the sense of perceived kinship) was not a major factor in how people in the ancient world understood their identities and that instead they tended to prefer "a more complex self-perception that incorporated mul-tiple mixtures and plural identities."[75]

Gruen succeeds in showing that ethnicity was unimportant for some people some of the time. But for others in other situations, perceived kin-ship did matter. By redirecting attention to what he calls "plural identities," Gruen actually shows the importance of looking at multiple types of iden-tity at once. The various identities constructed by Greek communities, by and large, would all be available to them at any given time, though not all would be salient at the same time. Syracusans always had the option of calling them-selves Syracusan, Dorian, Sicilian, or Greek, as the situation demanded. In Croton, the options were Crotoniate, Achaean, Italian, or Greek, and a sim-ilar list could be constructed for any *polis*. These identities did not stand in a vacuum but rather were part of a larger system. All four identities were con-stantly juxtaposed with one another, and a complete picture of identity in an-cient Greece must take account of the dynamic relationships among multiple types of identity.

Sometimes Greeks experienced these as four separate options, and in these cases, the analytical need for scholars to distinguish them aligns with the emic perception of identity. In these situations, understanding why one identity was emphasized requires also asking why other identities were less salient. Hermocrates's speech in 424, for instance, invited the Sicilian *poleis* not only to adopt a regional identity but also to reject ethnicity as a basis for political action. Similarly, a full appreciation of the significance and meaning of Greekness requires observing how it was often subordinated to rivalries between *poleis*. If we fail to recognize how Hellenic and *polis* identities inter-related, we miss the real significance of situations where Greekness did pre-dominate. In these cases, a complete grasp of the situation requires thinking about more than one identity.

---

75. Gruen 2016 (quote from 20); cf. Gruen 2020.

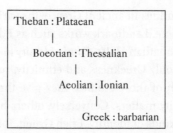

Theban : Plataean
|
Boeotian : Thessalian
|
Aeolian : Ionian
|
Greek : barbarian

FIG. 1.1 A hierarchy of identities in Thebes. By the author.

In other situations, however, Greeks experienced identities in overlapping combinations. Being Dorian was part of what it meant to be Syracusan, even though there were many other Dorians elsewhere. Similarly, being Greek may have been part of Sicilian regional identity. Although a criterion based on geography should have included the island's non-Greek inhabitants, there is little positive evidence that this logic was taken seriously, and as a result, Sicilian identity was most commonly experienced as a composite phenomenon. At panhellenic festivals, such as the Olympic Games, multiple types of identity were typically in play: on one level, they were a gathering of all Greeks, from which non-Greeks were at least sometimes excluded (Hdt. 5.22), but on another level, they were opportunities for athletes to compete for their cities and for *poleis* to display the prowess of their citizens—in other words, a showcase for *polis* identity. In these situations, it is still useful analytically to distinguish between different types of identity, because this enables us to recognize the greater complexity produced by these interactions.

Some sets of identities in Greece, such as the Theban identities shown in fig. 1.1, were interrelated in a hierarchical pattern. Here the two groups that are opposed at one level (Boeotians and Thessalians, for instance) combine to form a single group (Aeolians) at the next level. This is what anthropologists call a "segmentary hierarchy of comparison and contrast," because the two smaller groups together make up a larger group.[76] But other identities are not related hierarchically, including the four types of identity discussed in this book. While Greekness would be at the top of such a hierarchy and an individual *polis* at the bottom, ethnicity and regional identities do not relate to each other hierarchically: not all Dorians live in Sicily, and not all Sicilians are Dorians (fig. 1.2). Malkin therefore rightly rejects hierarchy as an organizing principle, and his visualization of various identities in Syracuse instead represents each

76. Jenkins 2008, 42–45.

FIG. I.2 Non-hierarchical identities in Syracuse. By the author.

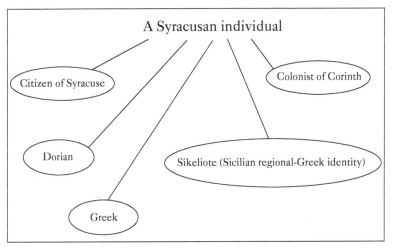

FIG. I.3 Malkin's visualization of identities in Syracuse. From Malkin 2011, 19.

identity as a separate circle (fig. 1.3).[77] Although Malkin describes the networks represented by the circles as overlapping, his diagram links them only to the individual Syracusan citizen, giving little sense of the complex juxtapositions and interactions between that citizen's various identities.

By contrast, I propose a series of overlapping circles, resembling a Venn diagram (fig. 1.4). Greekness forms the largest circle, with the *polis* as the smallest circle inside all the others. Dorian ethnicity contains Syracusan *polis* identity entirely, while another circle for Achaean ethnicity (not shown) would contain other *poleis* such as Croton.[78] Finally, Sicilian regional identity contains Syracuse, partly overlaps with Dorian ethnicity, and emerges narrowly beyond the surface of Greekness to account for the possibility that non-Greek Sikels

77. Malkin 2011, 17–19.

78. Not every citizen of Syracuse was necessarily of Dorian origin, especially since influxes of population were common, but notionally and ideologically, Syracuse portrayed itself as a Dorian community (see further in chapters 3 and 6).

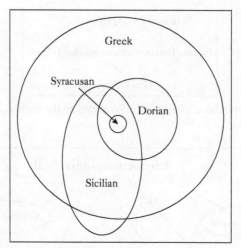

FIG. 1.4 Overlapping identities in Syracuse. By the author.

might sometimes be considered Sicilian. These various visualizations are powerful tools that reflect quite different conceptualizations of the relationships between different identities. What they all share is a sense that identities cannot be understood in isolation.

Seeking Identities in Antiquity

Since identity is such a slippery concept and so difficult to pin down even in the modern world, how can we identify and analyze identities in antiquity? For the study of ancient identities, the difficulties multiply, since the sources available to us are, of course, limited, fragmentary, and difficult to interpret. To make headway, what is needed is an interdisciplinary approach that makes full use of every possible source, taking into account historiography, epinician and other poetry, archaeology and material culture, inscriptions, visual evidence, coinage, myths, religious practices, and more. Literary sources vary widely—historiography, for instance, was written under different circumstances and with different goals from epinician poetry, and the two can answer quite different questions—and so combining evidence from different genres is already a step toward the kind of interdisciplinary study I am envisioning here. Numismatics, epigraphy, archaeology, history of religions, and the study of mythology all have their own contributions to make as well. Bringing together many types of evidence and a variety of subfields can help us build a deeper and more nuanced picture of how ancient communities perceived themselves and their place in the world.[79]

Each of these sources has both strengths and weaknesses, and they all require analysis that is sensitive to the different peculiarities of working with such varied material. Texts, for example, are well suited to transmit subjective ancient ideas about identity to us;[80] on the other hand, they are often late or written by outsiders and in many cases express only the viewpoint of a narrow elite. Material culture, by contrast, was produced and used by everyone in a society, and hence archaeological evidence is sometimes seen as a more objective window into the daily realities of ancient life.[81] Moreover, archaeologists have now begun to focus on how people in antiquity actively articulate and communicate their identities through objects, a process Carla Antonaccio has called a "discourse of things."[82] But the archaeological record is always incomplete; new excavations may change the picture, and perishable items such as wood, textiles, and food are rarely preserved, though any of them may have been central to past identities.[83] Since no one source has a complete picture of any ancient identity, analyzing all of these sources in conversation with one another can counteract their weaknesses and build on their strengths.

Two key methodologies will guide my analysis of all these disparate sources. First, we must pay careful attention to which type of identity is being expressed. The typology outlined above has shown that the various identities were all relevant to Greeks at different times, and we cannot assume which was relevant in a particular situation without carefully analyzing the evidence. Second, identifying objective facts or patterns in the evidence is not enough to draw conclusions about identities that were subjectively perceived. Rather, the key factor is salience, and hence I will be looking for evidence that ancient people found a particular fact or pattern salient for their identities. In fact, as many scholars have noted, the material record often substantially diverges

---

79. Malkin 2011 and Demetriou 2012 are good examples of this method.

80. Hall 1997; Hall 2002.

81. See broadly Jones 1997; Emberling 1997; Morgan 1999a; Morgan 2009; Antonaccio 2001; Antonaccio 2004; Antonaccio 2010; Lucy 2005; Hakenbeck 2007; Hall 2012; Mac Sweeney 2011; Shepherd 2014; Knapp 2014.

82. Antonaccio 2010; cf. Antonaccio 2005.

83. For critiques of archaeological approaches to identity, see Hall 2002, 19–29; Hall 2012. A particular risk is the so-called positivist fallacy, equating what is archaeologically visible with what is historically important: Snodgrass 1987, 37–39; cf. Jones 1997, 106–110. On food and identity, see Broekaert, Nadeau, and Wilkins 2016; Beck 2020, 82–95.

from or even outright contradicts what we read in texts.[84] For example, the importance of Greekness and a dichotomy between Greeks and barbarians emerge strongly from the literary sources on fourth- and third-century southern Italy. But scholars have shown (based on archaeological evidence as well as a closer reading of those same literary texts) that, in fact, southern Italy in that period would be better described as an environment of cultural mixing and exchange. Nicholas Purcell, therefore, has argued that the idea of "Greeks vs. barbarians" is nothing but meaningless rhetoric and should be ignored in favor of exploring the mixed cultures of the region.[85] Divergences like this rightly attract our attention, but I argue that they require explanations that go beyond elevating one source or methodology over another. Rather, they should be treated as an opportunity to seek a deeper understanding, based on all available evidence, of why the divergence occurred. Both the identities claimed by ancient peoples and the historical context in which they were expressed are critical elements of a full account of antiquity.

The subjective nature of identity creates a particular need for emic sources—those created by members of the communities concerned—since only insiders can directly express what it means to be a member of their community. Sicily and southern Italy produced a striking array of emic sources. Coinage, for instance, offers contemporary evidence that comes directly from the communities that produced it. Inscriptions and material culture, especially votive deposits, have similar advantages. Mythology must be reconstructed from a variety of (often later) sources and therefore comes down to us through a filter, but it, too, was often produced by insiders. Epinician poetry, while written by outsiders such as Pindar and Bacchylides, was commissioned by Sicilians and Italians and incorporated much local material. Sicilian historiography, especially the works of Antiochus and Philistus of Syracuse and Timaeus of Tauromenion, forms a significant body of work.[86] Since it has come down to us only in fragments, we do not have complete and unfiltered access to it, and this poses significant interpretive challenges. Each of these types of sources, in fact, raises particular methodological concerns, which will be addressed as they come up in the chapters that follow.

---

84. Antonaccio 2010, 34–35; cf. Antonaccio 2005, 107.

85. Purcell 1994, 393–394; cf. the more balanced treatment of Dench 2003, 300. See further in chapter 6.

86. Antiochus wrote in the late fifth century, Philistus in the first half of the fourth century, and Timaeus in the early third century. Besides the texts and commentaries in FGrH and BNJ, see Vattuone 2002 on Sicilian historiography as a whole; on Timaeus specifically, see Brown 1958; Vattuone 1991; Baron 2013.

The interdisciplinary methodology described here is indispensable to a nuanced and wide-ranging study of ancient identities. Communities in ancient Greece constructed multifaceted self-portraits, using numerous tools and mechanisms, ranging from myths to coins to material culture, to articulate their identities and drawing on a variety of elements to create a richly textured sense of who they were that goes far beyond a single criterion. Analyzing a variety of sources enables us to see many more dimensions of identity and to build a much richer picture of identities as they were perceived by Greeks.

Identity is perhaps the preeminent political and cultural issue of the twenty-first century, but it should be clear by now that studying identity in antiquity is not a matter of projecting our own preoccupations onto the Greeks, in an attempt to make them more like ourselves. Greeks discussed and debated their identities regularly, and the evidence for identity in the political sphere also suggests that they thought identity mattered enormously. The manner in which tyrants and politicians used identity for purposes of legitimacy presupposes that large swaths of the population took those identities seriously, and no city would change its political orientation for reasons of identity if the identity was not felt to be important. Ultimately, this should not be surprising. Appiah has recently described identity as a basic part of the human experience.[87] The practice of categorizing people, dividing them into in-groups and out-groups, and the need to belong to a community are as close to universals as the human experience gets. Greeks did not necessarily see their identities in the same way we do today, but denying that they perceived and articulated community identities at all is to disregard an important aspect of the Greek experience.

---

87. Appiah 2018, 20–32; cf. Jenkins 2014, 14.

2

Becoming Achaean in Italy

THE PEOPLE OF Croton, according to Herodotus (8.47), sent a single ship to the Battle of Salamis, captained by Phayllus, a three-time winner at the Pythian Games. Herodotus adds that "the Crotoniates are Achaean by birth (*genos*)." What does this mean? In what sense are the people of Croton Achaean? The historian's word *genos* suggests that the Crotoniates' status as Achaeans derives from their ancestry.[1] Herodotus sets the Crotoniates' Achaean identity alongside the Dorian and Ionian ethnicities of numerous other communities that fought at Salamis, suggesting that Achaeans are a collectivity of similar type: an ethnic group.

From which Achaeans are the Crotoniates descended? According to one story, Croton was founded in the late eighth century by Myscellus of Rhype, a town in the region of the northern Peloponnese known as Achaea.[2] Yet the Homeric Achaeans and similar figures from the heroic age were equally important: a Crotoniate coin of the late fifth century, which depicted Heracles with his club and lion skin and the legend ΟΙΚΙΣΤΑΣ, shows that he, too, was seen as a founder.[3] Croton was not alone in developing a whole series of foundation myths like this,[4] but the multiple levels on which Croton articulated its ethnic identity are particularly striking. A number of other cities in southern Italy shared this identification as Achaean; these included, most prominently, Sybaris, Metapontion, and Poseidonia but also smaller places such as Caulonia, Laus, Terina, and others.

---

1. Jones 1996; Hall 1997, 35–37. On Phayllus, see Cagnazzi 1996; Nicholson 2015, 196–201.

2. Antiochus F10 = Strabo 6.1.12; cf. 6.2.4; Diod. 8.17.

3. Rutter 2001, nos. 2139–2140. See fig. 2.2.

4. Mac Sweeney 2013.

The Politics of Identity in Greek Sicily and Southern Italy. Mark R. Thatcher, Oxford University Press. © Oxford University Press 2021. DOI: 10.1093/oso/9780197586440.003.0002

Herodotus, of course, also identifies Phayllus in another way, by his *polis*. His identity as a Crotoniate was likely just as important to him and his fellow citizens as their Achaean ethnicity. This *polis* identity incorporated a range of factors, but the city's great athletic success in the late sixth and early fifth centuries tops the list. Phayllus's status as a victorious athlete—which Herodotus thought was important enough to mention—helped contribute to a sense of what made Croton distinctive from other communities. These multiple levels of identity, both *polis* and ethnic, are a fundamental part of how Greeks identified themselves.

But the precise manner in which Croton articulated its Achaean identity repays closer attention. Many Greek ethnic groups such as the Boeotians or Phocians articulated their ethnic identity on the level of the group: through myths of common ancestors (Boiotos or Phokos) shared by various *poleis*, for example, or through festivals at a shared sanctuary. The Achaeans of southern Italy did not form a unified *ethnos* in this way. The foundation stories described above focus only on Croton, leaving other Achaean communities to tell their own stories, and they construct a vision of Croton as a *polis* that is defined partly through its ethnic origin. Ethnic and *polis* identity are articulated together: being Achaean is seen not as a separate identity but rather as part of what it meant to be Crotoniate. Coinage similarly expressed a sense of Achaean-ness—but, since it was minted by the *polis* of Croton and not by any federal authority, it, too, expressed the identity of the *polis*. And as we will see, some of the same stories that articulated Croton's belief in its Achaean origins also expressed its claim to athletic success. Thus, Croton's ethnic and *polis* identities cannot be neatly separated but overlap strongly, forming a network of varying self-identifications whose different strands interact in complex ways. Other cities—Metapontion, for instance—constructed similar overlapping ethnic and *polis* identities but in ways unique to their own *polis*.

Previous scholarship has made great strides in understanding the Achaeans' constructions of identity.[5] My argument builds on their work, yet they have usually treated the Achaeans as a single monolithic *ethnos*, rather than grappling with each city's separate construction of its plural identities, and without sufficient attention to the overlapping and intertwining strands of identity. The differences between Croton and Metapontion are worth considering, alongside their similarities. A second neglected angle is the relationship of identity to politics. As we shall see, these identities were created in response

---

5. See esp. Giangiulio 1989; Mele 1995; Mele 1998; Morgan and Hall 1996; Hall 2002, 58–64; Kowalzig 2007, 267–327; and the essays collected in Greco 2002.

to inter-*polis* conflict, they helped mediate relations (whether friendly or hostile) between cities, and they helped justify the hegemony of some cities over others. In fact, as we will see, conflicts and competition between different Greek cities in Italy (and not between Greeks and non-Greeks, as is sometimes thought) were the primary drivers of the creation and evolution of identities among the Achaeans. The best route to studying Achaean identities, therefore, is a comprehensive exploration of the multiple overlapping identities of individual *poleis*, using a wide range of sources and placing them in their historical context. Croton and Metapontion offer the richest surviving evidence, although this can sometimes be supplemented usefully with information from other Achaean cities. Therefore, case studies of these two communities, focusing on the intertwining of ethnic and *polis* identities, form the core of this chapter.

The First Achaeans

These Crotoniate, Metapontine, and Achaean identities were created in, by, and for those communities. They were not brought to Italy fully formed, nor did they spring into existence at the moment the first settler stepped off a boat onto the Italian shore. Instead, they arose over time and in specific historical and political contexts. So how did disparate settlers from the Peloponnese come to see themselves as a *polis* community? How and when did they first become Achaean? As we will see, scholars have proposed a number of events and conflicts as the original spark for the creation of Achaean identity. But since each *polis* constructed and articulated its sense of Achaean-ness in its own way, it makes little sense to think in terms of a single origin. Rather, Achaean ethnicity was created in response to the separate histories of each community and in conversation with the separate *polis* identities that were developing at the same time. There was not one ethnogenesis of the Achaeans but many.

The initial settlement in the Achaean regions of Italy began in the late eighth century, when both literary and archaeological evidence suggest that the earliest settlers arrived at Croton and Sybaris.[6] Decades of fieldwork at

---

6. Thapsos ware has been found at both sites, along with Corinthian material (Late Geometric at Croton and Subgeometric at Sybaris): Guzzo 1982; Sabbione 1982, 251–277; Spadea 2012. Eusebius dates both foundations to 709/8, while Ps.-Scymnus 360 offers 721/0 for Sybaris. For the following, see Cordano 1986, 56–64; Morgan and Hall 1996, 202–214; Yntema 2000; Yntema 2013, 101–106; Musti 2005, 84–90; Greco 2008, 33–43; La Torre 2011, 50–54; Guzzo 2011; and the articles on each city in *IACP*.

Metapontion, meanwhile, has suggested that the town and its *chora* evolved slowly, reaching a recognizable form by around 630.[7] Finally, the sub-colony of Poseidonia was founded from Sybaris around 600; a number of other subcolonies were also established, but little is known about them.[8] Archaeology has given us a much clearer picture of the earliest history of these communities, yet the identities they claimed at that time—how they subjectively perceived themselves—remain opaque. We should not assume that they saw themselves as Achaeans, as Crotoniates, or as Metapontines, because whatever subjective self-conceptions they had cannot easily be recovered archaeologically.

In fact, these early settlers are unlikely to have initially shared an identity at all. Recent approaches to Greek colonization have questioned the traditional model of colonization as a coherent series of centrally organized, state-run expeditions led by a single oikist (or at most a few) and populated from a single point of origin.[9] The early populations of places like Croton and Metapontion were likely a more diverse group than literary sources allow, hailing not only from a single mother city but from a larger region throughout the northern tier of the Peloponnese and perhaps beyond.[10] Such a diverse group would have needed time to forge themselves into a new community with its own identity.

This process becomes visible in the years around and after 600, when large public building projects were begun in a number of cities, all of which required the desire and the ability to mobilize labor and other resources. These include sanctuary structures and (slightly later) the first monumental temples.[11] Even more intriguingly, the so-called stone *ekklesiasterion* at Metapontion dates to the mid-sixth century and may have had a wooden predecessor as early as 600. These structures, if they are correctly identified, imply that the Metapontines at that date saw themselves as a political community.[12] The beginnings of coinage can also be placed at the end of this period,

---

7. De Siena 1999; Yntema 2000, 13–16; Carter 2006, 51–89.

8. Pedley 1990, 29–32; Morgan and Hall 1996, 211. Other Achaean subcolonies included Caulonia, Laus, and Terina (see fig. 0.1).

9. Osborne 1998; Yntema 2000, 43–45; *contra*, Malkin 2002; cf. Cordano 1986; Snodgrass 1994; Lombardo 2012; see now Donnellan, Nizzo, and Burghers 2016.

10. Morgan and Hall 1996, 202–211; Lomas 2000, 173–174; Kowalzig 2007, 298–301. On Achaean ceramic traditions, see Papadopoulos 2001.

11. E.g., Building B at the sanctuary of Hera Lacinia (Spadea 1996); the first stoa and the Treasury at Foce del Sele (Zancani Montuoro and Zanotti-Bianco 1937, 322–331; Pedley 1990, 61–75); cf. Yntema 2000; Yntema 2013, 101–115; Mertens 2006, 156–171.

12. Mertens and De Siena 1982; De Juliis 2001, 159–167; Carter 2006, 204–210.

around 550–530.[13] All of this suggests a heightened sense of communal solidarity in each city, and—while we cannot be sure—some form of *polis* identity was likely developing.[14]

Similarly, it is now firmly established that Achaean ethnicity was not brought to Italy fully developed by the initial settlers from the Peloponnese. No such thing existed at that time, in all likelihood, since a shared sense of ethnic identity in Peloponnesian Achaea cannot be traced farther back than the mid-sixth century.[15] Nor was there even a sense that the southern coast of the Corinthian Gulf constituted a unified region inhabited by a single *ethnos*. Instead, this area was thought of as several different regions that were more closely tied to places outside the later boundaries of Achaea (such as the Argolid or northern Arcadia) than to one another.[16] Thus, it is likely that conceptions of Achaean-ness developed in Italy first, in the sixth century, and then were exported back to the Peloponnese. How and under what circumstances did this process of ethnogenesis occur? Ethnic identity is frequently created through conflict and competition, by drawing ethnic boundaries between Self and Other, and the Achaeans were no exception. But which conflicts and which boundaries mattered most in Croton and Metapontion?

The encounter with non-Greeks, who spoke a different language and practiced a different culture, has often been seen as a key trigger for the development of new identities in colonial contexts. This was clearly relevant for some Greeks in Italy; at Taras, for instance, a foundation oracle described the colony as "a bane to the Iapygians," their indigenous neighbors.[17] This suggests that Hellenic identity was important to the Tarantines, who saw themselves as a bulwark against barbarians (a point to which we will return in chapter 6). But this idea has sometimes been overemphasized by scholars, based on modern preconceptions about the preeminence of a dichotomy between Greeks and non-Greeks that does not always apply in southern Italy. Explicit evidence such as we find at Taras is rare in Italy; nothing like it exists for Croton or

---

13. Stazio 1998; Rutter 2001, 108, 140, 144, 167; and see further below.

14. See esp. Morgan and Hall 1996, 211–214; Yntema 2000, 40–45.

15. Morgan and Hall 1996; Hall 2002, 62–63; Kowalzig 2007, 298–300; *contra*, Arena 2006–2007; cf. Walbank 2000; Goegebeur 1985.

16. Morgan 1999b, 417–420; Morgan 2002, 108–111; Kowalzig 2007, 284–290, 306–308.

17. Antiochus F13; cf. Diod. 8.21.3, with Nenci 1976; Malkin 1994, 115–127.

Metapontion, where an attitude of accommodation toward the natives is just as likely.[18]

Equally importantly, "Achaeans" was not simply another name for "Greeks in Italy," since a number of Greek cities (including Taras, as well as Locri, Elea, Rhegium, and many others) were excluded from the Achaean *ethnos*. Greekness and Achaean-ness seem to have been defined differently, and so it is crucial to keep the two forms of self-representation separate. At the same time, however, it is possible that contact with non-Greeks spurred a looser kind of rethinking of identities, of many kinds. In particular, the presence of Homeric heroes, which is such a prominent feature of the Achaean landscape, could be a way of staking a claim to the land on which their cities were built. As Irad Malkin and others have pointed out, myths of traveling Greek heroes acted as charter myths, allowing later Greek settlers to claim precedence over indigenous populations.[19] Greekness and Achaean-ness do seem to be intertwined in this way—being Greek was certainly felt to be one aspect of being Achaean—but other, more specific attributes acted to separate the Achaeans from other Greeks.

In fact, for early Crotoniates and Metapontines, the most salient contrasts may not have been with their indigenous neighbors but rather with other Greeks. They competed with these other cities—and among themselves—for land, prestige, and power. These boundaries between Greeks and other Greeks are likely the main force that ultimately generated Achaean ethnic identity. This is a particularly striking conclusion, because scholarship on Greek colonialism has tended to emphasize preconceived notions of quasi-nationalist solidarity among Greeks.[20] The history of this region in the sixth century is hazy, but three important threads of competition and conflict between the Achaeans and their non-Achaean neighbors should be discerned: those with Siris, Locri, and Taras.

Siris, an Ionian community lying between Metapontion and Sybaris, was founded from Colophon in the late seventh century, but in the mid-sixth century, it was attacked and apparently destroyed by a coalition of Sybaris, Metapontion, and Croton.[21] Jonathan Hall has identified the atmosphere of

18. Malkin 1998, 210–233; Hall 2002, 63, 97–103; cf. Morel 2002; Burgers 2004; Dominguez 2006b.

19. Malkin 1998; Malkin 2011, 119–141.

20. On this problem, see De Angelis 1998; De Angelis 2016, 4–25; Ceserani 2012; Urquhart 2014a; Urquhart 2020; cf. the potential inclusion of indigenous Sikels within Sicilian regional identity (chapter 4).

21. Foundation: Timaeus (*FGrH* 566) F51 = Athenaeus 12.25. Destruction: Lycoph. *Alex.* 978–992; Just. 20.2.3–10; cf. Moscati Castelnuovo 1989, 100–115. For the date: Huxley 1982, 35–37.

competition leading up to this destruction as a key catalyst for the initial development of Achaean identity. Hall places the Metapontine story of origins
from Homeric Pylos alongside similar claims made by Mimnermus about
Colophon, Siris's mother city. To Hall, this suggests an "environment of
claims and counter-claims" in which Metapontion tried to surpass Siris by
claiming direct descent from Homeric Pylos, rather than indirect descent via
Colophon.[22] Moreover, the decision on the part of several Achaean communities (and no one else) to take collective action might have resulted from a
sense of ethnic solidarity. Still, as an explanation for the ethnogenesis of all
Achaeans, the conflict with Siris leaves many unanswered questions. How
can we explain the complex overlap of Peloponnesian and heroic origins that
was so central to Achaean identity if Metapontion's rivalry with Siris was articulated only through Homeric Pylos? If the development of Achaean ethnicity
was prompted by a unified collective action, what accounts for the substantial
variation between different Achaean communities? Additional contexts must
be sought.

Also in the mid-sixth century, Croton fought the Battle of the River Sagra
against Locri, this time without other Achaean allies.[23] Locri was neither
Dorian nor Ionian (nor, of course, Achaean), but it often aligned with Dorian
states such as Syracuse and, on this occasion, Sparta. The richness of mythical traditions that grew up around this campaign suggests that the Sagra may
well have sparked a sense of distinctiveness that culminated in Croton's particular brand of Achaean identity.[24] According to several sources, the Locrians
asked for help from Sparta and received statues of the Dioscuri as allies.
Ajax, a Locrian hero, was also believed to have taken part in the battle. While
Croton's response can only be pieced together, this seems a likely context for
the development of the story that Menelaus had visited Croton's important
sanctuary of Hera Lacinia during his return from Troy, and Malkin has argued
that Croton in fact tried to claim Spartan origins at this time, as a way of
countering Locri's appeal for help.[25] Crucially, though, Menelaus's presence at

---

Literary sources use the language of destruction, but archaeological evidence suggests that
the site continued to be inhabited, albeit at a much lower level.

22. Hall 2002, 63–65, with Strabo 6.1.15; Mimnermus F9 West; cf. Kowalzig 2007, 313–316.

23. For the date, see Bicknell 1966.

24. Paus. 3.19.11–13; Diod. 8.32; Just. 20.2–3; Strabo 6.1.10, with Giangiulio 1983.

25. Malkin 1994, 62–64; cf. Giangiulio 1983; Paus. 3.3.1. Menelaus: Lycoph. *Alex.* 856–858.

Croton bridges the gap between Sparta and Croton's Achaean traditions: he is a Spartan hero, of course, but also an Achaean one. If Croton tried to innovate, it did so within the limits of its traditions, taking advantage of the hero's multiple valences.

Finally, Malkin also proposes that conflict with Dorian Taras (a Spartan colony) may account for another piece of the puzzle.[26] Conflict between Metapontion and Taras is attested in the 430s, surrounding the foundation of Heraclea on the former site of Siris.[27] Metapontion's claims of Achaean identity predate this war, but if, as Malkin thinks, such a conflict existed earlier as well, then the Dorian ethnicity ascribed to Taras may have led the Metapontines to develop their own ethnic identity as a contrast. Alternatively, the fifth-century conflict may have provided a context in which a preexisting Achaean identity gained additional and continuing relevance.

None of these three conflicts—with Siris, Locri, and Taras—consisted primarily of a single one-day hoplite battle. Rather, they were flashpoints in a broader pattern of ongoing competition for land, resources, and prestige.[28] These situations sparked the creation of stories that helped understand them, both to create legitimacy for one side's positions and to spur further action, and ultimately became part of a much lengthier process of identification over time. Moreover, each of the three conflicts involved a different cast of characters. Taras was of little concern to Croton, and Metapontion had nothing to do with Locri. Their ethnic unity was quite limited. As we will see, the Achaeans had no shared origin story (as many Greek *ethnē* did); they did not mint a federal coinage, nor did they worship at a single shared sanctuary. Though they were surely in frequent communication and knew of one another's thinking, each city arrived at its Achaean identity through its own separate path and based on its own unique concerns. A sense of being Achaean fulfilled different needs for different communities and at different times, beginning in the first half of the sixth century and developing through the fifth century, though the limitations of the available evidence do not permit a detailed diachronic study. Rather than choosing any one conflict as the primary driver behind the first

---

26. Malkin 1998, 211–212.

27. Antiochus F11 = Strabo 6.1.14. See further below.

28. Cf. the dedication at Olympia by Hipponion (a subcolony of Locri), together with Locri itself and another subcolony, Medma, for a victory over the Crotoniates: *SEG* XI.1211. Since the letter forms suggest a date in the late sixth or early fifth century, the dedication likely celebrates not the Sagra but another unknown battle: Maddoli 1996.

articulation of Achaean-ness, we should attribute the creation of Achaean ethnicity to several origins.

Of course, being Achaean was only one meaningful form of identification in these communities, and conflict among the Achaean *poleis* themselves was an equally important driver of the development of their various identities. Croton, Metapontion, Sybaris, and others fiercely guarded their statuses as separate *poleis*, and the political history of the sixth and fifth centuries also shows that they all tried to build up their own power at the expense of others. Through much of the sixth century, Sybaris was among the wealthiest and most powerful cities in the Greek world. According to Strabo, Sybaris "excelled so much in prosperity that it ruled four nearby *ethnē* and had 25 *poleis* as subjects."[29] Exactly which these were and what was the nature of this Sybarite empire has been the subject of great debate, but in all likelihood they included both Greek and non-Greek communities, including some other Achaeans. This power came to a sudden end in 510, after a crushing defeat by Croton, which maintained its new dominant role throughout the fifth century. Croton's authority was communicated in part by "alliance coins," which were minted by various cities under Crotoniate hegemony, including the refounded Sybaris itself. Each coin displayed a tripod (a symbol of Croton) on one side, with a local emblem on the other; their subordination was symbolized by the fact that they could not mint their own coins without including Croton.[30] Thus, shared Achaean ethnicity was fully compatible with conflict among themselves and the hegemony of some over others.[31] In fact, as we will see, the competition between Sybaris and Croton and their successive hegemonies lay behind much of the development of the multiple interwoven identities, both ethnic and *polis*, of Croton and Metapontion.

Croton: Athletes and Heroes

Croton is a useful place to start exploring the relationship among politics, ethnicity, and the individual *polis*, because of the relatively rich and varied

---

29. 6.1.13: τοσοῦτον δ' εὐτυχίᾳ διήνεγκεν ἡ πόλις αὕτη τὸ παλαιὸν ὥστε τεττάρων μὲν ἐθνῶν τῶν πλησίον ἐπῆρξε, πέντε δὲ καὶ εἴκοσι πόλεις ὑπηκόους ἔσχε. On the Sybarite Empire, see Dunbabin 1948, 153–159; Greco 1990; Greco 1993; Giangiulio 1992; Burgers 2004; Lombardo 2008; La Torre 2011, 84–90. While later writers used this wealth as a byword for the corruption of luxury, this anecdotal tradition seems to have little basis in fact: Gorman and Gorman 2014; cf. Simon 2012, 356–399.

30. Rutter 1997, 36–40; but see Mackil and Van Alfen 2006.

31. See Mac Sweeney 2013 for a similar phenomenon among the Ionians of Asia Minor.

body of evidence that survives. Foundation narratives, coinage, and cultic and ritual practices all combine to give a detailed picture of the city's multiple interweaving identities. Croton's claims of Achaean ethnicity were anchored by foundation narratives starring the city's two founders, Myscellus and Heracles. Yet these same stories also articulated what makes Croton distinctive among the Achaeans, especially its fame in the sixth and fifth centuries for its athletic success and the skill of its doctors. These factors became part of the self-definition of the Crotoniate community, in other words, its *polis* identity. Coinage and religious practices similarly show that the same performances of identity—the same coins, for instance—often express both ethnic and *polis* identities at once. Moreover, these claims of identity are rooted in and conditioned by the political contexts on which they were developed and deployed. They allowed Crotoniates to make strong statements both about the nature of their community and about their place in the world.

Burning the Ships

Strikingly, the Achaeans as a whole did not emphasize a single origin narrative for their entire ethnic group. By contrast, the Dorians were united by the myth of the Dorian Invasion and the Ionians by the story of the Ionian Migration.[32] The Achaeans focused instead on the separate origins of individual cities, not of the Achaean *ethnos* as a whole. An example, one that at first glance runs counter to what I have just suggested, actually helps bring out some of the possibilities. Strabo introduces his description of Croton with the following story (6.1.12):

ἐστὶ . . . ἄλλος ποταμὸς Νέαιθος, ᾧ τὴν ἐπωνυμίαν γενέσθαι φασὶν ἀπὸ τοῦ συμβεβηκότος. καταχθέντας γάρ τινας τῶν ἀπὸ τοῦ Ἰλιακοῦ στόλου πλανηθέντων Ἀχαιῶν ἐκβῆναι λέγουσιν ἐπὶ τὴν κατάσκεψιν τῶν χωρίων, τὰς δὲ συμπλεούσας αὐτοῖς Τρῳάδας καταμαθούσας ἔρημα ἀνδρῶν τὰ πλοῖα ἐμπρῆσαι βαρυνομένας τὸν πλοῦν, ὥστ' ἀναγκασθῆναι μένειν ἐκείνους, ἅμα καὶ τὴν γῆν σπουδαίαν ὁρῶντας· εὐθὺς δὲ καὶ ἄλλων πλειόνων εἰσαφικνουμένων καὶ ζηλούντων ἐκείνους κατὰ τὸ ὁμόφυλον, πολλὰς κατοικίας γενέσθαι, ὧν αἱ πλείους ὁμώνυμοι τῶν ποταμῶν ἐγένοντο.

---

32. On the Dorians, see Malkin 1994, 15–45; Hall 1997, 56–65; Hall 2002, 73–89. On the Ionians, see Mac Sweeney 2013. Of course, many Dorian and Ionian *poleis* told individual foundation stories as well.

Next, there is another river, the Neaethus, which they say got its name from what happened there: some of the Achaeans who had wandered from the expedition against Troy landed there and disembarked to take a look at the place, and when the Trojan women who were sailing with them learned that the ships were empty of men, they set them on fire, since they were tired of the voyage; the result was that the men were forced to remain there, and at the same time they saw that the land was excellent. And when immediately many others arrived, emulating them because of kinship, many settlements arose, most of which took their names from rivers.

This story purports to offer a myth of origin for the entire Achaean *ethnos* in Italy, not just for any one city, and it closely links settlement in this region with the greatest Achaean accomplishment, the sack of Troy.[33] The protagonists are not individual Achaean heroes but rather unspecified members of the Achaean fleet generally, and while "many settlements" are founded as an indirect result of the burning of the ships, none is named; what matters is only that the settlers are Achaean.

Yet, on closer examination, the story should be seen not as a broadly shared narrative of ethnic unity and equality but rather as an attempt by Croton to assert its primacy among the Achaean *poleis* in the late sixth and fifth centuries. The story is attached to the river Neaethus, whose name Strabo derives from *neas aithein* ("to burn ships"). In Archaic times, the Neaethus (today's Neto, about ten kilometers north of the city) probably formed the boundary of Crotoniate territory to the north, toward its most powerful rival, Sybaris.[34] This territory expanded northward following Croton's destruction of Sybaris in 510, as Croton assumed a position of leadership among the Achaeans. Hiding behind this story of common Achaean origins, therefore, is a claim by Croton that its territory was the *fons et origo* of Achaean colonization in Italy, giving themselves a precedence that served to justify Crotoniate hegemony.[35] Thus, in all likelihood, Strabo has preserved a Crotoniate myth that attempts to make

---

33. See Bérard 1963, 352; Mele 1995, 443; Roller 2018, 299–300. As pointed out by Fowler (2013, 567–568), Hornblower (2015, 387–388), and Scheer (2018, 131–132), versions of this "roving anecdote" were attached to a wide range of places; nevertheless, this is the version that was particularly relevant at Croton.

34. Sabbione 1982; Giangiulio 1989, 224–228; Osanna 1992, 175–176.

35. Cf. Quinn 2018, who argues that the Carthaginians proclaimed a shared identity as Tyrian colonists among various "Phoenician" colonies in the western Mediterranean in order to promote its imperial designs.

a statement about its relations with its neighbors in the late sixth and fifth centuries, in which Achaean ethnic identity became a vehicle for promoting Croton's own interests.

The "constructivist" approach that I adopt here focuses on the social functions of foundation myths at the time they were told and retold and seeks to recontextualize them in the societies in which they originated.[36] In this way, I sidestep the question of historical accuracy, which was once the primary focus of investigation into these narratives.[37] Rather than asking what grains of truth the various foundation stories preserve about eighth-century coloniza-tion or about Mycenaean contact with Italy,[38] I treat them as offering historical insight into the later times in which such stories were deliberately preserved, especially the sixth and fifth centuries.[39] What was it about the culture that produced these stories that led them to postulate these origins for themselves? What do they say about the identities articulated at various points in time?

This approach has the further advantage of applying the same analysis to both sets of Achaean narratives, the "historical" ones (starring characters from the eighth century or later, such as Myscellus) and the "mythical" ones (which focus on the heroic age). Earlier scholars long distinguished between these two groups, searching among the former for trustworthy elements and simply discarding the latter.[40] The Achaeans themselves, however, did not make such a distinction. To them, stories of Heracles or Menelaus founding their cities or sanctuaries were no less real or believable than those involving more recent Peloponnesian figures. Conversely, the supposedly historical Myscellus—whose stories include a number of tropes familiar from a variety of colonial narratives, such as an unwilling oikist, a Delphic consultation, and a riddling oracle whose solution proves the oikist worthy to found a city—is no

---

36. See esp. Hall 2008; Mac Sweeney 2013; cf. Osborne 1998; Nafissi 1999; Giangiulio 2001; Yntema 2011.

37. E.g., Graham 1964; Cordano 1986; Malkin 1987; Boardman 1999.

38. Such grains of truth might exist, of course, though work on oral traditions has highlighted the difficulties in this approach (e.g., Thomas 1989). Even if any of these narratives could be verified, however, my discussion focuses on the continuing relevance of foundation myths to the societies in which they were remembered and retold.

39. In this way, I differ from the entirely literary approach adopted by Dougherty 1993; cf. Calame 1990.

40. Bérard 1963; and cf. citations above in note 32. Another approach to the "mythic" narratives treated them as dim memories of Mycenaean contact with Italy, e.g., Sjöqvist 1973, 2–13; Pugliese Carratelli 1983, 8–27; *contra*, Guzzo 1990, 138–141; Mele 1995, 427–429; Leighton 1999, 184–186. For an important outline of various scholarly approaches with fur-ther references, see Hall 2008, 383–394.

less a legendary, heroic figure than the Homeric *nostoi*. Since both were clearly crucial to articulating identity among the Achaeans, we should ask the same questions of each of them.

Although the multiple foundation myths that existed for individual Achaean *poleis* seem contradictory to modern readers, they coexisted in antiquity with no apparent difficulty. Strabo, for instance, proceeds directly from his Neaethus story into one regarding Myscellus's foundation of Croton, so he sees no contradiction between the two layers of foundation. In fact, their coexistence was a critical means by which the Achaeans articulated their ethnic identity. This in itself was not unusual. As Naoíse Mac Sweeney has emphasized, foundation stories do not exist in a vacuum. Rather, the multiple origins claimed by a single community work together to create a larger "foundation discourse" that says much more about a community than one story alone.[41] At Croton, the burning of the ships secures its identity as Achaean, coexisting with other stories that did the same, while also claiming leadership among other Achaeans. Other stories, both at Croton and at Metapontion, sought to define the ethnic identity of one particular *polis* as Achaean, by tracing its origins either to the northern Peloponnese or to a mythical Achaean, and they usually also highlight a feature of the community in question that distinguishes it from others. Together, they produce a complex and layered set of identities that includes both civic and ethnic elements.

Myscellus

Ancient writers universally agreed that the eighth-century oikist of Croton was Myscellus of Rhype, a town located seven kilometers inland from Aigion, in the west-central part of Peloponnesian Achaea.[42] Two extant narratives about Myscellus, however, tell more complex stories. According to the first of these narratives, Myscellus is told by the Delphic oracle to found a city at Croton, but after scouting the coast of Italy, he prefers the site of Sybaris, which has already been founded and is flourishing. Apollo then tells him to "approve the gift which the god gives," and Croton is founded as ordered.[43] In the second, Myscellus visits Delphi together with Archias, the founder

---

41. Mac Sweeney 2013, esp. 14–16.

42. Morgan and Hall 1996, 179–180. On the stories of Myscellus, see Mele 1984, 17–21; Malkin 1987, 43–47; Giangiulio 1989, 134–148; Goegebeur 1990; Guzzo 2011, 227–233; Luraghi 2013a, F10.

43. Antiochus F10 = Strabo 6.1.12; Diod. 8.17.

of Syracuse in Sicily. Apollo asks the two men whether they prefer health or wealth. Myscellus chooses health, Archias chooses wealth, and as a result, each of them establishes a city that is appropriate to his choice.[44] Both stories stake a claim to the Achaean origins of Croton but also flesh out that claim by situating Croton in relation to other important western cities and highlighting Croton's distinctive qualities.

In each of these stories, the foundation of Croton is closely associated with that of another city but in different ways. In the first narrative, Croton is juxtaposed with Sybaris. While Sybaris appears a more prosperous community at first glance, Croton proves in the end to have the sanction of Apollo. This story likely developed during a period of competition between Croton and Sybaris, presumably the second half of the sixth century, which culminated in the destruction of Sybaris in 510, and serves to assert Croton's status against its rival.[45] Croton's relationship with Syracuse, on the other hand, appears cooperative and mutually beneficial, though not without some healthy rivalry. After all, this time both cities receive the divine stamp of approval. They are presented as equals, rather than enemies, albeit as very different places, adhering to a different set of values: health and wealth, respectively. This myth seems to belong to a context, probably in the early fifth century, when Croton and Syracuse occupied similar hegemonic positions in Italy and Sicily, respectively.[46] The two myths therefore serve to articulate Croton's relations with other *poleis* in its neighborhood, while also staking a claim to Achaean ethnicity.

Even as the stories of Myscellus demonstrate Croton's Achaean origins, however, they also outline a set of factors unique to Croton, articulating a clear sense of the community's self-image by interweaving ethnic and *polis* identities. First, Diodorus records three oracles supposedly given to Myscellus; one of them offers a description of the route from Delphi to Croton, culminating in the key features of Crotoniate territory itself: "This way I say that you will not miss the Lacinian Promontory, nor sacred Crimisa, nor the river Aesarus."[47] As has been pointed out, the Delphic itinerary would not actually help anyone sail

---

44. Strabo 6.2.4 (and cf. 6.1.12); Steph. Byz. s.v. Syrakusai; Suda s.v. Archias, Myscellus; Eust. in Dionys. Per. 369.

45. Malkin 1987, 45–46; Giangiulio 1989, 143–147; Morgan and Hall 1996, 206–207.

46. Dunbabin (1948, 27, 444) dates it to the early fifth century, while Mele (1984, 19–21) and Giangiulio (1989, 134) place it a century later; cf. Malkin 1987, 43; Morgan and Hall 1996, 206.

47. Diod. 8.17.1: οὕτω σ' οὐκ ἄν φημι Λακινίου ἄκρου ἀμαρτεῖν οὐδ' ἱερᾶς Κριμίσης οὐδ' Αἰσάρου ποταμοῖο. The oracle most likely postdates the foundation considerably: Giangiulio 1989, 142–144; *contra*, Malkin 1987, 45–47.

from the Corinthian Gulf to Italy.[48] Instead, the oracle defines the community that Myscellus will found through three important geographical features of its territory. The Lacinian Promontory, about ten kilometers south of Croton, was the site of the sanctuary of Hera Lacinia, one of Croton's most important civic sanctuaries and also an internationally prominent one. Cape Crimisa, site of the important sanctuary of Apollo Alaios, marked the northern frontier of the fifth-century *chora* of Croton.[49] Finally, the river Aesarus adjoined the city itself, marking out the site as the civic heart of the community.[50] The choice of these natural features both ties this new community to its territory and emphasizes the changes the settlers will bring to the land, by building temples and an urban environment.[51] All played crucial roles in articulating Croton's civic identity—very similar roles, in fact, to those played by landscape at Syracuse (chapter 3) and Camarina (chapter 5).

Similarly, the choice offered to Myscellus and Archias—either health or wealth—and Myscellus's decision to pursue health recall two of Croton's most famous achievements. At its peak in the late sixth and early fifth centuries, Croton was especially known for both its doctors (who restored health) and its athletes (who exploited it). Herodotus calls Democedes of Croton the best doctor of his time, describing his probably embellished career as chief physician first to Polycrates of Samos and then to Darius, king of Persia.[52] Alcmaeon of Croton, meanwhile, was one of the first to investigate medicine from a rational perspective, in the early fifth century, though he seems to have been more a natural philosopher than a practicing physician.[53]

Meanwhile, Croton produced an impressive string of victors at the panhellenic games, especially in running and fighting events, where physical training mattered more than in equestrian events. These victors included Astylus, who won the *stadion* and *diaulos* races in 488; Phayllus, a three-time Pythian victor in the *stadion* and pentathlon; and Milo, a boxer who won seven consecutive

---

48. Malkin 1987, 45–46; *contra*, Dougherty 1993, 19–20.

49. The actual boundary may have been the Hylias (today's Nicà) River, just north of Cape Crimisa: Thuc. 7.35, with Osanna 1992, 176. On Crimisa's non-Crotoniate connections, see Malkin 1998, 215–226.

50. On these three features, see Cerchiai, Jannelli, and Longo 2004, 107–112.

51. Cf. Beck 2020, 53–61, for other examples of foundation myths articulating ties to the land.

52. Hdt. 3.125, 129–137; Griffiths 1987; Davies 2013.

53. The fragments and testimonia are at DK 24; cf. Mansfeld 1975; Lloyd 1991; Longrigg 1993, 47–63.

FIG. 2.1 Stater of Croton, c. 550–530. Tripod, incuse. Courtesy of the American Numismatic Society.

Olympic victories in the late sixth century.[54] On one occasion, the first seven finishers in the *stadion* were all Crotoniates, giving rise to the proverb "The last of the Crotoniates is the first of the Greeks" (Strabo 6.1.12). Croton's pride in its athletic success was so great that it apparently tried, unsuccessfully, to establish an athletic competition that would eclipse the Olympic Games (Timaeus F45). Success in athletic competitions came to be thought of as part of what it meant to be Crotoniate. Thus, the single story in which Myscellus chooses health over wealth both articulates Croton's sense of Achaean ethnicity and embeds its success in athletics and medicine into a unique *polis* identity.

Croton's coinage, which regularly bore a distinctive tripod emblem (fig. 2.1), articulated a similar set of plural identities. Like those of many *poleis* and monarchs in Sicily and southern Italy, Croton's coins were a useful tool for disseminating ideological messages. Coins circulated widely both within a city's territory and often elsewhere and were used by a wide range of people. While not all coins were necessarily designed to express identities, the choice of types—the images on each side of a coin—often has much to say about the identities of the community that minted it, typically by depicting something that made the community distinctive.[55] They offered a city a means both of proclaiming its identity to the outside world and of reinforcing it domestically, including through complex messages that provided additional layers of

54. Mele 1984, 44–49; Giangiulio 1989, 102–121; Mann 2001, 164–191; Miller 2004, 216–218, 233.

55. Rutter 2000a; Papadopoulos 2002; Pretzler 2003; Skinner 2010; Skinner 2012, 134–140.

meaning available mainly to insiders.[56] Since we have few other sources that emerge so directly from Croton itself, this is a precious document for how Crotoniates saw themselves.

Of course, coinage served many practical purposes, especially economic ones, such as making state payments, including paying mercenaries, or facilitating trade, and many decisions about coinage must have been made on this basis.[57] Similarly, the choice of a weight standard—exactly how much a coin would weigh, whether a standard coin would be worth two or four drachmas (or use a different system entirely), and similar technical issues—could also send a message, since a number of such standards were available, but it is difficult to disentangle such a message from purely economic factors. From the beginnings of coinage in Italy, Croton was linked to a number of neighboring cities through the distinctive "incuse" technique, in which the reverse of the coin was struck in negative relief and was usually the same type as the obverse.[58] This was used by several Achaean cities, and also sometimes by Taras, Rhegium, and Zancle, up to the middle of the fifth century. Some (but not all) of these cities also shared a weight standard (the so-called Achaean standard), in which a standard coin weighed about eight grams and was divided into three drachmas.[59] The incuse technique is used nowhere else in the Greek world, and hence it may have contributed to some sense of commonality within the region of southern Italy. Yet the distribution of its use cuts across the Achaean/Dorian/Ionian ethnic boundaries, and moreover there were a number of variations in weight standards within this group.[60] It therefore seems that any sense of shared identity produced by the technical specifications of the coinage must have been very loose, and more likely regional than ethnic in nature.

Instead, it is the tripod type, which persisted for so long (nearly two centuries, from the origins of coinage in the second half of the sixth century down to the mid-fourth century),[61] that tells a deeper story about Croton's identities. Since these coins were minted by the *polis*, not by any larger federal authority,

---

56. Kurke 1999, 13; cf. Martin 1995, 265; Rutter 2000a, 74.

57. On early uses of coinage (a much-debated topic), see Kraay 1964; Wallace 1987; Howgego 1990; Martin 1996; Kim 2001; cf. Martin 1995; Kurke 1999; Schaps 2004; von Reden 1995; von Reden 2010.

58. Gorini 1975; Kraay 1976, 163–164; Rutter 1997, 17–33.

59. Rutter 1997, 17.

60. Rutter 1997, 32, 52–53.

61. Rutter 2001, 166–175.

they should contribute to the ideology and identity of the *polis*. Yet what is striking is that Croton's tripods also have important meaning as Achaean emblems; they serve to remind Crotoniates of the origins of their community and its double claim of Achaean-ness, both Peloponnesian and Homeric. While tripods were familiar objects used throughout the Greek world, they would have evoked a particular set of associations for the Achaeans of Croton. First, the coins recall the tripod on which the Pythia sat at Delphi and therefore the stories of Myscellus's oracular consultation which resulted in the foundation of Croton.[62] The coinage thus offers a reminder to Crotoniates of the origin of their city, an origin that stemmed from Peloponnesian Achaea and was sanctioned by Apollo. The tripod was prominent on Croton's coinage precisely in the period when the various stories of Myscellus were developing, and the role of Delphi in the foundation of the city is surely one layer of meaning behind the Crotoniate tripod. The images might, however, also suggest a connection with Olympia and a broader northwest Greek custom of dedicating tripods. Numerous Archaic examples of these dedications have been found at Olympia, at Delphi, and at the Polis Cave on Ithaca, where the dedicators may have thought they were following in the footsteps of Odysseus.[63] The appearance on coins of such a prestigious dedication also helps tie Croton back to its origins in the Peloponnese.

But tripods have another very strong set of resonances in Homeric society. Achilles sets a tripod, along with an enslaved woman, as the first prize for the chariot race at the funeral games for Patroclus. They are also given as prestige gifts from one *basileus* to another—Odysseus receives thirteen of them from the Phaeacian elders—as well as being used for practical purposes.[64] These Homeric resonances add to the prestige associated with tripods in Greek society and suggest that the Crotoniates were attempting to link themselves not only with a prestigious symbol of wealth and power but also with their heroic ancestry. The tripod coinage might remind a Crotoniate athlete, preparing to race at Olympia or elsewhere, that he was following in the footsteps of his ancestors. Since tripods were offered as prizes at some competitions (though famously not at Olympia), he might even hope to carry home the same prize as Diomedes, victor at Patroclus's funeral games. The tripod image, much like

---

62. Lacroix 1965, 158–159; Kraay and Hirmer 1966, 310; Gorini 1975, 148; Rutter 1997, 29; Papadopoulos 2002, 32–33.

63. Head 1911, 99; Gorini 1975, 77–78; Malkin 1998, 94–119; Papadopoulos 2002, 32–33.

64. Prizes: *Il.* 23.259–264, 485, 513, 702, 718; cf. 9.407, 11.700. Gift exchange: *Il.* 8.290; *Od.* 13.13, 217–218, 15.84. Practical uses: *Il.* 18.344–348, 22.443, 23.40; *Od.* 8.434–437, 10.359–361.

the stories of Myscellus, thus conveys to Crotoniates a distinct sense both of the dual ethnic origins of their community and of its contemporary culture and *polis* identity.

Heroes

The Homeric resonances of the coins brings us to the other element of the ethnicity claimed by the Achaeans: tracing their roots back to the Heroic Age. By naming Heracles as their founder, the Crotoniates declared that the origins of their community lay deep in the mythical past, with the greatest of the Achaean heroes.[65] Philoctetes was also reported to have settled in Croton's territory after the Trojan War; although he was not explicitly labeled an oikist, he played a similar role, and both heroes contributed in different ways to Croton's unique version of Achaean-ness.

Heroes like these certainly played other roles as well, for instance, by linking Croton to a panhellenic network of Greeks who honored the same heroes. As Malkin has argued, such networking contributed to a developing sense of Greekness across the Mediterranean.[66] Nevertheless, in Croton, this Hellenic identity was inflected with a particularly Achaean flavor. Moreover, Croton was not alone in constructing an identity through heroic predecessors; virtually all Greek communities tried to tie themselves to heroes in one way or another, and Heracles in particular had been active in many parts of the western Mediterranean.[67] Still, Heracles enjoyed a particular salience for the Crotoniates, who claimed a special relationship with him as their founder, beyond that enjoyed by most other cities. Linking themselves to him gave the Crotoniates increased prestige and helped them define their community. Stories about Heracles and other heroes thus allowed the people of Croton to articulate their identities in particularly interesting ways, supporting the same discourse of interlocking ethnic and *polis* identities that we have already seen for Myscellus.

A pair of coins dating to c. 420 are the earliest evidence from Croton explicitly labeling Heracles as oikist, and they evoke clearly the interwoven nature of

---

65. Giangiulio 1989, 70–76, 185–186; Malkin 1994, 134–135.

66. Malkin 2005b, 64–66.

67. Giangiulio (1989, 185–186) adduces similar foundation stories involving Heracles at Solous, Abdera, and Heraclea Pontica.

FIG. 2.2 Stater of Croton, c. 420. Obverse: Heracles as oikist. Reverse: Apollo and Pytho with tripod. © Trustees of the British Museum.

Crotoniate identity (fig. 2.2).[68] The obverse type, shared by both coins, shows the hero with his club and lion skin; he is sacrificing at a flaming altar and holding a branch, while his bow and quiver lie behind him. The scene is labeled *oikistas*, which testifies clearly to a fifth-century claim of Heracles as Croton's founder and thus asserts the city's ethnicity by ascribing its origins to Heracles. Intriguingly, this obverse type is paired with two different reverses, both of which link Heracles with other elements of Crotoniate identity. The first shows a tripod and the abbreviated name ϘΡΟΤ. Thus, the innovative obverse is paired with a long-standing emblem of the *polis*, and naming the city further reminds viewers that Heracles was the founder of Croton alone, not the other Achaean cities. The second reverse goes even further, adding to the tripod a standing figure of Apollo who aims his bow across the tripod at the snake Python. In this instance, the tripod clearly refers to Delphi and therefore to the stories of Myscellus, yet it is combined with the image of Heracles as founder on the obverse. As Colin Kraay has said, "two traditions of the foundation of Croton are here mingled," and the dual Peloponnesian and heroic origins that make them Achaean are literally two sides of the same coin.[69] Moreover, this is not a proclamation of ethnic identity alone but also of *polis* identity, since the figure of Myscellus had no meaning beyond Croton, while

---

68. Rutter 2001, nos. 2139 and 2140, respectively; cf. Lacroix 1965, 78–79; Kraay 1976, 181; Holloway 1978, 59; Mele 1984, 35–37; Giangiulio 1989, 71–72; Malkin 1998, 217–218.

69. Kraay 1976, 181. If the branch held by Heracles is the Delphic laurel, as Kraay suggests (cf. Rutter 1997, 38–39), the mingling of traditions would be even stronger.

Heracles elsewhere lacked the special significance he bore at Croton.[70] The *oikistas* coins thus bring together a number of facets of Croton's identities, both ethnic and *polis*.

Although these coins do not appear until the late fifth century, Heracles's prominent role at Croton probably dates from at least the late sixth century. According to Diodorus, Milo the boxer, now chosen as general, marched off to war with Sybaris wearing a lion skin as a new Heracles. If this story can be trusted, the Crotoniates thus called upon Heracles as their civic hero to support them in this war; alternatively, it represents how the Crotoniates commemorated the event in subsequent decades.[71] Soon afterward, the Crotoniates took possession of what was believed to be a heroic relic, the bow and arrows of Heracles, which had supposedly been dedicated after the Trojan War at a local shrine in the newly conquered territory; they rededicated it in their own temple of Apollo, thereby claiming Heracles as its patron and divine helper.[72] Both of these episodes would have far greater point if Heracles was understood as a founder figure at the time.

Despite all this evidence, however, the literary tradition does not actually say that Heracles founded the *polis* of Croton. Instead, he founded the sanctuary of Hera Lacinia, Croton's most important religious site. According to Diodorus:

ὁ δ' Ἡρακλῆς μετὰ τῶν βοῶν περαιωθεὶς εἰς τὴν Ἰταλίαν προῆγε διὰ τῆς παραλίας, καὶ Λακίνιον μὲν κλέπτοντα τῶν βοῶν ἀνεῖλε, Κρότωνα δὲ ἀκουσίως ἀποκτείνας ἔθαψε μεγαλοπρεπῶς καὶ τάφον αὐτοῦ κατεσκεύασε· προεῖπε δὲ καὶ τοῖς ἐγχωρίοις ὅτι [καὶ] κατὰ τοὺς ὕστερον χρόνους ἔσται πόλις ἐπίσημος ὁμώνυμος τῷ τετελευτηκότι.

After Heracles crossed over into Italy with the cattle, he proceeded along the coast; there he killed Lacinius as he was stealing some of the cattle. But when he killed Croton by accident, he gave him a magnificent funeral and built a tomb for him. And he foretold to the locals that in the future a famous city would arise that would have the same name as the deceased.[73]

---

70. For example, two coins of Metapontion (Rutter 2001 nos. 1494–1495, which he dates to c. 440–430) show Heracles sacrificing, but crucially he is not labeled an oikist.

71. Diod. 12.9.5–6; accepted by Dunbabin 1948, 363; Malkin 1998, 217; cf. Giangiulio 1989, 70. The story is certainly no less credible than that of Pisistratus and his false Athena (Hdt. 1.60).

72. Ps.-Arist. *Mir. Ausc.* 107; see below for further discussion.

73. Diod. 4.24.7; cf. the parallel version of Serv. *ad Aen.* 3.552.

The presence of the eponym Lacinius clearly indicates that Heracles was understood to have established the sanctuary, a detail confirmed by Servius; on the other hand, he only foretold the foundation of the city.[74] Yet, as we will see further below, this sanctuary was such an important part of the social fabric of Croton that its foundation was felt to be equivalent to that of the city itself. The paired deaths of Lacinius and Croton closely link the two epichoric figures, and Croton's death occurs only because of Lacinius's actions. This unusual pattern makes the sanctuary actually precede the city, and the city is subordinated to it.[75] Croton's existence, which depends on that of the sanctuary, is therefore sanctioned by its veneration of Hera. Yet, as we have seen, Heracles was also regarded as the oikist of Croton, implying that the city and the sanctuary were inextricably intertwined. Heracles's relationship with the sanctuary was expressed on coins as well, in a series that combines an obverse of a scene depicting Heracles with a head of Hera Lacinia on the reverse.[76] As a civic sanctuary founded by a mythical hero, the Lacinion adheres closely to patterns of identification that are by now familiar. It boasts an Achaean pedigree, and yet it is bound to the *polis*, not the ethnic group as a whole.

Of course, Heracles was not typically seen as Achaean in the same way as the Homeric heroes, who are regularly called by that collective name, though his family's roots in the Argolid connect him, in a prior generation, to the world of Agamemnon. Still, as the greatest hero of the heroic age—an Achaean in a looser sense—he was useful for the Crotoniates in defining their community, in both an ethnic and a civic manner. We should therefore see Heracles's role in Croton's foundation myths as a variation on a theme, a particularly flexible local instantiation of a general pattern of Achaean heroic foundation myths, and one particularly suited to Croton. After all, Heracles was also the founder of the Olympic festival and patron of Croton's successful athletes; his appearance on coins and in myths proclaims the city's distinctive athletic culture and its link with Olympia. The Crotoniates thus simultaneously follow a common Achaean pattern and also assert their civic distinctiveness.

Aside from Heracles, a number of Homeric heroes were said to have visited southern Italy during their return from Troy. These included Diomedes, Menelaus, Tlapolemus, Philoctetes, and Epeius, the builder of the Trojan

---

74. On the prophetic role of Heracles here, see Giangiulio 1982, 56–57. Iambl. *VP* 50, who does have Heracles found Croton, has most likely transformed the story into a more common type.

75. Cf. Giannelli 1963, 144, who, however, takes far too historicizing an approach to this text.

76. Rutter 2001, nos. 2159–2161.

Horse. Not all of these were closely connected with Achaean ethnic discourse, but the last two bear particular significance. Philoctetes came to be linked with Croton and Epeius with Metapontion, but they function in such similar ways that I discuss them here together.[77] While neither *polis* claimed Philoctetes or Epeius as a founder, both cities maintained sets of heroic relics in their temples: the bow and arrows of Heracles, brought to Italy by Philoctetes after the Trojan War, and the tools of Epeius used to build the Trojan Horse.[78] These relics (and the myths attached to them) acted as proof positive of both Croton's and Metapontion's assertions of their Achaean origins.

Malkin has argued convincingly that the wanderings of both Epeius and Philoctetes were originally localized in non-Greek communities, at a time (the seventh century) when they remained independent of the Greek colonies. Epeius dedicated his tools at a temple of Athena at Lagaria, a non-Greek site near Metapontion. Philoctetes supposedly founded several non-Greek communities and deposited Heracles's bow at the temple of Apollo Alaios (at Cape Crimisa, north of Croton); this area, too, lay outside Croton's control in the seventh century. In Malkin's reading, the stories of Epeius and Philoctetes originally functioned to mediate between Greeks and non-Greeks in these communities.[79] This changed, however, around the end of the sixth century, as the Greek *poleis* expanded their territories. Malkin argues that the temple of Athena at Lagaria eventually became an extra-urban sanctuary belonging to Metapontion, in which case the relics of Epeius came under their control. Croton, too, took possession of the bow and arrows after its victory over Sybaris in 510 and rededicated them at its own temple of Apollo. In this latter phase, their meaning changed considerably. Croton's rededication of the bow and arrows, in particular, should be understood as a collective religious act that loudly proclaimed not only Croton's political power but also its Achaean identity. It was also a political maneuver much like the Spartan repatriation of the bones of Orestes or Cimon's of the bones of Theseus,[80] and allowed Croton to claim Heracles as its patron and divine helper (and likely as its founder).

---

77. On these two figures, see Bérard 1963, 330–341; Maddoli 1980; Malkin 1998, 214–226; Genovese 2009; Hornblower 2015, 343–350; and the articles in De La Genière 1991, esp. Musti 1991 and Giangiulio 1991.

78. Philoctetes: Ps.-Arist. *Mir. Ausc.* 107; Lycoph. *Alex.* 911–913, 919–920; Strabo 6.1.3. Epeius: Ps.-Arist. *Mir. Ausc.* 108; Lycoph. *Alex.* 930, 946–950; Strabo 6.1.14. One late source (Just. 20.2.1) does give Epeius as the founder of Metapontion, but this is likely a confusion.

79. Malkin 1998, 210–233; cf. Genovese 2018.

80. Hdt. 1.67–68; Plut. *Thes.* 36, *Cim.* 8.5-6; cf. Malkin 1994, 26–33; Boedeker 1993; Higbie 1997.

It represented an assertion of control over its newly conquered territories and also a boast that they were more Achaean than their neighbors, since they now possessed a direct link to the greatest mythic hero.

Epeius and Philoctetes were particularly appropriate figures of reverence for the Achaeans, since both the heroes and the relics themselves played crucial roles in ending the Trojan War and thereby beginning the *nostos* phase of the epic myths. They therefore act as liminal figures, mediating between the two phases and creating the conditions under which the foundations of Croton and Metapontion could take place. At Croton, the role of Philoctetes, whose illness due to snakebite was legendary, might perhaps highlight the fame of their doctors, as Simon Hornblower suggests.[81] More important, the bow and arrows of Heracles represent an inheritance passed down first to Philoctetes and then to the Crotoniates themselves. By keeping these objects safe, the Achaeans of Croton established a continuum between themselves and the heroic past, in which they continued to perform the same deeds of reverence to Heracles that Philoctetes once did. Moreover, the physical objects that were understood as heroic relics provided evidence, for all to see, of the presence of these heroes in their respective territories and of the Achaeans' strong and lasting connection with their heroic ancestors. Telling stories was one thing; pointing to physical proof of their truth—a truth affirmed by Apollo and Athena, to whom the objects were dedicated—offered a deeper means of understanding and proclaiming the heroic origins of both Croton and Metapontion.

Cult and Identity on Cape Lacinia

The Crotoniates worshipped the full range of Greek deities, of course, but one stood out above the rest: Hera Lacinia, whose sanctuary was located on the Lacinian promontory (modern Capo Colonna) about ten kilometers south of the city.[82] This location meant that it was visible far out to sea and offered a stopping point for any shipping traffic up and down the coast of Italy; this gave it a certain degree of international prominence. Cult activity, in the form of dedications, is visible beginning in the mid-seventh century, although the first building does not appear until about 600. Over the next few centuries, the site was frequently expanded and embellished: a temple was built in the

---

81. Hornblower 2015, 344.

82. On the site, see Spadea 1996; Spadea 1997, 236–251; Spadea 2006; on its cult, see esp. Giangiulio 1982; Maddoli 1984; Camassa 1991, 458–461.

fifth century, and both a *katagogion* and a *hestiaterion* (which provided housing
and dining for visitors) were built in the fourth. The sanctuary maintained
its importance into the early Roman period, even after the establishment of a
Roman colony at Croton in 194; Hannibal notably retreated there for several
years late in the Second Punic War (see this book's conclusion).

Cult sites like this one and the religious practices performed there often
play a significant role in the articulation and maintenance of identities; think
of, for example, the Acropolis at Athens and the various rituals that surrounded
it.[83] As has long been recognized, rituals often act as a force for social cohe-
sion.[84] They can strengthen and reinforce an existing sense of community, as
well as passing it down to younger generations or even creating a new sense of
community where none had existed before. By choosing to participate in a sacrifice or to make a dedication to one of their shared deities, individuals actively
affirmed their membership in a community and validated the social order
communicated by the ritual. This performative aspect of ritual implicated each
individual participant in a web of relationships with his or her fellow citizens
and with the traditions of the community. Rituals thus serve to validate a social
order and to claim legitimacy for the existence of a particular community. As
such, religious practices frequently contributed to articulating a community's
identity, whether an ethnic identity, a *polis* identity, or something else.

Which type of identity was expressed through a particular ritual or cult
varies and must be explored on a case-by-case basis and in the local context.
Although Greek religious sites were generally open to all, cults and rituals frequently had additional meaning to the members of one community that was
not accessible or significant to outsiders. Most *poleis* throughout the Greek
world worshipped most of the main deities of the Greek pantheon, but some
were always more important to a community's self-definition than others.[85]
The specific cults a community chose to honor therefore sent a more precise message about the nature of the community. At Croton, the sanctuary of

---

83. Although recent work on Greek religion has emphasized its diversity of forms and multiplicity of practices and beliefs (Parker 2011, 224–264; Kindt 2012; Mackil 2013), I focus
especially on public cults, involving rituals that were shared by a community. However, this
community was not necessarily the *polis*, and by taking a larger view of communities of cult,
I avoid the pitfalls of the *polis* religion model, originally developed by Sourvinou-Inwood
1988; Sourvinou-Inwood 1990; for critiques, see Parker 2011, 57–61; Kindt 2012; Mili 2015,
6–12. On religion and identity more broadly, see Parker 1998; Robertson 2002; Mitchell
2006; Funke and Haake 2013; Mili 2015.

84. This line of investigation goes back to Durkheim; see more recently Parker 1998;
Kowalzig 2007, 32–55; Mackil 2013, 147–236; Wijma 2014.

85. On patron deities and *polis* identity, see Cole 1995; Burkert 1995.

Hera Lacinia (or the Lacinion, as the site is often known) bore a double significance: it was closely tied to the articulation of a *polis* community, and yet worshipping Hera Lacinia also allowed the Crotoniates to define themselves ethnically as Achaean.

We have already seen how the Lacinion is tied to the foundation of the city through the myth of Heracles, which presents the sanctuary as inherently linked to the *polis* and Crotoniate identity. Its relationship with *polis* ideology and civic politics is further demonstrated by the careers of two individual Crotoniates, both Olympic victors. Astylus, who won two running events at Olympia in 488, was honored with a statue at the Lacinion itself (Paus. 6.13.1). Victory statues in one's home city were normally erected at important locations in civic life, such as the agora,[86] so the choice of the sanctuary of Hera Lacinia suggests that the temple occupied a similar space in Croton's civic life. The remainder of Astylus's story is equally illuminating. For his second and third victories, he competed as a Syracusan, not a Crotoniate, in order to please the Deinomenids (see further in chapter 3). In response to this, the Crotoniates savagely attacked and tore down his statue and decreed that his house be turned into a prison. Astylus's attempts to gain the favor of the tyrants of Syracuse were understood as a rejection of his Crotoniate identity. This episode should be placed in the context of ongoing conflicts between Croton and Syracuse, in which the Deinomenids were trying (with some success) to gain influence in southern Italy at the expense of Croton.[87] What has been less recognized is the role of the sanctuary in this political rivalry, which was seen as a locus of that contestation. Whereas at first the sanctuary had been the site of honors bestowed by the *polis*, it now became the scene of the repudiation of those honors. This important civic site was considered an appropriate place for someone to be stripped of his membership in the community.

A generation earlier, Milo—the most famous Crotoniate of his day, six-time Olympic champion in wrestling, and victor in the war against Sybaris—also served as priest of Hera Lacinia. Athletic accomplishment and religious authority thus went hand in hand. We do not know how Milo acquired the priesthood (and we should not assume it was directly tied to his victories), but once he had it, it is easy to imagine that his fellow citizens felt an Olympic victor to be a particularly appropriate person to preside over Croton's most important cult. Moreover, his statue at Olympia apparently depicted him in this role, wearing a fillet as a priest and holding a pomegranate, an important cult

---

86. Giangiulio 1989, 296–299.

87. Luraghi 1994, 349–351; Bonanno 2010, 85–95; Nicholson 2015, 91–97.

attribute of Hera.[88] Thus, Milo's official presentation to the outside world, at a major panhellenic sanctuary, showed him integrated into Croton's civic cult. Olympic victories were always crucial to cities' pride in their accomplishments, but rarely were they so important an aspect of civic identity as in Croton. These stories of Milo and Astylus thus suggest a nexus between the cult of Hera Lacinia and Croton's articulation of a sense of itself as a *polis* community. In both stories, we see how the Crotoniates relate to the sanctuary of Hera Lacinia: she is essential in defining the boundaries of the Crotoniate community, in honoring the athletes whose successes make them the quintessential Crotoniates, and in projecting an image of Croton to the outside world.

Yet we must also locate Hera Lacinia in a larger Achaean context. Croton was not alone in situating Hera prominently in its pantheon, and so comparative evidence from other sites can help pin down the Achaean aspects of Hera's role at Croton. At both Metapontion and Poseidonia, temples to Hera were highly visible features of the urban core, adjacent to the agora and therefore placed in the civic center of each city. Poseidonia also featured the major extra-urban sanctuary of Hera at Foce del Sele, and Metapontion had one at Tavole Palatine as well. Sybaris, too, probably had both an urban and a rural sanctuary. Like Croton, these cities had many other important temples as well, but Hera cut a much higher profile than other deities.[89] It is therefore particularly striking, as several scholars have noted, that Hera is almost entirely absent from Peloponnesian Achaea, whereas Poseidon and Zeus Homarios are the chief gods at places like Helike and Aigion.[90] Clearly, Hera was not brought to Croton as its chief deity by settlers from Rhype or its environs; instead, her importance was created and articulated in Italy. Moreover, the stress placed on Hera by the Achaeans also distinguishes them sharply from the other Greek cities of Italy, such as Taras, Locri, and Rhegium, where Hera is not so prominent.[91] The worship of Hera thus forms a singular element in the cultic landscape of the Achaean cities, joining them together while separating

88. Philostratus *VA* 4.28; cf. Paus. 6.14.5–6. The existence of the statue is usually accepted, but Keesling (2005, 49–57) argues that the sources, writing some seven hundred years later, may have misunderstood the iconography. But Philostratus's interpretation of the iconography requires the outside information that Milo was a priest of Hera; this much probably derives ultimately from Timaeus and is trustworthy.

89. For overviews of these cults and sanctuaries, see Giannelli 1963; Maddoli 1988; Maddoli 2000; Camassa 1991; Camassa 1993; La Torre 2011, 291–298, 322–326; and the articles in De La Genière 1997, esp. Greco 1997; Cipriani 1997.

90. Osanna 1996, esp. 303–312; Osanna 2002; Giangiulio 1989, 174–178.

91. Giannelli 1963; Hall 2002, 61–62.

them from their neighbors—in other words, she helped define their shared Achaean ethnicity.

Hera's ethnic resonances can be seen especially through widely noted parallels with the religious system of the Argolid. Hera had a number of major cult sites in and around the Argive Plain—the famous Argive Heraion, the shrines at Prosymna and Tiryns, and others—as well as at Perachora, near Corinth, and in Sicyon. Moreover, the precise personality of Hera appears very similar at all these sites, both Peloponnesian and Italian.[92] As a warrior goddess, she received warrior figurines as dedications and at the Lacinion was also called Hoplosmia. She oversaw human, animal, and vegetal fertility, signified at the Lacinion by a sacred grove and by her cult attribute, a pomegranate. She also had a special link to bovines, which recalls her Homeric epithet "ox-eyed Hera," and it is no accident that one of the Achaean sanctuaries, at Foce del Sele near Poseidonia, was dedicated specifically to Argive Hera.[93] Thus, it seems that the Crotoniates, along with other Achaeans, were looking to the Argolid as they developed their cults of Hera. To explain this, Hall has pointed to ethnic boundaries between Achaeans and Dorians in the Iron Age and Archaic Argolid, which he argues were articulated there in part through cults of Hera. The Achaeans of southern Italy would thus be inscribing themselves within a similar framework, with Taras standing in for Dorian Argos, and modeling their religious landscape on one that carried an imported ethnic valence. This technique of constructing identity by looking to a far-off region of mainland Greece is strongly reminiscent of Syracuse's maintenance of ties to the Peloponnese (chapter 3) and especially to Corinth (chapter 6). Hall's argument may be part of the story, but it is equally likely that the Crotoniates would focus on the Homeric, rather than the contemporary, Argolid.

After all, the Argolid was one of the heartlands of Homeric Greece, home to Agamemnon and Diomedes, along with numerous other mythical figures, especially Heracles. The distribution of Hera cults outlined above maps closely onto the domain of Agamemnon as delineated in the Catalogue of Ships (*Il.* 2.559–580)—a region that would clearly be of great interest to the Crotoniates. It would be easy for the Crotoniates to interpret Hera's role across this region in the Archaic and Classical periods as reflecting the religious preferences of

---

92. These links can be traced through a variety of data, including myths and votive offerings, among other evidence; see Giangiulio 1982; Giangiulio 2002, 294–297; Greco 1998; Hall 2002, 61–62.

93. Strabo 6.1.1; Plin. *N.H.* 3.70; Solin. 2.12. The same sources report that the temple was established by Jason during the return of the Argonauts, another instance of Achaeans claiming heroic origins; cf. Bérard 1963, 212–214, 385–389.

the Heroic Age and then to follow in their footsteps. The Crotoniates would certainly know well Hera's prominent role in the *Iliad*, where she is one of the foremost divine proponents of the Greek cause. Along with other deities, such as Poseidon and Hera's frequent sidekick Athena, Hera champions various Greek warriors, and in Book 14, she deceives Zeus to prevent a complete Trojan victory. At one point (4.52), she lists her favorite cities as Argos, Mycenae, and Sparta, two of which are in the Argolid. For the Achaeans who worshipped Hera, these elements of the Homeric poem would stand out even more than for other Greeks. They would certainly feel that worshipping Hera allowed them actively to claim their inheritance as Hera's favorites and to position themselves as the descendants of these heroes.

The act of worshipping Hera—in other words, rituals, especially ones repeated regularly and carried out publicly—offered an opportunity for Crotoniates to reinforce and re-emphasize their identity as Achaeans. While relatively little is known about the rites for Hera conducted by the Crotoniates,[94] another ritual at the Lacinion offered even more symbolic resonance for Achaean and Crotoniate identity. This ritual is described by Lycophron (*Alexandra* 856–865), as part of a prophecy by Cassandra of the future wanderings of Menelaus:

ἥξει δὲ Σῖριν καὶ Λακινίου μυχούς,
ἐν οἷσι πόρτις ὄρχατον τεύξει θεᾷ
Ὁπλοσμίᾳ φυτοῖσιν ἐξησκημένον.
γυναιξὶ δ' ἔσται τεθμὸς ἐγχώροις ἀεὶ
πενθεῖν τὸν εἰνάπηχυν Αἰακοῦ τρίτον   860
καὶ Δωρίδος, πρηστῆρα δαΐου μάχης,
καὶ μήτε χρυσῷ φαιδρὰ καλλύνειν ῥέθη
μήθ' ἁβροπήνους ἀμφιβάλλεσθαι πέπλους
κάλχῃ φορυκτούς, οὕνεκεν θεᾷ θεὸς
χέρσου μέγαν στόρθυγγα δωρεῖται κτίσαι.   865

He [Menelaus] will come to Siris and the inner corners of Lacinion,
in which a heifer [Thetis] will prepare a grove,

---

94. Only one, a bull sacrifice mentioned by Theocritus (*Id.* 4.20–22), has attracted much comment. Maurizio Giangiulio has argued that this represented a symbolic rebirth of the city, reconstituting its civic order through sanctioned violence, much like the Athenian Bouphonia: Giangiulio 1982, 59–61; Giangiulio 1989, 73–77; Giangiulio 2002, 284–285; cf. Graf 1982, 167–170; Burkert 1983, 161–167. The decision to dedicate such a sacrifice to Hera, rather than another deity, underscores her importance as Croton's patron.

adorned with trees, for the goddess Hoplosmia [Hera].
And it will be forever an ordinance for the women of the land
to mourn the nine-cubit hero [Achilles], third in descent   860
from Aeacus and Doris, whirlwind of the destructive fight,
and not to beautify their shining limbs with gold,
nor clad them in fine-spun robes dyed with purple,
because a goddess [Thetis] to a goddess [Hera] presents
that great spur of land [Cape Lacinia] to settle.   865

Lycophron combines his description of a ritual of mourning for Achilles
with an alternative account of the origins of the sanctuary; according to this
version, it was established by Thetis, who dedicated a sanctuary to Hera alongside a cult for her son Achilles.[95] Since the passage seems to link the foundation to Menelaus's visit to Italy, he has sometimes been understood loosely as
a cofounder of the sanctuary (and thus perhaps also of Croton itself), bringing
an additional layer to Croton's narratives of heroic origins.[96]

The ritual described here implies the existence of a separate *heroon* for
Achilles on the Lacinian promontory, adjacent to or even within the sanctuary of Hera. This is not at all unusual in the context of larger Greek sanctuaries; compare the cult of Pelops alongside that of Zeus at Olympia or that of
Erechtheus on the Athenian Acropolis.[97] Although the cult is not attested prior
to Lycophron, it is unlikely to be a late or unimportant development. Instead,
as Maurizio Giangiulio has pointed out, the paired cults of Hera and Achilles
at the Lacinion are mythically integrated, since both were established together: Thetis ordained the mourning ritual as a condition of her gift of coastal
land to Hera for her sanctuary.[98] The development of a foundation myth shows
the importance of this particular hero cult within the Crotoniate religious
landscape. Placing the establishment of the cult in the Heroic Age, during the
nostos phase of the epic cycle (as shown by the presence of Menelaus) and soon
after Achilles's death, establishes a continuum between the heroes of that time

---

95. On the passage, see Hornblower 2015, 327–332; on the role of Achilles in the literary architecture of the *Alexandra*, see McNelis and Sens 2016, 101–128.

96. Malkin 1994, 61–64; for a more cautious view, see Giangiulio 1989, 183–184.

97. Giangiulio 1989, 69.

98. Giangiulio 1982, 41–52; Giangiulio 1989, 67–69, 123–126; Giangiulio 2002, 287–288;
cf. Giannelli 1963, 148–149; Maddoli 1984, 317–318. Moreover, its repeated performance
perpetuates Croton's claim of Achaean identity, even if (as Graf 1985, 351n4 argues) it originated as a late response to the epic tradition.

and the later community of Croton, who continue to mourn his death. This kind of continuity is a critical element of the discourse of ethnicity, which we will also see later for Metapontion, in Bacchylides 11.

The ritual apparently required women to abstain from wearing jewelry or luxurious clothing, perhaps on a prescribed day every year, but the identity of these women is unclear; it is merely γυναιξὶ . . . ἐγχώροις, "the women of the land." This vagueness perhaps suggests broad participation by any Crotoniate woman who wanted to—indeed, at least notionally, by all of them. Alternatively, as Giangiulio has argued, the women might be a college of priestesses, who would notionally represent the whole community.[99] In either case, the ritual was conducted on behalf of the *polis*, which gave its support to the participants, perhaps supplying them with funds or equipment; this implicates the entire community in its embrace. The ritual action of mourning for Achilles thus makes a major statement about the identity of the community that conducted it. Similar mourning rituals for heroes are known from other places, as are Achilles cults, especially in the Black Sea region.[100] Yet even the closest single parallel, from Elis, may not offer the primary resonance as seen by the people of Croton. The cult on Cape Lacinia is likely to have held much additional meaning for the Achaean participants, especially when placed in the Homeric context emphasized by the myth of Thetis.

Women's mourning rituals are common in Homer, and lamenting the dead is a typical role for women to play in Homeric society. Thetis on several occasions foresees the day when she will mourn for her son, and Briseis laments his coming death as well, while the lamentations of Hecuba, Andromache, and Helen for Hector in *Iliad* 24 bring the poem to its conclusion.[101] A woman from Croton who participates in the ritual therefore temporarily steps into the role of Thetis, Briseis, or Andromache. Therefore, the significance of this ritual is to be found especially in its performative aspect: by mourning for Achilles, the best of the Achaeans, these women are performing their identity and actually *become* Homeric Achaean women.[102] It is difficult to imagine a more eloquent way for a community to proclaim its identity.

99. Giangiulio 1982, 43–45; Giangiulio 2002, 287–288, on the basis of a parallel from Elis.

100. Mourning rituals: Giangiulio 1982, 42–43. Achilles in the Black Sea: Burgess 2009, 126–131; Ivantchik 2017; Kozlovskaya 2017a; Braund 2018, esp. 41–48.

101. The Cyclic scene of lament of Thetis and the nymphs for Achilles (in the *Aithiopis*) is alluded to at *Od.* 24.15–94; Pind. *Isthm.* 8.62–64. For Homeric laments more generally, see, e.g., *Il.* 24.707–804.

102. Farnell 1921, 288–289.

Religious practices were thus crucial to the performance of ethnic identity, yet the precise manner in which this ethnic identity was mediated through religious practices is worth noting. The role of religion in uniting Greek *ethnos* states such as Boeotia and Phocis has been well studied. Each of those regions developed one or more shared sanctuaries—those of Athena Itonia and Poseidon at Onchestos in Boeotia or at Kalapodi in Phocis—that acted as a focal point of regional and ethnic identity. Meetings of political institutions were held at these sanctuaries, festivals drew participants from throughout the region, and myths developed that linked the sanctuary to the ethnic origins of its people.[103] However, neither the sanctuary of Hera Lacinia nor any other religious site played such a role among the Achaeans (at least, until much later), and there were essentially no federal institutions until the emergence of the Italiote League (which also included non-Achaean members) in the fourth century.[104] The Achaeans simply were not an *ethnos* state like Boeotia or Phocis, and so the role of Hera among the Achaeans differed substantially as well: it was mediated through the *polis*. The cult of Hera on the Lacinian promontory, therefore, stands at the intersection of ethnic and civic identity, as indeed does the hero cult of Achilles associated with it, since both were central to the construction of both Crotoniate and Achaean identity. By linking their most important *polis* sanctuary to Heracles, Menelaus, Thetis, and Achilles, the Crotoniates defined themselves as Achaean.

Thus, as we have seen, Croton articulated its identity in a range of ways—myths, coins, and cults—that mutually supported one another to present a remarkably consistent picture. While the dual definitions of Achaean ethnicity—Peloponnesian and Homeric—have long been recognized, the striking ways in which *polis* and ethnic identities interlocked in Croton have not. It is clear that both types of identity were equally important for Crotoniates as they thought about the nature of their community. Moreover, we can now recognize the role of politics in the development of these identities. Myths of identity were a key way Greeks articulated their relationships with their neighbors, and new stories emerged as those relationships changed. When Croton's rivalry with Sybaris dominated the politics of southern Italy, a story of Myscellus that articulated that rivalry gained prominence. When Croton had replaced Sybaris as the hegemonic power, another story (of the Achaeans on the Neaethus) emerged to create legitimacy

---

103. Morgan 2003, 113–134; McInerney 2013; Mackil 2013; Funke and Haake 2013; Mili 2015.

104. Wonder 2012; Fronda 2013; Fronda 2015.

for this situation. More broadly, the Crotoniates sought to paint the most prestigious possible portrait of themselves for both domestic and international consumption, showing and enacting their identities as Achaeans and as Crotoniates through myths of Heracles and rituals for Achilles, both of which had special significance in Croton. As we will see next, the people of Metapontion constructed a remarkably similar set of identities, but the city's less powerful stature meant that political dynamics affected their identities quite differently.

Metapontion: Insiders and Outsiders

Metapontion, located on the instep of the Italian boot, northeast of Sybaris and sandwiched between Dorian Taras and Ionian Siris, was an average Greek *polis*, a prosperous but not very powerful community that, unlike Croton, never made any pretensions at regional dominance. Its historical experience differed drastically from that of Croton, as we can observe Metapontion trying to maintain an independent place for itself among its larger neighbors. Its sense of identity and the dynamics of its development were therefore also quite different from Croton's, even though we can trace some similar strands of Achaean-ness. In particular, powerful outsiders, such as Athens and Thurii, frequently tried to define Metapontine identity for their own purposes, and we can trace to some extent how the Metapontines tried to push back and reassert their own identity.

Precisely because of these competing emic and etic definitions and the changing political environments in which they developed, Metapontion's myths of identity and origins are (even more than for most cities) a confusing welter of contradictory ideas. Some traditions make the Metapontines Achaean; they were founded by a historical oikist from the Peloponnese, who was perhaps named Leucippus, or by Homeric heroes returning from Troy. Alternatively, Metapontion could be portrayed as stemming from the Aeolian *ethnos* via the figures of Melanippe and Neleus, who also tie the city to Ionia and thus to the Athenian Empire. These complex traditions have been thoroughly discussed by a number of scholars,[105] and so I focus here only on two elements in this mixture: first, the role of politics in shaping Metapontion's sense of identity, and second, the overlapping of *polis* and ethnic identities.

---

105. See esp. Mele 1998; Giacometti 2005; Kowalzig 2007, 267–327.

Sybaris, Thurii, and Leucippus

Two separate stories found in a single passage of Strabo (6.1.15) both define Metapontion as ethnically Achaean, through its roots in the Peloponnese of the Archaic period.[106] Both of these foundation narratives emerge out of identifiable political contexts, and both place Metapontion in specific relationships with other nearby cities. Both, for instance, present Taras as an enemy, likely in response to the loose political control that Taras exercised over Metapontion, in some form, in the mid-fifth century.[107] Yet the political implications of the two stories are strikingly different. One, which Strabo attributes to Antiochus of Syracuse (F12), gives Sybaris responsibility for the foundation of Metapontion, using a discourse of Achaean ethnicity to put the colony in a subordinate position. The second, for which no source is given, highlights Metapontine agency in its own creation through the figure of the oikist, Leucippus. Comparing the two narratives reveals a striking and highly politicized debate over the nature of Metapontion's Achaean identity in the late fifth century.

Antiochus, the earliest major historian of the Greek West, wrote in the late fifth century and covered both Sicily and Italy down to 424. Although his work is preserved only in fragments, the extant pieces constitute a major source for the foundation legends of the Greek cities of Italy.[108] His version of Metapontion's foundation presents Sybaris as the prime mover, summoning Achaeans to settle the site of Metapontion as part of its struggle with Taras:

Ἀντίοχος δέ φησιν ἐκλειφθέντα τὸν τόπον ἐποικῆσαι τῶν Ἀχαιῶν τινας μεταπεμφθέντας ὑπὸ τῶν ἐν Συβάρει Ἀχαιῶν, μεταπεμφθῆναι δὲ κατὰ μῖσος τὸ πρὸς Ταραντίνους τῶν Ἀχαιῶν τῶν ἐκπεσόντων ἐκ τῆς Λακωνικῆς, ἵνα μὴ Ταραντῖνοι γειτνιῶντες ἐπιπηδήσαιεν τῷ τόπῳ.

Antiochus says that some Achaeans were summoned by the Achaeans in Sybaris and resettled the site, which was abandoned, but that they were summoned because of hatred for the Tarantines on the part of the Achaeans who had been thrown out of Laconia, so that the Tarantines, who were neighbors, would not pounce upon the site.

---

106. Other sources concur without giving details: e.g., Ps.-Scymn. 327–9; Solin. 2.10; Euseb. *Chron. Arm.* under Olympiad 1; cf. Bérard 1963, 171.

107. Lepore 1974, 317–318; Giacometti 1990, 284; cf. Brauer 1986, 31.

108. His fragments are at *FGrH* 555; cf. Luraghi 2002; Luraghi 2013a.

The choice of site, according to Antiochus, was dictated by territorial concerns. Both Sybaris and Taras wanted to control the territory of Siris, which lies between Sybaris and Metapontion, and planting a colony at Metapontion would secure the site of Siris for the Achaeans. On the surface, Antiochus's story appears to be a narrative of Achaean ethnic solidarity and cooperation against Dorian enemies.[109]

Yet, as in the Neaethus story discussed earlier, cooperation seems to involve hegemony: Sybaris is presented as responsible for the settlement of Metapontion and even assumes the role of mother city, since no point of origin in the Peloponnese is specified. Such a role would make the colony subordinate to some degree, obliged to maintain loyalty and traditional ties to its metropolis. Meanwhile, the Metapontines play no role in their own foundation, and the story relies on suppressing any sense of Metapontion as a separate *polis* in favor of viewing it as a dependency of Sybaris. It is clearly told for the benefit of Sybaris, not Metapontion.[110]

Antiochus's version, while recorded in the late fifth century, could have originated in the second half of the sixth century, during the heyday of Sybarite power before its sack by Croton in 510. However, a more secure context places this story in the 430s, when a well-attested period of conflict occurred between Thurii—the *polis* founded a decade earlier on the former site of Sybaris—and Taras.[111] This conflict concerned precisely the territory that had once belonged to Siris and resulted in the foundation of Heraclea as a Tarantine colony on the site of the destroyed city. Although disputes over territory were common, the parallels between the historical situation and the foundation narrative are too great to be coincidence. The latter would have been enormously relevant—and perhaps newly created—in the second half of the fifth century, precisely when Antiochus was writing his history.

Although the narrative concerns the long-defeated Sybaris, rather than Thurii, the new panhellenic colony represented itself in important ways as a

---

109. On Antiochus's story, see Musti 1983, 274–281; Mele 1998, 69–74; Luraghi 2002, 69–71; Luraghi 2013a, F12.

110. Some scholars (Musti 1983, 274–281; Mele 1998, 69–70; Nicholson 2015, 293) instead see the story as pro-Tarantine: Antiochus says the site was empty, which (in their view) gives Taras an equal claim to it. But Greek colonial thought could equally well deploy the concept of the *terra nullius*, according to which the emptiness of the site legitimizes the claims of the first Greek settlers: Dougherty 1993, 1–2, 21–22.

111. Antiochus himself is known to have discussed this war (F11 = Strabo 6.1.14); further sources and discussion in Luraghi 2013a, F11; cf. Brauer 1986, 29–31. Antiochus's story is linked to this war by Bérard 1963, 170–171; Mele 1998, 70; Morgan and Hall 1996, 210; *contra*, Dunbabin 1948, 31.

FIG. 2.3 Stater of Sybaris, c. 530–510. Bull, incuse. Courtesy of the American Numismatic Society.

successor to Sybaris, especially through its appropriation of Sybarite imagery on its coinage. The symbol of a bull had appeared on Sybarite coinage since its inception and was remarkable for its longevity (fig. 2.3).[112] Surviving Sybarites tried several times in the fifth century to refound their city, and bulls consistently appear on the coins of each incarnation, helping them maintain their civic identity.[113] Thurii's coins also showed a bull, helping them stake a claim to the Sybarite past (fig. 2.4).[114] In the same way, a story about Sybaris might be used to make a claim about the present. The Thurians could easily have developed this story about Metapontion in the 430s as a way of creating legitimacy for their territorial ambitions by projecting them into the distant past.

Thus, we see in Antiochus's narrative how a story that defines Metapontion's identity as Achaean is imposed from outside. While Metapontion did undoubtedly claim Achaean identity for themselves—such an identity was certainly not invented by the Thurians—the details of the foundation story and the precise nature of the identity it describes were not chosen by the Metapontines and (as we will soon see) were likely rejected there. Moreover, we know of this story because it was recorded by Antiochus, a Syracusan—also an outsider. Since Syracuse and Taras were rivals at this time, he would have been eager to tell a story that strengthened Thurii at the expense of Taras.[115] For both Antiochus and the Thurians, Metapontion's attitude was unimportant.

112. Gorini 1975, 103–114; Rutter 1997, 22–27, 39–44; Papadopoulos 2002, 28–31.

113. Laus and Poseidonia, colonies of Sybaris that received refugees from the sack in 510, also began minting bull coins soon afterward: Rutter 1997, 40–42.

114. Rutter 1997, 43–45.

115. On Antiochus's political leanings, see esp. Nafissi 1985; Luraghi 2002, 76–78.

FIG. 2.4 Distater of Thurii, c. 410–330. Obverse: Athena with Scylla. Reverse: bull.
Courtesy of the American Numismatic Society.

It is the second story, which is retold by Strabo (6.1.15) without referencing
a source, that hints at those attitudes, offering completely different political
implications:

> ἔστι δέ τις καὶ οὗτος λόγος ὡς ὁ πεμφθεὶς ὑπὸ τῶν Ἀχαιῶν ἐπὶ τὸν
> συνοικισμὸν Λεύκιππος εἴη, χρησάμενος δὲ παρὰ τῶν Ταραντίνων τὸν
> τόπον εἰς ἡμέραν καὶ νύκτα μὴ ἀποδοίη, μεθ᾽ ἡμέραν μὲν λέγων πρὸς
> τοὺς ἀπαιτοῦντας ὅτι καὶ εἰς τὴν ἐφεξῆς νύκτα αἰτήσαιτο καὶ λάβοι,
> νύκτωρ δ᾽ ὅτι καὶ πρὸς τὴν ἑξῆς ἡμέραν.

> There is also this story, that the man sent by the Achaeans to help settle
> it was Leucippus, and that, after obtaining the place from the Tarantines
> for a day and night, he would not give it back, saying by day to those
> who asked for it back that he had asked and taken it for the next night,
> and by night that he had asked and taken it for the next day.

In this version, the focus on the figure of Leucippus, the oikist (whose native city is not named), emphasizes the Metapontines' control over their own
foundation and legitimizes the existence of Metapontion as a separate and
independent community.[116] The historicity of the story has been strongly (and
rightly) questioned, since Dionysius of Halicarnassus reports the same story

---

116. On the Leucippus story, see Bérard 1963, 172–173; Musti 1983, 274–281; Mele 1998, 69–
74; Morgan and Hall 1996, 211; Giacometti 2005.

regarding the foundation of Callipolis, a town in the territory of Taras.[117] Yet at the same time, Leucippus does appear as a bearded and helmeted head on Metapontion's coinage in the second half of the fourth century, when he was certainly recognized officially as the city's oikist.[118] Thus, the story, too, was probably accepted, if not created, in Metapontion itself.

The political implications of this narrative have been seen in various ways, either pro- or anti-Tarantine. On the one hand, the story presupposes a site controlled by Taras, which was able to lend the site to Leucippus, and this might seem to favor Taras's contemporary claim to the region, as the original occupant.[119] Yet a prior claim need not always remain the best claim. The story depicts the wily Leucippus defeating an enemy, the Tarantines, through trickery, displaying his intellectual superiority in order to succeed in founding Metapontion. As Carol Dougherty has argued, Greek foundation narratives frequently involve exactly this sort of mental gymnastics, especially in the form of a riddle, which the oikist typically solves, enabling the foundation to proceed.[120] The story of Leucippus involves the same sort of wordplay and cunning as in many examples Dougherty analyzes; in fact, she analyzes the somewhat fuller version applied by Dionysius to Callipolis in exactly this way.[121] Thus, the story shows how the oikist rightfully took the land from Taras, which both requires and defuses the idea that Taras previously claimed it, and establishes Metapontion as the legitimate possessor of its own land.

The story of Leucippus thus was highly relevant in the late fifth century, retrojecting the contemporary conflict with Taras into the distant past. Resistance to Taras is made a core part of Metapontion's foundation and

---

117. Dion. Hal. *Ant. Rom.* 19.3; cf. Dunbabin 1948, 31–32; Bérard 1963, 172–173; Malkin 1994, 119n13.

118. Rutter 2001, nos. 1552–1553, 1555, 1562, 1573–1576, 1622; cf. Lacroix 1965, 85–89; Rutter 1997, 93–96.

119. As emphasized by Musti 1983, 288–290; Mele 1998, 71–72. The same scholars (as well as Dunbabin 1948, 32) also argue that since Dionysius's Leucippus is a Spartan, and a Spartan hero by the same name is also known, the Metapontine Leucippus must be Spartan or Tarantine. But this has been conclusively rejected by Giacometti (2005, 182–183), who points out that the name Leucippus is attested across the Greek world, and the Spartan figures need not be relevant; cf. Bérard 1963, 172–173.

120. Dougherty 1993, esp. 45–60.

121. Dougherty 1993, 53. Dionysius's more extended version, applied to Callipolis, has the Tarantines accept that they have been properly bamboozled and recognize the rightful claims of the new colonists; conceivably, this was part of Metapontion's narrative as well but has been shortened by Strabo, as suggested by Bérard 1963, 172–173.

identity, which endures from its foundation to the present. This identity is presented as Achaean but in a rather different way from what we saw earlier. Unlike in Antiochus's story, where any trace of a *polis* identity is subsumed within the larger collective, here Metapontion uses its self-identification as Achaean in order to separate itself from other Achaeans in the present. Ethnic and *polis* identities are both deployed in different combinations to intervene in ongoing conflicts, not only with Taras but also among themselves. The Metapontine story of Leucippus emerged not only in response to conflict with Taras but also in conversation with Antiochus's alternative story, and it represents an attempt by Metapontines to assert their own identity and independence against the attempt by Thurii to define it from the outside. Whether the dueling narratives about its foundation were newly created in the 430s or merely found renewed relevance, they do provide a window into the dynamic processes through which politics continued to shape Achaean identity, even well into the fifth century.

By way of comparison, another Achaean city shows a strikingly similar pattern, despite the scanty available data about its foundation. Caulonia, located on the Ionian Sea south of Croton, is said by most sources to be a subcolony of Croton, yet one source, Pausanias, instead names as the oikist Typhon of Aigai, from Peloponnesian Achaea.[122] Such a specific report should not be attributed to late developments or mistaken information in Pausanias's day. Rather, these variants most likely emerged from the struggle over Crotoniate control of much of Magna Graecia in the early fifth century. Croton attempted to legitimize its control over Caulonia by claiming to be its mother city, while Caulonia resisted by asserting its higher status as a colony founded directly from the Peloponnese.[123] Regardless of which version, if either, may be historically accurate,[124] it is clear that Achaean ancestry in Caulonia, just as in better-documented Metapontion, represented a way of articulating and contesting the relative statuses of different communities.

---

122. Croton: Ps.-Scymn. 318–322; Solin. 2.10; Steph. Byz. s.v. Aulon. Typhon of Aigai: Paus. 6.3.12. Strabo (6.1.10) refers to it more generally as a foundation of Achaeans. Another tradition referred to an eponymous founder, Aulon or Caulon, son of an Amazon: Steph. Byz. s.v. Caulonia; Serv. *ad Aen.* 3.553; Lycoph. *Alex.* 1002–1004; cf. Bérard 1963, 352–353.

123. Morgan and Hall 1996, 208–209; De Sensi Sestito 2001.

124. On this question, see Dunbabin 1948, 27–28; Bérard 1963, 158–160; Giangiulio 1989, 221–224.

Neleus, Pylos, and Melanippe

A second set of stories describe Metapontines' ethnic ties in a completely different manner, labeling them not Achaeans but Aeolians.[125] First, Metapontion features prominently in the myth of Melanippe, who (at least in some versions) was the daughter of Aeolus and wife of the eponymous king Metapontos. Second, the Metapontines also wove themselves into the stories of the family of Neleus, a Thessalian hero and grandson of Aeolus, who founded Pylos in the Peloponnese and whose descendants (according to one tradition) settled Metapontion after the Trojan War. The two myths of Melanippe and the Neleids thus worked together to establish an Aeolian past and identity for Metapontion—though, as we will see, they also had important Achaean resonances. In the fifth century, this Aeolian identity came to be closely linked with Athens and Athenian imperial ideology, as Metapontion became one of Athens's key western allies. This identity was thus highly politically charged; it was also hotly contested, as two writers, Euripides and Antiochus of Syracuse, attempted to redefine Metapontine identity from the outside.

The story of Melanippe was told by Euripides in his lost tragedy *Captive Melanippe*, written probably in the 420s.[126] While the play has not survived, the essentials of its plot can be reconstructed as follows. Melanippe, the daughter of Aeolus, bore two sons to Poseidon, who were called Aeolus the Younger and Boiotos. Melanippe's father threw her in prison and exposed her twins, who in turn were rescued and adopted by Metapontos, king of Italy (and eponym of Metapontion). The king's first wife, whom Euripides probably named Siris, was at first childless but later bore twins of her own; as a result, she plotted against the adopted sons in favor of her own. In a happy twist, however, Melanippe's sons survived, Siris committed suicide, and Melanippe not only was released from prison but married Metapontos.[127] This myth existed in a variety of versions: some call the wife Theano instead of Siris, while others name Melanippe's father Desmontes. Moreover, as we will see, Antiochus of Syracuse wrote a fierce polemic against Euripides's play, denying that Melanippe had anything to do with Metapontion. Still, the Aeolian matrix from which this myth emerged is clear, since Melanippe is the daughter

---

125. On these stories as a unit, see Giacometti 1990; Nafissi 1997; Kowalzig 2007, 310–324.

126. For the date, see Giacometti 1990, 288–289n25, with further references.

127. For this reconstruction, which is based largely on Hyg. *Fab.* 186, see Giacometti 1990, 280–282; Kowalzig 2007, 308–310; Stewart 2017, 145–146. Euripides also wrote a second play, the *Clever Melanippe*, which was apparently unrelated to Metapontion. The fragments of the two plays are *TrGF* V F480–514.

of Aeolus, and her two sons are called Aeolus and Boiotos, the eponym of Boeotia; the myth probably originated there.[128] Euripides's play thus represents Metapontion as an offshoot of the Aeolian *ethnos*.

Meanwhile, Strabo reports that Metapontion had been founded by men from Pylos returning with Nestor from the Trojan War, and he adds as evidence of this a sacrifice to the Neleids conducted by the Metapontines.[129] These claims and rituals similarly proclaimed Metapontion's participation in a world of Aeolic traditions. According to the Neleid myth, the family patriarch originated in Thessalian Iolcus but departed after a dispute over the kingship and went on to found Pylos in the Peloponnese. Those Pylians, who founded Metapontion, could thus be understood as ancestrally Aeolian. After the Trojan War, meanwhile, the sons of Neleus led the Ionian migration to Asia Minor and founded a number of cities there. Their route to Asia, according to a tradition that was prominent in the fifth century, included a sojourn in Athens. On this basis, the Athenians claimed to be the mother city of all the Ionians, a claim that underpinned the legitimacy of the Athenian Empire.[130] If Metapontion, too, had been founded by the descendants of Neleus, then it shared in this strong and natural bond with Athens.[131]

This way of understanding Metapontion's identity as Aeolian, through Melanippe and the Neleids, benefited both sides. The Athenians' eyes had been on the West for much of the fifth century, forging alliances with Rhegium and Leontini in the 430s and (according to Herodotus) laying claim to the territory of Siris, adjacent to Metapontion.[132] While Metapontion was never a tribute-paying member of the empire like the Ionians, it did provide troops to the Athenian relief expedition to Sicily in 413 "in accordance with the alliance,"

---

128. Other versions of Melanippe's myth also demonstrate that she was originally Aeolian: Nafissi 1997, 341–345; Stewart 2017, 147–150.

129. On the Pylian story, see Giacometti 1990; Giacometti 2005, 169–176; Mele 1998, 77–78; Nafissi 1997; Malkin 1998, 211–213; Kowalzig 2007, 310–319. On the sacrifice, see Nafissi 1997, 349–352; Giacometti 2005, 170–175; cf. Ghinatti 1974, 555–557, with references to older scholarship.

130. See esp. Zacharia 2003a, 48–55; Mac Sweeney 2013; Fragoulaki 2013, 210–220.

131. Moreover, several important Athenian families, including the Pisistratids and the Alcmaeonids, traced their own lineage to Homeric Pylos, and this, too, had the effect of binding the Ionian cities to Athens: Hdt. 5.65.3–4; Paus. 2.18.8–9; Giacometti 1990, 293–294.

132. Hdt. 8.62.2; cf. Hornblower, *CT* III.5–6; Hornblower 2011, 169–172; Smith 2003, 89–116; Cataldi 2007; Mele 2007; Mattaliano 2010.

which had probably been formed in the 430s or 420s.[133] For Athens, a strong alliance with Metapontion protected its interests in the West. Meanwhile, for Metapontion, which was sandwiched between hostile Taras and Thurii, an alliance with a faraway power, unlikely to trouble them in their neighborhood, was highly desirable. The existence of this alliance thus strongly encouraged a strategy of myth-making that would legitimize this friendly relationship. The claim of Aeolic identity and Neleid origins for Metapontion did exactly that, by assimilating its status (and its relationship with Athens) to that of the Ionians. In this way, Metapontion and Athens were engaging in kinship diplomacy, a process of justifying alliances by invoking identity that, as we will see in chapter 5, was particularly prominent during the Peloponnesian War.

Nevertheless, it is important to observe that the original impetus for this myth-making came from Athens. The Neleid story as a whole was primarily an Athenian development. Its center of gravity, so to speak, lies between Athens and Ionia, with Metapontion somewhat uneasily grafted onto it. Many Metapontines clearly found the story persuasive, as shown by their willingness to sacrifice to the Neleids, and this is no doubt because they found it beneficial to have Athens as an ally, but it was not a native Metapontine idea.

The story that Melanippe came to Metapontion shows this pattern even more starkly; it was discussed and debated primarily by outsiders, and it is not clear whether Metapontines adopted it at all. As we saw above, her larger myth originated not in Italy but (probably) in Boeotia. There is no real evidence that Euripides was drawing on a prior Metapontine version by bringing her to Italy,[134] and it is not unusual for Euripides to make substantial innovations in his plays. Regardless, as we will see, it was Euripides's play and not any earlier texts that provoked the ire of Antiochus of Syracuse, producing a situation where two outsiders, Euripides and Antiochus of Syracuse, were debating Metapontion's identity for their own purposes. Massimo Nafissi has further pointed out that the negative portrait of the character Siris in the play supports Metapontion's claims in its contemporary conflict between Metapontion and

---

133. Thuc. 7.33.4–5; cf. 7.57.11. Metapontion was one of the only western cities to support Athens during the Sicilian Expedition.

134. Scholars continue to debate the issue: I follow Nafissi 1997, 344–347; Stewart 2017, 146–151; *contra*, Mele 1998, 75–77; cf. Kowalzig 2007, 318. Certainly, earlier Metapontine traditions included some Aeolian elements, and, as Barbara Kowalzig has argued (Kowalzig 2007, 308–310), the play seems to have linked its action to the cult of Artemis, which was prominent in Metapontion (and elsewhere, including in Athens), but this does not prove that the myth was native to Metapontion.

Taras, over Heraclea, the successor city founded on the former site of Siris.[135] Alternatively, the portrait of Siris may create legitimacy for the destruction of that city more than a century earlier.[136] Either of these interpretations of Euripides's intentions is possible, but what both of them presuppose is that Euripides intended to make an intervention in local Italian politics.

Equally important, however, is that Euripides was an Athenian writer with Athenian perspectives, writing for a primarily Athenian audience. Tragedies were, of course, performed and re-performed across the Greek world, and in a few cases, such as Aeschylus's *Aetnaeans* and Euripides's *Archelaus*, ancient testimony shows that tragedies were written at the behest of non-Athenian rulers. It is likely that local knowledge and interests were taken into account in those cases, but there is no evidence that the *Captive Melanippe* was one of them.[137] Instead, Euripides's choice of storylines was likely shaped not so much by the concerns of Metapontion itself but rather by his own city's desire to build ties with communities in the West. This should not be taken too far, of course, and the *Captive Melanippe* should not be reduced to a one-dimensional political tract. Like all extant tragedies, it was undoubtedly a complex literary composition, weaving together numerous ideas, themes, and attitudes.[138] Nevertheless, Euripides frequently uses myth to explore political issues and even to make patriotic points, alongside the many other ideas with which he is concerned.[139] In crafting a mythical past and an identity for Metapontion, Euripides put Athenian imperial interests at center stage, while in the play the Metapontines themselves are silent.

Meanwhile, Antiochus's strong reaction against Euripides's play suggests that he, too, saw it as pro-Athenian and that he saw representations of Metapontion's identity as an important battleground between Athens and Syracuse.[140] He denied that Melanippe came to Metapontion or married Metapontos; in fact, he disputed even the existence of Metapontos,

---

135. Nafissi 1997.

136. Giacometti 1990; Mele 1998, 76–77.

137. *Pace* Stewart 2017, 151–158.

138. See esp. Kowalzig 2007, 308–310.

139. The *Ion* and the *Trojan Women* are good examples: Zacharia 2003a; Wohl 2015. For similar approaches to fragmentary tragedies, see Vickers 1995; Zacharia 2001.

140. As has long been recognized, the wording of the citation at Strabo 6.1.15 indicates that Antiochus was responding directly to Euripides's *Captive Melanippe*: ἐνταῦθα δὲ καὶ τὸν Μετάποντον μυθεύουσι καὶ τὴν Μελανίππην τὴν δεσμῶτιν καὶ τὸν ἐξ αὐτῆς Βοιωτόν; cf. Nafissi 1997, 345–346.

substituting as eponym a hero Metabus. As proof, he apparently pointed to a *heroon* for Metabus located there, as well as a line from the Archaic genealogical poet Asius of Samos that places Melanippe in "the halls of Dius," not those of Metapontos.[141] From our perspective, all this line proves is that mythical variants existed, but for Antiochus, this argument severs the tight mythical connection between Metapontion and Athens. For a Syracusan in the late fifth century, Athens was a competitor and sometime enemy, and so a myth that strengthened Athens's position in the West was likely to harm Syracuse. Antiochus's polemic thus emerges as an attempt to delegitimize Metapontion's alliance with Athens and thus a further attempt to redefine Metapontine identity for political gain. As a Syracusan, Antiochus was no less an outsider to Metapontion than Euripides, and he is unlikely to have considered their own beliefs. For both authors, Metapontine identity is deployed to score political points, but neither author is interested in Metapontion for its own sake. Their dispute is, at its core, about staking out pro- or anti-Athenian positions. The existence of this polemic shows that in the late fifth century, Metapontion's identity became the object of politicized controversy among non-Metapontines, a critical example of the impact of politics on the identities of less powerful communities.

Thus far, we have read these myths as Aeolian, but they could also be interpreted as bolstering Metapontion's Achaean credentials. Above, we saw how the myth of a foundation from Pylos, together with the Neleid sacrifice, tied Metapontion to Ionia and the Athenian Empire. But those men of Pylos were also, of course, Homeric Achaeans, and Strabo's text calls them "Pylians sailing from Troy with Nestor." His description of them returning from the Trojan War with their leader, one of the great Homeric heroes, highlights this angle more than their Aeolian background. By claiming descent from Nestor's Pylians, the Metapontines were tracing their origins to what was perhaps the second-most-prominent region of Homeric Greece, after the Argolid, and all of this increases the city's prestige. In following this line of thought, the Metapontines would be taking a very similar view to those of Croton and other Achaeans.[142] Either interpretation, Aeolian or Achaean, need not exclude the other; both could be emphasized or de-emphasized as any individual desired or as a situation required.

---

141. Antiochus F12 = Strabo 6.1.15; Asius F2 PEG; on Antiochus's polemic, see esp. Giacometti 1990; Nafissi 1997; cf. Musti 1983, 276–279.

142. On the possible origins of the Pylos story in the sixth-century conflict between the Achaean cities and Siris, cf. Hall (2002, 64–65), who sees that conflict as the wellspring of Achaean identity in Italy.

FIG. 2.5 Stater of Metapontion, c. 530–510. Ear of barley, incuse. Courtesy of the American Numismatic Society.

Strabo offers two pieces of evidence for the Pylian origins of Metapontion: first, the Neleid sacrifice and, second, the dedication of a "golden harvest" at Delphi by the Pylian colonists. This dedication, presumably a gold sculpture of an ear or sheaf of grain, shows that the Metapontines were proud of the fertility of their agricultural land and wanted to proclaim it to the world at Delphi. Dedications by *poleis* in panhellenic spaces like Delphi frequently presented an image of the city to the world, allowing the dedicators to publicly define their city and to express civic ideology and *polis* identity. This dedication's message about fertility and prosperity echoes that found on Metapontion's copious coinage, which also depicts an ear of grain (fig. 2.5).[143] This emblem, consistent over centuries like Croton's tripod, often stood alone as a symbol of the city but could also be combined with other elements that distinguish it from others. For example, when Metapontine coins began depicting Leucippus in the fourth century, he was typically paired with an ear of barley on the coins' reverse.[144] While agricultural productivity was the foundation of the economy of nearly every Greek city, the Metapontines seem to have taken their pride to another level. The dedication and the coinage work together to emphasize Metapontion's image of itself as a farming community, rich in land and grain. There is no reason to deny that such a dedication existed, although we may doubt whether it was actually made by Pylians. Rather, later Metapontines developed this attribution in order to suggest that their agricultural prosperity

143. Noe and Johnston 1984; Rutter 1997, 27–29, 47–51; cf. Lacroix 1965, 112–114; Papadopoulos 2002, 31.

144. Rutter 2001, nos. 1552–1553, 1555, 1562, 1573–1576, 1622; cf. Rutter 1997, 93–96.

went back to their most distant Achaean forebears. By projecting their civic self-image of fertility back onto the Achaeans of Pylos who founded the city, the dedication promoted a message combining their civic and ethnic identities into one and the same story.

The Neleid sacrifice, too, has more implications than I have discussed so far. While some aspects of the Neleid family story, such as his Thessalian birth and his descendants' Ionian foundations, emphasize their Aeolian ties, it is equally possible to highlight Neleus's role as founder of Homeric Pylos and father of Nestor, who in the *Iliad* frequently bears the epithet "son of Neleus." The ritual, which probably occurred annually, thus enabled Metapontines to reinforce their identity, reminding themselves regularly of their Pylian origins and the Achaean identity of their community. It could also, of course, remind them of their ties to Ionia and Athens. In fact, the multivalent nature of the Neleid traditions is part of what enabled Metapontion's traditions of identity to become so varied: one and the same ritual could support both angles.[145] This suggests a limit within which the flexibility of identity operates; it is far more flexible when existing traditions can be reinterpreted rather than starting *ab nihilo*.

Barbara Kowalzig has argued that the Ionian/Aeolian traditions form an earlier sixth-century layer, which was later reinterpreted through an Achaean lens. Since much of the evidence is difficult to date, however, it is impossible to say with certainty whether one is earlier than the other.[146] But it is worth noting that Bacchylides 11, to which I turn next, is actually the earliest date-able text that explicitly articulates any form of identity for Metapontion—and Bacchylides makes the city Achaean.[147] We would be on firmer ground to say simply that Metapontine identity enjoyed enormous flexibility but was also highly contested. Aeolian and Achaean thinking coexisted for long stretches, each promoted by different parties for their own reasons.

Hera, Artemis, and Alexidamus

Bacchylides 11, which is in some ways the most impressive surviving written source for Metapontine identity, makes them Achaean in more ways than

---

145. Cf. Kowalzig 2007, 317.

146. Moreover, much of her evidence either relates to Italian cities other than Metapontion or describes loose cultural ties rather than identity.

147. The exact date is not known (likely mid-fifth century or earlier), but it certainly predates the works of Euripides and Antiochus: cf. Maehler 2004, 9–10; Cairns 2010, 1–4, 101.

one, deriving them both from the Homeric Achaeans and from the people of Lousoi, a town and sanctuary of Artemis in the mountains south of the Corinthian Gulf.[148] The poem concludes thus (11.113–126):

ἔνθεν καὶ ἀρηϊφίλοις
ἄνδρεσσιν <ἐς> ἱπποτρόφον πόλιν Ἀχαιοῖς
ἕσπεο· σὺν δὲ τύχᾳ   115
ναίεις Μεταπόντιον, ὦ
χρυσέα δέσποινα λαῶν·
ἄλσος τέ τοι ἱμερόεν Κά-
σαν παρ' εὔυδρον †πρόγο-
νοι ἐσσάμενοι† Πριάμοι' ἐπεὶ χρόνῳ   120
βουλαῖσι θεῶν μακάρων
πέρσαν πόλιν εὐκτιμέναν
χαλκοθωράκων μετ' Ἀτρειδᾶν. Δικαίας
ὅστις ἔχει φρένας, εὑρή-
σει σὺν ἅπαντι χρόνῳ   125
μυρίας ἀλκὰς Ἀχαιῶν.

From there [Lousoi] you [Artemis] followed
war-loving Achaean men to their horse-raising city,   115
and you dwell with happy fortune in Metapontion,
O golden queen of the people. And [they established . . .]
a pleasant grove for you by the well-watered Casas
when by the plans of the blessed gods   120
they finally sacked the well-built city of Priam
with the bronze-girt sons of Atreus. He who has a just mind
will find throughout all time countless deeds of valor of   125
    the Achaeans.

As Hall has aptly put it, Bacchylides draws "an uninterrupted ethnic continuum" from the Achaeans who sacked Troy down to the fifth-century Metapontion from which hails his honorand, Alexidamus, a victor in boys'

148. I discuss my approach to epinician poetry in chapter 3. Briefly, epinician poets familiarized themselves with local traditions and issues and deployed this knowledge in a way that would make their patrons happy. Thus, such poetry can be analyzed as a source for local identities. On the ode in general, see Burnett 1985, 100–113; Seaford 1988; Maehler 2004; Giacometti 2005, 52–75; Cairns 2005; Cairns 2010, 101–128, 268–299; Kowalzig 2007, 267–327; Nicholson 2015, 277–307.

wrestling at Delphi.[149] It is highly likely that this conception of Metapontine origins represents a local myth rather than a poetic innovation.[150] Moreover, in maintaining their identity despite travel and relocating their community, the Metapontines mirror a number of examples we will see later, especially Camarina (chapter 5) and Sicilian Greeks under Deinomenid rule (chapter 3).

This ethnic continuum connects Metapontion with both the Peloponnese and the Homeric heroes through its central myth, which tells the story of the daughters of Proetus, king of Tiryns. The daughters (the Proetids) angered Hera by claiming that their father was wealthier than the queen of the gods. As a result, they were driven mad by Hera, fled Tiryns, and ended up at Lousoi in northern Arcadia. There they were reconciled with Hera through the intervention of Artemis and founded a sanctuary and festival in honor of Artemis; later, their descendants founded Metapontion. Thus, the Proetids' madness begins the movement to Italy, linking the city to the Argolid, and their descendants soon become the *progonoi* of the Metapontines.[151] These ancestors align the Metapontines with the Achaeans of the Trojan War.

This alignment occurs both on the level of ancestry, thereby defining the ethnic identity of the Metapontines as Achaean, and on a cultural level. The Metapontine-Achaean community is described as "horse-raising" and especially as warlike; the sack of Troy in particular provides a model for later Metapontines to emulate.[152] While neither of these points is by any means unique to Metapontion, they nonetheless represent how the city wanted to be seen, as part of its self-image. Continuity between past, present, and future is further emphasized by a strong sense of timelessness, summed up in the phrase "countless deeds of valor through all time." These deeds include both the sack of Troy and the victory of Alexidamus.[153] Bacchylides's praise for the Metapontine boy thus situates him in relation to his Achaean ancestors— he has lived up to their example—and also closely integrates him with his community and its Achaean identity. In fact, the poet closes the entire poem with the word Ἀχαιῶν, strongly emphasizing the Achaean identity, while also leaving unclear which Achaeans are meant. Is it the Homeric Achaeans or the

---

149. Hall 2002, 61.

150. So Cairns 2010, 107–112; Maehler 2004, 133, 156, is more doubtful.

151. If the text has been established correctly; see Carey 1980; Cairns 2010, 298.

152. Maehler 2004, 155–156; Cairns 2010, 295–299.

153. Cairns 2005.

Italian Achaeans? Or is there a difference at all?[154] This blurring of categories is foundational to the Metapontines' self-image.

Bacchylides's use of the Proetid myth also points to another aspect of Metapontine identity, one closely tied to religious practice. According to the poem's narrative, the Proetids' original insult to Hera occurred in a sanctuary of Hera; although the poet does not specify which one, the Argive Heraion is a likely option.[155] Their eventual reconciliation with Hera occurs through the intervention of Artemis, and they go on to found a sanctuary and festival in honor of Artemis at Lousoi. Thus, both Hera and Artemis play crucial roles in the poem, in the cultic landscape of Metapontion, and in constructing Metapontine identity.

Although Hera appears as the divine antagonist, her role in the creation of Metapontine society is nonetheless crucial.[156] The maiden daughters of Proetus go through a typical three-phase rite of passage: first they are expelled from their Tirynthian community, then they wander through the wilderness for thirteen months, and finally they rejoin human society in a new form. Hera is central to all three of these phases, and the new community that ultimately becomes Metapontion can only come into being through Hera's agency. Thus, future Metapontines must propitiate Hera to ensure the continuation of their community and social order. This is exactly what they did at two cult sites, one adjacent to the agora and another three kilometers from town at Tavole Palatine, where cult activity stretches back to the earliest days of the colony. Temples were built at both sites in the mid-sixth century, and the two sanctuaries remained the focus of activity for centuries.[157] Much as at Croton, Hera was one of the most important deities in Metapontion.

Bacchylides's choice to give Hera such an important role is especially significant in light of other attested versions of the Proetid myth, many of

---

154. Cf. Maehler 2004, 156: "The 'Achaeans' are, of course, the Homeric heroes of the Trojan War, whose heroic exploits B[acchylides] claims for the Peloponnesian Achaeans who founded Metapontion."

155. Maehler 2004, 146; Cairns 2010, 279. The cult of Hera at Tiryns itself is another possibility, with (as I suggest below) tight connections to the Argive Heraion; the broader implications would be similar.

156. Seaford 1988; Kowalzig 2007, 275–283; Cairns 2010, 291; cf. Segal 1976, 122–128.

157. The identification of Tavole Palatine as a sanctuary of Hera is epigraphically secure: Nenci 1966. Which of the various temples in the urban sanctuary should be attributed to Hera continues to be debated: for Temple A, see De Siena 1998; Mertens 1999; De Juliis 2001, 138–146; Giacometti 2005, 105–111; Carter 2006, 198–201; for Temple B, see Maddoli 1988, 119; Camassa 1991, 473; La Torre 2011, 292–295.

which exclude Hera (attributing the Proetids' madness to another deity, such as Dionysus) and keep them in the Argolid, rather than having them travel.[158] Hera's expanded role in the Metapontine version must have had particular significance there, which can be seen through the links it constructs with the Argolid. Bacchylides's myth has a strikingly Argolic flavor. Its opening, with its mention of Tiryns, Argos, and perhaps the Heraion, is firmly fixed in that region. Moreover, the poet rehearses at length the conflict between the brothers Proetus and Akrisius over the throne of Argos, which led Proetus to found Tiryns. This is a story with important significance in the Argolid but normally less so elsewhere.[159] Its use by Bacchylides suggests that the Metapontines found it relevant also, since it tied the origins of their community to the Argolid. Much as at Croton, where the cult of Hera Lacinia linked the Crotoniates to an "Achaean" worshipping community in the Argolid, the worship of Hera authorized by Bacchylides's myth articulates the Metapontine community in a similar way.

Artemis's role in the articulation of Metapontine Achaean identity is equally prominent. After the daughters of Proetus have been driven mad by Hera, it is Artemis who reconciles them. The Proetids then establish a sanctuary and festival for Artemis at Lousoi, in northern Arcadia, and the goddess later accompanies the Achaeans from Lousoi to Metapontion.[160] In Bacchylides's admittedly poetic rendering, the establishment of the sanctuary of Artemis at Metapontion is equivalent to the foundation of the city, implying a tight connection between the two; Artemis acts as a focal point of civic identity at Metapontion, much as Hera does at Croton. Artemis's sanctuary by the Casas River (today the Basento) is usually identified with the site of San Biagio della Venella, about six kilometers from the town (see fig. 2.6).[161] The sanctuary, where cult activity begins in the late seventh century,[162] has yielded a number of terracotta plaques and figurines suggesting worship of a female

158. On these other versions, see Dowden 1989, 71–95; Hall 1997, 97; Maehler 2004, 134–136; Cairns 2010, 113–119.

159. Hall 1997, 93–99. Significantly, another early source for the Proetid myth is Akousilaos, a local historian of Argos (*FGrH* 2 F28).

160. On Artemis in the poem, see Giacometti 1999; Kowalzig 2007, 283–290.

161. On San Biagio and its relationship to the poem, see Giacometti 2005, 61–75; Kowalzig 2007, 291–297; but cf. the recent identification of Bacchylides's sanctuary with the one at Pantanello: Carter 2018.

162. Osanna 1992, 79–80; Carter 1994, 168–174.

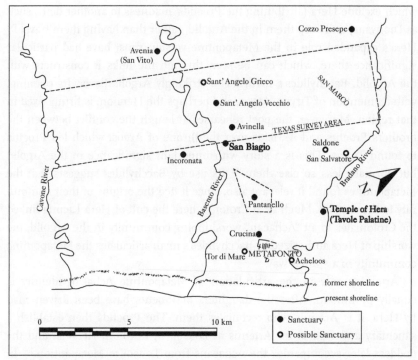

FIG. 2.6 Map of the *chora* of Metapontion. Drawing by D. Weiss, after Carter 1994, 163.

divinity combining kourotrophic and Mistress of Animals functions, much like Artemis in the Proetid myth.[163]

Bacchylides traces the origins of Artemis's worship at Metapontion to Lousoi, further linking the city to a different region of the Peloponnese. This sanctuary was located in northern Arcadia, very close to what would later be defined as the border with Achaea. In the early Iron Age, however, this border had not solidified, and the work of Catherine Morgan has demonstrated that Lousoi drew worshippers from a wide area in Arcadia and western Achaea.[164] Several scholars have come to the conclusion, based on this passage, that a substantial fraction of the settlers of Metapontion came from western Achaea and brought the cult of Artemis with them from Lousoi.[165] While this may

163. Osanna 1992, 48–52; Giacometti 1999, 418–420; De Juliis 2001, 97–106.

164. Morgan 2003, 182–184; Kowalzig 2007, 285–290.

165. Bérard 1963, 173–174.

or may not be historically accurate, what concerns me more is the impact of this belief on fifth-century Metapontine conceptions of their identity. The profession of religious ties with Lousoi demonstrates that the claim of Peloponnesian origins was a powerful one in Metapontion and was closely tied to Metapontine Achaean identity. In this way, Artemis represents a connection back to the Peloponnese that mirrors Hera's links to the Argolid discussed earlier, but in a uniquely Metapontine way.[166]

Strikingly, Metapontion is the only Achaean community known to rank Artemis so highly among its civic cults. While this sets the Metapontines apart from the other Achaeans, the manner in which they articulated their identity is quite similar. For the Metapontines, worshipping Artemis at San Biagio perpetuated the ethnic continuum linking them with the Proetids. Performing sacrifices to Artemis, dedicating small figurines, or singing in choruses (such as the one that may have performed Bacchylides's ode) allowed the Metapontines temporarily to become their Achaean ancestors, performing this identity in order to remember and reinforce their ethnic ties with various regions of the Peloponnese and with the heroic world in which their civic organization originated. Similarly, Bacchylides's poem and its myth speak to Metapontion alone, defining a *polis* community. While their community is defined as Achaean, other members of the ethnic group do not partake of this story. The complex relationship between Artemis and Hera allowed the Metapontines to construct through religious practices their own unique version of Achaean identity, distinguishing themselves from Croton just as much as it links them.

Conclusion

As we have seen in this chapter, in both Croton and Metapontion, ethnicity and *polis* identity were closely interwoven. The various foundation myths discussed here—ranging from Myscellus's Delphic consultations and Leucippus's trick to Heracles's murder of Lacinius and the arrival of the Pylians at Metapontion—typically articulate both an ethnic and a *polis* identity, and coins often do the same. Religious practices, too, served both to unify the citizens and to separate themselves from others. There were, naturally, differences in content and emphasis: Metapontion did not really see athletics as part of its *polis* identity, even in Alexidamus's victory ode, while Croton

---

166. Cf. also Syracusan references to Corinth and the Peloponnese (chapter 3 and chapter 6).

did not much emphasize the fertility of its land. But even beyond this, we can observe systematic differences in meaning between the two communities, much of which stems from their respective political environments. There was little unity to the Achaean ethnic group: to the extent that Crotoniates thought about the larger *ethnos* beyond their borders, it meant claiming hegemony over the others. The Metapontines tended to see it from the reverse position, often subordinated to others. Their experience hints at one crucial aspect of identity: it need not be articulated only by members of the community but can also be defined by others.

3

Syracusan Tyranny and Identity Politics

THROUGHOUT THE TWO decades of Deinomenid rule in Syracuse, both
Gelon (485–478) and Hieron (478–467) faced a major problem in securing
their power there: they were not Syracusan. They came instead from Gela,
a major rival that had recently dealt Syracuse a serious blow in the Battle of
the Heloros River in 492 (Hdt. 7.154.2–3). Gelon, in fact, had fought against
Syracuse in that battle, as second-in-command to Hippocrates, the tyrant of
Gela, and after Hippocrates's death, first Gelon and later Hieron themselves
ruled Gela (Hdt. 7.156.1). Gelon captured Syracuse and moved his capital there
in 485, but his family, as non-Syracusan tyrants of Syracuse, had an uphill
battle to be accepted as Syracusans.[1]

Despite their immense power, the Deinomenids faced a constant need
to create legitimacy for their positions. In this, they differed little from later
Sicilian tyrants, including Dionysius I (405–367), who at first struggled to
establish his power after half a century of democracy. More broadly, recent
work on Greek monarchy has shown that successful tyrants did not depend
on raw power alone. Rather, they engaged in self-representation and dialogue with their people, developing ideologies that presented themselves as
legitimate rulers.[2] A number of stories about the birth and youth of tyrants
serve to mark them out as special and worthy to rule. Dionysius's court
historian Philistus, for example, told how the future tyrant lost his horse
while crossing a river; when he later recovered the horse, a swarm of bees
had settled in its mane, which was interpreted as an omen of his coming

---

1. Portions of this chapter previously appeared in *BICS* as Thatcher 2012.

2. Lewis 2009; Luraghi 2013b; Mitchell 2013; Morgan 2015; Nicholson 2015.

The Politics of Identity in Greek Sicily and Southern Italy. Mark R. Thatcher, Oxford University Press. © Oxford University
Press 2021. DOI: 10.1093/oso/9780197586440.003.0003

success.[3] Similarly, monarchs placed great emphasis on displaying their *arete* through military success, athletic victories, and civic accomplishments; these qualities also justified how far they rose above others.[4] Such claims should not be understood as propaganda, a term that suggests one-way control by the tyrants over a passive target audience. Instead, these claims emerge as strategies for creating legitimacy for one-man rule within a *polis* framework, through a two-way discourse in which people actively accept their rulers' arguments and restrict the possible range of such strategies.

The Deinomenids' identity politics formed another strategy in the same toolkit. Gelon, victor over Carthage at Himera, presented himself as a champion of Greekness who enabled the Greeks of Sicily to remain Greek. Hieron's foundation of Aetna enhanced the ability of its Dorian inhabitants to prosper under its Dorian *nomoi* and invested him with the ethical qualities and political *eunomia* often associated with Dorians. At his new home of Syracuse, Hieron also co-opted elements of *polis* identity, linking himself to the city's landscape. Thus, three forms of identity—Greekness, Dorian ethnicity, and Syracusan *polis* identity—offered ways for the Deinomenids to shape public perceptions of themselves by appealing to their subjects' preexisting identities.[5] The tyrants supported and promoted these three identities in order to increase their salience and thereby to encourage their subjects to see the tyrant as "one of us" and as a legitimate ruler. Moreover, the Deinomenids also worked actively to reshape these preexisting conceptions of identity among their people in order to place themselves at the heart of those identities. Mediated through a number of channels, including epinician poetry, coinage, and public dedications, the discourse of identities helped define and structure the relationship between ruler and ruled and ultimately create legitimacy for their monarchical power in Sicily.

Much later, in the fourth century, Dionysius I used a very similar set of strategies, demonstrating that both the tactics used by the Deinomenids and the underlying dynamics of identity in politics continued to be available several generations later. Nevertheless, this dynamic relationship between tyranny and identity also evolved over time and left a lasting legacy. Although much of what the Deinomenids had implemented was overturned by the new,

---

3. Philistus (*FGrH* 556) F58 = Cic. *Div.* 1.73; cf. Plin. *N.H.* 8.158; Ael. *VH* 12.46; with Lewis 2000; Lewis 2009, 58–65; Pownall 2013, F58.

4. Mitchell 2013, 57–90.

5. They made use of Sicilian regional identity as well, but I reserve that discussion for chapter 4.

more democratic regime in Syracuse after the fall of the tyranny in 466, some aspects survived the political upheaval. The tyrants' identity politics did not simply vanish but were adapted by the citizenry to meet the needs of the new regime. Thus, the effects of tyranny on collective identities in Sicily were both broad and long-lasting, even when the tyrants themselves were gone.

The Tyrant's House and Syracusan Identities

Syracuse during the Deinomenid period was marked by enormous social change and disruption on a scale not seen before in Sicily. The tyrants not only imported thousands of mercenaries but also augmented the city's population with thousands of Sicilian Greeks. Gelon, according to Herodotus (7.156.2–3), destroyed the nearby *poleis* of Camarina, Megara, and Euboea and brought portions of their populations, along with half the people of Gela, to Syracuse.[6] Both the mercenaries and the Sicilians received full Syracusan citizenship.[7] As a result, within a few years, the tyrants had built up the city into a mega-lopolis that included a body of citizens larger than any other in Sicily, a worthy capital for a powerful dynasty.[8] But this citizen body also thereby became more diverse, less unified, and potentially a greater threat to Deinomenid su-premacy. The new citizens came from communities that had long traditions as independent *poleis* and took pride in their individual cultures. At Gela, for instance, the prominent temple of Athena Lindia celebrated the city's Rhodian origins—origins notably not shared with Syracuse. While such a Geloan iden-tity might be weakened by distance from that temple, how could Geloans truly become Syracusan? The tyrants needed to integrate their new citizens with the existing Syracusans, welding disparate groups of people into a single, cohesive community that would be loyal to the dynasty.

To solve this problem and establish themselves as the legitimate rulers of Syracuse, the Deinomenids successfully co-opted the Syracusans' preex-isting *polis* identity and inscribed themselves within a new concept of what it meant to be Syracusan. As seen in Pindar's odes and on Syracusan coinage, certain symbols of the city of Syracuse—especially its most distinctive physical

---

6. Dunbabin 1948, 416–418; Consolo Langher 1988, 244–247; Consolo Langher 1997, 9–12; Demand 1990, 47–48; Luraghi 1994, 288–304; Vattuone 1994, 95–107; Mafodda 1990, 60–65; Mafodda 1996, 71–80; Morgan 2015, 52–56; De Angelis 2016, 105–106. The town of Euboea has not been conclusively located, but it was probably in southeastern Sicily.

7. On these mercenaries, see Harris 2020 and see further below.

8. Luraghi 1994, 288–304; Mertens 2006, 310–315; De Angelis 2016, 180–186.

features, the island Ortygia and its spring Arethusa, as well as its Dorian ethnicity—became symbols of the tyrants themselves. Most (though not all) of the new citizens were of Dorian origin, and even those who were not now lived under Dorian *nomoi*—institutions such as tribes, festivals, and the calendar—that forced them to act (and perhaps begin to feel) Dorian. A city's unique to-pography, meanwhile, was something all residents could take pride in, and so all could join in this sense of being Syracusan. The community's *polis* identity was thus reoriented to focus around the tyrants and their house in an attempt to legitimize their rule by building up a sense of identification of the people with their rulers.

Hieron the Dorian

Syracuse had been founded from Dorian Corinth, and the city's Dorian ethnicity ultimately stemmed from this nucleus of early settlers.[9] The Deinomenids, however, radically altered the demographics of the city. Of the Sicilian cities whose populations contributed to the new Syracuse, only Camarina (settled from Syracuse itself and later refounded by Hippocrates of Gela) even partly shared its Corinthian ancestry. Megara Hyblaea and Gela did claim Dorian ethnicity, based on their foundations from mainland Megara and from Rhodes and Crete, respectively. But Euboea, a colony of Leontini, was Chalcidian (the Sicilian equivalent of Ionian). Many of Gelon's mercenaries came from Arcadia and hence were not Dorians; many others came from elsewhere in the Peloponnese and may or may not have been Dorians. Thus, while some of the new citizens were, in fact, just as Dorian as the original Syracusans, the population did become much more diverse. From an objective perspective, Syracuse was no longer a purely Dorian city (if, in fact it, ever was).

However, identity is always a subjective and ideologically constructed phe-nomenon; it is based less on any objective reality and more on the ideas that a group has about itself. If they wished, the Syracusans could choose to ignore the origins of their new compatriots and merely posit that logically, the new citizens are now Syracusans; Syracuse is a Dorian city; hence, the new citi-zens are Dorians. This is precisely what Hieron hoped to encourage. Although the community's ethnic identification was an established fact and could not

---

9. Thuc. 6.3.2. The exact identities of the original colonists cannot be known, and it is un-likely that all came from Corinth: Dunbabin 1948, 14–15; De Angelis 2016, 69–71, 160. By the 480s, the population was in all likelihood quite heterogeneous, including Greeks of all origins and probably even Hellenized Sikels, but the community's origins in Dorian Corinth, to which others were assimilated, maintained primacy.

easily be changed, its salience did vary substantially. If most Syracusans privileged their status as Syracusans above other forms of identity, then neither a
Geloan ruler nor an imported population could last long. But if the Syracusans
could be convinced to emphasize instead their Dorian identity, which the
Deinomenid family and many of the new citizens shared, then their presence
and rule could be seen as legitimate.

Pindar was an excellent candidate to help Hieron deal with this problem,
since his poetry repeatedly demonstrates his familiarity and engagement
with local sociopolitical issues of importance to his honorands and their communities.[10] In particular, the victory odes written for successful athletes by
poets such as Pindar regularly incorporated elements of civic ideology into
their praise of the victor; they often emphasized how an athlete's glory reflected on his city and thereby constituted a key locus for the expression of
the community's identities.[11] These poems were written for public, choral
performance and were usually performed repeatedly, especially in the victor's
home city,[12] and thus were good vehicles for conveying a message to a fairly
wide group.[13] Who determined the nature of that message: the poet or the patron? While the poems were written by outsiders (such as Pindar, a Theban),
they were commissioned by local patrons, such as Hieron, whom the poets
needed to keep happy. Pindar familiarized himself with the tyrant's needs and
preferences, paid close attention to local traditions and ideologies (as we can
often see by comparing other sources), and deployed them carefully. While
epinician poems cannot quite be called emic sources—the situation is more
complex than that—they are very nearly so.

The epinician genre thus allowed a community to celebrate itself and the
achievement of the great citizen it produced and to maintain a sense of pride
in itself—essentially, its *polis* identity—centered around the person of the
victor. As Leslie Kurke has shown, the victor's great achievement, which has
moved him above the level of ordinary mortals, requires his reintegration into

---

10. This engagement with local issues is not limited to identity: cf. Morgan 2015 on ideas of
monarchy and Eisenfeld forthcoming on local religious practices.

11. Kurke 1991; Morgan 2015; Nicholson 2015; Lewis 2020; cf. Bundy 1962, I.20–22, II.35;
Hirata 1996. For detailed analyses of non-western examples, see Dougherty 1994; Fenno
1995; Sevieri 2000; Fearn 2003; Fearn 2011.

12. Harrell 2002, 439–440; Athanassaki 2004; Currie 2004; Morrison 2007. For the debate
over the intended audiences of epinician performances, see the overviews of Robbins 1997,
256–257; Pelliccia 1999, 243–247.

13. What matters here is the circulation of the ideas in the poems, rather than the texts themselves; cf. Nagy 1990, 382–413; Harrell 2002, 439–440; Athanassaki 2004; Hubbard 2004.

the community as an ordinary citizen. For Hieron, this phenomenon operates at an even deeper level, since, as a foreign ruler of Syracusans, he requires not so much reintegration as integration in the first place.[14] I suggest that Pindar's emphasis on certain aspects of Syracusan civic identity constitutes a response to a social problem that was actively being discussed and contested not only in Hieron's court but also among the broader population. In several odes, Pindar took advantage of his genre to proclaim Hieron's ethnic bona fides and convince people that his patron was the right person to rule Syracuse.

Pythian 1, nominally written for Hieron's victory in the chariot race of 470, equally celebrates Hieron for his political and military achievements, and especially as the founder of Aetna, a new city founded in 476 on the site of Catana, the population of which Hieron had expelled (Diod. 11.49.1–2). Because Catana was a Chalcidian city (Thuc. 6.3.3) and the new foundation of Aetna was explicitly intended to be Dorian, Hieron's action had an unmistakable, if perhaps latent, ethnic valence.[15] While few scholars today would argue that ethnic tension actually caused Hieron's expulsion of the Chalcidians of Catana (and Naxos),[16] nonetheless an important element of the discourse at the time (represented by Pindar) emphasized, if not the conflict, then at least the Dorian end product.

In a key passage, Pindar praises Hieron for giving Aetna a Dorian constitution (*Pyth.* 1.60–66):

ἄγ' ἔπειτ' Αἴτνας βασιλεῖ	60
φίλιον ἐξεύρωμεν ὕμνον·	60b
τῷ πόλιν κείναν θεοδμάτῳ σὺν ἐλευθερίᾳ	
Ὑλλίδος στάθμας Ἱέρων ἐν νόμοις ἔ-	
κτισσε· θέλοντι δὲ Παμφύλου	
καὶ μὰν Ἡρακλειδᾶν ἔκγονοι	
ὄχθαις ὕπο Ταϋγέτου ναίοντες αἰ-	
εὶ μένειν τεθμοῖσιν ἐν Αἰγιμιοῦ	
Δωριεῖς. ἔσχον δ' Ἀμύκλας ὄλβιοι	65
Πινδόθεν ὀρνύμενοι, λευκοπώλων	

---

14. Kurke 1991. Hieron, of course, also required integration for other reasons, such as his anomalous status as a monarchical ruler (Morgan 2015), but here I focus only on his foreign origins.

15. Cf. Hubbard 1992, 107–108, 111.

16. Actual factors probably included the need to secure the kingdom's northern borders, the desire to maintain a body of loyal troops, and Hieron's desire to become an oikist (Diod. 11.49.2): Luraghi 1994, 335–341; Bonanno 2010, 127–134; Morgan 2015, 56–61.

Τυνδαριδᾶν βαθύδοξοι
γείτονες, ὧν κλέος ἄνθησεν αἰχμᾶς.

Come then, let us devise a friendly song for Aetna's king,   60
for whom Hieron founded that city with god-built freedom,
according to the laws of Hyllus's rule;
for the descendants of Pamphylus and of the Heracleidae,
dwelling under the peaks of Taygetus,
wish always to remain under the laws of Aegimius, as Dorians.
Setting out from Pindus, blessed with prosperity, they took
     Amyclae,   65
and were far-famed neighbors of the white-horsed Tyndarids,
and the fame of their spears flourished.

This lengthy passage is remarkable for its sustained emphasis on the
Dorian nature of Hieron's new city, a character that is closely associated with
the founder himself.[17] Pindar defines Dorian ethnicity through its origins,
telling the story of the Dorian Invasion in lines 65–66 and referencing a
number of founder figures: Hyllus, son of Heracles; Aegimius, companion of
the Heracleidae and close relative of Dorus, the eponym of the Dorians; and
Pamphylus, son of Aegimius. Moreover, Hieron is thus presented as a successor to these legendary originators of Dorian *nomoi*, continuing their work
and even joining the ranks of the ancestral Dorians.

While the defining features of Dorian identity are common ancestry and
shared origins, however, being a Dorian meant far more than that. Intermixed
with Pindar's emphasis on origins, we also see a number of key features of
Dorian culture.[18] The collective name of the ethnic group, Δωριεῖς, is not only
withheld for a time but is then displayed prominently at the beginning of a line
(65) and emphasized further by enjambment. Their ancestral homeland, the
region of Doris in central Greece, not far from the Pindus range, receives prominent attention, as does their claim to the Peloponnese by right of conquest.[19]

Pindar's references to Hyllus and Pamphylus also bring to mind the three
characteristic Dorian tribes (Hylleis, Pamphyloi, and Dymanes) into which the

17. Burton 1962, 103; Gentili 1998, 349–352; Morgan 2015, 333–336; Fearn 2017, 205–207;
Lewis 2020, 171–177.

18. Gentili 1998, 349–352; Morgan 2015, 333–336. On Dorian ethnicity, see Malkin 1994,
33–45; Hall 1997, 56–107; Robertson 2002.

19. Malkin 1994, 33–45; Hall 1997, 56–107.

citizen bodies of many Dorian *poleis* were divided. Dorians were often thought to excel in *eunomia*, which is celebrated as the "laws of Hyllus's rule" and the "laws of Aegimius" (62, 64), and Dorians typically felt that this social order, combined with their success in war (66), allowed them to enjoy a high degree of freedom (61). Pindar thus brings together the idea of kinship or common descent—the criterion that defines the Dorians as an ethnic group—with additional elements or dimensions that are felt to be typical of the Dorian community writ large. These latter features, which are all broadly speaking cultural, do not define the ethnic group per se, but they might in any given circumstance be highly salient parts of what it meant to be Dorian. Certainly in this case, the implications of social order, obedience to law, and military success would be of great interest to Hieron.

Within this encomium on Dorian history and identity, references specific to Sparta—Amyclae, one of Sparta's five constituent villages; Mount Taygetus, which overhangs the city; and the Tyndarids (i.e., the Dioscuri), heroes particularly important at Sparta—closely link Hieron to the preeminent Dorian state of the age. In fact, the text seems to describe the desire of the Aetnaeans to remain Dorian but refers to them as Spartans, since only they live under the heights of Taygetus. Thus, Hieron's settlers are actually assimilated to Spartans, and his kingdom becomes a new Sparta and a new focal point for Dorian identity. Of course, Sparta was known for its system of dual kingship; the references to Sparta have the added effect of suggesting an authoritative parallel for Hieron's rule. In fact, Nino Luraghi sees this as the primary reason for Pindar's inclusion of these Dorian founders.[20]

But Pindar seems to have in mind not only Sparta but also a broader ethnic discourse, since he uses very similar language to describe Dorians at Thebes and Aegina, two cities without monarchies in the historical period.

(*Isthm.* 7.12–15)
ἢ Δωρίδ' ἀποικίαν οὕνεκεν ὀρθῷ
ἔστασας ἐπὶ σφυρῷ
Λακεδαιμονίων, ἕλον δ' Ἀμύκλας
Αἰγεῖδαι σέθεν ἔκγονοι, μαντεύμασι Πυθίοις;   15

Or because you [Thebes] set the Dorian colony
of the Lacedaemonians on a firm footing,

---

20. Luraghi 1994, 358–360; cf. Bowra 1964, 133; Bonanno 2010, 149–153.

and your descendants the Aegeidae captured Amyclae
according to the Pythian oracles?   15

(F1.1–6 Bowra)

σὺν θεῶν δέ νιν αἴσᾳ
Ὕλλου τε καὶ Αἰγιμιοῦ
Δωριεὺς ἐλθὼν στρατός
ἐκτίσσατο· τῶν μὲν ὑπὸ στάθμᾳ νέμονται
οὐ θέμιν οὐδὲ δίκαν   5
ξείνων ὑπερβαίνοντες.

With the fortune of the gods,
the Dorian people of Hyllus and Aegimius
came and founded [Aegina];
they lived under their rule,
transgressing neither the law   5
nor the rights of guests.

In these passages, as in *Pythian* 1, Pindar invokes Dorian identity by referring to allegedly historical events (the capture of Amyclae and the settlement
of the Peloponnese) and personages (Hyllus and Aegimius) and refers to
Dorian institutions as a *stathma*. These parallels suggest that the mythical
Dorian figures and other references in *Pythian* 1 locate Hieron within a much
broader discourse of Dorian identity and work to solidify the tyrant's connection to Dorians everywhere. An audience of Syracusans, proud of their Dorian
heritage, would recognize Hieron as one of their own.

Hieron's Dorian nature is further emphasized by his connection to
the Peloponnese, whence many of the new Syracusans originally came, in
Olympian 1 (17–24).

    ἀλλὰ Δωρίαν ἀπὸ φόρμιγγα πασσάλου
    λάμβαν', εἴ τί τοι Πίσας τε καὶ Φερενίκου χάρις
    νόον ὑπὸ γλυκυτάταις ἔθηκε φροντίσιν,
    ὅτε παρ' Ἀλφεῷ σύτο δέμας   20
    ἀκέντητον ἐν δρόμοισι παρέχων,
    κράτει δὲ προσέμειξε δεσπόταν,
    Συρακόσιον ἱπποχάρ-
        μαν βασιλῆα· λάμπει δέ οἱ κλέος
    ἐν εὐάνορι Λυδοῦ Πέλοπος ἀποικίᾳ.

Come, take the Dorian lyre from its peg,
if the splendor of Pisa and of Pherenicus
has brought the sweetest thoughts to your mind,
when beside the Alpheus he sped along,   20
offering his body ungoaded in the race,
and brought his master to victory,
the horse-delighting king of Syracuse, whose fame shines forth
in the colony of fine men founded by Lydian Pelops.

Although many more groups besides Dorians inhabited the Peloponnese
(seven *ethnē*, according to Hdt. 8.73), it was already seen as the quintessential
Dorian land: the two were inextricably linked.[21] In the ode, the colony of Lydian
Pelops is clearly the Peloponnese, as the topographical references to Pisa and
the Alpheus show: both are not only actual features of the Peloponnesian landscape but also traditional poetic ways of referring to the Olympic festival.[22]
Moreover, the ode's central myth recounts the foundation of the Olympic
Games by Pelops. Hieron's fame most immediately shines across the region
in which he won his victory.

But Peloponnesian origins were also of great importance to Sicilians and
especially Syracusans. Several decades later, Thucydides has the Syracusan
statesman Hermocrates describe his fellow citizens as "free Dorians from the
autonomous Peloponnese, inhabiting Sicily."[23] Moreover, it was common to
refer to citizens of a colony as members of their mother community; thus,
Corcyreans were actually Corinthians (Thuc. 7.57.7), and Pindar's Aetnaeans,
as discussed above, were actually Dorians from Sparta (perhaps metonymically for the Peloponnese). Thus, I suggest, the "colony of Pelops" across
which Hieron's fame shines could also include Sicily, and the island is thereby
said to partake in the characteristics of the Peloponnese, including its association with Dorians.

---

21. This connection is fully established by the time of Thucydides (see 1.12.3–4, 5.9.1, 6.77.1,
with Vlassopoulos 2007), but the roots of it can be found even in Tyrtaeus F2 West (see Hall
2002, 85–86) and in the myth of the division of the Peloponnese among the Heracleidae
(attested as early as Pind. *Pyth.* 5.69–72). Although the Dorians and the Heracleidae could be
seen as ethnically distinct (Hdt. 5.72.3–4), they were closely associated from an early period
(e.g., Pind. *Pyth.* 1.60–66). On the complex associations of Dorians, Heracleidae, and the
Peloponnese, see generally Malkin 1994, 33–43; Hall 1997, 56–65.

22. E.g., *Ol.* 7.15, 8.9, 9.18, 13.35, with Gerber 1982, 46; Kirkwood 1982, 50; Griffith 2008.

23. 6.77.1: Δωριῆς ἐλεύθεροι ἀπ᾽ αὐτονόμου τῆς Πελοποννήσου τὴν Σικελίαν οἰκοῦντες; cf.
chapter 6 for the same idea in a third-century context.

Moreover, the reference to the Alpheus would have added resonance to a Syracusan audience: the myth in which the River Alpheus traveled under the sea to emerge in the spring of Arethusa on Ortygia, in the center of Syracuse (see below), suggests a tight connection between the region of Olympia and Sicily.[24] Emblematic of this close connection is the story, which likely dates back to Ibycus (F323 *PMG*; cf. Timaeus F41), that after the River Alpheus flooded the sanctuary at Olympia, a golden bowl and a quantity of cow manure turned up in the spring of Arethusa after traveling underwater from the Peloponnese. Certainly, if the ode was performed in Syracuse,[25] its Sicilian audience may have been primed to hear a deeper layer of meaning, that Hieron's fame shines out across its own Dorian island.

The close connection between Sicily and the Peloponnese would also bear additional meaning for those new citizens, a substantial group, who had come there from the Peloponnese. Pindar also emphasized this aspect in two poems written for Hieron's courtiers Chromius and Hagesias (*Nem.* 9 and *Ol.* 6, respectively).

(*Nem.* 9.1–3)

κωμάσομεν παρ' Ἀπόλλωνος Σικυωνόθε, Μοῖσαι,
τὰν νεοκτίσταν ἐς Αἴτναν, ἔνθ' ἀναπεπταμέναι ξείνων νενίκανται θύραι,
ὄλβιον ἐς Χρομίου
   δῶμ'.

Let us go, Muses, in a revel march
from Apollo's temple at Sicyon to newly founded Aetna,
where the wide-open doors are overrun by guests
at the prosperous home of Chromius.

(*Ol.* 6.98–100)

σὺν δὲ φιλοφροσύναις εὐ-
   ηράτοις Ἁγησία δέξαιτο κῶμον
οἴκοθεν οἴκαδ' ἀπὸ Στυμ-
   φαλίων τειχέων ποτινισόμενον,
ματέρ' εὐμήλοιο λείποντ' Ἀρκαδίας.   100

---

24. Kirkwood 1982, 250; Harrell 1998, 156–159; Eckerman 2007, 235–238; Griffith 2008; Baldassarra 2010, 101–103; Morgan 2015, 62–63; Lewis 2020, 49–57; cf. Paus. 5.7.2–3.

25. Athanassaki 2004, 337; Morrison 2007, 59–61, 93; Griffith 2008, 5–6.

May he [Hieron] welcome Hagesias's revel band with friendly cheer
as it goes from one home to another, leaving the walls of Stymphalus,
the mother city of Arcadia rich in flocks.   100

The revel processions (*kōmoi*) of the victors from the Peloponnese to Sicily
mirror the journeys made by migrants—including Hagesias himself, by birth
an Arcadian from Stymphalus—first to Syracuse and later to Aetna, and
Pindar presents them as joyous occasions for all.[26] Moreover, in *Olympian* 6, it
is Hieron himself who welcomes Hagesias to Syracuse and seals his identity
as a transplanted Syracusan.[27] By emphasizing Syracuse's—and Hieron's—
connections to the Peloponnese in both of these odes, as well as *Olympian* 1,
Pindar both draws together all Syracusans and shows many of them that their
ruler shares their strong ties to their ancestral land.

Scholars have also noted the close parallels that Pindar, in *Olympian*
1, draws between Hieron and Pelops.[28] Toward the end of the ode (90–93),
Pelops appears as the oikist of Olympia, with a tomb in the sanctuary he
founded, and Pindar earlier describes his settlement of the Peloponnese as
an *apoikia*.[29] Hieron, like Pelops, is also an oikist; in fact, his colony of Aetna
was founded in 476, precisely the same year as the victory commemorated in
Olympian 1, and his grand plans of colonization must have been a major focus
of attention that year.[30] Syracuse, too, was a colony, and the representation of
Hieron as the oikist of Dorian Aetna serves to link Hieron closely to the ancient origins of Syracuse as a Dorian *polis*. It is as if he has been in Syracuse
from the beginning.

Hieron's association with Dorians, moreover, is strengthened by Pindar's
description of his song as Dorian (*Ol.* 1.17), a statement whose interpretation
has defied scholarly consensus.[31] While the passage has sometimes been

---

26. Hubbard 1992, 80–82, who also suggests that Chromius's very decision to enter the local
games at Sicyon may have been the result of a desire to promote ties between Sicily and the
Peloponnese.

27. An identity that is made explicit at line 6 (where he is συνοικιστήρ τε τᾶν κλεινᾶν
Συρακοσσᾶν) and line 18 (where he is ἀνδρὶ κώμου δεσπότᾳ . . . Συρακοσίῳ).

28. E.g., Gerber 1982, xiv–xv; Sicking 1983; but cf. Verdenius 1987, II.1–4.

29. Harrell 1998, 217–221; Eckerman 2007, 68–72.

30. Hieron celebrated the foundation of his new city not only with the commission of *Pythian*
1 (in 470) but also with that of Aeschylus's *Aetnaeans* and a reperformance of his *Persians*; cf.
Herington 1967; Bosher 2012a; Morgan 2015, 96–105.

31. Gerber 1982, 41–42; Verdenius 1987, II.13–14; Morrison 2007, 61; Gentili 2013, 360–361.

taken to refer to the Doric features of his poetic dialect, this can hardly be the whole story, especially since later in the same poem, he refers to it as an "Aeolian melody" (102).[32] Pindar's language is actually an artificial amalgam of elements from many dialects, with a strong Doric component but also admixtures of Aeolic and epic forms and vocabulary.[33] Thus, even if Pindar is referring particularly to dialect, he is selecting elements that are significant for his purposes and ignoring others.[34] This purpose is most likely to suggest that a Dorian song is appropriate for his subject, Hieron. The tyrant is therefore connected to Syracuse's old and proud status as a Dorian city.

Thus, Pindar presents Hieron not merely as a Dorian but as a ruler who actively and energetically promotes and maintains the Dorian identities of his subjects. What is remarkable is that this portrait occurs at precisely the historical moment when the Syracusan population became, from an objective perspective, substantially more diverse and open to outside influences. Since there is no particular evidence prior to the Deinomenid period that Syracusans considered Dorian ethnicity so central to their identity (as opposed to having a more general awareness of Dorian origins), it may even be the case that Hieron was the first to connect these two ideas so strongly. This shows the necessity of approaching identity as a discursive construct, and it is precisely the difference between representation and reality that makes Hieron's Dorian ideology important to the study of identity.

The Syracusan Landscape

The urban landscape of Syracuse provided two major focal points for its *polis* identity (fig. 3.1). The city's distinctive island citadel, Ortygia, and its sacred spring, Arethusa, were frequently used as metonyms for the city itself and were closely enough associated with the city that Hieron's emphasis on them rewards attention. The island of Ortygia was the original nucleus of Greek settlement at Syracuse, and, although a second nucleus, known as Achradina, quickly emerged on the mainland immediately opposite,[35] "the Island"

---

32. Guildersleeve 1885, 131; Harrell 1998, 217.

33. Guildersleeve 1885, lxxvi–lxxxvi; Farnell 1932, xix–xx.

34. Conceivably, Pindar could be referring not to his dialect in particular but to the more broadly Dorian mode of choral lyric in general; see Gerber 1982, 41.

35. *IACP*, 228–229; Evans 2009, 9–24.

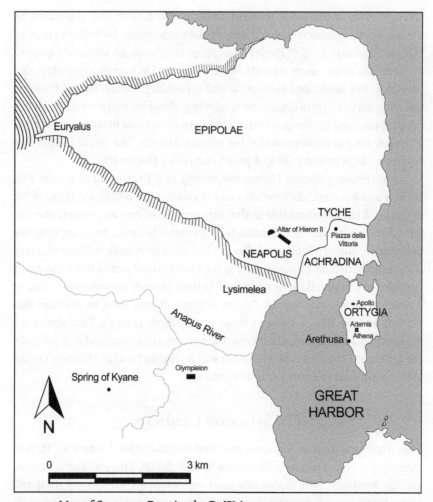

FIG. 3.1 Map of Syracuse. Drawing by D. Weiss.

remained the center of the city for centuries, both in terms of the location of prominent monuments and in terms of mental associations.

One of its most famous features, the spring of Arethusa, is at least as closely associated with Syracuse as the island itself. These two features, in fact, frame a description of the site of Syracuse, reported by Pausanias (5.7.3) as part of the city's foundation oracle:

> Ὀρτυγίη τις κεῖται ἐν ἠεροειδέι πόντῳ,
> Θρινακίης καθύπερθεν, ἵν' Ἀλφειοῦ στόμα βλύζει
> μισγόμενον πηγαῖσιν ἐυρρείτης Ἀρεθούσης.

A certain Ortygia lies in the misty sea by Trinacria, where the mouth of
Alpheus bubbles, mingled with the springs of fair-flowing Arethusa.

Rather than an authentic eighth-century document, I take this to be a later
(perhaps sixth-century) expression of what really mattered about the city's location.[36] Much as we saw for Croton in chapter 2, this oracle suggests that
Ortygia and Arethusa contribute to making Syracuse distinctive. The myth of
Alpheus and Arethusa (discussed above), which features prominently in the
oracle, appears also to be referenced in Gelon's first issue of coinage after his
arrival in Syracuse in 485, which shows a river god who has been identified
as the Alpheus. The myth and the significance of Arethusa must already have
been well known at that time.[37] The fact that the spring quickly developed a mythology of its own is suggestive of the prominence it enjoyed in civic identity.

This prominence is further indicated by the appearance on Syracusan
coinage, from the first issues well before the arrival of Gelon, of a head of
Arethusa (fig. 3.2). At first, this was a small element among others, but on coins
of the Deinomenid period, it became the central element on the reverse (fig.
3.3).[38] Moreover, on these coins, the head was surrounded by four dolphins,
which have often been taken to represent the watery setting of Ortygia itself; the coin thereby "expresses in a flight of fancy the site of Syracuse."[39]
By increasing the prominence of the city's key topographic features on its
coinage, the tyrants encouraged their Syracusan subjects to take pride in these
distinctive aspects of their city.

Pindar closely associates Hieron with both Arethusa and Ortygia. Perhaps
the most direct association appears in *Pythian* 2 (5–7):

εὐάρματος Ἱέρων ἐν ᾷ κρατέων   5
τηλαυγέσιν ἀνέδησεν Ὀρτυγίαν στεφάνοις,
ποταμίας ἕδος Ἀρτέμιδος.

---

36. See Braswell 1992, 33–34 (with further references); Griffith 2008, 4; cf. my approach to
Achaean foundation myths in chapter 2.

37. Arnold-Biucchi and Weiss 2007; Morgan 2015, 62–63; Lewis 2019.

38. Morgan 2015, 61–63; Lewis 2020, 38–41; cf. Boehringer 1929, 98–102. The Arethusa
types were normally paired with a quadriga on the obverse. Horsemanship was, of course, a
traditional pursuit for Greek aristocrats, including the Syracusan Gamoroi (cf. Rutter 1997,
114–115), and Deinomenid athletic victories made it particularly salient. In fact, they added
a Nike figure crowning the charioteer (fig. 3.3) to celebrate their victories and further align
themselves with preexisting Syracusan (elite) ideologies.

39. Kraay 1976, 210; cf. 218, 222–223; Lacroix 1965, 105–106.

FIG. 3.2 Tetradrachm of Syracuse, c. 500–485. Obverse: Quadriga. Reverse: Head of Arethusa in incuse square. Courtesy of the American Numismatic Society.

FIG. 3.3 Tetradrachm of Syracuse, c. 482–480. Obverse: Quadriga with flying Nike. Reverse: Head of Arethusa with dolphins. Courtesy of the American Numismatic Society.

> Victorious Hieron, possessor of fine chariots,   5
> crowned Ortygia with far-shining wreaths,
> seat of Artemis the river goddess.

The glory of Hieron's victory attaches to Syracuse.[40] The city has already been named in the poem's first line, when the poet addresses μεγαλοπόλιες ὦ Συράκοσαι, and Pindar now represents it through its outstanding physical features. Normally, we would expect the victor to crown his city; here, Hieron crowns Ortygia in particular because the island is such an integral part of

---

40. Carey 1981, 25–26; Lewis 2020, 45–46.

Syracusan civic identity that it stands for it by metonomy. By suggesting that Hieron has won even more glory for this oldest and most prestigious part of the city, Pindar helps to incorporate him into Syracusan identity.

Pindar's mention of "Artemis the river goddess," meanwhile, references the spring of Arethusa and the cult of Artemis on Ortygia. The myth is given slightly fuller expression in the opening of *Nemean* 1 (1–6):

ἄμπνευμα σεμνὸν Ἀλφεοῦ,
κλεινᾶν Συρακοσσᾶν θάλος Ὀρτυγία,
δέμνιον Ἀρτέμιδος,
Δάλου κασιγνήτα, σέθεν ἁδυεπὴς
ὕμνος ὁρμᾶται θέμεν   5
αἶνον ἀελλοπόδων
    μέγαν ἵππων, Ζηνὸς Αἰτναίου χάριν.

Ortygia, holy resting place of Alpheus,
scion of famous Syracuse,
couch of Artemis
sister of Delos, from you
a sweetly worded song arises to give great praise   5
to storm-footed horses for the glory of Zeus Aetnaeus.

This passage is usually interpreted as indicating the place of the poem's original performance (i.e., in Syracuse),[41] but it also reflects the interplay of city and victor. In this ode for Hieron's general Chromius, it is Ortygia and Arethusa—that is, the city of Syracuse—that praise the victor.[42] Although the tyrant himself is not mentioned, his close association with his courtiers (Chromius was Hieron's brother-in-law) allows their glory to rub off on him. Thus, the association of Hieron and his court with Syracuse's topography is deepened: not only does he bring glory, but he is himself glorified by the city.

In two further passages, Ortygia and Arethusa appear as the seat of Hieron's power and as places especially associated with him:

(*Pyth.* 3.68–70)
καί κεν ἐν ναυσὶν μόλον Ἰονίαν τάμνων θάλασσαν
Ἀρέθοισαν ἐπὶ κράναν παρ' Αἰτναῖον ξένον,
ὃς Συρακόσσαισι νέμει βασιλεύς.   70

41. Morrison 2007, 24.

42. Cf. Carey 1981, 104–105; Braswell 1992, 32–35; Morgan 2015, 384–385; Lewis 2020, 42–46.

And I would have come on a ship, slicing through the Ionian Sea,
to the spring of Arethusa and to my Aetnaean guest-friend,
who rules Syracuse as king.   70

(*Ol.* 6.92–94)
εἶπον δὲ μεμνᾶσθαι Συρα-
    κοσσᾶν τε καὶ Ὀρτυγίας·
τὰν Ἱέρων καθαρῷ σκάπτῳ διέπων,
ἄρτια μηδόμενος.

Tell [the chorus] to remember Syracuse and Ortygia,
which Hieron rules with a pure scepter,
devising straight counsels.

In the first passage, the spring is given physical valence as the location
where the poet would go to find Hieron, while in the second passage, written
for Hieron's close associate Hagesias, Ortygia is recalled specifically as the seat
of the ruler. Even as Hieron is described as Aetnaean, not Syracusan, and even
in an ode for his courtier's victory, the tyrant is inscribed in the physical landscape of Syracuse—a landscape whose significance for the city's identity is
clear.[43]

Both Ortygia and Arethusa were felt to bear particular meaning as part of
what made Syracuse unique. Everyone who lived there shared in the experience
of inhabiting its distinctive topography. Residents must have crossed regularly
by bridge from the island to the mainland and back, and being surrounded
by the sea would have affected their daily lives. While they were on the island,
Arethusa would have been a key source of fresh water, as it was for the original
settlers. Pindar placed these two sites at the heart of Syracusan identity, using
their names in place of the city's by metonymy and linking them closely to
Hieron. These daily experiences would be shared by the new citizens brought
to Syracuse by Gelon and Hieron just as much as those who had lived there
for generations. Focusing attention on the city's topography thus helped them
unify the citizen body and weld these disparate groups into a community of
Syracusans. Much as we have already seen at Croton (chapter 2) and will see at

---

43. Foster 2013, 314–316; Adorjáni 2014, 291–292; Lewis 2020, 47–49. Moreover, the connection drawn here between Hieron and Ortygia is even stronger if νιν (*Ol.* 6.96) refers to
Ortygia and not Hieron, as argued by Friis Johansen 1973.

Camarina (chapter 5), landscape played a key role in articulating *polis* identity; here this process was facilitated by the tyrant.

Hieron is thus portrayed in the odes of Pindar as a Dorian ruler firmly localized in the urban landscape of Syracuse. Both of these elements are key factors in Syracusan civic identity, and Pindar's victory odes crucially illustrate the ways in which Hieron legitimated his status in Syracuse. Though not born a Syracusan, he became one, and Syracusan civic identity was refashioned to center on the tyrant and his house. By closely associating himself with two newly crucial aspects of Syracusan identity, Hieron encouraged his fellow citizens to look to him for their self-definition. In particular, Hieron wanted to avoid alienating the new citizens introduced primarily by Gelon and instead to integrate them within the expanded citizen body. He thereby sidestepped the question of descent. One did not have to have been born of Syracusan parents to be a true Syracusan. Rather, Syracuse's redefined identity focused on elements that were more broadly shared. Most of Gelon's new citizens were Dorians; by focusing on Syracuse's Dorian identity, Hieron included those new citizens. Topography is even more general: it can be shared by all Syracusans alike. It was this manipulation of Syracusan identity that allowed Hieron both to secure his role as the non-Syracusan tyrant of Syracuse and to unite the diverse citizen body into a formidable force.

One more element deserves further emphasis: the role of geography in shaping these multiple identities, a factor that recurs often throughout this book.[44] The interplay between the landscape of a *polis* and its identity as a civic community—seen throughout Syracusan history and also at Croton (chapter 2) and Camarina (chapter 5)—gives a deeper window into the kind of self-fashionings that Greek communities engaged in. *Polis* identity consisted of far more than legally defined citizenship, and as we will see in chapter 4, geographical features (the shores of the island and the towering presence of Mount Etna) played a key role in articulating Sicilian regional identity as well. Moreover, communities also drew attention to distant geographies. In the case of Syracuse, repeated references to Corinthian and Peloponnesian origins contribute massively to their Dorian and *polis* identities, much as we saw in chapter 2 for the Achaeans. In these latter cases, it is the mobility that comes with overseas settlement that makes the far-off lands of mainland Greece relevant, and the effect of travel on identity will be critical in the next section.

---

44. Cf. Lewis 2020; Beck 2020, 43–74.

Mercenary Mobility

While the conception of the Syracusan community that Hieron put forth is clear, we have much less evidence for how it was received. The high level of stability in Syracuse during his reign might suggest that his ideas were popular. Soon after his death, however, many of the cities destroyed by the Deinomenids were refounded by their original inhabitants, suggesting that those other identities remained strong, if temporarily hidden (Diod. 11.76.4–6). We do, however, have information about the self-representations of four Deinomenid mercenaries and courtiers, many of whom not only physically left their home communities but also began to call themselves Syracusans, just as Hieron wished.[45] Much like the former Megarians and Geloans, these new citizens had the tyrants to thank for their new status and for the high positions some of them acquired in the tyrants' court, and so the result of their personal mobility is the recentering of identity around the person and court of the tyrant.[46] The four individuals are Astylus (from Croton), Phormis (from Maenalos in Arcadia), Praxiteles (from Mantinea), and Hagesias (from Stymphalos). All of these men were of high status, wealthy enough to compete at Olympia and commission either a statue or an epinician ode (or both), and so they may not be representative of rank-and-file Deinomenid mercenaries. Still, their experiences provide some limited evidence for the variety of responses to Deinomenid identity politics.

Astylus of Croton was proclaimed a Crotoniate at his first Olympic victory in 488, but at the two subsequent Olympiads, he had himself proclaimed a Syracusan, in order "to please Hieron" (as Pausanias tells us, although most scholars substitute Gelon's name, since Hieron did not succeed his brother until 478).[47] Astylus is generally understood to be one of a number of mercenary captains who also functioned as Gelon's courtiers, and Pausanias's explanation for Astylus's behavior shows how the tyrant was at the center of the rearrangement of identities. The extent to which Astylus's choice to follow Gelon entailed a break with his prior Crotoniate identity was shown by the response of his former fellow citizens: as discussed in chapter 2, they tore down his statue at the temple of Hera Lacinia and turned his house into a prison, a striking

45. On these mercenaries, see Luraghi 1994, 291–296; Harrell 1998, 177–196; Morgan 2015, 53–55.

46. Consolo Langher (1997, 12–13) suggests that the purpose of settling so many mercenaries in Syracuse was to create a loyal cadre of citizens; cf. Mafodda 1990, 65–68; Péré-Noguès 2004.

47. Paus. 6.13.1; Nicholson 2015, 161–196. Astylus's change of identity was likely interpreted in antiquity as indicative of corruption and was therefore associated with Hieron, the "bad"

repudiation of their former Olympic victor (Paus. 6.13.1). There was no going back; Astylus had made his move for the tyrants, and they were all he had left.

Yet Astylus was the only one of the four mercenaries to abandon his prior identity so thoroughly. Another of Pausanias's Olympic dedicators, Phormis, instead emphasized his multiple concurrent identities (5.27.2):

> Φόρμις ἀνέθηκεν
> Ἀρκὰς Μαινάλιος, νῦν δὲ Συρακόσιος.

> Phormis dedicated this,
> an Arcadian from Maenalos, but now a Syracusan.

Pausanias describes his career: he came to Sicily from Arcadia to Gelon specifically and served both Gelon and Hieron gloriously in war. Luraghi suggests that the νῦν δὲ is emphatic and emphasizes the contrast between his former Arcadian identity and his new Syracusan status.[48] Nevertheless, Phormis still considered not only his Arcadian ethnicity but also his *polis* of origin important enough to record on his dedication at a panhellenic sanctuary. Thus, a man whom Pausanias explicitly describes as a mercenary in service to the tyrants maintained his multiple identities.[49]

A fragmentary inscription from Olympia (*IvO* 266) expands on this same pattern of migration:

> Πραξιτέλες ἀνέθεκε Συρακόσιος τόδ᾽ ἄγαλμα
> καὶ Καμαριναῖος· πρόσθα <δ>ὲ Μαντινέαι
> Κρίνιος hυιὸς ἔναιεν ἐν Ἀρκαδίαι πολυμέλō<ι>

> Praxiteles, a Syracusan and Camarinaean, dedicated
> this statue; but the son of Krinis
> previously lived in Mantinea in sheep-rich Arcadia.

---

tyrant, rather than the universally beloved Gelon (cf. Diod. 11.67); equally possible is that stories dealing with athletics tended to accrete around Hieron, the patron of Pindar.

48. Luraghi 1994, 291.

49. Pausanias (5.27.7) adds an epilogue: three statues, representing Phormis himself in battle, were dedicated by his friend or relative Lycortas of Syracuse. Since Lycortas is a common Arcadian name (e.g., the father of Polybius), Luraghi (1994, 291) suggests that he, too, may be one of the new citizens; but this must remain speculative.

Praxiteles is usually taken to be one of Gelon's Sicilian new citizens, brought to Syracuse from Camarina. In fact, his origin in Arcadia, the source of numerous mercenaries, suggests that he was once in the pay of a tyrant, quite possibly Hippocrates, who resettled Camarina in 492.[50] Praxiteles's career thus shows both the complexities of mobility in Sicily and the difficulties of the Deinomenids' project to unify new citizens into a single Syracusan community. Although claiming to be Syracusan, he also retained his Camarinaean identity, despite presumably having lived there only a few years, and moreover, he still considered his Mantinean origin to be worth recording. In fact, the placement of Συρακόσιος first suggests that he now primarily identifies as Syracusan, while the delayed placement and enjambment of Καμαριναῖος gives his second identity added emphasis: he is not just any Syracusan but a Camarinaean Syracusan.[51] Praxiteles is precisely the sort of Sicilian the Deinomenids needed to win over to solidify their rule, and his triple identity is thus suggestive of the extreme flexibility of *polis* identities in Deinomenid Sicily.

Finally, Hagesias of Stymphalos, an Arcadian mercenary who became a courtier of Hieron and the recipient of Pindar's *Olympian* 6,[52] shows in more detail the complex shifting of identity—hinted at by the "recurrent duality" that has been observed in the poem[53]—that occurred at the court of the tyrants. Hagesias was proclaimed a Syracusan at the Olympic festival and is explicitly described as Syracusan at line 18. He is even described as a "cofounder of famous Syracuse," a term of disputed meaning.[54] Moreover, he is linked into Syracusan identity by the mention of Ortygia—and the lengthy reference to Hieron—in a passage quoted above (lines 92–96).

But Hagesias is equally treated as an Arcadian. The central myth of the poem is a celebration of the origin of the Iamids, a Peloponnesian clan of seers, to which Hagesias presumably belonged. More important, Pindar strongly evokes Hagesias's ancestral roots in Arcadia (lines 77–81):

---

50. Luraghi 1994, 161–162.

51. Cf. Luraghi 1994, 295, who suggests that the emphasis is on the contrast between the old and new identities.

52. Luraghi 1994, 292–293; Foster 2013; Morgan 2015, 399–411.

53. Kirkwood 1982, 80; cf. Guildersleeve 1885, 171–172; Morrison 2007, 71.

54. *Ol.* 6.6: συνοικιστήρ τε τᾶν κλεινᾶν Συρακοσσᾶν; see Foster 2013; Morgan 2015, 400–402; cf. Guildersleeve 1885, 173; Farnell 1932, 41; Kirkwood 1982, 85; Harrell 1998, 188–191.

εἰ δ᾽ ἐτύμως ὑπὸ Κυλλά-
   νας ὄρος, Ἀγησία, μάτρωες ἄνδρες
ναιετάοντες ἐδώρη-
   σαν θεῶν κάρυκα λιταῖς θυσίαις
πολλὰ δὴ πολλαῖσιν Ἑρμᾶν εὐσεβέως,
   ὃς ἀγῶνας ἔχει μοῖράν τ᾽ ἀέθλων,
Ἀρκαδίαν τ᾽ εὐάνορα τιμᾷ·
   κεῖνος, ὦ παῖ Σωστράτου,   80
σὺν βαρυγδούπῳ πατρὶ κραίνει σέθεν εὐτυχίαν.

If truly, Hagesias, your maternal ancestors,
dwelling beneath Mount Cyllene,
piously gave many prayers and sacrifices
to Hermes, herald of the gods, who watches over
the contests and the allotment of prizes,
and who honors Arcadia, land of brave men;
then he, son of Sostratus, with his deep-thundering father   80
brings about your good fortune.

This passage evokes not only Mount Cyllene, a famous landmark that in literature often stands metonymically for Arcadia, but most especially Hermes, a patron deity of the region and a key focal point for Arcadian identity.[55] Thus, Hagesias retains his ancestral identity as well as acquiring a new one.[56]

However, it is Hieron who binds Hagesias's two identities together. Pindar emphasizes the role of the tyrant in bringing Hagesias to Syracuse, in a passage already discussed (98–100):

σὺν δὲ φιλοφροσύναις εὐ-
   ηράτοις Ἀγησίᾳ δέξαιτο κῶμον
οἴκοθεν οἴκαδ᾽ ἀπὸ Στυμ-
   φαλίων τειχέων ποτινισόμενον,
ματέρ᾽ εὐμήλοιο λείποντ᾽ Ἀρκαδίας.   100

May he [Hieron] welcome Hagesias's revel band with friendly cheer
as it goes from one home to another, leaving the walls of Stymphalus,

---

55. Harrell 1998, 199–200; Gentili 2013, 455–456.

56. Foster 2013, 309–317; Adorjáni 2014, 290; Morgan 2015, 405–408.

the mother city of Arcadia rich in flocks.   100

The *kōmos* that Hieron is to welcome is clearly that of the returning Olympic victor. But it also evokes a previous welcome that Hieron at least notionally gave to his courtier when he originally arrived in Sicily from Arcadia. Thus, it is Hieron who is in control of Hagesias's shifting identities. The structure of the passage imitates Hieron's position: Pindar begins by linking Hagesias with "Syracuse and Ortygia" (92) and then moves on to praise of Hieron himself (93–97) before returning to Hagesias in Arcadia (98–100). The movement from Syracuse to Arcadia is the reverse of movements that took place both in the past, when Hagesias originally arrived, and in the poem's future, when the victor will return to Sicily. This reversal is evocative of the back-and-forth mobility of some individuals and of the flexibility of identity in the age of tyrants.

These mercenaries who moved to Syracuse and adopted Syracusan civic identity provide an excellent backdrop for understanding two monuments dedicated by Gelon himself. After winning the Olympic chariot race as tyrant of Gela in 488, he dedicated a bronze chariot statue with the inscription Γέλων Δεινομένεος Γελῷ]ος : ἀνέθēκε.[57] Naturally, since this was before his move to Syracuse, Gelon had himself proclaimed as a Geloan. But a decade later, the preserved inscription on Gelon's victory monument for the Battle of Himera at Delphi reads quite differently:[58]

Γέλον ὁ Δεινομέν[εος]
ἀνέθεκε τὀπόλλονι
Συραϙόσιος.

Gelon, son of Deinomenes, a Syracusan, dedicated [this] to Apollo.

Unlike three of the figures discussed above, Gelon chooses not to mention his previous identity; he instead called himself a Syracusan only and even puts that adjective in a highly emphatic position, on a line by itself, separated from the name and patronymic. By proclaiming himself a Syracusan on this monument, he merges himself with his new city and his new citizens, who have also experienced similar changes of identity. Yet he does so even more thoroughly

---

57. *Syll.*³ 33; the supplement comes from Paus. 6.9.4–5. See Harrell 1998, 168–169; Harrell 2002, 451.

58. *Syll.*³ 34 = ML 28; Harrell 2002, 453–454; and see further below.

than they do, since most of them did not efface their prior identities entirely. For Hagesias, Phormis, and Praxiteles, their Arcadian heritage still mattered. Here the tyrants' identity politics, while mostly quite successful, show their limits.

In fact, the examples discussed here display a typical range of ways in which mobility impacts identities. There certainly are cases where travel leads ultimately to a change of identities, such as the arrival of colonists to found a new city (as discussed in chapter 2), but such examples are, in fact, rare. While the Deinomenid-era new citizens at Syracuse appear to have changed their identities, in fact, the mercenaries discussed here added new identities to their self-representation, rather than replacing prior ones. The new citizens who had come from other Sicilian cities, meanwhile, returned home to refound their cities after the fall of the Deinomenids, demonstrating that they had maintained their separate *polis* identities through a period of exile.[59] In many cases discussed elsewhere in this book, in fact, identities remained firm despite travel. Bacchylides 11 presents the settlers of Metapontion as still Achaean, still the same ethnic community as they were back in the northern Peloponnese. The people of Camarina, as we will see in chapter 5, maintained their identity despite repeated exiles and refoundations. And in a poem of Theocritus discussed in chapter 6, a Syracusan woman, despite finding herself in Alexandria, emphasizes that she is still Syracusan. Scholars have until recently tended to downplay the role of mobility and travel in Greek history, perhaps taking an Athenocentric viewpoint that saw foreigners as forever foreign and therefore as unimportant.[60] Nevertheless, as Thucydides's Alcibiades saw but fatally misunderstood,[61] these factors were central to the Greek colonial world and its shifting identities.

The remarkable phrase οἴκοθεν οἴκαδ' at *Ol.* 6.99 well illustrates the flexibility of identity in Classical Sicily. Enormous social changes came to Syracuse, and particularly to the makeup of its citizen body, throughout the first half of the fifth century.[62] The Deinomenid redefinition of Syracusan identity was quite successful at its primary goal of solidifying the dynasty's power, as the tyrants inscribed themselves within a Syracusan identity built around widely

---

59. See Souza 2020 for two striking examples of communities (Naxos and Motya) retaining communal identities even after being enslaved by Dionysius I; cf. Beck 2020, 71–74.

60. See recently Montiglio 2005; Lane Fox 2009; Garland 2014; Costanzi 2020.

61. Thuc. 6.17.2–3: "The cities are full of a mixed multitude of men, and they easily have changes and influxes of citizens, and because of this no one feels that he is fighting for his fatherland"; cf. Lewis 2020, 58–63.

62. Lomas 2006; Evans 2016, 66–78.

shared criteria. As the boundaries of the community shifted, however, some dissent remained, as the evidence of the mercenaries shows, which would emerge fully after the fall of the last Deinomenid.

Greeks and Barbarians

Hellenic identity proved equally useful to a series of Sicilian tyrants. Uniting a nation by focusing attention on an outside enemy has been a key strategy of leaders from antiquity to the present. For the Deinomenids, their self-representation as protectors of panhellenic identity was central to their claim to legitimacy; decades later, Dionysius I reinvigorated this same strategy with (as we shall see) a twist. In the early fifth century, both Gelon's victory over Carthage at Himera in 480 and Hieron's defeat of an Etruscan fleet at Cumae in 474 were trumpeted as examples of the tyrants' abilities and virtues. They cast themselves as defenders of Greek freedom against "barbarian" aggression and in the process redefined Greek identity in Sicily. A very similar process was happening on the mainland at the same time, of course, in the wake of the Persian Wars.[63] Yet Sicilian conceptions of Greekness in the 470s differed from those in Athens or Sparta, due to the central role of tyranny in the process. To be Greek in Sicily in the 470s meant supporting the Deinomenids, who (so they claimed) ensured the ability of Greeks to remain Greek.

All of this, it should be stressed, was a retrospective construction, articulated during the 470s and mostly by Hieron (although Gelon may have begun the process before his death soon after Himera, in 478).[64] The reality of the two battles was quite different from the rhetoric. The Carthaginian invasion of Sicily in 480 resulted from a cascading series of calls for help among various tyrants who enjoyed ties of *xenia* with each other. According to Herodotus (7.165), Terillus, the tyrant of Himera, had been expelled by Theron of Akragas and appealed for help to his son-in-law, Anaxilas of Rhegium. Both men then used their influence with Hamilcar, ruler of Carthage, to induce him to lead a large force to restore Terillus. Theron, who now controlled Himera, appealed for help to Gelon, who quickly arrived there with his army. In the subsequent

---

63. Hall 1989; Hall 2002, 172–189; Mitchell 2007. On the West, see Smith 2003, 29–74.

64. Luraghi (1994, 354–357) argues forcefully that this ideological program does not predate Hieron's accession and that references to Gelon engaging in it are retrojected; but see below for Gelon's dedications at Delphi and Olympia, with Yates 2019.

battle (narrated by Diod. 11.20–26), many Carthaginian ships were burned, Hamilcar was slain, and the Greeks were victorious.[65] The Carthaginians sent envoys to ask for a peace treaty, which was granted on favorable terms; the Greeks undertook no reprisals or further military action. The Battle of Cumae, six years later, is less well understood but seems to have followed similar lines. The people of Cumae requested Syracusan help against the Etruscans, who held naval supremacy. Hieron sent a fleet to join the Cumaeans and other local forces; together they defeated the Etruscans in a sea battle, and the Syracusan ships returned home without further action.[66] Although Hieron certainly celebrated his own victory at Cumae, his commemoration of Himera is more prominent and will be the primary focus here.

In its short duration, small scale, and lack of serious military or political consequences, the Himera campaign offered little that was different from previous conflicts between Greeks and non-Greeks in Sicily, which had been minimal. Although Sicilian Greeks of Archaic times were surely aware that their culture differed from that of the Phoenicians, a true dichotomy between Greeks and barbarians had never been especially salient in Sicily.[67] Phoenician settlement was limited to far western Sicily, centered on the three cities of Motya, Panormus, and Solous, and there had been little or no long-term confrontation that would lead to such a self-conception. The attempts by Pentathlos in the 580s and Dorieus around 510, for example, to establish a Greek presence in western Sicily were relatively small in scale and short in duration.[68] When Carthage slowly became involved in Sicilian affairs in the late sixth century, the scale of its commitments remained small. Moreover, there is some evidence for genuinely positive contacts between Greeks and Carthaginians. Hamilcar, the general at Himera, had *xenia* ties with Terillus of Himera and Anaxilas of Rhegium and apparently was himself the offspring of a mixed marriage between a Carthaginian father and a Syracusan mother (Hdt. 7.165–166).

Nevertheless, discourse frequently differs from history, and the memory of the Battle of Himera quickly came to be dominated by the perception that

---

65. Luraghi 1994, 304–310; Mafodda 1996, 119–131; Krings 1998, 314–326; Evans 2016, 32–42.

66. Diod. 11.51; schol. Pind. *Pyth.* 1.137c; Asheri 1992b, 151–152; Consolo Langher 1997, 37–40; Bonanno 2010, 159–172; Evans 2016, 49–50.

67. Hall 2002, 90–124; Smith 2003, 25–27; De Angelis 2016, 46–53.

68. Pentathlos: Antiochus F1 (= Paus. 10.11.3); Diod. 5.9; Merante 1967. Dorieus: Hdt. 5.42–48; Diod. 4.23; Malkin 1994, 203–218. Cf. also Dunbabin 1948, 326–354; Krings 1998, 20–32, 188–215.

it had been fought as a panhellenic war against a barbarian enemy, a perception that was fostered, if not outright created, by the Deinomenids themselves. Unlike Dionysius (and others after him), Gelon did not pursue further wars with Carthage. In fact, at no point did the Deinomenids contemplate counterattacks against Carthaginian possessions, and Sicily returned to its essentially stable status quo for some three-quarters of a century.[69] Instead, Gelon and Hieron both used the memory of their past victory to remind their subjects of their past great deeds on their behalf.

This new and unprecedented discourse of Greekness was fostered by the Deinomenids as a means of securing their power. In commemorations of Himera, both in the form of dedications at panhellenic sanctuaries and in the poetry of Pindar, the Deinomenids emphasized their personal role in safeguarding the Greeks of Sicily. In other words, the newly relevant sense of Greekness that Hieron tried to instill in his subjects was built around the figure of the tyrant himself: he is their champion, without whom it would be impossible to remain Greek. In this way, Sicilians' sense of their Greek identity was not only heightened but also reshaped around the person and family of the tyrants. Moreover, the tyrants placed their deeds safely within a *polis* framework by associating the Syracusan people with their victories. By convincing their subjects that they should think of themselves as Greeks and by reminding them that they had achieved a great victory for them as Greeks, the Deinomenids presented themselves as the legitimate rulers of Sicily.

Pindar's Himera

Comparison between the Deinomenid victories in the West and the Persian Wars in the Aegean was critical to this ideology. Under Deinomenid sponsorship, some congruence of basic facts—Greek victories over foreign enemies in the same year—led to a sense that the victories were ideologically equivalent. Ten years after Himera and four after Cumae, Pindar's *Pythian* 1 drew this comparison explicitly. We have already seen how this poem supports Deinomenid claims to Dorian ethnicity; now we add panhellenic rhetoric to the mix. The fact that the same poem appeals to its audience in the form of two different identities shows the multifaceted nature of Hieron's identity politics.

Pindar begins with a description of the naval battle at Cumae before elucidating its significance (*Pyth.* 1.71–80):

---

69. In fact, the year 409, when a Carthaginian army destroyed the cities of Selinus and Himera, represents a much more important breaking point than 480.

λίσσομαι νεῦσον, Κρονίων, ἥμερον
ὄφρα κατ' οἶκον ὁ Φοίνιξ ὁ Τυρσανῶν τ' ἀλαλατὸς ἔχῃ, ναυσίστονον ὕβριν ἰδὼν τὰν πρὸ Κύμας,
οἷα Συρακοσίων ἀρχῷ δαμασθέντες πάθον,
ὠκυπόρων ἀπὸ ναῶν ὅ σφιν ἐν πόν-
   τῳ βάλεθ' ἁλικίαν,
Ἑλλάδ' ἐξέλκων βαρείας δουλίας. ἀρέομαι   75
πὰρ μὲν Σαλαμῖνος Ἀθαναίων χάριν
μισθόν, ἐν Σπάρτᾳ δ' <ἀπὸ> τᾶν πρὸ Κιθαιρῶ-
   νος μαχᾶν,
ταῖσι Μήδειοι κάμον ἀγκυλότοξοι,
παρ<ὰ> δὲ τὰν εὔυδρον ἀκτὰν
   Ἱμέρα παίδεσσιν ὕμνον Δεινομέν<εο>ς τελέσαις,
τὸν ἐδέξαντ' ἀμφ' ἀρετᾷ, πολεμίων ἀνδρῶν καμόντων.   80

I pray, son of Cronus, grant that the Phoenicians' and Etruscans'
   war cry
may stay quietly at home, after they saw their ship-lamenting
   hubris at Cumae
and what they suffered when they were conquered by the
   commander of the Syracusans,
who hurled their finest men from their swift ships into the sea,
and rescued Greece from harsh slavery.   75
From Salamis I will earn the Athenians' thanks as my reward
and in Sparta from the battle before Cithaeron,
in which the Medes who shoot with curved bows were distressed,
and by the well-watered bank of Himera
when I have completed a song for the sons of Deinomenes,
which they received because of their courage when their
   enemies suffered.   80

Hieron's and Gelon's battles against barbarian enemies frame the two decisive battles of the Persian Wars, Salamis and Plataea, and the four are explicitly compared.[70] While, strictly speaking, much of the passage describes
Cumae alone, the intricately interlocking structure brings the four battles

---

70. This has been widely noted; see, e.g., Burton 1962, 105–107; Gentili 1998, 354–357;
Harrell 2006, 130–133; Morgan 2015, 336–340; Fearn 2017, 211–216.

into unity. The Phoenician and Etruscan war cry (ὁ Φοίνιξ ὁ Τυρσανῶν τ' ἀλαλατός: 72) are merged, producing a single threatening enemy, and the Persians themselves clearly lurk in the background. They are, in fact, mentioned a few lines later, producing an effect in which Greece (75) is surrounded by its enemies, spaced equally apart (72, 78). The Etruscan fleet demonstrated "ship-lamenting hubris" (ναυσίστονον ὕβριν: 72), which would apply equally well to the Persians at Salamis; moreover, the attribution of hubris to Xerxes as the cause of his downfall had already entered the tradition, in Aeschylus's *Persians*.

All of this suggests that the meanings of all four battles, and particularly the accomplishments of the poem's dedicatee and his family, are similar: that victory "rescued Greece from harsh slavery" (75). These words echo a number of epigrams commemorating the Persian Wars.[71] One for the Corinthians who fell at Salamis, for example, claims that they saved "all Greece," while another for Adeimantus, the Corinthian admiral, says that his efforts enabled "all Greece to put on the crown of freedom." Since Syracuse maintained close ties with Corinth as its mother city, these may have been particularly relevant. Closer to home, an epigram known from the literary tradition and supposedly (but improbably) linked to the Deinomenid monument at Delphi declares that the sons of Deinomenes "defeated barbarian peoples" and "provided great assistance as an ally to the Greeks for freedom."[72] Here, too, the stakes of Himera and Cumae are set as freedom for the Greeks. Moreover, it judges the enemy harshly, calling them "barbarian peoples" without naming them; this, too, allows a certain slippage: Phoenicians, Etruscans, and Persians all merge in this conception of a single barbarian enemy.

Moreover, Sicily and the West are defined as "Greece" (Ἑλλάδ': 75). Pindar could easily have chosen to emphasize Syracuse here, or the island of Sicily, but instead the scope of Hieron's victory is presented much more broadly. Not only does this choice of terminology redefine the land Hieron rules, but

---

71. E.g., VIII, X–XII, XIV–XV, XXIII–XXIV, LIII *FGE*. To be sure, the authenticity and dates of most of these epigrams have been questioned; see discussion in Molyneux 1992, 147–211; Raaflaub 2004, 62–64. Few are likely to be authentically by Simonides (but this makes no difference to my argument), and some are of quite late date, but others are nearly contemporary. On the discourse of freedom, newly developing at this time, see Raaflaub 2004; cf. also Morgan 2015, 150–157.

72. XXXIV *FGE* = schol. Pind. *Pyth.* 1.152b; a variant is at *Ant. Pal.* 6.214. The epigram is attributed to Simonides but is perhaps more likely a Hellenistic exercise, which exaggerates a representation of the battle that dates to the 470s. Authenticity questioned by Page (*FGE*, 247–250); Luraghi 1994, 314–315; Privitera 2003, 410–416; cf. Molyneux 1992, 220–224; Harrell 1998, 248–251; Smith 2003, 32–33; Raaflaub 2004, 301n27; Morgan 2015, 42–45.

it also redefines the people who inhabit it. In this section of the poem, they are Greeks, rather than Syracusans or Sicilians, and they share the experience of freedom with all Greeks across the world. By focusing attention on specific aspects of their victories and presenting them as fights against barbarians that preserved Greek freedom from slavery, the Deinomenids were attempting to promote a view of the battle and their own role in it that emphasized their subjects' Greek identity.

Who was responsible for these victories? The focus in this passage is on the personal heroics of Hieron himself.[73] Although not mentioned by name, he should be understood as the "Syracusan commander" (73), the only individual singled out for praise, and the only active agent in the battle. The Phoenician and Etruscan sailors, by contrast, do not act but are passively hurled from their ships. More broadly, first Hieron and later the (significantly plural) sons of Deinomenes are placed at the center of the brief descriptions of both Cumae and Himera (73, 79). In the latter passage, it is not merely the now-deceased Gelon but the entire Deinomenid house who take center stage. Thus, Hieron and his family are portrayed as great defenders against barbarians: they are at the center of Greek identity in Sicily, and this constitutes one of their greatest claims to legitimate rule. Yet, on the other hand, the Syracusans are partly responsible as well; Hieron is named in line 73 only by a very significant periphrasis, as the commander of the Syracusans. By sharing his glory with them, Hieron is reintegrated into the framework of the *polis*, which further secures the legitimacy of his position. Just as the Deinomenid is the leader of Syracuse, so, too, Syracuse is the leader of the Greeks in protecting Sicily against barbarian threats. As we shall see, the Deinomenid public dedications did the same.

Finally, Pindar explicitly envisions the possibility of a renewed invasion, since he expresses the hope that the Etruscan and Phoenician war cry will stay at home. This presses the listeners to remain vigilant and keep their sense of Greekness at the forefront of their minds. While such an invasion never materialized, Pindar ensures that Hieron, as the first line of defense against barbarian attack, will remain central to Greek identity in Sicily indefinitely.

Deinomenid Dedications and the Memory of Himera

A similar message emerges from the Deinomenid dedications at Delphi and Olympia. These panhellenic sanctuaries attracted a wide audience from across

73. Harrell 2002, 453.

the Greek world and therefore represented prime locations for dedications that would present Deinomenid ideology to a diverse audience in perpetuity. Despite being located in mainland Greece, across the Ionian Sea from Sicily, the two sanctuaries were frequented by many Sicilian Greeks. Olympia, in particular, served as a pan-Sicilian meeting place, a common ground that belonged to no individual city—something that did not exist in Sicily itself.[74] Dedications by the Deinomenids at Olympia and Delphi would therefore be seen by many of their subjects who traveled there; moreover, news of these dedications, some of which were presented as jointly dedicated by the tyrant and the city, would quickly make its way back home. Public dedications played a major role as part of the larger Deinomenid strategy to commemorate the Battle of Himera as a victory of Greeks over barbarians.

The so-called Treasury of the Carthaginians represented Gelon's major investment at Olympia; in it, he dedicated a large statue of Zeus and three linen breastplates, taken as spoils.[75] Pausanias's brief description (6.19.7) allows us to recover something of the ideological program of the building:

ἐφεξῆς δὲ τῷ Σικυωνίων ἐστὶν ὁ Καρχηδονίων θησαυρός, Ποθαίου τέχνη καὶ Ἀντιφίλου τε καὶ Μεγακλέους· ἀναθήματα δὲ ἐν αὐτῷ Ζεὺς μεγέθει μέγας καὶ θώρακες λινοῖ τρεῖς ἀριθμόν, Γέλωνος δὲ ἀνάθημα καὶ Συρακοσίων Φοίνικας ἤτοι τριήρεσιν ἢ καὶ πεζῇ μάχῃ κρατησάντων.

Next to the treasury of the Sicyonians is the treasury of the Carthaginians, the work of Pothaeus, Antiphilus, and Megacles. The dedications in it are a statue of Zeus, great in size, and three linen breastplates, a dedication of Gelon and the Syracusans after they had defeated the Phoenicians in a fight either with triremes or on foot.

Pausanias seems to have no information other than what the inscription conveyed, which allows us to reconstruct it with some confidence;[76] in particular, it must have mentioned Phoenicians (or perhaps Carthaginians) as the defeated enemy. The term "Treasury of the Carthaginians" is equally suggestive. All other treasuries at both Olympia and Delphi were built by individual cities to celebrate themselves and were described as *belonging to* the city that

---

74. Philipp 1994; Harrell 1998, 162–165; Antonaccio 2007a.

75. Paus. 6.19.7. On this building, see Luraghi 1994, 317–318; Harrell 1998, 171–173.

76. Luraghi 1994, 317–318, 355; Pettinato 2000, 127–128; Harrell 2006, 128–130.

built them.[77] The Treasury of the Carthaginians was unique among these treasuries in commemorating a victory *over* a defeated enemy. This suggests that a strong emphasis was placed on the identity of the defeated, a non-Greek people.[78] Here in this panhellenic sanctuary, where all Greeks came together and where (at least in theory) non-Greeks were barred from competing, Gelon's new treasury was part of a carefully orchestrated attempt to focus attention on Greek identity by representing Himera as a victory over barbarians.[79]

Moreover, the inscription (if Pausanias accurately transmits it) stated that the treasury was dedicated "by Gelon and the Syracusans." Here Gelon shares the glory of his victory with the Syracusans, merging his own achievement with theirs and integrating himself into the *polis* as its leader. Similarly, Hieron followed in his brother's footsteps by dedicating three Etruscan helmets taken at Cumae; inscriptions on each stated that "Hieron, son of Deinomenes, and the Syracusans [dedicated this] to Zeus, from the Etruscans at Cumae."[80] Here, too, the name of the defeated people is mentioned, framing the battle as a war against non-Greeks. Yet two of the three lines are devoted to the dedicators, with Hieron only slightly more emphasized than his fellow Syracusans. Syracuse, too, is a defender of the Sicilian Greeks against barbarian domination.

The Deinomenids were also well positioned at Delphi. Gelon and Hieron made their own individual dedications, similar in form and sharing a single foundation, located on the terrace at the east end of the Temple of Apollo. Each consisted of a bronze column on a campaniform base, topped by a gold Nike and, above that, a gold tripod.[81] An inscription on the left-hand base indicates that "Gelon, son of Deinomenes, the Syracusan, dedicated this to Apollo" and also names the artist (Bion of Miletus), while the more mutilated inscription on the right-hand base gives the patronymic "son of Deinomenes" and mentions

---

77. Of course, Pausanias's terms may not always reflect usage at the time the buildings were constructed. On the idea of treasuries, see Neer 2003.

78. Harrell 1998, 172–173.

79. Cf. Pettinato 2000, 128–131.

80. *hιάρον ὁ Δεινομένεος* | *καὶ τοὶ Συρακόσοι* | *τοῖ Δὶ Τυράν᾽ ἀπὸ Κύμας*: ML 29; *SEG* 33.328. On two of the helmets, the last line reads Τυρρανόν for Τυράν᾽. Cf. Bonanno 2010, 172–173.

81. The Nike and tripod are attested epigraphically, while the bronze columns are reconstructed from markings on the bases: Amandry 1987, 81–97. The dedications are also described in the literary tradition by Bacchylides (3.17–19) and Athenaeus (6.231f–232b, citing Phainias of Eresus and Theopompus). See also Jacquemin 1992; Molyneux 1992, 221–223;

a weight of seven minas (Syll.³ 34, 35). According to Diodorus, Gelon's tripod was a "thank offering" (charistērion: 11.26.7) for the victory at Himera.[82] Yet neither inscription mentions the victory for which it was erected or identifies the defeated enemy. The monuments therefore derive meaning from their context and should be read against a series of other dedications erected by other cities commemorating their achievements in the Persian Wars.

In the 470s, Delphi was crowded with Persian War monuments. No fewer than eight states and individuals made dedications that proclaimed their contribution to the defeat of the invaders and the defense of Greece. Each of these parties desired, in competitive Homeric fashion, to show that their own arete equaled or even surpassed that of others.[83] For example, the most famous Persian War monument, the Serpent Column, lists thirty-three poleis that fought the Persians, thereby excluding all others as Medizers. It stood just a few meters from the Deinomenid monument and took a very similar form: a bronze column (this time in the form of coiled snakes) supporting a tripod. While it is unclear which of these monuments was erected first and therefore which responds to the other, any visitor to the temple terrace would immediately see them in dialogue with each other. The Deinomenid tripods claim the same status for Gelon and Hieron as the Serpent Column does for its dedicators.

The "culture of emulation" or of competition expressed at Delphi fits exactly the Deinomenid program of self-promotion. On this terrace, where claims and counterclaims jostled within a space measured in meters, Gelon and Hieron could easily project their self-image as defenders of Greece. It is noteworthy that the two inscriptions highlight the names and patronymics of Gelon and Hieron, without mentioning the Syracusans as co-dedicators. It is the tyrants and their family alone who have safeguarded the Greeks of Sicily. When viewed in this larger context of competitive emulation, the Deinomenids' dedications make a claim about the nature of their achievement: Himera, just as much as Salamis and Plataea, kept Greece safe from the barbarians, and it was the tyrants themselves who accomplished this. The message is very similar to the one conveyed by Pindar in Pythian 1; the two different media reach slightly different audiences but

---

Zahrnt 1993, 361–368; Luraghi 1994, 314–317; Harrell 1998, 237–258; Privitera 2003; Privitera 2014; Bonanno 2010, 173–177.

82. Diodorus's attribution is usually followed, though see Adornato 2005.

83. Scott 2010, 88–91; Morgan 2015, 32–45; Yates 2019; but cf. the reservations of Krumeich 1991, 49–52.

also reinforce each other. For any Sicilians who came to Delphi, the Deinomenid monument would show their leader as the champion of Greek identity.

Thus, the Deinomenid dedications, together with Pindar's epinician celebration, developed a conception of the victories at Himera and Cumae that reshaped what it meant to be Greek in Sicily. Both monuments and text focus the audience members' attention on their shared identity as Hellenes in a way that few had before. The Deinomenids appear prominently in this discourse, enabling the audience members to appreciate the *arete* of Gelon and Hieron themselves and encouraging them to unite around the leaders who have preserved their freedom. The tyrants show that they hold legitimate power in exchange for the services they provide to their people, a legitimacy that is rooted in a newly prominent Hellenic identity.

Although our main evidence for the widespread salience of this identity is the top-down rhetoric of the tyrants, such a strategy could not have been successful, as it was for more than a decade, without widespread buy-in from the population at large. In fact, the Deinomenids' strategy was so successful that later traditions developed linking the Sicilian battles with the Persian Wars even more closely. By the end of the fifth century, Herodotus reported a Sicilian belief that the battles of Himera and Salamis took place on the same day (7.166); Diodorus instead synchronizes Himera with Thermopylae (11.24.1). Diodorus also reports that Persia and Carthage had colluded to attack Greeks in Sicily and the mainland in the same year, an idea that goes back at least to Ephorus.[84] While these synchronizations and interpretations are clearly invented and tendentious, they did have earlier antecedents. The two "barbarian" invaders of 480, Persia and Carthage, could be seen as two branches of the same enemy, and the struggle against each of them was the same struggle for Greek liberty. In this aspect, as in others we have seen, Deinomenid identity politics had effects that long outlasted the tyranny itself.

Dionysius I and Hellenic Identity

Defending Sicilian Greekness also played a critical role in the rise of the next Syracusan tyrant, Dionysius I, at the end of the fifth century. Like Gelon and Hieron before him, Dionysius secured and legitimated his power through identity politics, using some recognizably similar rhetoric. But fourth-century Sicily was a very different place from what it was in the early fifth century, which meant that Dionysius's identity politics also differed from those of

---

84. Diod. 11.1.4, drawn from Ephorus (*FGrH* 70) F186; cf. Gauthier 1966; Asheri 1992a; Zahrnt 1993; Harrell 1998, 130–137; Feeney 2007, 44–52; Prag 2010, 58–59.

his predecessors in important ways. An examination of Dionysius's use of Hellenic identity shows both the similar use of identity politics between the two periods of tyranny and also how changing circumstances affect the deployment of these strategies.

The so-called First Carthaginian War of 409–405 was a watershed moment in Sicilian history.[85] In 409, Carthage invaded western Sicily in order to assist Segesta against Selinus (Diod. 13.43–44). The Carthaginian army besieged and sacked Selinus and did the same to Himera for good measure (13.54–62), thus avenging their defeat in 480. Three years later, Carthage sent another force to Sicily, which sacked Akragas (13.80–91). Gela fell in the following year, and Camarina was also evacuated (13.108–111). At this point, the Carthaginians stopped and agreed to a peace treaty.[86] Nevertheless, in only five years, Syracuse had gone from a position of great power, flush with the defeat of Athens and able to send a naval squadron to pursue that war in the Aegean, to ruling nobody and barely clinging to independence. The rest of Greek Sicily was lost. A second war began in 397, when Dionysius (now tyrant) captured the Punic city of Motya.[87] The Carthaginians responded forcefully by invading eastern Sicily. Although they failed to capture Syracuse, several years of back-and-forth actions followed before a treaty was signed (14.96). In the end, Carthage remained a major Sicilian power, controlling a substantial province based in western Sicily, for another century and a half. While there is no reason to conclude that ethnic hatred, on the part of either Greeks or Carthaginians, was the cause of these wars, nonetheless the rhetoric that surrounded them was suffused with the language of barbarians and panhellenic identity.[88]

Dionysius appeared on the Syracusan political scene in 405, soon after the fall of Akragas. At this point, there was no doubt that the war with Carthage was a war of survival and that the Greeks of Sicily needed to unite just to survive;[89] in fact, they had already begun this process before Dionysius seized power. He accomplished this by presenting himself, much as the Deinomenids had done generations earlier, as the leader who could successfully defend his subjects' Greekness. Yet the circumstances of the war required a different approach

---

85. Stroheker 1958, 35–47; Caven 1990, 27–79; Consolo Langher 1997, 112–115.

86. Diod. 13.114, with Stroheker 1958, 49–52; Caven 1990, 75–79; Anello 2002b, 352–355; Anello 2008a, 88–91.

87. Diod. 14.47–53, with Stroheker 1958, 64–85; Caven 1990, 98–131.

88. Cf. the different views of Luria 1964; Barceló 1994, 6–7; Prag 2010; for a historiographical approach to Diodorus's narrative, see Cusumano 2012.

89. Cf. Caven 1990, 36–38.

from what was possible in the early fifth century, when Gelon and Hieron commemorated their past victories. Dionysius instead depended on his present and even future accomplishments. This strategy worked well at the time, but as we will see, it contained a crucial weakness: unlike the Deinomenids, who made use of victories they had already achieved, Dionysius opened himself up to the possibility of failure.

In the first few years of the war, the Greeks of Sicily had already begun to think of themselves primarily as a single community bound together by opposition to Carthage. This can be seen especially through their response to the massive refugee crisis created by the Carthaginian march across Sicily. Some 2,600 Selinuntines were received at Akragas and given food and shelter not only by the government but by individual citizens (Diod. 13.58.3). A Syracusan naval squadron helped half the population of Himera escape to Messina (13.61.4–5). A "great crowd" of refugees from Akragas fled under armed escort to Gela and were later given new homes at Leontini (13.89.3–4). Diodorus has elaborated the plight of these refugees into several set-piece scenes on the horrors of war, but the underlying facts must be more or less correct: as the war proceeded, the remaining Greeks welcomed the refugees with open arms and treated them as members of a single community. By the time Dionysius arrived on the scene, the shared experience of war had the Sicilians well on their way to thinking of themselves as a single community of Greeks, united by their opposition to Carthage. Dionysius therefore did not need to encourage the Syracusans to consider their Greek identity salient, because they already did. Everyone knew they needed to fight the Carthaginians; the relevant question instead was how to wage the war, and especially who could properly lead them.

In early 405, in an atmosphere of recriminations following the failure to relieve Akragas, Dionysius in the Syracusan assembly accused the city's generals of colluding with the enemy (Diod. 13.91.3–92.1).[90] This accusation was all the easier to believe because of the initial allied successes in the campaign; they had defeated the Carthaginians on the march but had failed to follow through on this victory, which led the army to harshly criticize the generals (13.87). As a result of Dionysius's successful accusation, the generals were deposed, and Dionysius was chosen in their place. By attacking the generals in this way and presenting

---

90. Diodorus adds a number of other rhetorical *topoi* appropriate to demagogues, which may or may not be authentic, but this charge seems likely to reflect the actual claims at the time; cf. Caven 1990, 53–54.

them as unsuitable leaders of a Greek city, Dionysius offered the Syracusans a better way to act on their Greek identity: by uniting around him as their leader against the barbarians. The Syracusans enthusiastically gave him a chance to prove this, and their support for him was tied to his expected ability to protect them as Greeks. As we shall see in more detail below, this strategy worked only temporarily.

Although military exigencies forced Dionysius to sign an unfavorable peace treaty in 405 and spend the next several years putting down a revolt against him and securing his corner of eastern Sicily, what he really needed to solidify his power was another war with Carthage, which would allow him to reclaim his position as protector of the Greeks. When he finally embarked on the Second Carthaginian War in 397, Dionysius used the rhetoric of barbarians and of Greek identity to encourage the Syracusans to support him.

Dionysius's ultimatum to Carthage in that year announced that "the Syracusans declare war on the Carthaginians unless they free the Greek cities that they have enslaved."[91] This clearly represents the official government position on the purpose of the war and would surely have been proclaimed loudly at home as well. It draws heavily on the language of Greek freedom in opposition to barbarian enslavement[92] and therefore builds on Deinomenid precursors. Moreover, this rhetoric of Greek identity and liberation from barbarians resonates strongly with Agesilaus's campaigns to free the Greeks of Asia from the Persians, which were going on at precisely this time,[93] and with Isocrates's rhetoric of panhellenism slightly later. This view of Greek identity was widespread at the time, and by presenting his war in this way, Dionysius was encouraging all his subjects and allies to unite behind him.

Diodorus also presents a speech of Dionysius to the Syracusan assembly, in which he declares that the Carthaginians were "most hostile to the Greeks in general and especially that they were plotting against the Greeks of Sicily at every opportunity." The tyrant adds that "they would not refrain from attacking the Sicilian Greeks, against whom they had been plotting since ancient times," and points out that "it was terrible to ignore the Greek cities that had been enslaved by barbarians."[94] The powerful invective in this speech is very much in line with

---

91. 14.46.5: Συρακόσιοι καταγγέλλουσι πόλεμον Καρχηδονίοις, ἐὰν μὴ τὰς ὑπ' αὐτῶν καταδεδουλωμένας Ἑλληνίδας πόλεις ἐλευθερώσωσιν.

92. Cf. Stroheker 1958, 69–70; Caven 1990, 99.

93. Caven 1990, 99.

94. 14.45.2–4: ἀποφαίνων αὐτοὺς καθόλου μὲν τοῖς Ἕλλησιν ἐχθροτάτους ὄντας, μάλιστα δὲ τοῖς Σικελιώταις διὰ παντὸς ἐπιβουλεύοντας . . . αὐτοὺς οὐκ ἀφέξεσθαι τῶν Σικελιωτῶν, οἷς ἐξ

the ultimatum discussed above, urging a crusade (under Dionysius's leadership, of course) to free fellow Greeks from barbarian slavery. If, as some suppose, it derives from Philistus, Dionysius's collaborator and friendly historian, then it may well represent rhetoric that was deployed at the time.[95]

By emphasizing that his proposed war would restore the freedom of the Greeks of Sicily, Dionysius placed himself in the position of the defender of Greekness. The Syracusans at the time seem to have recognized this, since the war was quite popular.[96] Diodorus gives us a large set-piece description, no doubt exaggerated but unlikely to be wholly invented, of the preparations for war. Large portions of the population were put to work building weapons, and they set to it enthusiastically (14.41–43). Thus, it is reasonable to assume that they supported the goal for which they were working and that they were receptive to Dionysius's self-representation via panhellenic rhetoric.[97] Diodorus does report that the Syracusans supported the war in part so that they could revolt against Dionysius if an opportunity arose. Even if this accurately records Syracusan public opinion in 397, however, they never subsequently followed through on that desire. Although the war as a whole had mixed success—Dionysius captured Motya and repelled a Carthaginian siege of Syracuse but failed to dislodge Carthage from much of the rest of Sicily—Dionysius's tyranny remained secure for the rest of his life.

In fact, Dionysius's strategy of appealing to Greek identity by fighting ongoing wars with Carthage, as opposed to Deinomenid appeals to the memory of past victories, was ultimately so successful that it remained a major piece of the blueprint for a successful tyranny in Sicily for some two centuries to come (see chapter 4). Although Greek identity based on hostility to Carthage was not always the most salient form of identity in Sicily, it frequently returned to the fore throughout the fourth century and down to the reign of Hieron II (see chapter 6).

Yet even for Dionysius, there were limits, and a close look at Dionysius's failures shows the constraints that reality placed on identity politics. His strategy required continued success in war against Carthage, which was

---

ἀρχαίων ἐπιβουλεύουσιν . . . ἅμα δὲ συνίστα δεινὸν εἶναι περιορᾶν τὰς Ἑλληνίδας πόλεις ὑπὸ βαρβάρων καταδεδουλωμένας. Cf. Stroheker 1958, 69.

95. Sanders 1987, 141–149. On the other hand, it is equally possible to see the speech as a later rhetorical elaboration: Pearson 1987, 174–175 (who attributes it to Timaeus).

96. Cf. Stroheker 1958, 69; Caven 1990, 99.

97. Stroheker 1958, 62–65; Caven 1990, 88–91; and cf. also Diodorus's description of the fortification of Epipolae a few years earlier (14.18).

conspicuously lacking in his tumultuous early years. In his very first campaign, in 405, he lost a battle to defend Gela and had to withdraw to Syracuse, evacuating the populations of Gela and Camarina as he went. According to Diodorus, the refugee situation that ensued caused the troops to begin to hate the tyrant (13.111.5–6); certainly, his failure to defend these cities was a major factor in his inability to maintain popular support at this time.[98] The cavalry class at once revolted, pillaging his house and eventually going into exile. Although Dionysius quickly regained control at Syracuse, it is clear that rebellion raised its head when the tyrant no longer seemed capable of defending the Greeks of Sicily against the barbarians. An even more serious revolt occurred once Dionysius came to terms with Carthage in late 405, since the barbarians were no longer such an imminent threat.

Dionysius seems to have recognized this possibility and attempted to find a new enemy against whom to rally his subjects. He therefore led his army against the Sikels, probably (as Diodorus says) under the pretext of their former alliance with Carthage.[99] This suggests that Dionysius wanted his people to continue to place their Hellenic identity foremost, allowing him to bolster his credentials as their leader with a simple substitution of enemies. In this, his policy was an abject failure: no sooner had Dionysius's Syracusan troops arrived to besiege the Sikel town of Herbessus than they began to revolt (Diod. 14.7.6–7). In all likelihood, this failure of identity politics occurred simply because it went a step too far. The Sikels were not the Carthaginians. Relations between the Greeks and the Sikels had been tense and even hostile on occasion over the past half-century, especially during the war with Ducetius (461–451, with a resurgence in 440). But numerous Sikel towns had been allied with each side during the two Athenian invasions and had even supported the Syracusans during their overthrow of the Deinomenids.[100] They were simply not enough of a threat to cause the Syracusans to subordinate their desire for liberty to the need for resistance. Dionysius's swift pivot from one enemy to another while continuing to promote a Greek identity in opposition to barbarians was unsuccessful.[101]

The career of Dionysius thus shows both the possibilities and the limitations of the exploitation of Greek identity in politics. For a time, Dionysius was able to convince the Syracusans that he could play the central role in defending

---

98. Stroheker 1958, 47–49; Caven 1990, 73–74.

99. Diod. 14.7.5; Stroheker 1958, 54; Caven 1990, 80.

100. Thuc. 3.103.1, 115.1; 6.65.2, 88.3–4, 98.1, 103.2; 7.1.4–5, 32.1–2, 57.11, 58.3; Diod. 11.68.1–2.

101. For a similar (and more successful) tactic by Hieron II, see chapter 6.

them. Like the Deinomenids, he not only focused on Greek identity but tried to insert himself into it so that his subjects would rally around him. But unlike his predecessors, Dionysius had no memories of past victories to promote; he had to place his hopes on future victories. The tyrant did not have completely free rein; not all non-Greeks were readily portrayed as dangerous barbarians, and military failures meant that the difference between rhetoric and reality became too great to ignore. Only when he finally had victories to proclaim did Dionysius's manipulation of Greek identity prove successful.

Hellenic identity thus proved useful to a series of Syracusan tyrants, from Gelon and Hieron to Dionysius and even, as we will see in chapter 6, later rulers such as Hieron II. Circumstances certainly contributed to making Greekness a particularly powerful tool. Opposition to an Other is always an effective cognitive strategy for the creation or mobilization of an identity, and events such as the Battle of Himera and the Carthaginian wars under Dionysius I made this form of identification highly salient. Yet we should not discount the choices made by rulers, ranging from Deinomenid dedications and Pindaric poetry to Dionysius's rhetoric, in promoting this sense of identity among Syracusans and other Sicilians. The prominence of Greekness required both the right historical context and political leadership to encourage it. Finally, a proper evaluation of the place of Greekness in Syracusan politics, especially in the Deinomenid period, requires placing it alongside the other identities—Dorian, Syracusan, and (discussed in chapter 4) Sicilian identity—that were also deployed in service of the tyrants' legitimacy.

Responses to Tyranny

What happens when a tyrant loses power, either permanently (as when the Deinomenid dynasty fell in 466) or temporarily, during a revolt (as Dionysius experienced in 405)? Responses to tyranny in such times provide some insight into the attitudes of non-elites, as they negotiate their positions in a new (actual or desired) reality. Do they reject the identities promoted by the tyrants and resume prior ones, or have the tyrants made a permanent impact on how identities are perceived? As so often, the answers are complex and often contested.

Hieron died in 467, and the reign of his brother, Thrasybulus, lasted only a matter of months before the dynasty was overthrown.[102] Civil strife quickly followed. On one side were former Deinomenid mercenaries who had been

---

102. Diod. 11.67–68; Arist. *Pol.* 5.1315b; cf. 5.1312a–b. The exact chronology of the years 466–461 is uncertain; see Manganaro 1974, 9–16; Sinatra 1992, 353–356; Evans 2016, 56–78.

granted citizenship by Gelon; on the other side were the "original citizens" (ἀρχαῖοι πολῖται) who traced their ancestry in Syracuse back beyond the Deinomenid period. At issue was the question of who could hold office in the new, more democratic constitution;[103] according to Diodorus (11.72.3), office-holding was restricted to the original citizens, while another group of citizens of different origins was specifically excluded.[104] This latter group then took up arms, seized central portions of the city, and remained in open revolt for some time until they were militarily defeated and agreed to leave Sicily.[105] This conflict has usually been explained as a political or institutional dispute between different groups vying for power.[106] But the episode has much more to offer the social historian. Closer examination of the civil war at Syracuse in the 460s reveals a struggle, in the aftermath of the Deinomenid tyranny, over the nature of Syracusan identity and over the question of what it meant to be Syracusan, as both parties attempted to redefine Syracusan civic identity.

On the surface, much that was contested in Syracuse revolved around cit-izenship: Gelon granted citizenship to several groups, and so they became Syracusan; later, this citizenship—defined by the right to hold office—was stripped from them. At first sight, this seems a purely legal, constitutional matter. But simple definitions of citizenship as a mere juridical category, sus-ceptible to adjustment by fiat, fail to capture the complexities of the situation. As we have seen, the Deinomenids went to great lengths to reshape the iden-tities of their people, in order to weld them into a single, cohesive community; only then would the Syracusans consider these changes in citizenship legiti-mate. Why, some time later, was this redivision of the citizen body considered appropriate by a group large enough to ensure its enactment through military force? To treat this episode from an exclusively legal perspective is to ignore something much more significant, namely, the social attitudes that underlie both this decree and the mercenaries' reaction to it.

In fact, as discussed in the introduction, scholars in recent decades have rightly moved away from a focus on a sharp, legally defined boundary between

---

103. The exact nature of this new regime is disputed; see Rutter 2000b; Robinson 2011, 57–92.

104. This has generally (and probably accurately) been taken to indicate that the mercenaries were stripped of their citizenship.

105. Diod. 11.72–73, 76, is the unique narrative source for this episode; Aristotle's brief notice (*Pol.* 5.1303b) contains nothing useful for my purposes here.

106. Rizzo 1970, 16–20; Sinatra 1992, esp. 354–356, 360–363; Berger 1992, 37–38; Consolo Langher 1997, 44–45.

citizen and noncitizen that changes only through legislation and toward a social paradigm of citizenship, in which membership in a community is defined
instead through social practice.[107] Such a definition develops through an informal process of negotiation among community members, sometimes aided
by the ideology of a leader such as Hieron, to arrive at a consensus of who is
in and who is out. In other words, the struggle over citizenship in the 460s
was, in fact, a reflection of a struggle over a larger phenomenon, namely, civic
identity.

In Greek society, determining who could hold office was no mere political
decision or sterile constitutional debate. Rather, like citizenship itself, it was
an institutional reflection of a much larger debate over who belonged to the
community, and access to magistracies was a key indicator of group membership. For Aristotle in the *Politics*, it is one of two fundamental activities
separating citizens from noncitizens, although Aristotle also admits that no
one can agree on a definition of citizenship.[108] Moreover, the crucial importance of office-holding to the mercenaries' self-conception as Syracusans is
shown by the vehemence of their reaction to the new citizenship law. Even if
they retained citizenship in other senses, they had been demoted to the status
of second-class citizens; they were no longer considered true Syracusans and
instead were outside the community. The criteria used to determine access to
offices therefore have enormous significance for determining the nature of
civic identity. In post-Deinomenid Syracuse, these criteria were precisely what
was at issue. By redefining who was eligible for magistracies, the Syracusans
were redefining the boundaries of their community and therefore what constituted their civic identity.

For the original citizens, the sole criterion for access to magistracies seems
to have been a familiar one: descent. As in a number of Greek societies (such
as Athens, most familiarly), membership in the community was hereditary,
and only those with ancestral heritage in the city were considered sufficiently
Syracusan to hold public office. This constituted a radical redefinition of
Syracusan identity from the inclusive, explicitly nonhereditary version that
prevailed under the Deinomenids.

The mercenaries, though, immediately disputed this redefinition of civic
identity and offered their own criterion: shared history. The evidence for this is

---

107. Davies 1977; Manville 1990; Manville 1994; Connor 1994; Lape 2010; Wijma 2014, 13–27;
Blok 2017; Cecchet and Busetto 2017.

108. 3.1275a23: the citizen is one who μετέχειν κρίσεως καὶ ἀρχῆς; cf. more broadly 3.1274b–
1276a; Blok 2017, 187–248.

admittedly circumstantial. But by the time of these events in the late 460s, they had been living in Syracuse as citizens for perhaps as long as twenty years. Not all of them valued this. Some of their number had departed at the fall of the tyranny itself, but some seven thousand *chose* to remain (Diod. 11.68.5, 72.3). They had evidently decided that although they had been born elsewhere, they had made their lives at Syracuse, and they belonged there more than anywhere else. They believed, I suggest, that the set of experiences they had shared with the other Syracusans entitled them to membership in the community. This is a much less familiar criterion for civic identity than that of descent favored by the original citizens. But I suggest that it may have seemed more suitable in the context of colonial and Deinomenid Sicily. Gelon and Hieron had essentially founded a new community, which happened to share a name, a physical location, and a portion of its people with a previous one. In this estimation, there is no such thing as "original" citizens or newcomers; there are merely coequal members of the community. Moreover, Gelon and Hieron had relied on their large mercenary armies to establish and maintain their power; the mercenaries perhaps believed that this entitled them to membership in the community they had been instrumental in creating. This shared history became their criterion for Syracusan identity; they insisted that they fulfilled this criterion and were willing to fight for it.

How did the original citizens react to these claims? Therein, I suggest, lies the answer to the larger question of why the restrictions on office-holding were passed. The new democracy evidently wanted to make a clean break with the previous regime; not only did they expel the mercenaries, but they also expelled tyrants from other cities (Diod. 11.68.5) and at home set up a colossal statue of Zeus Eleutherios and an annual festival in honor of their liberation (11.72.2).

Many Sicilian Greeks also wanted a fresh start. Many of them who had become citizens of Syracuse returned home to liberate and re-establish their home cities, almost precisely reversing the forced migrations carried out by the Deinomenids; the tyrants were literally wiped off the map.[109] As with the mercenaries discussed above, it appears that their acceptance of new identities only went so far. Similarly, Leontini had previously been tightly controlled by the Deinomenids, forced to receive refugees from Naxos and Catana and to mint coins that displayed a Syracusan quadriga on the obverse; even the name

---

109. Diod. 11.76.4–5; Asheri 1980; Demand 1990, 52–55; Consolo Langher 1988, 253–258; Lomas 2006, 108–110.

of the *polis* was written on the coins in the Syracusan alphabet. Once freed, its new regime abandoned that emblem in favor of a head of Apollo, with a lion's head on the reverse, punning on the name of the city. Although the lion type had been used under the Deinomenids, its revival strongly emphasized the Leontinians' control over their own image—with their name written in the Chalcidian alphabet. These types remained in place until Syracuse regained control of Leontini in 422 and represent a strong rejection of Syracusan domination.[110]

But it is by no means clear that all Sicilian Greeks departed Syracuse. Megara Hyblaea, for instance, was not refounded, and the Megarians presumably remained Syracusan citizens—at least, the legislation is said to have been passed specifically against the mercenaries, and only two groups are envisioned in Syracuse at all: the mercenaries and the original citizens.[111] What of the Megarians and other Sicilian Greeks who were new citizens but not mercenaries? The drafters of the law on office-holding seem not to have considered them a problem.

In fact, it is clear that the new Syracusan regime did not want to reject all aspects of its recent tyrannical past; instead, its response to tyranny was much more complex. For example, Deinomenid influence remained heavy in Syracusan coinage, which retained the Arethusa-and-dolphins motif for decades. More important, however, it was only under Deinomenid rule, as a result of the influx of population, that Syracuse had become such a large and powerful city. If the Syracusans wanted to maintain the position of leadership to which they had become accustomed—and of course, we know from later in the fifth century that they did maintain it—they would need to retain a large population. How could they manage this while going back to a hereditary model of citizenship? Here the flexibility of a paradigm for citizenship based on identity is crucial. Since identity is inherently malleable, focusing on criteria that can easily change, I suggest that Syracusan identity was sufficiently flexible to include one group of citizens of Sicilian origin (who had been Syracusan for less than twenty years) under the rubric of "original citizens" while excluding another, similar group, the mercenaries.

The *stasis* at Syracuse and the denial of citizenship to the former mercenaries have several lessons to teach us about the intersection of political and social forces and about concepts of citizenship and, above all, identity. Most important,

---

110. Rutter 1997, 129–132, 135; Nicholson 2015, 262–265.

111. *Contra*, Berger 1992, 37–38, who insists that other Sicilian Greeks were expelled; and Green 2006, 143n279, who professes ignorance. But the Megarian case is instructive.

political and constitutional debates, and even political violence, take place in a social matrix governed in part by questions of identity. These questions involve different, and often hotly contested, criteria, such as heredity or shared history, for defining who belongs to the community and who does not. Conversely, competing conceptions of civic identity were highly politicized and were used as a tool in a complex and multifaceted struggle. Syracusan citizenship was a valuable commodity, and each side had a tangible interest in the success of its respective ideology. It is therefore no surprise that defining what it meant to be Syracusan was the subject of ongoing contestation.

In fact, half a century later, the boundaries of the Syracusan community were still ripe for debate. Diodorus's narrative of the so-called Great Revolt against Dionysius, which occurred near the beginning of his career in late 405, suggests that both sides deployed offers of citizenship as tools to gain advantage. Although the account in Diodorus is less detailed than that of the earlier *stasis*, it is nevertheless possible to discern two competing views of what sort of person could legitimately join the Syracusan community.

Diodorus lists a number of actions Dionysius took to safeguard his tyranny from possible revolt. Along with fortifying both the island of Ortygia as a whole and a smaller citadel within it (14.7.2–3), the tyrant distributed land to many of his supporters, including his commanders, his mercenaries, and members of the general population, in order to enrich those who supported him and strengthen their ability to do so, as well as to reward and solidify their devotion to the tyranny.[112] Among the groups who received land were freed slaves newly enrolled as citizens; these were called νεοπολίται, a word explicitly attributed to Dionysius (14.7.4). This is the only reference to these new citizens, and it might be considered untrustworthy, a mere *topos* of demagogic politics, except that Diodorus had preserved this detail of the name. The specificity suggests a source with genuine information. If Dionysius did indeed free slaves and enroll them as citizens, this was surely intended to stack the citizen body in his favor. Dionysius's view of the criteria for Syracusan citizenship was therefore much like Gelon's and Hieron's: the tyrant and the state were the same, so anyone who supported the tyrant was a supporter of the state and therefore deserved to be a citizen and a full member of the community.

The Syracusans, on the other hand, "promised citizenship to any mercenaries who would come over to them."[113] They, too, were redefining the boundaries of their community. By offering citizenship to the mercenaries,

---

112. Cf. Stroheker 1958, 53; Caven 1990, 78–79.

113. Diod. 14.8.3: τοῖς μεταβαλομένοις τῶν ξένων ἐπηγγείλαντο μεταδώσειν τῆς πολιτείας.

they were proclaiming a conception of Syracusan identity that was precisely opposed to that of Dionysius but also closely related to it. For them, anyone who fought alongside the Syracusans against the tyranny was legitimately a member of their community. Unlike in Athens, where at almost precisely the same time, fighting against the Thirty Tyrants was not considered enough for enfranchisement by the democracy,[114] in Syracuse, the boundaries of the community were much more flexible. On one level, both Dionysius and the Syracusans understood the shared experience of fighting together as the basis for the community, but their underlying conceptions of Syracusan identity shaped how they interpreted that shared experience.

For both Dionysius and his opponents, the foremost motivation for their offers of citizenship was clearly military expediency. Yet a precious commodity like citizenship could not be given away without consideration of the legitimacy of such actions, in the context of the changing and contested definitions of citizenship and identity discussed above. This episode cannot be understand apart from the politics of identity and its relationship with tyranny.

Conclusion

A tyrant's power rested ultimately on popular foundations. If the citizens of his *polis* considered him a legitimate leader, then he could stay in power; otherwise, he would not last long. Identity politics were a critical tool for establishing this legitimacy. While much of the evidence for Sicilian identity politics describes ideas promoted from the top, it is clear that those ideas had a real impact on average people. When Hieron framed himself as a Dorian or Dionysius as a champion of Greek freedom, those identities shaped what people thought about the tyrant—and also how they saw themselves. Hellenic identity was not very prominent prior to the 470s, for instance, but Deinomenid ideology brought it to the forefront, and Dionysius later capitalized on this. The attention tyrants paid to identity thus had long-lasting effects, reshaping for generations how the people of Syracuse saw their identities. The dynamics of identity and tyranny thus remained remarkably similar between the two regimes discussed here.

Of course, those dynamics were not identical, and the changes that occurred between the fifth and fourth centuries are equally important. The experience of major wars with Carthage between 409 and 392 (a period of nearly two decades) made Hellenic identity far more important than it had been in

---

114. E.g., Bakewell 1999.

the past, at the expense of other types of identity. The salience of ethnicity, in particular, was radically reduced. Ethnicity had played an important role in Sicilian politics as recently as the Athenian invasion of 415 (see chapter 5). But Dionysius made no discernible attempt to represent himself as a Dorian. This shift can be ascribed to changing circumstances; the explosive Carthaginian rampage across Sicily caused all Sicilian Greeks, Dorian and Chalcidian alike, to unite against their common enemy. Intra-Hellenic ethnicities were simply not important in this situation. The population of Sicily was changing, too, due to wartime disruption and Dionysius's mercenary settlements, and so the old ethnic groups based on notions of descent no longer meant much.[115] The whole issue slipped away, and by the third century, the conflict between Dorians and Chalcidians was only a memory.

The evolution of identity in mainland Greece experienced many of the same phenomena as Sicily, such as the creation of Greekness in the aftermath of the Persian Wars and the decline of intra-Hellenic ethnicity in the fourth century. Yet the relationship between identity and tyranny sets Sicily apart from the rest of the Greek world. Tyranny was far less prominent elsewhere in Greece during the fifth century, and so factors such as the Athenian Empire and the conflict between Athens and Sparta were what conditioned the evolution of various forms of identity. In Sicily, by contrast, tyranny had an outsized impact on the evolution of concepts of identity. The figure of the tyrant played a critical role in the development of Hellenic identity, with little parallel in the Aegean. Meanwhile, *polis* identity took on a much more flexible form than the more familiar Athenian variety. As we will see in the next two chapters, however, identity and politics remained deeply intertwined even in the absence of tyrants.

115. Cf. Giuffrida 2002. On Dionysius's colonies, see Demand 1990, 100–105; Giuliani 1994.

4

Ruling Grain-Rich Sicily

PINDAR'S FIRST NEMEAN *Ode* includes a striking image (13–18). Writing in
the 470s for Chromius, a close associate of Hieron, tyrant of Syracuse, the
poet asks the Muse to:

σπεῖρέ νυν ἀγλαΐαν
   τινὰ νάσῳ, τὰν Ὀλύμπου δεσπότας
Ζεὺς ἔδωκεν Φερσεφόνᾳ, κατένευ-
   σέν τέ οἱ χαίταις, ἀριστεύοισαν εὐκάρπου χθονός
Σικελίαν πίειραν ὀρθώ-
   σειν κορυφαῖς πολίων ἀφνεαῖς·   15
ὤπασε δὲ Κρονίων πολέμου
   μναστῆρά οἱ χαλκεντέος
λαὸν ἵππαιχμον, θαμὰ δὴ καὶ Ὀλυμ-
   πιάδων φύλλοις ἐλαιᾶν χρυσέοις
μιχθέντα.

scatter glory over the island which Zeus, lord of Olympus,
gave to Persephone, and promised, nodding with his hair, that
he would raise up fertile Sicily with its high and prosperous cities
to be the best on the fruitful earth.   15
And the son of Cronus gave her a people who fight on horseback,
wooers of bronze-armored war, and often acquainted with the
   golden leaves
of Olympic olive.

In the epinician tradition, it is not unusual to ascribe the key advantages
of the victor's *polis*, such as its fertility, its military tradition, and its Olympic

The Politics of Identity in Greek Sicily and Southern Italy. Mark R. Thatcher, Oxford University Press. © Oxford University
Press 2021. DOI: 10.1093/oso/9780197586440.003.0004

success, to the favor of its most prominent deity. Indeed, Pindar describes Sicily as uniquely blessed with agricultural fertility and military and political power, and he attributes this prosperity to the fact that Sicily is sacred to Persephone—a status approved by Zeus in the phrase "nodding with his hair," with all its Homeric resonances of divinely ordained order.[1] Yet Sicily is not a *polis*. Pindar offers praise not of Syracuse or of Aetna, the colony founded by Hieron which Chromius proclaimed as his hometown, but of Sicily as a whole. His praise falls initially on the word "island," while its name is first delayed and then emphasized at the start of a line. It is this island, not any of the "high and prosperous *poleis*" located there, that was given to Persephone. What defines this community of Sicilians is not citizenship in a *polis* but rather the shores of their island and the deities especially revered there. Pindar is, in fact, describing a regional Sicilian identity.

It is no accident that this image appears in a poem dedicated to one of Hieron's courtiers. As we will see, Persephone, together with her mother, Demeter, figured prominently in the Deinomenids' ideology of kingship. In fact, they promoted these two goddesses—often called Demeter and Kore locally—in both myth and cult, as a way of legitimizing their rule across much of the island. Although this sense of Sicilian-ness was encouraged by the tyrants, they likely did not invent it, because (as we saw in chapter 3) this technique for creating legitimacy typically builds on preexisting foundations. So when and how did a sense of pan-Sicilian identity first emerge? What were the criteria on which it was based, and how did it differ from other types of identity? Moreover, after the Deinomenid period, a sense of island-wide unity re-emerged time and again, often with the encouragement of later tyrants and leaders. In fact, as this chapter's title (which quotes Bacchylides 3.1) suggests, Demeter and Kore were a useful tool for anyone who wanted to rule this grain-rich island. But what circumstances led Sicilian identity to regain salience, and what does this tell us about its defining features? Placing the Deinomenids' deployment of Sicilian identity in its full cultural and historical context will help us understand its nature and its political valence.

Under the shared name of Sikeliotai, first attested in Thucydides and often translated as "the Greeks of Sicily," Sicilians articulated their sense of Sicilian uniqueness in various ways, each with separate implications. This chapter will focus on two criteria that have not been fully explored. First, the two goddesses Demeter and Persephone form a recurrent motif in pan-Sicilian contexts.

---

1. Braswell 1992, 41–44, citing *Il.* 1.524–530; cf. Magrath 1974, 42–53; Morgan 2015, 384–385; Lewis 2020, 116–135.

Their mythology, for instance, suggests that Sicilians frequently thought of them as an island-wide possession, rather than pertaining to any one specific *polis*, and the Deinomenids appropriated them as a way of legitimizing their authority over (as they liked to see it) the whole island. This discussion also shows that Sicilian identity predates by at least half a century its first explicit attestation in Thucydides. Second, Sicilian identity was especially invoked in situations where the island was threatened with invasion from overseas. From the Athenian invasion in 415 to the repeated Carthaginian incursions of the fifth and fourth centuries, Sicilians drew attention to the natural maritime boundaries of their land and to the special status this gave it. These two contributing factors could even be linked—for example, in Timaeus's narrative of the Sicilian Expedition, which claimed that Persephone made an intervention in favor of her own island (F102b). Sicilians were held to be separate from all other peoples who lived overseas, both Greek and non-Greek.

Of course, these two criteria are by no means the only ways of conceptualizing the Sicilian community. Irad Malkin, for instance, has pointed to the altar of Apollo Archegetes at Naxos, which was set up by the first Greek settlers there.[2] According to Thucydides (6.3.1), *theoroi* from all of Sicily sacrificed at this altar whenever they sailed back to Greece. This criterion emphasized the links of all the Greek *poleis* of Sicily back to the mainland and their shared heritage as Hellenic *apoikiai*.[3] Moreover, Sicily was far from unique in developing this sort of island identity: a number of other multi-*polis* islands in the Aegean, such as Rhodes, Lesbos, and Crete, did something similar.[4] Moreover, as I have emphasized throughout this book, identities were multiple and fluid, and Sicilian identity was never the only or even the dominant way in which people in Sicily perceived themselves. Rather, it was one choice out of a menu of options, and one that deserves more attention for its interesting implications, as a regional identity that cut across familiar ethnic categories.

We saw in chapter 3 how both the Deinomenids and Dionysius deployed a series of identities—Syracusan, Dorian, Hellenic—to create legitimacy for their rule, and Sicilian identity also played a similar role. Yet I have chosen to discuss it separately because it raises a somewhat different set of issues. Rather than concentrating only on the relationship between identity and

---

2. Malkin 2011, 97–117; cf. Malkin 1986; Fragoulaki 2013, 77; with the critiques and modifications of Antonaccio 2001, 134; Antonaccio 2007b; Hall 2002, 122; Donnellan 2012; Murray 2014; Sammartano 2015, 235–246.

3. See also Willi 2008, an account of Sicilian culture through language.

4. See esp. Malkin 2011.

tyranny (as chapter 3 did), I here expand the focus to include a wider chronological range and a broader view of the sociopolitical function of Sicilian
identity, including its cultural and religious components. Regional identities have traditionally been an understudied topic, and for this reason, too,
Sicilian identity deserves separate and sustained attention.[5] The first part of
this chapter therefore explores the role of Demeter and Kore in constructing
and articulating Sicilian regional identity and brings out some further
implications of this self-conception. The second part then traces the role
of regional identity in Sicilian politics, drawing on both criteria (the two
goddesses and overseas enemies) as they ebbed and flowed across several
centuries.

Myth and Cult

Four centuries after the Deinomenids, Diodorus and Cicero both describe
Sicily as entirely sacred to Demeter and Persephone, claiming that they were
the patrons of the island as a whole.[6] Although these sources are relatively late,
there is ample earlier evidence that links the two goddesses with a rhetoric of
pan-Sicilian identity. We have already seen, for example, how Pindar made
the island Persephone's wedding gift from Zeus, and Simonides likely gave
Demeter possession of Sicily. Demeter and Kore were also extremely prominent in cult practice: across the island, Sicilians (especially women) conducted
rituals such as the Thesmophoria that recalled those myths and enacted their
close and reciprocal relationship with the goddesses. Myth and cult together
thus articulated a privileged association between the two goddesses and the
island of Sicily, which stood at the heart of Sicilian regional identity. Moreover,
this construction also posed difficult questions about who counted as Sicilian
(only Greeks, or non-Greeks as well?) that, as we will see, challenged traditional Greek ethnic concepts.

---

5. See, e.g., Reger 1997; Constantakopoulou 2005; Vlassopoulos 2007; Kowalzig 2007, 224–
266; Malkin 2011, 65–95; Kouremenos 2018; on Sicily, see Shepherd 2006, 441–442; Frisone
2009; Malkin 2011, 97–118. Much recent work has focused on regions that are also *ethnē*,
such as Boeotia and Phocis, which present some separate issues: see, e.g., McInerney 1999;
Morgan 2003; Nielsen 1999; Larson 2007; Greaves 2010; Mackil 2013. The unique characteristics of islands have also received much attention: see Broodbank 2000; Constantakopoulou
2007; Knapp 2007; Knapp 2009.

6. Diod. 5.2–5, esp. 2.3; Cic. *Verr.* 2.4.106–108, esp. 106; cf. Anello 2008b. For broad
introductions to Demeter and Kore in Sicily, see Shapiro 2002; Sfameni Gasparro 2008;
Greco 2013.

Myths of Demeter and Kore

A number of Sicilian myths of Demeter and Kore emphasize the goddesses' standing as a common possession of all Sicilians. They do not merely belong to one particular city (though sometimes they do that, too) but rather to the entire island. This mythical discourse promotes both a sense of Sicily as a single unitary region and the idea of a community encompassing all inhabitants of Sicily, who share in this special relationship with the goddesses of grain. The particular favor shown to them by the two goddesses makes the Sicilians distinctive, setting them apart from the rest of the world, and their myths boldly proclaim the pride they take in it.

The sources for these myths are various and problematic, and some are quite late. The fullest sources are Diodorus (5.2–5) and Cicero (*Verr.* 4.106–108), but the extreme similarity of these two texts makes it likely that they go back to a common source, probably Timaeus in the late fourth or early third century.[7] Furthermore, Pindar, Bacchylides, and Simonides seem to show familiarity with various elements that appear more clearly later, and other sources provide occasional corroboration. Thus, the core claim of a special relationship between the island of Sicily and its two goddesses must date to the early fifth century, even if some of the details may have developed later.[8] Moreover, the main sources are all either Sicilians themselves or (like Pindar) had detailed knowledge of Sicilian ideas and attitudes. Myths such as these are some of the closest sources we have to an emic informant to tell us about Sicilian identity.

One of the earliest expressions of a pan-Sicilian myth is also one of the most tantalizingly difficult. In an unknown poem, Simonides described a contest between Demeter and Hephaestus, judged by the nymph Aetna, "over the land" of Sicily (περὶ τῆς χώρας ἐρίσαντας), suggesting a conception of the deity taking possession of the island. Although the scholiast who preserved this information did not mention the winner, it is hard to imagine Demeter falling short.[9] We do not have even a single word directly quoted, and we do

---

7. So Jacoby in *FGrH*, on Timaeus F164; Romano 1980; Baldo 1999, 17–18; Sfameni Gasparro 2008, 31, 35; Casevitz and Jacquemin 2015, xxviii–xxx, 119; though Champion (2010 on Timaeus F164) and Robert (2012, 53–56) are more hesitant. Jacoby's F164 (which encompasses a large part of Diodorus Book 5) need not be entirely Timaean to accept the origin of the smaller segment at issue here.

8. Lewis 2020, 82–84.

9. Σιμωνίδης δὲ Αἴτνην φησὶ κρῖναι Ἥφαιστον καὶ Δήμητραν περὶ τῆς χώρας ἐρίσαντας: F552 *PMG* = schol. Theocritus 1.65/66a; cf. Molyneux 1992, 229–231; Dougherty 1993, 91–93.

not know the date or circumstances of this poem's composition (beyond a pre-sumptive Deinomenid connection). This myth is clearly related to (if not de-liberately modeled on) the well-known Athenian story of the contest between Athena and Poseidon, and its existence speaks to a growing sense of unity among Sicilians in the early fifth century: they would not have felt a need for a single island-wide patron if they did not consider that a meaningful social unit.[10] However, the Sicilian story offers an important contrast: whereas the Athenian myth resulted in the choice of a patron for a single *polis*, the Sicilian story references no *poleis* but rather the entire island. Demeter is chosen not by the citizens of a *polis* (as in the Athenian story) but by a local nymph, who represents a crucial element of the Sicilian landscape. Equally interestingly, the alternative deity in the contest is Hephaestus, god of fire and clearly asso-ciated with Mount Etna in this period.[11] That he was felt a legitimate contender to become the foremost god of all Sicily is suggestive of the impact the tow-ering presence of Mount Etna had on the entire island.

This should not be surprising. After all, while some parts of the Greek world, such as Lemnos and the Bay of Naples, displayed volcanism, no other region boasted such an impressive mountain, with such remarkable capabil-ities. The existence of Mount Etna thereby served to distinguish Sicily from the rest of the Greek world, and Sicilians could take pride in a feature that made their island unique. In this way, the volcano played the same role for the Sicilian community as the local landscape did for *polis* communities at Croton (chapter 2), Syracuse (chapter 3), and Camarina (chapter 5). Crucially, how-ever, Mount Etna as a whole was claimed by no single *polis*. It stood between Catana and Naxos, and its lower slopes were certainly cultivated by these com-munities, but the mountain's peak, visible across wide swaths of eastern and central Sicily, belonged to all. Hieron's emphasis on the cult of Zeus Aetnaeus thus usurped this position, associating himself and his rule with a shared Sicilian possession.[12] It is therefore no accident that Pindar associates three deities—Demeter, Kore, and Zeus Aetnaeus—as the objects of Hieron's rev-erence (*Ol.* 6.92–96). Like Mount Etna, the two goddesses are shared by all Sicilians alike, and their Sicilian myths emphasize their regional appeal. They are worshipped not merely by one particular city but by the entire island com-munity that takes first place in piety toward the goddesses.

10. Cf. also the Argive story of a contest between Hera and Poseidon, judged by Phoroneus, son of the river Inachus (Paus. 2.15.5).

11. Pind. *Pyth.* 1.25–28; Aesch. *PV* 365–367.

12. On Zeus Aetnaeus, see Luraghi 1994, 339–341; Nicholson 2011.

Next, the most important event in Persephone's mythical biography, her rape by Hades, was placed in various places by various writers, but for Sicilians, it occurred on their island. This localization appears most explicitly in Cicero and Diodorus, but, as we have already seen, Pindar alludes to it in *Nemean* 1, describing Sicily as "the island which Zeus, lord of Olympus, gave to Persephone."[13] The scholiast (line 17) adds that this was a wedding present (*anakalupteria*); Diodorus draws on the same tradition, ascribing it to "some poets" (5.2.3). Persephone's marriage was, of course, to Hades, and the *Homeric Hymn to Demeter* (77–80) similarly describes the rape as a marriage approved by her father, Zeus. In the hymn, the event occurred in the mythical plain of Nysa (17), so the Sicilian tradition offers a local variant, one of substantial importance. Locating in Sicily such a formative event in the mythic biography of the goddess creates a special connection between the place and its deity, forming a charter myth for the future cultic landscape. At least sixteen other places also claimed to be the site of the rape, and undoubtedly for Greeks in those places, their hometown claim held just as much meaning as this one did in Sicily, but for Sicilians, only their own claim mattered.[14]

In Pindar, the specific location within Sicily does not matter: since the entire island (νάσῳ: 13) is Persephone's wedding present, the event that sparked it impacts all of Sicily. Other writers do specify the precise location of the rape, and their accounts highlight the significance of mythical geography in articulating identities. Both Diodorus (5.3.2–3, 4.1–2) and Cicero (*Verr.* 2.4.106–107) connect two locations with it: first, the Lago di Pergusa near Enna, a non-Greek indigenous city in the center of the island, and second, the spring of Kyane, just outside Syracuse.[15] These authors incorporate both sites into their mythical narratives by suggesting that Hades emerged from the ground and seized Persephone near Enna, then traveled aboveground to Syracuse and returned to the underworld there. The myth in this version thus serves to link the geographic center of the island with its coasts through the movement of Hades and Persephone across its landscape, thereby neatly integrating the whole island within a single religious framework. Moreover, the description of Enna as Sicily's *omphalos* (Cic. *Verr.* 2.4.106) gives it not only geographic but also cultural centrality, imbuing geography with cultural meaning. The term implies a tight relationship between the center and the whole, between Enna's

---

13. *Nem.* 1.13–14: νάσῳ, τὰν Ὀλύμπου δεσπότας Ζεὺς ἔδωκεν Φερσεφόνα, with references above at note 1.

14. Richardson 1974, 148–150.

15. For Kyane, see fig. 3.1.

FIG. 4.1 Litra of Enna, c. 450. Obverse: Demeter riding a chariot holding a torch. Reverse: Demeter sacrificing. © Trustees of the British Museum.

famed Demeter cult and the entire region that looks to it as its religious heart. What happened in Enna matters to all of Sicily.[16]

Yet there are signs that this story represents a rationalization and systematization of two originally separate myths.[17] According to Diodorus (5.4.2; cf. Cic. *Verr.* 2.4.107), Hades's action at Kyane caused the creation of the spring itself. The Syracusans commemorated this event annually with a public sacrifice of bulls, which were thrown into the spring, a very rare form of sacrifice supposedly established by Heracles.[18] The bulls enter the spring just as Hades and Persephone did, and so the story thus offers a tight etiology not only for the existence of the spring but also for the specific sacrificial procedure; this version is complete and self-consistent without a link to Enna.

Where did the version set at Enna come from? Although proof is impossible, it may be a local development. A coin of Enna from the mid-fifth century, depicting Demeter riding on a chariot and carrying a torch, searching for her daughter, seems to offer corroborating evidence that Enna's myth existed that early (fig. 4.1).[19] Although the coin does not actually depict the rape of Persephone, much less its localization at Enna, it does suggest that by that time, the people of Enna were claiming a special connection to the goddess.

---

16. Lewis 2020, 84–89.

17. Cf. Casevitz and Jacquemin 2015, 126.

18. Casevitz and Jacquemin 2015, 126.

19. Jenkins 1975, 78–83; Rutter 1997, 139–140; Borba Florenzano 2005, 15; Manganaro Perrone 2007; Lewis 2020, 82–84.

Conceivably, a story localized at an indigenous site could have been invented by Greeks in order to mythically take possession of the site. In that case, however, it seems unlikely that the people of Enna would have become sufficiently invested in such a story to depict it on their coins. Moreover, although the obverse and reverse types are partly modeled on Greek examples, there is no parallel up to that time for depicting Demeter as a charioteer.[20]

If these two localizations did, in fact, originate separately, they may have done so in a climate of competition between Syracuse and Enna, in which each attempted to outdo the other in piety and the closeness of its connection to Persephone. Such a sense of competition may also account for the notice in Stephanus of Byzantium (s.v. Enna) that Enna was actually a colony of Syracuse, founded in the mid-seventh century. The site is sufficiently inland and distant from Syracuse that this is unlikely to be accurate, especially at a time when Syracuse's attention was focused on southeastern Sicily.[21] Instead, it most likely reflects an invented tradition that attempted to subordinate Enna to Syracuse. The date of such competition, and thereby the date of the myth, is difficult to determine. Enna is listed among several indigenous communities conquered by Dionysius during a campaign in 397, creating a plausible situation in which Syracuse may have attempted to claim superiority on a mythical as well as a military level.[22] Yet the numismatic evidence suggests that Enna's myth already existed by the mid-fifth century. In any case, the fact that competition between communities was articulated through competing claims to be the site of the rape of Persephone shows that such localizations brought great prestige to Greek and non-Greek Sicilians alike.

Sicily played a prominent role in Demeter's biography as well, when she traveled through the island on a chariot, lighting her way with torches, in search of her daughter; this is the episode depicted on Enna's coins. According to both Diodorus and Cicero, Demeter lit her torches in the fires of Mount Etna.[23] These torches were a widely recognized symbol of Demeter's worship; as we will see below, they played important roles at both the Thesmophoria festival and the Eleusinian Mysteries, and they frequently appear as attributes on the terracotta figurines that are ubiquitous as votive dedications across Sicily

---

20. Jenkins 1975, 80.

21. Rejected by Dunbabin 1948, 136; Schipporeit 2008, 41; accepted by Calciati 1987, 229; Manganaro 2003. On Syracusan expansion, see Thuc. 6.5.2–3; Dunbabin 1948, 95–112; Di Vita 1956; and further in chapter 5.

22. Diod. 14.14.5–8, cf. 78.7; Schipporeit 2008.

23. Diod. 5.4.3; Cic. *Verr.* 2.4.106; cf. *Hom. Hymn Dem.* 48–61.

(see further below).[24] In Sicilian myth, the most emblematic landform on the island acts as the original source of this sacred fire, giving the island pride of place among Demeter's worshippers; her rituals could not occur without Sicily's role in their origin.

Demeter is also tied to Mount Etna in a remarkable fragment from the fourth-century tragedian Carcinus, a shadowy figure who was most likely Athenian by birth but spent significant time in Syracuse at the court of Dionysius II and who may also have become a citizen of Akragas.[25] Diodorus introduces this passage in order to demonstrate that his version of the rape of Kore was attested by earlier poets (F5 Snell = Diod. 5.5.1):

λέγουσι Δήμητρός ποτ' ἄρρητον κόρην
Πλούτωνα κρυφίοις ἁρπάσαι βουλεύμασι,
δῦναί τε γαίας εἰς μελαμφαεῖς μυχούς,
πόθῳ δὲ μητέρ' ἠφανισμένης κόρης
μαστῆρ' ἐπελθεῖν πᾶσαν ἐν κύκλῳ χθόνα.   5
καὶ τὴν μὲν Αἰτναίοισι Σικελίαν πάγοις
πυρὸς γέμουσαν ῥεύμασιν δυσεμβόλοις
πᾶσαν στενάξαι, πένθεσιν δὲ παρθένου
σίτων ἄμοιρον διοτρεφὲς φθίνειν γένος.
ὅθεν θεᾶς τιμῶσιν εἰς τὰ νῦν ἔτι.   10

They say that once upon a time, Pluto, by hidden plots,
seized Demeter's daughter, whom none may name,
and sank beneath the dark-lit folds of the earth.
Her mother, from longing for the disappeared girl,
came in search to every land in turn.   5
And the entire land of Sicily by the peaks of Etna
groaned, full of unapproachable streams of fire,
and the people beloved by Zeus were perishing
with grief for the maiden, without a share of grain,
whence they honor the goddesses even now.   10

The passage is completely bereft of context (not even the play's title is known), but it nonetheless emerges from a Sicilian environment and thus provides a critical window into Sicilian attitudes. Carcinus brings together

24. Richardson 1974, 165–167; Foley 1994, 38; Parker 2005, 350.

25. The *Suda* (s.v. *Karkinos* = *TrGF* I 70 T1) lists two tragedians named Carcinus, one Akragantine and one Athenian; for the identification of the two, see Kannicht 1991, 146–147.

Demeter and Kore, Mount Etna, and an etiological explanation for Sicilian devotion to the two goddesses. Volcanic flame again plays a pivotal role, in this case symbolizing Demeter's grief over the theft of her daughter. In fact, the entire land of Sicily itself shares in this grief (6–8: τὴν Σικελίαν γέμουσαν πᾶσαν), as do its people. Carcinus's myth-making thus shows how, through the mediation of the volcano, Demeter's mythic experiences build a reciprocal relationship with her favored island and its people. Moreover, the passage appears to draw heavily on a choral ode from Euripides's *Helen*, which also describes Demeter's wanderings; the Euripides passage does not mention Sicily, and so Carcinus's refocusing of the myth on Sicily would have been quite striking.[26]

Finally, Sicilians claimed that they were the first recipients of Demeter's gift of grain to humanity.[27] The Athenians, of course, claimed the same for themselves, and so this Sicilian claim directly challenged a core element of Athenian civic ideology. Because of this element of rivalry inherent in the myth, I will discuss it more fully below as a form of cultural competition. For now, we should observe that for both Cicero and Diodorus, it is the entire island of Sicily, not any specific *polis*, that received this gift. Thus, like the other myths we have discussed, this claim presents a special relationship between all Sicilians and the two goddesses. This, in turn, implies that they are a single community, distinguished from others by their relationship with the goddesses.

Cult Practices

When Diodorus described Sicily as the land most favored by Demeter and Kore, he demonstrated the truth of this claim by drawing not only on myths but also on Sicilian festivals (5.4). In his mind, myth and practice were closely interrelated: myths commemorated the goddesses' special relationship with the island, while the festivals and sacrifices in their honor maintained and enhanced that divine favor. We, too, should read myths in conjunction with rituals, and vice versa. Demeter and Kore were extremely popular recipients of cult throughout Sicily. What might these religious practices have contributed to Sicilian regional identity?

We must be careful: there is nothing inherently and objectively Sicilian about festivals of Demeter and Kore, especially the Thesmophoria, which was celebrated throughout the Greek world. Nevertheless, Sicilian participants might well disagree, since they would understand these rituals through the

---

26. Eur. *Hel.* 1301–1368; cf. Xanthakis-Karamanos 1980, 87–89; Allan 2008, 292–310.

27. Diod. 5.2.4–5, 4.3–5; Cic. *Verr.* 2.4.106, 108.

lens of the myths discussed above. Cult practices performed within a mythical discourse of regional identity might well bring to mind a sense of Sicilian-ness, not for every participant on every occasion but for some people some of the time. As a result, paying attention to cult practice begins to reveal another dimension of Sicilian identity, a performative one, through which Sicilians might proclaim their special relationship with Demeter and Kore. Ritual prac-tice thus gives us a deeper window into the functioning of identity.

The most widely celebrated festival for the two goddesses, in Sicily and elsewhere, was the Thesmophoria. This was an annual fertility festival cel-ebrated by women, normally all the married citizen women of a particular *polis*.[28] The festival has been reconstructed as follows. Women departed from normal society for a period of days, living in tents at small sanctuaries. There they conducted a series of secluded rituals, especially one that involved the sacrifice of piglets. The piglets were then buried, while the decomposed re-mains of the previous year's piglets were excavated and used in the fields as a sort of sacred fertilizer. Meanwhile, the women enacted an experience of grief, by fasting and by abstaining from sexuality and the comforts of civilized life; they also engaged in obscene talk, made special cakes in the form of gen-italia,[29] and finally celebrated with a feast. While the ritual was performed by women alone, it actually involved the whole community, since (as evidence from Athens attests) it was paid for by men and sponsored by the *demos*.[30] More broadly, the festival was thought to promote fertility (both agricultural and human) and thereby safeguard the future of the entire community. If the Thesmophoria contributed in any way to a sense of Sicilian identity, it would do so for all Sicilians, not just women.

As has long been recognized, the Thesmophoria rituals are tied very closely to the myth of the rape of Kore.[31] The festival's arc imitates Demeter's

---

28. For the following, and on the Thesmophoria generally, see Burkert 1985, 242–246; Clinton 1992, 29–37, 59–63; Goff 2004, 125–138; Parker 2005, 270–283; Stehle 2007; Johnston 2013, esp. 374–378; in Sicily specifically, see Hinz 1998; De Miro 2008; Greco 2013. This broad summary necessarily elides differences between *poleis*, a few of which will be mentioned below.

29. The Hellenistic writer Heracleides of Syracuse (cited in Athenaeus 14.647a) informs us of a specifically Sicilian form of cake made in the shape of female genitalia, called *mylloi*, which was used in the Thesmophoria there. The existence of a separate word at least hints at the distinctiveness of Sicilian celebrations.

30. *IG* II² 1261, 1290; Isaeus 3.80; 8.19–20; cf. Winkler 1990, 194; Parker 2005, 278; Johnston 2013, 375.

31. See, e.g., Richardson 1974; Clinton 1992, 29–37, 59–63; Clinton 1993; Lowe 1998; Parker 2005, 272–275; Johnston 2013.

experience as narrated in the *Homeric Hymn to Demeter* and various other sources: her grief at the loss of her daughter followed by joy at their reunion and the use of coarse language by a character (Baubo or Iambe, in different versions) who cheered up Demeter with obscenities. Torches were a key element of Thesmophoric iconography, because Demeter was thought to have carried torches to light her way while searching for her daughter.[32] Further, the role of piglets was thought to derive from a swineherd, Eubouleus, whose pigs were swallowed up by the earth along with Hades's chariot.[33] Thus, performing the Thesmophoria ritual would have had added meaning in Sicilian eyes, since they were re-enacting the mythical events that took place in Sicily and made the island sacred to the two goddesses. Myth and ritual formed two pieces of an interlocking whole that, for many Sicilians, promoted Sicilian distinctiveness.

This may help explain why Sicilians were especially enthusiastic in celebrating festivals of Demeter and Kore. Diodorus describes in great detail (5.4.5–7) a pair of festivals celebrated by "those in Sicily"—thus, in theory, by all Sicilian communities, though he may be describing Syracusan practice in particular.[34] These consisted of the Thesmophoria, which was scheduled to coincide with the sowing of grain, and a second festival for Kore at harvest time, celebrating her return from the underworld and significantly bookending the agricultural cycle. Sicilians demonstrated the Thesmophoria's particular significance for them by celebrating it more elaborately than other Greeks: at Athens, the Thesmophoria lasted three days, but in Sicily, ten days were devoted to it. According to Diodorus, it was a festival "most magnificent because of the splendor of their preparation for it," and he also highlights the Sicilians' "strictness and zeal" in celebrating the Koreia.[35] These two festivals invited such enthusiasm and public investment because they offered the community a way of publicly proclaiming its relationship with the goddesses.

---

32. Richardson 1974, 167–168.

33. Eubouleus is a character from Eleusinian myth (Clinton 1992, 56–63), and the sources are likely thinking of the Athenian Thesmophoria, which might differ from Sicilian versions. Still, the differences were unlikely to be enormous, and there is no reason to postulate a separate explanation for the well-attested role of piglets in the Sicilian Thesmophoria; cf. Johnston 2013, 374–375.

34. 5.4.5: οἱ δὲ κατὰ τὴν Σικελίαν. See Polacco 1986; Hinz 1998, 96–99; Kowalzig 2008, 138.

35. 5.4.7: πανήγυριν . . . τῇ τε λαμπρότητι τῆς παρασκευῆς μεγαλοπρεπεστάτην; 5.4.6: μετὰ . . . ἁγνείας καὶ σπουδῆς.

Although Syracuse provides the best literary evidence for the Thesmophoria in Sicily, it was also widely celebrated across the island. For example, at the site of Bitalemi, just outside Gela, a fragment of an Attic vase (possibly the cover of a *pyxis*) of the mid-fifth century was inscribed "sacred to Thesmophoros, from the tent of Dikaio."[36] Not only does the inscription demonstrate that the sanctuary was a Thesmophorion, but it also suggests that the participants stayed in tents during the festival. The role of such temporary structures is also supported by the layout of the sanctuary, which consisted of a small *sacellum* surrounded by ample open space. Equally important, the excavators found numerous piglet bones in and around the sanctuary's hearth. On top of these were found numerous ceramic vessels (such as *kylikes* and *hydriai*) that would be used for banqueting, as well as cutlery and cookware. These have rightly been interpreted as the remains of a ritual banquet, which would have occurred on the third and final day of the Attic Thesmophoria and which clearly was part of the ritual at Gela as well.[37] Similar assemblages have been found at sites across the island, including at Syracuse, Heloron, Akragas, Entella, and many more.[38]

The widespread popularity of the Thesmophoria can also be seen from the huge number of small terracotta figurines depicting Demeter or Kore, which had been dedicated at sanctuaries of the two goddesses by, most likely, Sicilian Greek women as they celebrated the Thesmophoria festival. Mold-made and mass-produced, these figurines come from numerous sites across Sicily and are a common sight at any museum there (fig. 4.2). While there were many variations, the figures typically represent either a standing or seated female figure wearing a *polos* (a large ritual headdress) and carrying a piglet and/or a torch, two attributes that make specific reference to the Thesmophoria.[39] Each votive figurine represents a gift to the deities by one or more individuals, and

---

36. Orlandini 1968, 20–21; Hinz 1998, 56–57; De Miro 2008, 50; cf. also Fiorentini 1993–1994, 721. Several other graffiti on vases were also found, with portions of the names Demeter and Thesmophoros: Orlandini 2008, 174.

37. On the Bitalemi site, see Orlandini 1968; Orlandini 2008; Kron 1992; Hinz 1998, 56–64; De Miro 2008, 47–53; Scibona 2012.

38. Hinz 1998; De Miro 2008; cf. esp. Micciché 2020; Sojc 2020 on the faunal remains at S. Anna near Akragas.

39. The identification of the figure represented by the votives (whether the dedicant or one of the goddesses) is debated: Bell 1985; Portale 2008; Ferruzza 2013. See the cautionary remarks of Uhlenbrock 2016; Uhlenbrock 2019 (who, however, does not refer to the Thesmophoric imagery on the group of figurines discussed here); Patera 2020.

FIG. 4.2 Terracotta figurine with piglet and torch, from Catania. Used by authorization of the Parco archeologico e paesaggistico di Catania e della Valle dell'Aci.

in toto they testify to the widespread devotion to Demeter and Kore felt by ordinary Sicilians over the centuries.[40]

Of course, the reasons any individuals would have had for dedicating a Demeter and Kore figurine must have varied widely. Some might have been celebrating their Greekness (rather than Sicilian-ness) or their identities as women; others might not have been thinking of an identity at all but simply their religious devotion or their desire to ensure a good harvest by keeping the goddesses happy. In many cases, all of these must have been wrapped up

40. Cole 1994, 203–204.

together. Nevertheless, the island-wide distribution pattern suggests that the figurines, and the religious practices to which they testify, may have contributed to articulating a Sicilian regional identity, in conjunction with the mythical discourse of regionalism mediated by the two goddesses. The figurines give us a window into the lives and perceptions of the women who made up half of the communities in question, from all points on the socioeconomic spectrum, who are mostly ignored by the (elite, male) literary sources, and thus they tell a richer and more inclusive story of Sicilian identity. It is clear that the worship of the two goddesses was not merely an elite phenomenon, and the meanings and identities it supported must also have been widespread.

Another passage from Diodorus's account of Sicilian worship of Demeter and Kore brings myth and ritual even closer together (5.4.2; cf. 4.23.4). He describes an annual festival held at the spring of Kyane near Syracuse, at which sacrifices were conducted both by private citizens and by the state. This festival and the particular manner of sacrifice—throwing bulls into the spring— were believed to have been ordained by Heracles and thereby held particularly high status. Moreover, as we saw above, the spring of Kyane was also held up as the location of the rape of Kore, and three other festivals mentioned in various sources—the Theogamia, the Anakalypteria, and the Anthesphoria—also highlight this claim through their reference to Persephone's "marriage."[41] The development of two separate myths placing both Heracles and Kore at Kyane suggests that this site was particularly evocative for Syracusans and central to their religious landscape, where myth and cult were tightly interwoven. Each year, the Syracusans would commemorate and, in a sense, re-enact the myth that made the site so special; this festival, performed by the community as a whole, proclaimed their distinctiveness to themselves and to the world. This reciprocal relationship between myth and cult allowed both to take on additional layers of meaning.

Of course, that community would most naturally be the *polis* of Syracuse, which celebrated the festival. But there was a strong tendency for the Syracusans to merge their own interests and ideologies with those of the island as a whole, and it was Syracuse's (self-proclaimed) embodiment of everything that was Sicilian that made its claims to rule over the whole island possible. Syracuse's imperial ambitions made it unusual among Sicilian communities, and we

---

41. Pollux 1.37; Strabo 6.1.5; schol. rec. Pind. *Ol.* 6.161g (Abel). The Anthesphoria may recall the story that Persephone was gathering flowers when she was abducted: Martorana 1982; Hinz 1998, 28–30; Kowalzig 2008, 138.

cannot simply extrapolate from Syracuse to other cities whose practices and ideologies are much less well known. Still, Pollux says that the Theogamia and the Anthesphoria were celebrated "among the Sikeliotai," which perhaps implies that they were celebrated in other cities as well.[42] Moreover, as we have seen, the rape of Kore was often represented as possessing island-wide significance, and so the rituals that celebrated it might well hold similar meanings across Sicily.

Across the island, in fact, the archaeological record shows striking similarities.[43] Most Sicilian communities had more than one cult site for Demeter and Kore, and many of them followed a similar chronological trajectory: cult activity began in the sixth century (or in some cases earlier) and expanded substantially in the fifth. At Syracuse, for example, at least four more cult sites are known besides Kyane. Some of these date back to the late sixth century, while others originated in the fifth; one, at Piazza della Vittoria, received a temple in the fifth century, which may have been built by the Deinomenids.[44] The Bitalemi sanctuary at Gela went through a series of phases beginning in the second half of the seventh century and was rebuilt in the early fifth century after a fire. At least eight other small sanctuaries ring the urban center.[45] Similarly, at Akragas, cult activity began soon after its foundation in 580 and expanded through the sixth century. The so-called Chthonic Sanctuary at the western end of the same ridge on which the famous fifth-century temples sit was the initial focus of development, with a complex series of buildings, altars, and votives. Elsewhere at Akragas, high on the slopes of the acropolis, the "rock sanctuary" at San Biagio is also Archaic and received a temple in the early fifth century.[46] The cult was important enough to Akragas's self-image that Pindar could describe Akragas as the "seat of Persephone" (*Pyth.* 12.2). At Catana, cult activity may have begun slightly later: a votive deposit from the early fifth century was excavated at the foot of the acropolis, while a late-fifth-century dedication inscribed "to Demeter and Kore" shows that the cult

42. Pollux 1.37: ἑορταὶ ἔντιμοι . . . Κόρης παρὰ Σικελιώταις θεογάμια καὶ ἀνθεσφόρια.

43. See the overviews (including all of the sites mentioned below) of Hinz 1998; Veronese 2006; De Miro 2008; Lewis 2020, 74–79.

44. Polacco 1986; on Piazza della Vittoria, see Voza 1976–1977, 553–560; Voza 1980–1981, 680–684; Voza 1999, 94–99.

45. On the Bitalemi site, see above, note 36.

46. On Demeter and Kore at Akragas, see Marconi 1933; de Waele 1971; Siracusano 1983; Cole 1994, 214–215; Genovese 2020; Sojc 2020.

included both goddesses by name.[47] All of these examples (and more could be adduced) show that the worship of Demeter and Kore enjoyed particular prominence and stature within their respective communities, and their cult was the object of ongoing communal investment over a long period of time. Moreover, although the worship of the two goddesses became even more prominent during the Deinomenid period, it was widespread long before their rise to power.

How exactly, then, did rituals and cult practices in honor of Demeter and Kore contribute to a sense of Sicilian unity and regional identity? As discussed in chapter 2, many Greek *ethnē* and federal states had a central shared sanctuary, such as those of Athena Itonia and of Poseidon at Onchestos in Boeotia or Kalapodi in Phocis, where individuals from across the region would come together to celebrate joint festivals and reinforce their sense of community.[48] The various *poleis* of Rhodes and Lesbos similarly built shared sanctuaries (for Athena Lindia and at Mesa, respectively). It is therefore striking that no such sanctuary of Demeter and Kore existed in Sicily. Instead, the Thesmophoria and other rituals were performed separately in each *polis*, and there was no opportunity for them to physically come together to worship their goddesses as a single community. Parallels can be found, however, in the Apatouria and Karnea festivals, since both of these were celebrated in many *poleis* separately but nonetheless created a sense of shared culture among the Ionians and Dorians, respectively,[49] and also in the cults of Hera among the Achaeans discussed in chapter 2. This suggests a model where identity is generated not from the experience of worshipping the same deities at the same site but rather from sharing a common ritual practice at separate locations: it is the performance, not the location, that marks the worshippers as Sicilian.

Moreover, as I suggested earlier, exactly what the two goddesses meant to any individual Sicilian depended heavily on context. A participant in the Thesmophoria may have focused on her concern for agricultural fertility, the afterlife, or the *polis* community in which she was celebrating—or all of these at once. Which of these meanings was foremost would depend on context and would vary from one person or occasion to another. Rituals honoring Demeter and Kore only took on the specific connotation of pan-Sicilian unity when

---

47. Rizza 2008, 187–188; Pautasso 2009; cf. more broadly Rizza 1960. No Archaic evidence is known, perhaps due to the existence of the modern city on top of ancient Catana.

48. Morgan 2003, 113–134; McInerney 2013; Mackil 2013; Funke and Haake 2013; Mili 2015.

49. Apatouria: Hdt. 1.147.2; Hall 1997, 39–40; Parker 2005, 458–461. Karnea: Thuc. 5.54.2; Paus. 3.13.4, 26.7; Malkin 1994, 149–158; Robertson 2002, 36–74.

they were deployed in the context of a larger discourse of regional identity, a discourse articulated primarily through myth.[50] More specifically, I suggest that the contribution of cults of Demeter and Kore to a shared pan-Sicilian sense of identity can be located in the reciprocal relationship between cult and myth. Deities do not stand in a vacuum; when stories are told and sacrifices are conducted for the same goddesses, myth and ritual work together to shape ideas about them. For participants familiar with the mythical discourse of regional identity discussed earlier, the claims made by those stories would structure their understanding of the rituals in which they were engaged. Through this mutually reinforcing dynamic, cults became salient for Sicilian identity when they were interpreted in the context of pan-Sicilian myths, while those myths gained the most authority when they were grounded in real-life cult practices. This mutually reinforcing dynamic helped cement a sense of Sicilian-ness among participants.

Focusing on the performance of rituals can also give us a broader view of how identity was constructed by different groups within society. The Thesmophoria, of course, was conducted by women, whose role was seen as critical for the continued fertility and prosperity of the community. Women such as Dikaio, whose dedication was found at Bitalemi, played a key role in the articulation and maintenance of Sicilian identity through cult. By worshipping Demeter and Kore, they were declaring themselves Sicilian just as much as the men who wrote and commissioned our poetic sources.

Who Were the Sikeliotai?

Who counted as Sicilian, according to these criteria? By constructing Sicilian-ness as a regional identity, defined through the island's natural boundaries, the concept of Sicilian identity would seem logically to encompass everyone who lived on the island, including its non-Greeks. What of the Sikels, Sikanians, and Elymians who lived throughout the interior?[51] This question gets to the heart of the dynamics of Sicilian regional identity. If non-Greeks were excluded, this would imply that the geographical definition of Sicilian-ness worked in tandem with other ethnic or cultural criteria, so that only Greeks counted as Sicilian. But if non-Greeks could be considered Sicilian, then this

---

50. Cf. the approach of Konstan 1997 to the relationship between genealogy and ethnicity.

51. Cf. Hall 2004, 49; Sammartano 2015, 261–265. I reserve discussion of the Phoenicians in western Sicily for the end of this chapter.

would suggest that Sicily's island nature dominated other criteria, producing an identity that cuts across familiar categories.

Scholars have often downplayed this possibility, due especially to a modern preconception that sees the dichotomy between Greeks and barbarians as paramount and as a way of thinking that overrides other possible modes of identification.[52] As we have seen throughout this book, that is a considerable oversimplification and one that draws heavily on modern preconceptions. A second modern preconception works from a model of nation-states, seeing Greek and native Italian populations as inherently separate.[53] Notably, some Italian scholars have taken a very different view, emphasizing the contributions of Sikels to broader Sicilian culture and to the Greeks who settled there; this, too, is based in part on Italian nationalism.[54] Analyzing the relationship between Greeks and non-Greeks in terms of multiple identities challenges these modern preconceptions; it allows these peoples to join together under a regional identity under some circumstances and to keep separate under the banner of Greekness when that was desired. Since identities were so flexible, an open-minded approach pays dividends.

Roman authors such as Cicero and Livy perceived all inhabitants of Sicily alike—whether from originally Greek cities such as Syracuse and Catana or non-Greek ones such as Centuripae and Entella—as *Siculi*. Diodorus Siculus, a Sicilian from Agyrion, uses *Sikeliotai* in exactly the same way; this is strikingly different from Thucydides's use of that term, which he applies to the Greeks of Sicily alone.[55] Diodorus describes how the originally "barbarian" natives came to be called Sikeliotai after they learned the Greek language and customs (5.6.5). Indeed, these processes of cultural change can be traced archaeologically back into the Archaic period.[56] By the first century BCE, the

---

52. For Sicily, see De Angelis 2003; Hall 2004.

53. De Angelis 1998; De Angelis 2016, 4–25; Smith 2011; Urquhart 2014a; Urquhart 2020; cf. the role of conflict between Greeks in the creation of Achaean identity (chapter 2), as well as Quinn's (2018) striking analysis of Phoenician identity in modern nationalisms and its impact on scholarly perceptions of Phoenicians.

54. E.g., Pace 1935–1949; for discussion, see De Angelis 2016, 14–16; De Angelis 2020b; and above all Ceserani 2012.

55. In other passages, Diodorus uses *Sikeloi* and *Sikeliotai* interchangeably, as do epigraphic sources: Prag 2013.

56. As Willi (2008, 17–18) points out, the process could not have been as simple as Diodorus presents it. An enormous bibliography has developed around these issues, of which I can cite only a small selection: Albanese Procelli 2003; De Angelis 2003; Antonaccio 2004; Cusumano 2009; Giangiulio 2010; Hodos 2010; Ampolo 2012; Spatafora 2013; Shepherd 2014; Frasca 2015; Baitinger and Hodos 2016; Malkin 2017.

distinction between Greeks and non-Greeks in Sicily had been erased. How did this situation arise? How far back can the blurring of this boundary be traced?

Demeter and Kore might provide a way into this question. As we saw above, the myths that relate Demeter and Kore to Sicilian identity include a striking emphasis on Enna, a non-Greek community, as one of the sites of the rape of Kore and as the *omphalos* of Sicily as a whole.[57] Although those literary sources were written much later by Greeks, we should not assume that the cult did not exist earlier or that only Greeks worshipped the goddesses there. Rather, the mid-fifth-century coin discussed above implies not only that the cult was at least that old but also that it mattered to the people of Enna themselves. We are dealing either with a Greek cult that was adopted locally or with a native deity of fertility and vegetation, who eventually came to be understood as Demeter and/or Persephone.[58] And Enna was far from the only indigenous community to worship similar deities; in fact, archaeological evidence from across Sicily suggests that the worship of Demeter and Kore was not limited to Greeks.

A large number of indigenous sites have produced votive deposits, often beginning in the second half of the sixth century, indicating worship of female divinities very similar to Demeter and Kore. For example, in western Sicily, a recently discovered extramural sanctuary at Entella has been interpreted as a Thesmophorion, on the basis of recovered material including lamps, *kernoi*, and figurines holding piglets; activity begins in the late sixth century and continues down to the third century.[59] In the center of the island, a cult site at Sabucina from the seventh century onward displays a fusion of Greek and indigenous architectural forms; among the ritual remains are pig bones, suggesting sacrifices similar to those for Demeter and Kore, and (in one corner of the site) typical terracotta votive figurines.[60] At Morgantina, excavations in the huge complex at San Francesco Bisconti, which originated in the second half of the sixth century and was arrayed on a series of terraces on a steep slope, have produced votive deposits and a number of early cult buildings.[61] Sculpture in the form of late Archaic antefixes (one made of imported Thasian

57. On Enna, see Dunbabin 1948, 136–137, 180–181; *IACP*, 195–196.

58. Holloway 1991, 86.

59. Spatafora 2008; Öhlinger 2015, 106–109.

60. Leighton 1999, 262–263; Fischer-Hansen 2002, 159–162; Öhlinger 2015, 76–85; but cf. the reservations of Hodos 2006, 125–129.

61. See esp. Hinz 1998, 124–127; Raffiotta 2007; Raffiotta 2008; Caruso 2013; Greco 2015.

marble) and the so-called Goddess of Morgantina demonstrates the level of investment that was put into this sanctuary.[62] In the mid-fifth century, when the Archaic settlement on the Cittadella hill was destroyed and refounded on the Serra Orlando ridge, San Francesco Bisconti remained in use and even expanded, indicating its importance to the community, while a new Sanctuary of the Chthonic Deities was established in the Classical agora.[63] These are only a few of the numerous indigenous sites that have produced similar finds.[64]

How to interpret this material is a difficult puzzle. Not much is securely known about native Sicilian religion, due to lack of good evidence, and moreover, it is often unclear which features of religious practice were truly indigenous and which had been adopted from Greeks. The indigenous peoples of Sicily had been deeply influenced by Greek culture over many centuries, as far back as the Bronze Age.[65] It is a red herring, in fact, to try to identify a stratum of indigenous religion uncontaminated by contact with Greeks; that contact had been influencing their religious traditions as early as we have evidence. We should therefore focus not on the origins of such practices but rather on how they fit into the religious systems of indigenous communities synchronically. Even if the worship of a pair of agricultural goddesses had not been part of their inherited traditions, they had certainly entered many native pantheons. It is, of course, entirely possible, if not likely, that the native populations had somewhat different ideas about the female divinities they were worshipping, based on their own traditions, from those of the Greeks. Nevertheless, regardless of the origins of these practices, Demeter and Kore (or similar deities by other names) were part of the religious life of communities such as Morgantina and Entella, in many cases from the mid-sixth century onward.

How would Greeks respond to this? Might they consider the natives who worshipped the two goddesses to be Sicilians just like themselves? Without direct testimony, it is difficult to know with certainty, and Greek perceptions of the natives surely varied over time and in different places and situations. Still, these shared cult practices—including, most important, the role of pigs as sacrificial victims and as attributes on terracotta figurines of the deity, as well

---

62. Marconi 2008; Marconi 2013.

63. Hinz 1998, 127–134; Sposito 2008.

64. See, e.g., Hinz 1998; Fischer-Hansen 2002; Patanè 2008; Patanè 2009; Spigo 2009, 70–72.

65. Brelich 1965, 34–35; Leighton 1999, 261–268; Anello 2008b, 15–17; Urquhart 2014b; Öhlinger 2015.

as the broader agricultural context—offer an important point of similarity between Greeks and non-Greeks in Sicily. Greeks who observed such practices at Entella in the late sixth century, for instance, would likely have concluded that the Entellans were worshipping Demeter and Kore. These similarities would initially have allowed agricultural goddesses to mediate between Greeks and natives, a process that would eventually facilitate the identification of native deities with Greek ones in a form of *interpretatio graeca*.[66] In this way, the worship of the two goddesses invited, but did not dictate, the inclusion of indigenous communities alongside Greeks within a pan-Sicilian identity and surely facilitated the eventual erasure of the ethnic boundaries between Greeks and non-Greeks in Sicily.

We should also look for the indigenous perspective. Did the people of Entella or Sabucina believe they were worshipping the same Demeter and Kore as the Greeks did, and did they ever take the further step of self-identifying as Sicilians? After all, it is one thing for Greeks to ascribe Sicilian identity to Sikels from the outside, which is what I have just been discussing, and quite another for Sikels to call themselves Sicilians. Unfortunately, the types of evidence available do not allow us to answer this question. We must admit frankly that we know little about what indigenous Sicilians thought on this or most other questions, and their voices must again remain silent. This discussion, in fact, raises more questions than it answers. Nevertheless, these questions are important to ask, because they illustrate the complexities and challenges of interpreting ancient identities. Cross-cultural relations in Sicily were far more complicated than a Greek versus barbarian politics of exclusion.

It is worth asking, finally, why Demeter and Kore were so popular in Sicily, and what this can tell us about the construction of identity. Earlier explanations for the goddesses' prominence—the survival of a pre-Greek religious substrate or the perpetuation of what was originally a Deinomenid family cult—no longer enjoy much support.[67] Another line of thinking sees the cult as a cultural reflex of economic factors: the breadbasket of the Mediterranean would naturally worship the goddesses of grain. Sicily was an exporter of grain to the Greek mainland as early as the Peloponnesian War, and it became one of Rome's main suppliers before being supplanted by Egypt in the Augustan age.

---

66. Cf. the Palici, a pair of Sikel deities who, I have argued elsewhere, function similarly in Aeschylus's *Aetneans*: Thatcher 2019.

67. Pre-Greek survival: e.g., Freeman 1891–1894, I.169–182; Manni 1963, 105–117; further references with critique at Urquhart 2014b, 1–2; cf. Brelich 1965; Jourdain-Annequin 2006. Deinomenids: Dunbabin 1948, 179–181; Manni 1963, 117–118; White 1964, 261–266. See overall Hinz 1998, 19–25.

In fact, it is to the Roman period that we owe the familiar image of Sicily as a monoculture, growing field after field of wheat and little else. There are, however, problems with this explanation. As Franco De Angelis has shown, this image is a mirage: Sicilian agriculture (and its economy more generally) was just as diverse as any other region of the Mediterranean, growing olives, vines, pulses, and numerous other crops; conversely, many regions elsewhere (such as Metapontion; see chapter 2) enjoyed a similarly high level of productivity.[68] Nevertheless, Sicilians' devotion to Demeter and Kore may indeed reflect their agricultural wealth. Despite the fact that on a purely objective economic level, Sicily scarcely differed from other regions, Sicilians nevertheless took pride in the fertility of their land and the abundance of their crops. We see here a clear example of the difference between emic and etic perceptions: objectively and from the outside, agriculture cannot distinguish Sicily from other lands in any meaningful way, but for the Sicilians themselves, this factor bore enormous subjective meaning and helped define their identity.

Sicilian Politics

We have now seen how Demeter and Kore helped articulate what made Sicilians distinctive and construct a sense of Sicilian-ness that was defined by geography and bolstered by shared myths and religious practices. This regional identity played an important and ongoing role in the island's politics, sometimes drawing on ideas of the two goddesses and sometimes not. Demeter and Kore helped create legitimacy for Deinomenid power, giving religious sanction to their regime. A number of leaders and tyrants followed their example over the subsequent centuries, using the two goddesses to unify the island against invasions from overseas. This brings in a second major criterion of Sicilian regional identity, which was oppositional in nature, contrasting Sicily with mainland Greeks, especially Athens. The two goddesses played a role here as well, but, as we will see at the end of the chapter, they are absent from the single clearest exposition of Sicilian identity, the speech of Hermocrates at Gela during Athens's First Sicilian Expedition. Regional identity thus emerges as a flexible and multivalent tool for Sicilian political figures, available to be used and reshaped according to the needs of the moment and also shaping their political choices and strategies.

---

68. De Angelis 2006; De Angelis 2016; cf. Walthall 2020.

Demeter and the Deinomenids

The Deinomenids were careful to foster the ideas of Sicily as the favored land of Demeter and Kore and of themselves as its protector. This can be seen most clearly in the opening of Bacchylides 3 (1–4):

ἀριστο[κ]άρπου Σικελίας κρέουσαν
Δ[ά]ματρα ἰοστέφανόν τε Κούραν
ὕμνει, γλυκύδωρε Κλεοῖ, θοάς τ' Ὀ-
　[λυμ]πιοδρόμους Ἱέρωνος ἵππ[ο]υς.

Of Demeter, ruling grain-rich Sicily,
and of Kore, crowned with violets,
sing, Klio, giver of sweetness, and of
the swift horses of Hieron, who run at Olympia.

The poet's inspired song brings together Hieron and his Olympic victory with the two goddesses and their island.[69] It is Demeter who "rules grain-rich Sicily," but the phrase evokes the extent of Hieron's rule as well, and the Muse is asked to sing equally of the two goddesses and Hieron's horses. Bacchylides thus articulates a triangular relationship between the tyrants, Demeter and Kore, and the island of Sicily, which drew on the preexisting patterns that we saw earlier but also reshaped them to promote the legitimacy of Deinomenid power.

The tyrants were instrumental in the initial articulation of Sicilian regional identity. It was once thought that they had actually spread the cult of Demeter and Kore across their domains from an original home in Gela, but as we saw above, new archaeological discoveries have definitively disproven this idea. Rather, much as we saw with other types of identity in chapter 3, they took advantage of the cult's preexisting ubiquity to heighten the unity of their domains and inscribe themselves within it. In fact, this element of their ideology—the relationship between Demeter and Kore, Sicilian regional identity, and the legitimacy of authority—would prove to be long-lasting, even after the fall of their regime.

The conception of Sicilians as a single unified people was especially advantageous to the Deinomenids, because, although they did not in reality control the entire island, they did sometimes present themselves as pan-Sicilian

---

69. Cairns 2010, 197–198; cf. broadly Lewis 2020, 108–116.

authorities. Pindar's *Olympian* 1, for example, describes Hieron's power as extending over all Sicily: "Hieron wields the scepter of righteousness in sheep-rich Sicily."[70] The phrase "in Sicily" does not necessarily imply a claim to rule all of Sicily, but, especially since Pindar did not have to mention Sicily at all, the word choice paints an idealized portrait of the island-wide scope within which Hieron's scepter holds sway.[71] Since the Deinomenid domains were large and diverse (even if not literally the entire island), building a sense of Sicilian regional identity helped legitimize the combination of so many cities within a single kingdom. Thus, the Deinomenids' promotion of the myths and cults of Demeter and Kore was designed primarily to help solidify and legitimize their power across a wide region, not only in Syracuse but across the rest of Sicily as well. Building on preexisting ideas, they spurred the artic-ulation of a new regional identity, a strategy that had both substantial success and, as we will see later, long-lasting consequences.[72]

Demeter and Kore were particularly useful deities for the Deinomenids because the family already boasted a special connection with them, due to the hereditary priesthood of "the chthonic deities" which they held in their home-town of Gela.[73] They apparently retained this priesthood when Gelon relocated to Syracuse in 485, and it became a key source of legitimate religious authority for them. Pindar's description of Hieron as priest suggests some of the possi-bilities (*Ol.* 6.93–96):

τὰν Ἱέρων καθαρῷ σκάπτῳ διέπων,
ἄρτια μηδόμενος, φοινικόπεζαν
ἀμφέπει Δάματρα λευκίπ-
    που τε θυγατρὸς ἑορτάν   95
καὶ Ζηνὸς Αἰτναίου κράτος.

Hieron, ruling [Syracuse] with a pure scepter,
devising straight counsels, honors crimson-footed Demeter

---

70. 1.12–13: θεμιστεῖον ὃς ἀμφέπει σκᾶπτον ἐν πολυμήλῳ / Σικελίᾳ; cf. Harrell 2002, 441–444; Morgan 2015, 231.

71. Morrison 2007, 59; *contra*, Gerber 1982, 34. Herodotus also twice describes Gelon as "ruler of Sicily," which may reflect contemporary thinking: 7.157.2 (ἄρχοντί . . . Σικελίης); 7.163.1 (Σικελίης τύραννος); but contrast 7.161.1 (βασιλεῦ Συρηκοσίων); cf. Luraghi 1994, 365–366; Sammartano 2015, 355–358; Lewis 2020, 97–104.

72. On the Deinomenids' religious politics, see White 1964; Privitera 1980; Scibona 2003.

73. Hdt. 7.153; on the priesthood, see esp. Lewis 2018.

and the festival of her daughter of the white horses,   95
and the might of Zeus Aetnaeus.

Pindar brings into focus Hieron's ideology of good rulership, deploying several traditional elements: the scepter symbolizing kingship, the Hesiodic focus on "straight" or just decision-making, and his piety toward Demeter and Kore.[74] The word *heortē*—the festival that Hieron honors—can include a great variety of activities, from processions to sacrifices to meals, and his usage surely implies active participation, perhaps as a "master of ceremonies" (to use Michael Flower's phrase) orchestrating the community's piety.[75] This would allow the citizens of Syracuse (and perhaps elsewhere) to see their ruler in action, honoring their gods, underscoring their religious authority and the legitimacy of their rule. The priesthood of Demeter and Kore is thus represented as a key aspect of the legitimacy of his political power, as he manages their festival and wields his authority in their service. Their priesthood thus gave the Deinomenids a crucial claim to religious authority that was broadly acceptable throughout Sicily and one that came to be tightly bound up with their political authority.

This same claim to religious authority is visible in the story of their ancestor, Telines, the first to hold the priesthood. According to Herodotus, during a *stasis* in the early days of Gela, one faction withdrew from the city to a place called Mactorion. Telines brought this faction back and resolved the *stasis* by displaying the sacred objects of the deities; he received the hereditary priesthood as a reward for his services to the community (Hdt. 7.153). Even if this story has been embellished or invented outright, as some have suggested,[76] its retelling in the fifth century played an important role in Deinomenid ideology by mapping out an integrative function for the chthonic deities and their priests. Demeter and Kore were goddesses who bound communities together, not only the factions at Gela centuries earlier but also the larger community of Sicilians under Deinomenid rule.

In the present, too, the Deinomenids were eager to proclaim their devotion to Demeter and Kore. Most of the myths discussed above derive from poetry composed at the Deinomenid court. Pindar, Bacchylides, and Simonides were key mediating figures in the creation and dissemination of the idea of a special

---

74. Adorjáni 2014, 293–298; Morgan 2015, 406–408; Lewis 2020, 109–112.

75. Flower 2015, 296; cf. Parker 2005, 178–183; Parker 2011, 48–57.

76. Especially since Telines's story mirrors that of Gelon's arrival in Syracuse (Hdt. 7.155.2): Luraghi 1994, 120–125; cf. Petruzzella 1999; Scibona 2003; Lewis 2018.

relationship between the two goddesses and the island of Sicily. Whether these poets created or merely amplified such myths, they had a substantial impact on the concept of Sicily as an island, and it was Hieron's sponsorship of poetry that had made this possible. The tyrant himself was thus tightly linked to this newly emphasized Sicilian mythology. Furthermore, these myths were, most likely, widely disseminated through poetic performances and reperformances, and perhaps in other media as well, inviting wide swaths of the Sicilian population to accept the tyrant's conception of the two goddesses as the chief deities of the island and adding to his legitimacy as the ruler of Sicily.

Demeter and Kore also took center stage in the Deinomenids' building program. According to Diodorus (11.26.7), Gelon built "noteworthy temples of Demeter and Kore" out of the spoils from the Battle of Himera, and he (or more likely Hieron) also planned to build a temple to Demeter in Aetna, but he died before he could complete it.[77] As for the earlier temples, Diodorus gives no indication of where they were located, but the sanctuary at Piazza della Vittoria in Syracuse has been identified as a likely possibility, while another may have been built at Himera.[78] Such temples represented a substantial investment in commemorating the victory and gave the people of Syracuse and other cities a permanent reminder of the Deinomenids' piety. Moreover, the choice of deities hints that Demeter and Kore were seen as playing an active role in defending their island against outside aggression, a pan-Sicilian interpretation that became extremely popular over the next few centuries.

Invaders from Overseas

Over the next few centuries of Sicilian history, in fact, the political role of Demeter and Kore came to be directed at outsiders and thereby strengthened a heretofore dormant angle of Sicilian identity: opposition to others. Sicily's protective deities were believed to have intervened on several occasions when

---

77. 11.26.7: ὁ Γέλων ἐκ μὲν τῶν λαφύρων κατεσκεύασε ναοὺς ἀξιολόγους Δήμητρος καὶ Κόρης . . . ἐπεβάλετο δὲ ὕστερον καὶ κατὰ τὴν Αἴτνην κατασκευάζειν νεὼν Δήμητρος ἐννηὼς δὲ οὔσης τούτον μὲν οὐ συνετέλεσε, μεσολαβηθεὶς τὸν βίον ὑπὸ τῆς πεπρωμένης. It is widely suspected that Gelon's name is a mistake for Hieron's, since Gelon died before the colony at Aetna was founded.

78. The identification was made by the excavator: Voza 1976–1977, 553–560; Voza 1980–1981, 680–684; adopted by Gras 1990; Mafodda 1996, 92–95; Morgan 2015, 46; but caution is urged by Hinz 1998, 102–107; Polacco 1986; Luraghi 1994, 318.

the island was threatened with outside invasion.[79] For example, Timaeus (in a startling twist for those familiar with Thucydides) ascribed the Athenian defeat in 413 to divine intervention. Plutarch records that he wrote that "it was fitting that Heracles should aid the Syracusans, for the sake of Kore, through whom he captured Cerberus."[80] According to Timaeus, while Heracles (also an important hero in Sicily) was the agent of the Syracusan victory, Kore also played an important role as the instigator of his actions. For Plutarch, this is part of a larger critique of Timaeus's penchant for deploying divine machinery and mythological explanations, and some scholars have suggested that for Timaeus, this was more a literary game than a genuine Sicilian local tradition.[81] Still, this claim is no stranger than those attested for the Persian Wars, in which Demeter, Boreas, Pan, and numerous heroes aided the Greek cause, and suggests instead that the defeat of Athens had itself become mythologized. For Sicilians, Kore acted to protect her own island, and they owed their continued freedom in part to her.

Soon afterward, Syracuse became embroiled in a lengthy series of wars with Carthage, which lasted for years with seesawing fortunes (see chapter 3). The new tyrant, Dionysius, sacked the Phoenician colony of Motya in far western Sicily in 397, but in the very next year, a Carthaginian counterattack under Himilco reached Syracuse itself, placing the city under siege and capturing the Achradina quarter of the city.[82] Himilco's troops plundered a temple of Demeter and Kore (possibly the one at Piazza della Vittoria); soon afterward, a plague broke out, and the siege failed. Diodorus concludes that "he quickly paid a price worthy of his impiety toward the divinity."[83] Although Diodorus also reports mundane factors behind the plague (such as the swamp known as Lysimelea),[84] he insists that the root cause was the vengeance of the goddesses. While his interpretation certainly draws on broader historiographical patterns

---

79. White 1964, 266–269; Kowalzig 2008, 138–139; for Demeter's political-military role more broadly, see Boedeker 2007.

80. F102 = Plut. *Nic.* 1.1.3: ἔτι δ' εἰκὸς εἶναι τὸν Ἡρακλέα τοῖς μὲν Συρακουσίοις βοηθεῖν διὰ τὴν Κόρην, παρ' ἧς ἔλαβε τὸν Κέρβερον. Cf. Champion 2010 ad loc.; Baron 2013, 191–192; Lewis 2020, 93.

81. Schepens 1994; Baron 2013, 191–192.

82. On the fourth-century wars with Carthage, see Stroheker 1958, 58–85; Caven 1990, 88–123; Lewis 1994; Hoyos 2010, 149–177; De Vincenzo 2019; and here in chapter 3.

83. Diod. 14.63.1–2, 70.4, 77.5; quote from 14.63.1: ταχὺ τῆς εἰς τὸ θεῖον ἀσεβείας ἀξίαν ὑπέσχε τιμωρίαν.

84. Diod. 14.70.4–6; cf. Villard 1994.

of divine retribution, its specific instantiation here is distinctively Sicilian, as it is the island's two goddesses who protect Sicily against the invader from overseas. Even more interesting, Diodorus reports that the Carthaginians propitiated Demeter and Kore by building them a temple in Carthage. The Carthaginians at this time were amassing a large empire in western and central Sicily, and recognizing the cults of their new subjects may have been a step toward reconciling the Sicilians with their power.[85]

Half a century later, however, Sicily had fallen on hard times, and the Corinthian general Timoleon was invited to come to Sicily and put things right, especially by fighting Carthage. According to Plutarch, the priestesses of Demeter and Kore at Corinth had dreamed that the goddesses appeared to them and said they would be going to Sicily with Timoleon; the Corinthians who were outfitting his ship then named it the *Demeter and Kore*.[86] While he was on the voyage, moreover, a miraculous light appeared in the sky. Plutarch (*Tim.* 8.6–8) writes:

λαμπὰς ἀρθεῖσα ταῖς μυστικαῖς ἐμφερὴς . . . κατέσκηψεν. οἱ δὲ μάντεις τὸ φάσμα τοῖς ὀνείρασι τῶν ἱερειῶν μαρτυρεῖν ἀπεφαίνοντο καὶ τὰς θεὰς συνεφαπτομένας τῆς στρατείας προφαίνειν ἐξ οὐρανοῦ τὸ σέλας· εἶναι γὰρ ἱερὰν τῆς Κόρης τὴν Σικελίαν, ἐπεὶ καὶ τὰ περὶ τὴν ἁρπαγὴν αὐτόθι μυθολογοῦσι γενέσθαι, καὶ τὴν νῆσον ἐν τοῖς γάμοις ἀνακαλυπτήριον αὐτῇ δοθῆναι.

a torch, resembling the ones used in the Mysteries, lifted itself on high . . . and rushed down. The seers declared that the apparition bore witness to the dreams of the priestesses, and that the goddesses were taking part in the expedition and showing forth a flame from the sky; for Sicily, they said, was sacred to Kore, since mythology makes it the scene of her rape; and the island was given to her as a wedding present.

This scene of divine epiphany shows just how closely Timoleon aligned himself with preexisting idea of Sicilian identity. The light in the sky (perhaps a comet or meteor) is interpreted as a torch, a symbol of Demeter and Kore, and more specifically as one of the torches used by *mystai* of Demeter, rooting it firmly in cultic practice. Moreover, according to Plutarch, the *manteis* linked

---

85. Diod. 14.77.5; Xella 1969; Picard 1994, 376–377; Hoyos 2010, 96–97. On Carthaginian imperialism in Sicily, see Ameling 2011.

86. Plut. *Tim.* 8. Diod. 16.66.3–5 is similar in broad outline but differs in details; cf. Sjöqvist 1958; Talbert 1974, 32; Melita Pappalardo 1996, 265–267; Bearzot 2008.

the epiphany with Sicilian myths of the rape of Kore and her special care for the island, the cornerstones of Sicilian regional identity. Thus, the story clearly represents Timoleon's claim to be acting with the support of the two goddesses on behalf of an island whose local needs and identities he understood and respected. Later, after his victory over Carthage at the River Crimisus in c. 339, coins struck by a number of Sicilian cities commemorated the goddesses' support for Timoleon with coins that displayed a torch between two ears of grain.[87] Although Timoleon could easily have been seen as an outside invader himself, by co-opting the island's goddesses, he presented himself as a Sicilian fighting on behalf of the island against the Carthaginian outsiders.

The next major tyrant, Agathocles (317–289) took the fight against Carthage to Africa. When he landed in Carthaginian territory in 310, according to Diodorus, he burned his ships, ostentatiously declaring that they were a sacrifice to Demeter and Kore.[88] Although Agathocles was obviously taking the offensive and leaving Sicily, by deploying this familiar symbolic imagery, he nonetheless framed his invasion of Africa as a war in defense of his island. The immediate objective was to attack Carthage, but his invocation of the goddesses and his self-presentation as their priest, much like the case of Deinomenids, highlighted his long-term goal of protecting Sicily. In a separate development, Agathocles also minted coins that showed a head of Persephone with dolphins on the obverse, while the reverse offered a bull. Some scholars have suggested that this combination specifically references the sacrifice at Kyane, discussed above, where a bull was thrown into the spring for Persephone.[89] Although this cannot be taken as definite, it is highly suggestive. Other coins even included the inscription ΚΟΡΑΣ, ensuring that no mistake could be made: this was the city and island of Kore.

There is even some tantalizing, if limited, evidence that Demeter played a role in the First Sicilian Slave War in the 130s BCE. Eunus, a Syrian slave held at Enna who led the revolt, seized that city as an ideologically significant headquarters and minted bronze coins with a veiled image of Demeter on the obverse. Peter Morton, among others, has argued that this represents a coherent attempt to capitalize on preexisting Sicilian ideology and to portray his rebellion not as a slave uprising but rather as a quasi-nationalist act of resistance against Rome that sought to gain support among the free population of

---

87. White 1964, 267; cf. Head 1911, 126; Borba Florenzano 2005, 18–19.

88. Diod. 20.7; White 1964, 267–268; Kowalzig 2008, 139. On this campaign, see Meister 1984, 393–400.

89. Kraay and Hirmer 1966, 293; Rutter 1997, 172–173; Borba Florenzano 2005, 20–21.

Sicily as well.[90] If we accept this line of argument, it suggests that the conception of Sicilian identity outlined in this section remained relevant far beyond the Roman conquest.

Most of these examples of the political use of Demeter and Kore (all except Eunus, in fact) have been collected before, especially by Donald White (1964), but one point deserves further emphasis. They all appear at historical moments when Sicily was threatened by invaders from outside the island, whether Athens or Carthage, and thus when Sicily's island nature became particularly salient. The way politicians exploited such situations thus demonstrates the close link between the island's natural boundary, which defines its identity, and the goddesses who reinforce that identity.

Demeter's Favorites

This articulation of identity through opposition to those from overseas distinguished Sicilians from other Greeks in the cultural sphere as well. Demeter and Kore play their role here, too. While Sicilians claimed that their island was the site of the rape of Persephone and that their ancestors were the first to receive Demeter's gift of grain, others—especially the Athenians—claimed those honors for themselves. These competing claims took shape in a broader context of rivalry, both political and cultural, between Sicily and mainland Greece, especially Athens, which in the last decades of the fifth century erupted into war.

Demeter and Kore were, of course, worshipped by Greeks everywhere, from Cyrene to Cyzicus to Corinth, but one site surpassed them all in prestige and political significance: Eleusis. In the *Homeric Hymn to Demeter*, the goddess stops there in her wandering after Hades snatched her daughter, and it is the kings of Eleusis who receive special honors from the goddess, especially knowledge of the Mysteries (473–479). After Eleusis came under the control of the Athenian *polis*, the Athenians claimed a special status as the protector of this shrine.[91] This tight bond between Athens, Eleusis, and Demeter stood among the core aspects of Athenian self-presentation through the fifth

90. Morton 2012; cf. Manganaro 1982; Brennan 1993, 156–157; on the revolt more broadly, see Bradley 1989, 46–65. For the coins, see Calciati 1987, 237. I thank Dominic Machado for pointing me in this direction.

91. On the original relationship between Athens and Eleusis, see Richardson 1974, 5–11; Foley 1994, 169–175.

and fourth centuries and was enacted annually in the sacred procession from Athens to Eleusis that opened the celebration of the Mysteries.[92]

It is rather unsurprising, then, that Athens laid claim to being the site of the rape of Persephone. The Orphic Hymns (usually thought to incorporate fifth-century Eleusinian material) link the rape closely to the topography of the Eleusinian sanctuary, while Phanodemus, an Atthidographer writing in the mid-fourth century, placed it somewhere in Attica.[93] Sicilians, as we have seen, claimed that honor as well. From a Sicilian perspective, although at least fifteen other localizations are known,[94] Eleusis's worldwide prominence made this one stand out as a rival. Whether the Athenians meant it this way or not, their claims represented a challenge to Sicily's prestige.

The Athenians also claimed that they had been the first to receive Demeter's gift and then spread it to the rest of the world. This primacy was a strong source of Athenian pride in their past: if they had discovered agriculture, they had essentially invented civilization. Isocrates, for instance, declared to the panhellenic audience of the *Panegyricus* that the Athenians were "not only so beloved by the gods but also so benevolent to mankind that, having gained power over such great good things [i.e., both the Mysteries and grain itself], they did not begrudge them to others but shared with everyone what they had received."[95] For Isocrates, the gift of grain is inextricably linked with the establishment of the Eleusinian Mysteries, itself an Athenian institution. The invention of agriculture is made to serve the orator's goal of justifying Athenian leadership in Greece (20), alongside other familiar elements of Athenian greatness such as autochthony (23–25) and victory in the Persian Wars (85–98). Since Athens has made such a great contribution to civilization, Isocrates suggests, the rest of the world owes Athens a debt of loyalty.

Long before Isocrates, however, the figure of Triptolemus, who had spread knowledge of agriculture throughout the world, was used to articulate Athens's imperial ambitions. He is a popular figure on Attic black-figure and especially red-figure vases, typically depicted setting out for his mission to bring Demeter's gift to the world. The Great Eleusinian Relief, often dated

---

92. Richardson 1974, 194–196; Matheson 1994, 368–372; Clinton 1994.

93. Phanodemus (*FGrH* 325) F27; *Hymn. Orph.* 18.11–15; for further sources, see Richardson 1974, 150.

94. Richardson 1974, 148–150.

95. *Paneg.* 28–29: οὕτως ἡ πόλις ἡμῶν οὐ μόνον θεοφιλῶς, ἀλλὰ καὶ φιλανθρώπως ἔσχεν, ὥστε κυρία γενομένη τοσούτων ἀγαθῶν οὐκ ἐφθόνησεν τοῖς ἄλλοις, ἀλλ' ὧν ἔλαβεν ἅπασιν μετέδωκεν. Cf. Plato *Menex.* 237e–238a; Dem. 60.5; Xen. *Hell.* 6.3.6.

to c. 430, may depict him along with Demeter and Persephone, the so-called Eleusinian Triad.[96] From at least the late sixth century, he had a temple in the City Eleusinion, with a large cult statue, and he received first fruits at Eleusis, alongside Demeter, from both Athenians and allies.[97] His story was dramatized in Sophocles's *Triptolemus*, which won first prize in 468.[98] In a number of media, then, the Athenians proudly declared their claims on this matter, which would not have been lost on outside observers. The figure of Triptolemus symbolized the primacy of Athens in the invention of agriculture, which for the Greeks was one of the hallmarks of civilization, and secured a place for Athens as the most civilized city in the world.

Sicilian myth sharply challenged these Athenian claims, boasting that the Sicilians were the first of mankind to receive the gift of grain from Demeter.[99] Diodorus's account, for instance, promotes their primacy in agriculture over Athens specifically: "Since the Athenians had welcomed the goddess most benevolently, the produce of wheat was given to them first after the Sikeliotai."[100] Other peoples then received grain from the Athenians, but Sicily had it first. Cicero, too, distinguishes between the Athenians, to whom Demeter "brought" grain, and Sicily, where grain was "discovered."[101] The latter region, the orator claims, deserves much more respect and takes precedence over Eleusis. Both authors choose not to excise Athens's role entirely. Instead, they carefully insert Sicily into a position of priority: the Sicilians were the first to receive Demeter's gift, and the Athenians followed. The explicit contrast reminds the reader of Athens's rival claim, enhancing the specificity of the opposition.

---

96. Raubitschek and Raubitschek 1982; Schwarz 1987; Shapiro 1989, 67–83; Matheson 1994; cf. Clinton 1992, 39–55, who points out that the relief does not match well with the iconography of Triptolemus elsewhere and prefers to identify the youthful figure as Ploutos.

97. City Eleusinion: Paus. 1.14.1; Miles 1998, 37–58. First fruits: ML 73.

98. Vanotti 1979, 97–103; Zacharia 2003b, 64–66; Kowalzig 2008, 145–147.

99. Diod. 5.2.4–5, 4.3–5; Cic. *Verr.* 2.4.106, 108. The chronology of these stories, and hence whether Athenians were responding to Sicilians or the reverse, is unclear. The Deinomenid period, a fertile one for Sicilian myth-making and contemporary with the early phases of the Athenian Empire, seems most likely, although the fourth century is also a possibility. Probably, we should envision a process of co-development, in which both communities were aware of the other's claims and felt they had something to gain from pressing their claims with revamped myths.

100. 5.4.4: φιλανθρωπότατα δὲ τῶν Ἀθηναίων ὑποδεξαμένων τὴν θεόν, πρώτοις τούτοις μετὰ τοὺς Σικελιώτας δωρήσασθαι τὸν τῶν πυρῶν καρπόν.

101. *Verr.* 2.4.108: etenim si Atheniensium sacra summa cupiditate expetuntur, ad quos Ceres in illo errore venisse dicitur frugesque attulisse, quantam esse religionem convenit eorum apud quos eam natam esse et fruges invenisse constat?

Sicily, not Athens, emerges as the founder of civilization and the benefactor of the world.

This confrontation between Athenian and Sicilian claims even took tangible form at Enna, where Cicero describes a pair of large statues depicting Demeter and, remarkably, Triptolemus (*Verr.* 2.4.110):

> ante aedem Cereris in aperto ac propatulo loco signa duo sunt, Cereris unum, alterum Triptolemi, pulcherrima ac perampla. pulchritudo periculo, amplitudo saluti fuit, quod eorum demolitio atque asportatio perdifficilis videbatur. insistebat in manu Cereris dextra grande simulacrum pulcherrime factum Victoriae; hoc iste e signo Cereris avellendum asportandumque curavit.

> In front of the temple of Demeter, in an open and uncovered place, there are two statues, one of Demeter and one of Triptolemus, very beautiful and very large. Their beauty was their danger, but their size was their salvation, because taking them down and carrying them away seemed very difficult. But a very beautifully made statue of Victory stood on the right hand of Demeter, and that man saw to it that this was torn away from the statue of Demeter and carried off.

Since the statues stood in a plaza in front of the temple, they were likely dedications, of monumental size, and they appear to have formed a pair. The Triptolemus statue, moreover, was depicted on bronze coins of Enna that date between the mid-fourth and late third centuries, so the pair of dedications must predate them. Sven Schipporeit has suggested a date in the fourth century, on the basis of the statue's pose and his interpretation of the likely political context, and this is probably the best we can do.[102]

The appearance of such a quintessentially Athenian hero in Sicily is striking, especially since no other large-scale depiction of Triptolemus is known from outside Attica until the Roman period.[103] The decision, whether by one or more wealthy citizens of Enna, by Syracusans, or even by the tyrant Dionysius I himself, to dedicate a monumental statue of Triptolemus must bear particular significance. Some scholars have suggested that a specifically Eleusinian-style mystery cult existed at Enna, which might have invited a depiction of Triptolemus. Yet there is no real evidence to support this theory,

---

102. Schipporeit 2008; cf. Calciati 1987, 229–240; Giuliano 1993; Manganaro Perrone 2007, 38–39.

103. Schwarz 1987; Schipporeit 2008, 44.

and in particular, if Verres had violated the secrets of the Mysteries, Cicero would have mentioned this.[104] More likely, Enna's choice of Triptolemus for its coins suggests that he bore some importance for its civic ideology. While the particular iconography of the coins may have been suggested by the statue, the choice to depict Triptolemus at all must have been based on the mythical significance of the hero himself. This significance, I suggest, lies precisely in his Athenian heritage: the dedication should be understood as an attempt to claim for Sicily not only Triptolemus himself but also Athens's great service to the world.

Meanwhile, the Demeter statue offers another Athenian connection, via the figure of Victory that stood on Demeter's right hand. Such placement of a Victory is rare in Greek sculpture. Only two parallels can be adduced, both by Pheidias: the Zeus at Olympia and the Athena Parthenos in the Parthenon.[105] The Demeter statue at Enna seems to be quoting one or both of those and thereby links Enna and Sicily to a network of major Greek cultural centers. Cicero does not specify whether the Demeter was seated or standing, but a standing Demeter would pair more easily with the Triptolemus, which coins show was standing. This would draw the statue closer to the standing Athena Parthenos than the seated Zeus. Pheidias's Athena Parthenos was a widely recognizable image, reproduced on vase paintings already in the fifth century, which suggests that knowledge of the Athenian statue could easily have spread to Sicily.[106] However, copies of the statue were always presented as Athena. Appropriating the Pheidian iconography but using it to represent Demeter suggests a subtler message: that the patron goddess of Sicily was the equal of the Athenian deity. Situating statues of both Demeter and Triptolemus in one of the most sacred Demeter sanctuaries in Sicily—the *omphalos*, the religious center of the island—stood as a challenge to Athenian primacy in the worship of Demeter. Viewed in light of the myths discussed above and the island-wide significance of Demeter, the statues seem to define a community of all Sicilians through opposition to Athens.

This competition in the worship of Demeter did not develop in a vacuum. Rather, it represented one key part of a much larger climate of competition and rivalry between Sicilians and mainland Greeks, which can be traced (in somewhat looser form) as far back as the Deinomenids. In particular, the memory of the Persian Wars was hotly contested, as Gelon and Hieron laid

104. Schipporeit 2008, 43; *contra*, Brelich 1965, 50–51; Hinz 1998, 122.

105. Cf. Carpenter 1953.

106. Gaifman 2006.

claim to a level of glory equal to that of the mainland Greeks for their victories at Himera in 480 and Cumae in 474. A famous passage of Pindar's *Pythian* 1 (75–80) makes this comparison explicit:

ἀρέομαι 75
πὰρ μὲν Σαλαμῖνος Ἀθαναίων χάριν
μισθόν, ἐν Σπάρτᾳ δ' <ἀπὸ> τᾶν πρὸ Κιθαιρῶ-
  νος μαχᾶν,
ταῖσι Μήδειοι κάμον ἀγκυλότοξοι,
παρ<ὰ> δὲ τὰν εὔυδρον ἀκτὰν
  Ἱμέρα παίδεσσιν ὕμνον Δεινομέν<εο>ς τελέσαις,
τὸν ἐδέξαντ' ἀμφ' ἀρετᾷ, πολεμίων ἀνδρῶν καμόντων. 80

From Salamis I will earn the Athenians' thanks as my reward 75
and in Sparta from the battle before Cithaeron,
in which the Medes who shoot with curved bows were distressed,
and by the well-watered bank of Himera
when I have completed a song for the sons of Deinomenes,
which they received because of their courage when their enemies
  suffered. 80

We have already seen, in chapter 3, how Pindar deploys the rhetoric of Greek identity in praise of Hieron, in language very similar to that used in mainland Greece. What we must add to the analysis here is the sense of competitive prestige. At the same historical moment when Athens and others were claiming to have freed Greece from slavery, Pindar appropriates the same glory for Hieron and for Sicily. The significant juxtaposition of Salamis, Plataea, and Himera, with the last as a capstone for the trio, suggests that the glory of Syracuse equals or even surpasses that of Athens and Sparta.

The Deinomenid dedications at Delphi expressed the same viewpoint. Soon after the Persian Wars, Delphi became the site of a series of competitive dedications by a variety of Greek cities, alliances, and rulers.[107] On the terrace in front of the Temple of Apollo, the Serpent Column—part of a larger dedication commemorating the Battle of Plataea—and the bronze statue of Apollo that commemorated Salamis were both prominent, along with individual dedications celebrating the *arete* of Aegina, Epidaurus, Carystus, and others. The golden tripod topped by a statue of Nike, which Gelon dedicated

---

107. Harrell 2006; Scott 2010, 81–91; Morgan 2015, 32–37; Yates 2019.

in honor of Himera, does not merely proclaim the glory of his victory; it spatially confronts the other Persian War dedications located nearby, claiming its place among them. Hieron's later additions to the same monument show an ongoing interest in this site and this message.[108] Herodotus also reports a Sicilian tradition that had developed within a few decades, according to which the Battle of Himera occurred on the same day as Salamis.[109] This synchronization expressed the Sicilians' conviction that their victory was equally as important and equally as glorious as that of Athens. A later tradition heightened this glory even further by synchronizing Himera instead with Thermopylae, implying that the Sicilians defeated their barbarian invaders earlier than the mainland Greeks.[110]

The sense of competition seen in the memory of Himera is much looser than that expressed in the dueling claims to Demeter. The extent to which Sicily as a whole represents one pole of the opposition, rather than Syracuse or the Deinomenids individually, is not nearly as clear, and there is quite a bit of slippage between them. And on the opposite side, Athens is prominent among the victors in mainland Greece, but it is only one of many. Nevertheless, this material provides an important precursor to the more specifically Sicilian ideologies we saw above. The climate of competition that is visible in the 470s helped shape Sicilian self-conceptions, encouraging Sicilians to take pride in their glorious achievements and separateness from mainland Greece.

Developments later in the fifth century, however, focused Sicilian attention on Athens in particular. The two Athenian expeditions to Sicily during the Peloponnesian War represented the culmination of a long-standing interest in Sicily and in the West more generally from the early fifth century onward. This interest can be traced as far back as the Persian Wars but picks up speed with the development of a network of friendships and alliances in the latter part of the fifth century, such as the alliances with Rhegium and Leontini in 434/3 and Segesta in (probably) 418.[111] The Athenians perceived that they had vital imperial interests in the West and took steps to cultivate

---

108. Morgan 2015, 40–42.

109. 7.166.1; cf. Gauthier 1966; Harrell 2006; Morgan 2015, 37–38.

110. Diod. 11.24.1, perhaps relying on Timaeus: Asheri 1992b, 58–60; Green 2006, 77–79.

111. Persian Wars: Hdt. 8.62.2; cf. Raviola 1986; Bowie 2007, 150. Alliances: ML 37, 63–64. For further discussion and evidence, see the convenient summary of Hornblower, CT III.5–6; cf. Smith 2003, 89–116; Cataldi 2007; Mele 2007; Mattaliano 2010; Hornblower 2011, 169–172; Péré-Noguès 2016.

them; this cannot have gone unnoticed by Sicilians at the time. On a cultural level, too, plays such as Sophocles's *Triptolemus* in 468 interpreted these imperial ambitions through the lens of myth, by sending the Athenian hero to the West, making him a benefactor to the peoples there, and thus placing Athens in a position of political and cultural superiority over the Sicilian and Italian Greeks.[112] In fact, the fifth-century idea of Athens as "the education of Hellas," a hub of Greek culture, itself represented a challenge to Sicilians. Sicily had long been a literary center, beginning with sixth-century poets such as Ibycus and Stesichorus; through Hieron's and Theron's sponsorship of Pindar, Bacchylides, Simonides, and Aeschylus; and continuing with the fifth-century luminaries Epicharmus, Empedocles, and Gorgias. The athletic achievements of Hieron and his circle, as well as those of the other tyrannical families, also suggest an attempt to claim cultural glory for Sicily on the panhellenic stage.

All of this led, I suggest, to a broader sense of rivalry and competitive emulation on both cultural and political levels. Of course, Sicilian responses to Athens's imperial ambitions undoubtedly varied. The people of Leontini, for instance, likely saw Athens as an important counterbalance to Syracusan power. Still, the rising power of Athens and particularly Athenian interest in gaining political influence in the West must have been noted with concern elsewhere, particularly in Syracuse, and in times of crisis, the Syracusan perspective came to dominate.

Not all of the ways in which Sicilians claimed a distinctive status as Demeter's most favored worshippers directly challenged specific Athenian claims. Sicilians saw themselves as set apart due to their piety toward Demeter and Kore, whether by comparison with Athens or not. But in setting Athenian and Sicilian claims side by side, another facet of Sicilian identity emerges. By presenting their whole island as the possession of Demeter and Kore, Sicilians reinforced the geographic predication of their regional identity through a shared culture. By contrasting their uniquely deep relationship with the two goddesses with that of Athens, they established a difference between themselves and others, a classic case of the creation of identity through opposition. This version of Sicilian identity arrived on the political stage during the Peloponnesian War.

---

112. Vanotti 1979; Zacharia 2003b; Kowalzig 2008, 145–149; cf. broadly Smith 2003, 116–135, and compare the discussion of Euripides's *Captive Melanippe* in chapter 2.

Hermocrates and the Sikeliotai

The speech Thucydides attributes to the Syracusan politician Hermocrates at Gela (4.59–64) presents the most explicit surviving articulation of Sicily's island identity in its fully developed form. It also gives us the earliest attestation of the collective name Sikeliotai, and as a result, this event, in the year 424, has sometimes represented the starting point for exploration of Sicilian identity.[113] It should be clear by now that this ignores important antecedents. Instead, I think, we should see the speech as a significant turning point in the development of Sicilian identity, one that built on the preexisting elements we have seen already, transforming and solidifying them in the face of Athenian invasion. Hermocrates's speech is also the earliest known articulation of Sicilian identity with no role whatsoever for Demeter and Kore. This was not a permanent change, since we have seen above the role of the two goddesses in defending their island over the subsequent centuries. Instead, we should ascribe their absence to Thucydides, who generally ignores religious elements.[114] Still, his treatment suggests how Sicilian identity could stand alone, apart from the two goddesses: by contrasting Sicily with Athens.

As reported by the Athenian historian, Hermocrates's speech highlights a regional conception of Sicily not only as an island bounded by the sea but also as a community sharply contrasted with the overseas invaders from Athens. In 427, the Athenians sent a fleet of twenty ships (later reinforced by forty more) to Sicily; their mission was to assist Leontini, an Athenian ally whose perennial struggle with Syracuse had flared up.[115] This ongoing war had engulfed almost all the Greeks of Sicily, who were fighting in support of one side or the other in what Thucydides describes as mainly ethnic blocs: Dorians on one side, Chalcidians (a local term for Ionians) on the other (3.86). I discuss this theater of war and Thucydides's account of it in greater detail in chapter 5; here I focus on the end of the Athenian expedition and its consequences for Sicilian identity.

After three years, representatives of all the Sicilian Greek *poleis* met at Gela to hammer out a peace agreement among themselves. Thucydides offers a rendition of Hermocrates's speech, whose goal was to unite all the Sicilian

---

113. Antonaccio 2001 (a deservedly influential article); but cf. the reservations of Malkin 2011, 107–112; Sammartano 2015.

114. Cf., by contrast, Timaeus's report of divine involvement in the defeat of the second Athenian expedition in 413 (F102 and see above).

115. 3.86.1, 115.4. On the First Sicilian Expedition, see Westlake 1960; Bosworth 1992.

poleis in order to end the Athenian military presence on the island.[116] In order to accomplish that, the speech evokes a pan-Sicilian community of Sikeliotai, a name that appears here in its earliest attestation, which transcends ethnic and civic divisions. The Sikeliotai are particularly urged to ignore the difference between Dorians and Chalcidians, since both sides are equally in danger from Athens. Hermocrates's speech represents one of the clearest expositions of a sense of regional identity to survive from ancient Greece and also highlights a clear political opposition between Sicily and Athens that strengthened the preexisting sense of Sicilian separateness.

Carla Antonaccio has argued that the Conference of Gela presents an example of ethnogenesis, the creation of an ethnic group where there was none before. While the experience of Athenian invasion undoubtedly transformed Sicilians' perceptions of their identities, Sicilian identity had important antecedents, as we have seen. Moreover, it is also clear that the Sikeliotai as conceived by Hermocrates are not an ethnic group, since the speech does not use kinship, the primary criterion of ethnicity, to define them.[117] On the contrary, the concept of kinship or *syngeneia* is dismissed as irrelevant: shared Ionian ethnicity will not protect the Chalcidians from Athens (4.61.2–3), and Dorians and Chalcidians should not work only with their kinsmen (4.64.3). Perhaps unsurprisingly for a Thucydidean character, Hermocrates does not create a new mythical common ancestor for the Sikeliotai—a common procedure in documented cases of ethnogenesis, such as that of the Triphylians in the 360s[118]—but focuses instead on other criteria. Describing the Sikeliotai as an ethnic group would require broadening the definition of the term *ethnicity* so much that it would no longer be useful.

Instead, the Sikeliotai, as described by Thucydides, are defined by geography. Hermocrates points out that "taken all together, we are all of us neighbors, fellow dwellers in one land, in the midst of the sea, all called by the single name of Sikeliotai."[119] This striking formulation represents the rhetorical peak of the speech, near its conclusion. According to this formulation,

---

116. 4.58–65. I discuss my approach to Thucydides and his speeches in chapter 5. To preview briefly: Thucydides meant his speeches to serve as a form of historical analysis, so the arguments presented in them must reflect real historical phenomena. The historian, a well-informed observer of contemporary Sicily, would not have written a speech about Sicilian regional identity unless Sicilian regional identity actually did play an important role in the events under discussion.

117. Sammartano 2015, 267–271; *pace* Antonaccio 2001, 118–121; Fragoulaki 2013, 96–99. For my discussion of definitions of ethnicity, see chapter 1.

118. Nielsen 1997.

119. 4.64.3: τὸ δὲ ξύμπαν γείτονας ὄντας καὶ ξυνοίκους μιᾶς χώρας καὶ περιρρύτου καὶ ὄνομα ἓν κεκλημένους Σικελιώτας.

what unites the Sikeliotai is not common descent, shared culture, or anything else: instead, the essential similarity that binds them together is geographical; they are those who inhabit the island of Sicily, separated from other Greeks (especially the Athenians) by the boundary of the sea. This makes them fundamentally different both from sub-Hellenic ethnic groups such as Dorians and Chalcidians and from the panhellenic identity shared by all Greeks. Indeed, Sicilian regional identity cuts across both of these by including both Dorians and Chalcidians but excluding other Greeks, especially Athens.

This same geographical conception is also prominent elsewhere in the speech. Hermocrates refers to the audience as "inhabitants of Sicily," thereby drawing a tight link between the island and its people.[120] Meanwhile, his deployment of the collective group name Sikeliotai at 4.64.3 is emphatic—it also appears at the opening (4.59.1)—but the toponym *Sikelia*, which appears no fewer than six times, is even more prominent. This usage—referring to a place, not a group of people—encourages the listeners to think about their identities in geographical terms and in terms of unity. The phrase τὴν πᾶσαν Σικελίαν appears three times, focusing attention on Sicily as an entire unit, and forms of *koinos* appear in conjunction with the name three times, inviting reflection on the audience's common interests as Sicilians.[121]

Moreover, Hermocrates carefully places the Sikeliotai in opposition to the Athenian invaders. Of course, in this context, it is not surprising that Athens is identified as Sicily's main opponent, but what is interesting is how that opposition is defined: the Athenians are an enemy from overseas, and they threaten all of Sicily, not merely certain cities. Hermocrates emphasizes that Athens is a threat not only to the Dorians but also to the Chalcidians (4.61.2). Twice he describes the whole island of Sicily as "plotted against" (*epibouleumenēn*) and a third time uses the same verb to describe the inhabitants of Sicily (4.60.1, 64.5; 61.1). Equally important, Hermocrates draws a sharp distinction between war among various Sicilians, which is acceptable though not desirable, and war between Sicily and foreigners, in which all Sicilians must unite to drive out the invader (64.4–5). In his conception, the island of Sicily constitutes a closed system from which outsiders must be excluded.

Finally, Hermocrates's phrase "one land, in the midst of the sea" is also highly evocative, emphasizing the precise nature of the boundary between Sicily and Athens, since it is the Sicilians' island home that separates them

120. 4.61.1: τὴν Σικελίαν, ἧς γε οἱ ἔνοικοι ξύμπαντες μὲν ἐπιβουλευόμεθα.

121. *Sikelia* alone: 4.61.1, **61.3**, 64.5. *tēn pasan Sikelia*: 4.**59.1**, 60.1, **61.2**. Bolded instances also include a form of *koinos*. Cf. Connor 1984, 121–122.

from the Athenians. The notion of the sea as a natural and often divinely established boundary was deeply embedded in Greek thought (compare Herodotus and the Hellespont), and it serves here to emphasize the legitimacy of Sicilian separateness. The same idea is also picked up by Nicias, who is portrayed by Thucydides as an astute observer of Sicilian affairs. In his first speech opposing the Sicilian Expedition, he urges the Athenians to keep to the boundaries that divide the Sicilians from them, namely, the Ionian and Sicilian Seas.[122] Another point of contact between Nicias and Hermocrates is the word *allophylos*, which Hermocrates applies to the Athenian invaders (4.64.4). Although the word sometimes carries an ethnic connotation, it need not, and in this case, the speech has well prepared us to see the "foreign" nature of Athens as primarily geographical. Nicias, meanwhile, twice advises the Athenians not to get involved in a conflict with "foreigners" (*allophylois*).[123] The two statesmen agree: Athens and Sicily should stick to their maritime boundaries.

Sicilian regional identity had never before been so highly politicized, and it was undoubtedly transformed by the experience of foreign invasion in the 420s. Both the nature of the Athenians' threat as an enemy from overseas and their tacit goal of conquering the entire island strongly encouraged a sense of island unity. The invocation of Sicilian unity in the crisis of external invasion drastically increased the salience of this form of identity, tightly focused around a binary opposition between Athens and Sicily, with long-lasting consequences. Sicilian regional identity thus cut across familiar ethnic categories by separating the Sicilian Greeks from those of the mainland.

It is also worth comparing the implications of Syracuse's wars against Athens, discussed here and in chapter 5, with the wars against Carthage discussed in chapter 3. Syracuse fought Athens in Sicily off and on from 427 through 413 (and continued the war in the Aegean for several more years); Carthage's invasion of western Sicily commenced in 409. Despite the almost continuous nature of these wars, they are not often compared.[124] We saw in chapter 3 how war with Carthage led to renewed focus on Greek identity,

---

122. 6.13.1: ψηφίζεσθαι τοὺς μὲν Σικελιώτας οἷσπερ νῦν ὅροις χρωμένους πρὸς ἡμᾶς, οὐ μεμπτοῖς, τῷ τε Ἰονίῳ κόλπῳ παρὰ γῆν ἤν τις πλέῃ, καὶ τῷ Σικελικῷ διὰ πελάγους, τὰ αὑτῶν νεμομένους καθ' αὑτοὺς καὶ ξυμφέρεσθαι.

123. 6.9.1: ἀνδράσιν ἀλλοφύλοις πειθομένους πόλεμον οὐ προσήκοντα ἄρασθαι; 6.23.2: πόλιν τε νομίσαι χρὴ ἐν ἀλλοφύλοις καὶ πολεμίοις οἰκιοῦντας ἰέναι. The first of these instances is often thought to refer to non-Greek Segesta: Hornblower, *CT* ad loc.

124. This is perhaps because the Carthaginian wars are conceptualized as part of the fourth century, along with the reign of Dionysius.

which had not been prominent over the previous two decades. A war against a Greek enemy naturally discourages thinking about shared Greekness, whereas fighting non-Greeks encourages exactly that. Syracusans and other Sicilians thus experienced a rapid shift in the salience of these identities due to changing circumstances. We will see more examples of this rapid switch in chapter 5. Nevertheless, as we saw earlier in this chapter, Sicilian identity became prominent during various Carthaginian wars, a further reminder that even when circumstances pushed one type of identity to the fore, multiple identities were still available and potentially relevant.

Conclusion

I have not yet made much mention of the Phoenicians who lived in western Sicily.[125] In fact, there is little evidence to suggest that Phoenicians were ever included in any fully articulated conception of Sicilian identity. This strongly suggests that the geographic criterion of Sicilian identity (which, logically, would require the inclusion of Phoenicians who inhabited the island) was not applied mechanistically. Rather, this criterion interacted with a variety of other factors. The Phoenicians did not adopt Hellenic culture to nearly the same extent as indigenous Sicilians and may thus have been perceived as too different to cross that boundary.[126] Their close connection with Carthage may have led to a perception that the inhabitants of cities such as Motya and Panormus were not truly Sicilian islanders but merely an extension of the North African power. Finally, and perhaps most important, the memory of the Battle of Himera and, in the fourth century, ongoing Carthaginian rule over much of the island most likely conditioned Sicilian perceptions of Carthage to such an extent that co-identifying with them became impossible.

As a result, we should conclude that the geographical criterion of Sicilian identity was heavily inflected by other considerations. It was also mediated through two further mechanisms: articulating contrasts between Sicily and mainland Greece, especially Athens, and highlighting cultural similarities among Sicilians. Attention was drawn to Sicilian cultural achievements, presenting the island as a center of Greek culture equal to anything on the mainland and even as superior to Athens in some ways. The experience of

---

125. See broadly Whittaker 1974; Aubet 2001; Delgado and Ferrer 2007; Hoyos 2010, 149–177; De Vincenzo 2019.

126. On the other hand, Carthage did adopt the cult of Demeter and Kore in the fourth century (Diod. 14.77.5), and Greeks assimilated the Phoenician Melqart in western Sicily to Heracles: Malkin 2005a.

Athenian invasion in the late fifth century solidified this perception of opposition. Not all Sicilians felt exactly the same way—Leontini undoubtedly welcomed Athenian intervention, for instance—but Syracuse's status as an imperial power lent its perceptions great weight, and Sicilian identity often reflected its point of view. Meanwhile, even as Sicilians separated themselves from mainland Greece, cultural similarities—particularly religious ones—were bringing different Sicilians together. Demeter and Kore in particular acted as important contributors to Sicilian identity. Myths and cult practices worked together to articulate a sense of shared distinctiveness that all Sicilians could be proud of.

Similarities and differences such as these form the core of any identity; once they have been identified and deemed salient by community members, they begin to define the boundaries of that community. In the case of Sicilian identity, the Deinomenids played a key role in heightening the salience of Sicilian identity. Building on preexisting cultural similarities among Sicilians (especially the widespread worship of Demeter and Kore), Gelon and especially Hieron promoted a sense of pan-Sicilian unity within their domains in order to shore up their rule. This policy produced long-lasting effects, expanding the range of identities that could be perceived as potentially relevant by a wide range of Sicilians.

5

Shifting Identities in Thucydides's Sicily

THE SMALL SICILIAN *polis* of Camarina offers a striking and overlooked window into the dynamic relationship between identity and foreign relations in the late fifth century. In 427, after four years of war with Sparta, Athens was drawn into an ongoing large-scale conflict between Leontini and Syracuse. Thucydides (3.86) reports that the other Sicilian Greek communities had joined the fight, in most cases choosing sides according to their ethnic identities: the Dorians sided with Syracuse and the Chalcidians with Leontini. Camarina alone, though Dorian and a colony of Syracuse, chose instead to fight with the Chalcidians. They did so, most likely, because of their long-standing hatred of Syracuse (6.88.1), which, I suggest, had altered Camarina's sense of its *polis* identity. What is noteworthy, however, is that at this time, every Sicilian Greek community had made a major political decision on the basis of one of its collective identities—either ethnicity or *polis* identity.

The Athenians sent twenty ships in the so-called First Sicilian Expedition, and the war continued for three years with little effect. In 424, however, a peace conference, organized at Gela, brought together the same Sicilian communities. At this conference, the Syracusan general and statesman Hermocrates made a speech that, in Thucydides's rendering (4.59–64), attempted to unite all the Sicilian Greeks against the Athenians: "We are all of us neighbors, fellow dwellers in one land, in the midst of the sea, and all called by the same name of Sikeliotai" (4.64.3). Thus, in a passage we encountered in chapter 4, Hermocrates appealed to a different, pan-Sicilian identity that was fundamentally different from either ethnicity or civic identity. As a result of this speech, the various cities, including Camarina, did make peace with one another, forcing Athens to withdraw.

A decade later, however, the Athenians returned in the Great Sicilian Expedition. Both sides sought allies; Camarina wavered, and Hermocrates

The Politics of Identity in Greek Sicily and Southern Italy. Mark R. Thatcher, Oxford University Press. © Oxford University Press 2021. DOI: 10.1093/oso/9780197586440.003.0005

made a speech in Camarina's assembly to persuade them to join Syracuse. The Thucydidean version of this speech (6.76–80), far from appealing to Sicilian unity, was a vicious ethnic screed insisting that Camarina should ally with Syracuse as fellow Dorians against the hated Ionian invaders. Although Camarina at first remained neutral, the city did eventually send troops to aid Syracuse (7.33.1). Thus, in the space of only thirteen years, the single *polis* of Camarina made momentous political decisions in contexts where no fewer than three different types of identity were relevant (civic identity in 427, Sicilian identity in 424, and ethnicity in 414). Camarina's experience well demonstrates the crucial role played by multiple collective identities in interstate politics in Greek Sicily.

The speed with which the people of Camarina rethought their identities makes it unlikely that ethnogenesis or the articulation of entirely new identities is the explanation for Camarina's changing policies; such changes take place on a much lengthier timescale. Moreover, other evidence shows that all three identities had already been articulated long before 427. What changed instead was the relative salience of the various identities claimed by the Camarinaeans. When faced with a major political decision, the citizens of Camarina selected which of their various identities to consider most important on that occasion and viewed the decision they had to make through the lens of one identity, temporarily ignoring others. I argue in this chapter that the range of identities claimed by Sicilian communities shaped and conditioned their responses to the political challenges they faced and the decisions they made. While considerations of identity rarely, if ever, positively determined political outcomes, they did influence the way the people of Camarina thought about their decisions and how they responded to the various political, strategic, and economic arguments presented to them. As a result, Camarina's *polis* identity pointed it toward an anti-Syracusan alliance in 427, but by 414, other considerations, such as Hermocrates's rhetoric of Dorian unity, superseded that. In this new context, the Camarinaeans no longer considered their civic identity especially salient.

Exploring these issues depends, more than in the previous chapters, on a careful and critical reading of historiographical evidence, especially Thucydides. Like all ancient historians, Thucydides was not an anthropologist or a sociologist, seeking to convey precise and accurate information about the functioning of identity in Greek Sicily and Italy. Rather, he was a literary author with his own agenda, who deliberately skewed, manipulated, altered, and omitted information in support of his literary and interpretive goals. Indeed, as many scholars have pointed out, every item Thucydides gives us has been carefully chosen for a purpose, which produces distortion in our picture of historical events.[1] Important recent work has emphasized that among Thucydides's literary goals is an exploration of ethnicity and identity, whether in the form of kinship diplomacy, colonial relationships, or his portraits of "the city on the move" in the Sicilian narrative and the "city at Samos" in Book 8.[2] The Sicilian narrative in particular is framed by two texts, the Sicilian Archaeology (6.2–5) and the Catalogue of Allies (7.57–58), which focus on colonial and kinship relations and thereby articulate an image of Athens's invasion as a colonial expedition.[3] His account contains much useful information on these topics, but, precisely because its inclusion is not merely incidental but deliberate, his presentation of it may be biased, especially through significant omissions or juxtapositions.

However, Thucydides's strong statement of his critical methodology (1.21–2) should give us some confidence. Important recent approaches have emphasized the rhetorical nature of Thucydides's text and even suggested that this claim of objectivity is itself a rhetorical stance and should not be taken at face value.[4] His methodological discussion certainly attempts to promote the authority of his text, perhaps above what it deserves, but to deny therefore any possibility of deriving accurate historical data from the text would be pushing too far. I prefer to see his rhetorical method as involving manipulation, rather than fabrication, of data. Therefore, we can retain some degree of confidence that what information he does give us, while not representing the total picture, is at least accurate in itself, and therefore that we can trust his factual statements, such as which cities were on which sides of a particular war. Moreover, Thucydides's statements should be read in a larger context of all that we know about identity in Greek Sicily, which provides a check of a different sort. If we had no outside evidence for the existence of Sicilian regional identity, for instance, we would be more cautious in evaluating Thucydides's testimony about it. Thucydidean narrative can thus provide important data about the function of identity in Greek politics. His speeches, of course, are an entirely different question, which I reserve for discussion below.

The Greeks generally navigated the treacherous waters of international politics by pursuing their self-interest, and the Sicilian *poleis* were no exception. Still, they viewed that self-interest and the decisions before them through

---

1. E.g., Hunter 1973; Dover 1983; Connor 1984; Woodman 1988, 5–40; Rood 1998.

2. Alty 1982, 3–7; Crane 1996, 147–161; Hornblower, *CT* II: 61–80; Luginbill 1999; Price 2001, 151–161; Taylor 2010; Fragoulaki 2013.

3. Avery 1973, 8–13; cf. Hornblower, *CT* III.262–263, 278–299, 654–670; Kallet 2001, 24–27.

4. See Connor 1984, 6–18; Smith 2004, 44–47.

the lens of their multiple identities, which created a framework within which to evaluate possible courses of action. As we will see, individual politicians frequently deployed appeals to identity in their rhetoric as a means of persuasion, a tactic that could not be successful without an audience receptive to these arguments. Moreover, Greek states frequently tried to create legitimacy for their actions by claiming to be motivated by concerns rooted in identity, and aiding ethnic kinsmen was a particularly common pretext for military expeditions. Through these mechanisms, collective identity played an important but underappreciated role in shaping the political events, decisions, and rhetorical strategies that make up Greek history.

Kinship Diplomacy

While his analysis of the politics of identity is sometimes more subtle than his overt focus on the dynamics of power, necessity, and self-interest, Thucydides nonetheless sees identity as an essential component of his account of Greek politics. The historian is particularly concerned with kinship diplomacy, a common Greek mode of international relations in which states that perceive themselves to be ethnically related (usually through a claim of mythical common descent) align themselves more closely together, provide mutual aid, and award each other various privileges.[5] Although kinship diplomacy gained special prominence in the Hellenistic period, it was well known in the fifth century and possibly even earlier. The Athenians, for example, relocated the myth of Tereus from Phocis to Thrace in order to draw connections between themselves and the Thracians; this, it was hoped, would allow them access to the resources, especially gold and timber, of the north Aegean littoral.[6] The Macedonian kings, especially Alexander I in the first half of the fifth century, also highlighted their claimed descent from Heracles to link themselves with Argos and the rest of Greece.[7] Even Herodotus's story of Xerxes's embassy to Argos, requesting the latter's neutrality due to their shared ancestor, Perseus, should be included under this heading. Although the historicity is the story is highly doubtful, the fact that Herodotus includes it suggests that

5. On kinship diplomacy, see Jones 1999, esp. 23–40; Zacharia 2001; Patterson 2010; Fragoulaki 2013.

6. Thuc. 2.29; Sophocles's *Tereus* also dealt with this theme, probably in the 420s; cf. Zacharia 2001; Patterson 2010, 53–59.

7. Hdt. 5.22; with Borza 1990, 110–113; Jones 1999, 36–41; Hall 2001, 167–168; Asirvatham 2008, 237–240.

its fundamental basis, that states might act on the basis of perceived kinship, would be plausible to his audience.[8]

Thucydides, as an observant student of fifth-century international norms, is certainly familiar with the custom of kinship diplomacy. He frequently reports that communities cited kinship as a motivating factor in forging alliances and going to war, as an argument in a request for military assistance, or as a reason they expected such assistance.[9] For example, in 427, the Athenians cited their *syngeneia*, or kinship, with Leontini as the official reason for sending military assistance, thereby declaring publicly that their common Ionian ethnicity was a valid reason for sending an expedition.[10] However, the historian gives alternative reasons—preventing Sicilian grain from reaching the Peloponnese and scouting out possibilities for conquest—which he thinks were Athens's real motives.[11] Kinship is thus a pretext, rather than a cause of action. But elsewhere in the same passage (3.86.2), Thucydides accepts without comment that Rhegium was allied with Leontini because of kinship. The juxtaposition of these two instances shows that he treats each such claim on a case-by-case basis, rather than rejecting kinship as a true motivating factor altogether.[12] This should be our procedure, too. Perceptions of shared ancestry most likely did have an impact on the decision-making processes of Greek states on some occasions, alongside numerous other factors, while at other times, kinship served as a convenient pretext for action.

Yet these pretexts matter greatly, since they provide crucial insight into attitudes that were widely shared among the Greeks. The point of a pretext is that it confers more legitimacy on an action than the real reasons would. Kinship diplomacy famously helped ensure the legitimacy of the Delian League: since so many members were Ionian, the Athenians emphasized

---

8. Hdt. 7.150–152; Jones 1999, 28–29; Patterson 2010, 46–53.

9. See, e.g., 1.26.3 (Epidamnus and Corcyra), 1.34.3 (Corinth and Corcyra), 1.71.4 (Corinth and Sparta), 3.2.3 (Lesbos and Boeotia), 5.80.2 (Macedonia and Argos), 5.104 and 5.108 (Melos and Sparta), 6.6.2 (Syracuse and the Peloponnesians), 6.20.3 (Athens, Naxos and Catana), 6.46.2 (Athens, Rhegium and Leontini), 6.80.2 (Camarina and Syracuse), 6.88.7 (Syracuse and Corinth); cf. further sources in Fauber 2001, 42n118. Cogan (1981, 283–285) downplays the importance of kinship diplomacy early on the war; *contra*, Alty 1982, 11–14; cf. also Lape 2010, 167–173.

10. 3.86.3; cf. Westlake 1960, 106. While Leontini cited both *syngeneia* and "the ancient treaty," Thucydides's account does not have the Athenians invoke the treaty.

11. For full discussion of Athenian motives, see Westlake 1960, 105–116; cf. Smart 1972, 146; Kagan 1974, 181–186; Zahrnt 2006, 640–641, with further references.

12. As argued by Will 1956, 65–69; de Romilly 1963, 83–84, 243–244; Cogan 1981, 283–285; Curty 1994, 194–195. My position follows that of Alty 1982, 5; Crane 1996, 151–161.

their mythical role as colonial mother city and ethnic matriarch of the Ionians, thereby justifying Athens's hegemony over them.[13] Similarly, at the time of the Second Sicilian Expedition in 415, Thucydides emphasizes that the Athenians' main goal was to conquer Sicily, but he reports that publicly they declared their intention of protecting their *syngeneis* and allies.[14] When the expedition arrived in Sicily, the Athenians proclaimed that they had come to restore the people of Leontini, who had been forcibly driven out of their city by Syracuse, despite the fact that (if we follow Thucydides) Leontini had not asked for such assistance.[15] That these pretexts had widespread publicity and even some resonance with at least one city in Sicily is shown by the great lengths to which Hermocrates goes to debunk them in his speech at Camarina, and Thucydides is clearly aware of their power to create legitimacy for military action.[16] Thus, the fact that states in the late fifth century frequently cited ethnicity as a reason for action suggests that going to war to defend one's kin was broadly acceptable—or even laudable.

At the same time, however, identity was subject to manipulation by any interested party. While the ethnic connection between Leontini and Athens was long-standing,[17] neither party in 427 was an uninterested bystander. Leontini wanted a powerful ally in its perennial struggles against Syracuse, and, as Thucydides himself points out, Athens had important interests in Sicily as well. The two cities did not fabricate the connection between them for this occasion, but neither city would have emphasized it if it had not had something to gain from an Athenian presence in Sicily. Ethnic and other identities

---

13. For the Delian League, Thuc. 1.95.1; Eur. *Ion* 1571–1594, with Barron 1964, 46–48; Schuller 1974, 112–118; Alty 1982, 8–9; Hornblower, *CT* I.141–142, 520–521, II.72–73; Zacharia 2003a, 48–55; see further in chapter 2. However, the idea of Athens as a leader of the Ionians existed as early as Solon F4a West; cf. Hdt 1.146–147, 8.44; Paus. 7.2.1–4, with Connor 1993; Mac Sweeney 2013; Fragoulaki 2013, 210–220.

14. Main goal: 6.1.1, 6.6.1. Intention: 6.6.1, 6.50.4. While "allies" could refer equally to Segesta and Leontini, the Athenians made no claims of kinship with Elymian (i.e., non-Greek) Segesta, and so the *syngeneis* must be the Leontinians. For the political maneuverings at Athens leading up to the expedition, see Smart 1972, 138–144.

15. Proclamation: 6.50.4; cf. 6.6.2, 6.8.2, 6.33.2, 6.63.3. Expulsion of Leontini: 5.4. Thucydides emphasizes only the role of Segesta in sparking the expedition, but Diod. 12.83.1–3 (followed by Kagan 1981, 159n11) reports that Leontini and Segesta sent a joint embassy; cf. Plut. *Nic.* 12.1.

16. 6.76.2–3, 6.77.1, 6.79.2.

17. Hornblower, *CT* I.492; Smart 1972, 145–146. Although a formal alliance did exist between Athens and Leontini, which had recently been renewed in 433/2 (ML 64, and cf. 63, the treaty with Rhegium), I am here concerned only with the ethnic aspects of this decision.

mattered greatly to the Greeks but could also be manipulated to suit specific goals.

Examples such as these provide critical context for Thucydides's description of the two alliances in Sicily in 427 (3.86.2):

οἱ γὰρ Συρακόσιοι καὶ Λεοντῖνοι ἐς πόλεμον ἀλλήλοις καθέστασαν. ξύμμαχοι δὲ τοῖς μὲν Συρακοσίοις ἦσαν πλὴν Καμαριναίων αἱ ἄλλαι Δωρίδες πόλεις, αἵπερ καὶ πρὸς τὴν τῶν Λακεδαιμονίων τὸ πρῶτον ἀρχομένου τοῦ πολέμου ξυμμαχίαν ἐτάχθησαν, οὐ μέντοι ξυνεπολέμησάν γε, τοῖς δὲ Λεοντίνοις αἱ Χαλκιδικαὶ πόλεις καὶ Καμάρινα· τῆς δὲ Ἰταλίας Λοκροὶ μὲν Συρακοσίων ἦσαν, Ῥηγῖνοι δὲ κατὰ τὸ ξυγγενὲς Λεοντίνων.

Syracuse and Leontini were at war with each other. All the other Dorian cities, apart from Camarina, were allies of Syracuse, and had also been allied with Sparta since the beginning of the war, although they had not actively taken part in it. The Chalcidian cities and Camarina were allied with Leontini. In Italy, Locri was on the side of Syracuse, while Rhegium was on the side of Leontini because of kinship.

The alliances that fell along ethnic lines go virtually without comment, as a normal and unremarkable phenomenon. Conversely, what he does emphasize, naming the city twice, is that Camarina was the only *polis* to act against the general practice of Dorians fighting alongside Dorians against Chalcidians (see fig. 5.1).[18] Kinship diplomacy, for Thucydides, is a normal and expected phenomenon of international politics, and he is particularly interested in cases, like that of Camarina, where these international norms are breached.

The catalogue of forces on each side before the final battle in the Great Harbor of Syracuse (7.57–58) similarly highlights exceptions to the standard of alliances based on kinship. Ethnicity and colonial relationships are at the heart of this passage, in which Thucydides lists each allied city, some fifty altogether, along with its ethnic affiliation and other relevant information.[19] This

18. In fact, by framing the alliances in ethnic terms, Thucydides elides some of the complexities of Sicily's ethnic landscape. In particular, Himera sided with the Dorians in 427 (3.115.1), but Thucydides elsewhere describes Himera as founded primarily by Chalcidians from Zancle, along with some exiled Syracusans. Himera's dialect, he says, was a mixture of Doric and Ionic, but its *nomoi* were predominantly Chalcidian (6.5.1). The suppression of this complex background at 3.86 suggests that describing the alliances as ethnic was thematically important to the historian.

19. On the complex organization of the Catalogue, see the detailed outline of Dover, *HCT* IV.432–436, with a helpful chart, and in general, see Hornblower, *CT* III.654–670.

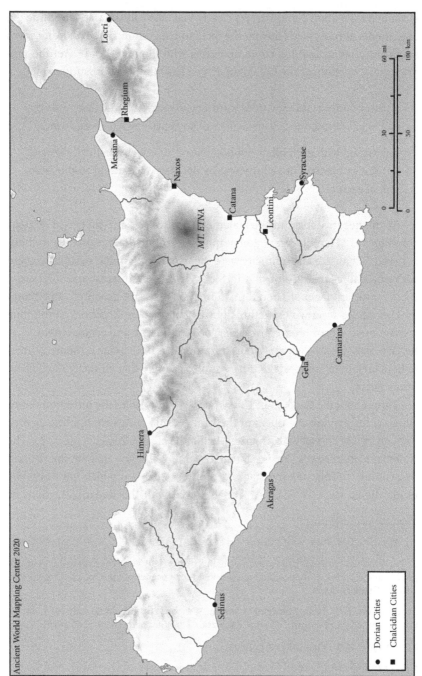

FIG. 5.1 Map of allies in Sicily, 427–424. By the Ancient World Mapping Center.

sustained exposition demonstrates clearly that ethnicity did not determine the alignments of most *poleis* during the Sicilian Expedition, and Thucydides was surely arguing against his contemporaries who thought it did.[20] Yet the programmatic opening of the Catalogue (7.57.1) has often been misunderstood:

οὐ κατὰ δίκην τι μᾶλλον οὐδὲ κατὰ ξυγγένειαν μετ' ἀλλήλων στάντες, ἀλλ' ὡς ἑκάστοις τῆς ξυντυχίας ἢ κατὰ τὸ ξυμφέρον ἢ ἀνάγκη ἔσχεν.

They stood with each other not because of justice or kinship [*syngeneia*] but rather because of self-interest or necessity, according to the situation of each city.

As the negative form of the statement—much like the rhetorical strategy common in Herodotean ethnography[21]—strongly suggests, Thucydides believed that justice and ethnicity were the usual and familiar reasons to stand with one's allies in war but that in Sicily in 413, self-interest and force were more important factors. Therefore, to treat this passage as simply an attempt by Thucydides to prove that ethnicity was not a factor in politics at the time is to ignore the broader picture.[22] His "polemical style and arrangement,"[23] as he describes the neglect and abuse of a normal and laudable mode of international relations, suggests that he was also arguing that ethnicity *should have been* a factor.

Throughout the Catalogue, Thucydides carefully notes the numerous cases where cities that are members of the same ethnic group are fighting against each other. He begins with an example that he clearly thinks is positive: "The Athenians themselves, being Ionians, came willingly against the Dorian Syracusans."[24] This sets the stage for the rest, many of which have negative implications, such as: "The Argives followed with the Ionian Athenians as

---

20. Alty 1982, 6–7; Price 2001, 156–157.

21. For example, "the Scythians [when sacrificing] do not light a fire, consecrate the victim, or pour libations" (Hdt. 4.60.2), which implies that the opposites of these practices are deeply familiar Greek customs.

22. As Dover, *HCT* IV.433, recognizes; *contra*, Will 1956, 65–68; de Romilly 1963, 83–84; Cogan 1981, 284; Crane 1996, 156–159; Price 2001, 156–161; Calligeri 2002, 260–261.

23. Alty 1982, 7; cf. Fragoulaki 2013, 91–92.

24. 7.57.2: Ἀθηναῖοι μὲν αὐτοὶ Ἴωνες ἐπὶ Δωριᾶς Συρακοσίους ἑκόντες ἦλθον; note the chiasmus which deliberately brings the names of the two ethnic groups together. Cf. also 7.57.4 (ὑπήκοοι δ' ὄντες καὶ ἀνάγκῃ ὅμως Ἴωνές γε ἐπὶ Δωριᾶς ἠκολούθουν), referring to Athenian allies in Euboea, Ionia, and the islands, which clearly implies that it is good for Ionians to fight Dorians, even when this happens under compulsion.

Dorians against Dorians, not so much because of the alliance as from hatred of the Lacedaemonians, and each of them came on account of quick individual profits."[25] Other particularly striking examples are those of the Boeotians (7.57.5) and of Corcyra (7.57.7). He even includes "a few Megarian exiles fighting [for Athens] against the Megarians of Selinus" (7.57.8); these could hardly have mattered in purely military terms and are included instead to highlight the breakdown of diplomatic norms. For Thucydides, the natural state of affairs is for members of the same ethnic group to ally with one another and to fight members of the opposite group, and his goal in the Catalogue is to highlight how this rule has broken down.

The two factors driving states to ignore their ethnic affiliations and fight against their kinsmen were, according to Thucydides, compulsion and self-interest, two factors that are central to Thucydides's political thought. In Sicily in 413, they represent a disruptive force preventing states from aligning with their ethnic kin, as they normally would.[26] Moreover, it is primarily the Athenian list of allies that draws such heavy scrutiny and disapproval. Thucydides pays special attention to identifying the precise status of each member of the Athenian *archē*, alongside its ethnic affiliations, as either a tribute-paying or an autonomous ally and as providing either ships or money. By pointing out the mechanisms of control in the Athenian Empire, Thucydides emphasizes the role of force in subverting normal state behavior with regard to ethnic alliances.[27] By forcing members of the same ethnic group to fight one another, the Athenians have disrupted what Thucydides sees as the normal workings of kinship diplomacy.

One of Thucydides's larger goals is to portray a world turned upside down by war.[28] At Corcyra, the outbreak of *stasis* causes words to change their

---

25. 7.57.9: Ἀργεῖοι μὲν γὰρ οὐ τῆς ξυμμαχίας ἕνεκα μᾶλλον ἢ τῆς Λακεδαιμονίων τε ἔχθρας καὶ τῆς παραυτίκα ἕκαστοι ἰδίας ὠφελίας Δωριῆς ἐπὶ Δωριᾶς μετὰ Ἀθηναίων Ἰώνων ἠκολούθουν; cf. also 7.57.5, 7.57.7. Athens has already been listed as Ionian, in case anyone needed reminding; its repetition here is emphatic and for effect. Cf. 7.57.6 for a similar repetition of Dorian Syracuse.

26. Cf. Alty 1982, 5–7; Crane 1996, 150–151.

27. See also, programmatically, 7.57.3: τῶν δ᾽ ἄλλων οἱ μὲν ὑπήκοοι, οἱ δ᾽ ἀπὸ ξυμμαχίας αὐτόνομοι, εἰσὶ δὲ καὶ οἳ μισθοφόροι ξυνεστράτευον, and 7.57.5, 7.57.7, with Dover, *HCT* IV.432–435, for whom status under the Athenian *archē* is a major organizing feature of the Catalogue.

28. Connor (1984, 195–196) explicitly compares the Catalogue to the Corcyrean *stasis*; cf. Cogan 1981, 120–169; Hornblower, *CT* I.477–491; Price 2001, esp. 207–236; Fragoulaki 2013, 91–92.

meanings and places faction ahead of family (3.70–85, esp. 82–83). At Athens, Pericles's vision of Athens solemnly and collectively burying its war dead is immediately overturned in the plague narrative, where burial customs are abandoned and the community nearly tears itself to pieces (2.34–54, especially 34 contrasted with 52). So, too, in Sicily, the Athenian war effort causes international norms to break down, which is why Thucydides so strongly emphasizes cases where ethnic brethren fight one another. In such a world, battles can go disastrously wrong, as happened in the night battle of Epipolae, when the Athenians were confused by the Dorian paeans sung by their Argive allies and ended up slaughtering one another (7.44.6–7). This project must be taken into account in evaluating the evidence on the role of identity in politics. In fact, it is precisely because Thucydides thinks identity matters in politics that we must be careful in using the evidence he provides. Thucydides has likely given us much reliable information on alliances, but what has he left out in pursuit of a coherent portrait?

Camarina's Polis *Identity*

We can begin to explore the role of multiple identities in Sicilian politics through the decisions of Camarina, a city that punches far above its political weight in Thucydides's narrative. Its prominence in the Sicilian sections of Books 3 and 4 helps prepare the reader both for Hermocrates's speech at Gela (4.59–64) and for the Camarina Debate (6.75–88); the latter is a pivotal pair of speeches that allows Thucydides to explore the role of small *poleis* in a world dominated by large ones.[29] This level of attention has given us a great deal of information that, if used with due caution, can tell us a great deal about the various identities claimed by Camarina and how they helped shape the city's decisions. In particular, in a context where every other Sicilian *polis* chose allies according to ethnic identity, Camarina's decision in 427 to fight not only against other Dorians but even against Syracuse, its own mother city, requires explanation. I suggest that the explanation lies in Camarina's *polis* identity, constructed around both its claim to the status of an independent *polis*, a status that Syracuse denied, and its resulting fear and hatred of Syracuse (cf. 6.88.1).

The foundation of Camarina in 598 represented the latest in a string of subcolonies established by Syracuse throughout southeastern Sicily: Heloron, around 700; Acrae, in 663; and Casmenae, in 643 (fig. 5.2). Camarina saw itself as being substantially different in purpose and status from these other

---

29. We can thus compare the position of Camarina to that of Metapontion; see chapter 2.

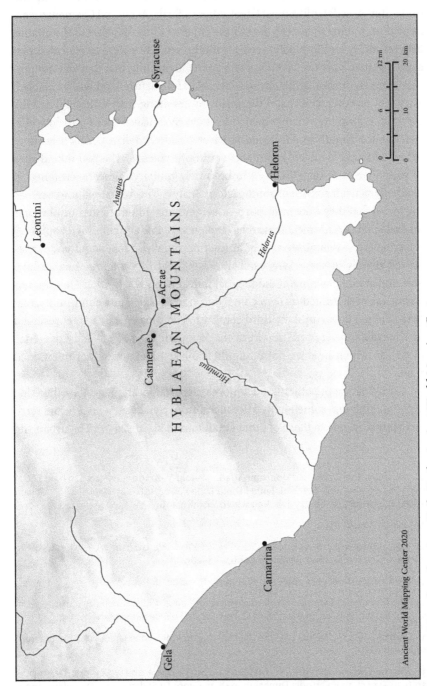

FIG. 5.2 Map of southeastern Sicily. By the Ancient World Mapping Center.

subcolonies, and comparison of Camarina with two of them brings out significant differences.[30] Unlike most Greek cities in Sicily, Acrae and Casmenae were located on hilltop sites deep within the interior of the Hyblaean Mountains, between thirty and forty kilometers from the sea. They were also located very close together, only twelve kilometers apart, suggesting that they did not possess large territories, although some arable and pasture land was available.[31] They did, however, command the major routes along river valleys toward the coast, including the Anapus, which leads to Syracuse. Heloron, meanwhile, stood at the mouth of the Heloros River (modern Tellaro), which leads to Acrae, and only eighteen kilometers south of Syracuse. The two inland sites in particular were once thought to be purely military outposts, designed to secure Syracusan control of southeastern Sicily.[32] New research, however, has suggested that they were multipurpose settlements, intended to control routes for trade and communications and to exploit available agricultural resources.[33] Nevertheless, although they were at least nominally independent *poleis*, they existed mainly to serve Syracusan interests, held in a degree of subordination, and at no known point did they act independently.[34] Neither Heloron nor Casmenae ever minted its own coins, one sign of a separate community, and Acrae did not do so until the third century.[35] Their lower status is represented in Thucydides's very brief report of the foundations of Acrae and Casmenae (6.5.2), in which he does not name their oikists; Heloron is not mentioned at all.

Camarina, on the other hand, enjoyed a coastal location, on the other side of the mountains, some eighty kilometers from Syracuse, with a fertile territory similar in size to those of other small-to-mid-sized *poleis*.[36] The urban site

---

30. For these three cities, see Dunbabin 1948, 99–104; Voza 1999, 113–120, 129–143; *IACP*, 189–190, 195, 205–206; Cerchiai, Jannelli, and Longo 2004, 216–223; Copani 2005; Copani 2009; Frasca 2015, 71–88, 125–128; Jonasch 2020b, 189–196.

31. Jonasch 2020b, 194.

32. E.g., Dunbabin 1948, 95–112; Di Vita 1956; Di Vita 1987; Graham 1964, 92–94; Anello 2002a, 63–70; Erdas 2006; Veronese 2006, 284–289.

33. Melfi 2000; De Angelis 2016, 163–164; Jonasch 2020b, 189–196.

34. The Gamoroi of Syracuse fled to Casmenae around 485 after a popular uprising (Hdt. 7.155.2), but this episode does not show Casmenae acting independently.

35. Graham 1964, 92; Di Vita 1987, 80. Of course, numerous other Greek *poleis* did not mint coins, either.

36. On the city and territory, see *IACP*, 202–205; Veronese 2006, 342–347; De Angelis 2016, 119–121; cf. more broadly Dunbabin 1948, 104–106; Di Stefano 1987; Di Stefano 2000; Mattioli 2002; Sulosky Weaver 2015, 45–63.

is large, although most likely not all of it was occupied in Archaic times, and its coinage is well known from the early fifth century onward.[37] Camarina is thus much more comparable than the other subcolonies to the fully independent Greek *poleis* of Sicily. Its higher status is evident from Thucydides's more detailed report of its foundation, including two oikists, Dascon and Menecolus. Dascon was likely from Syracuse, since he was apparently named after a topographical feature near the city, but Menecolus may have been a Corinthian.[38] If so, this would group Camarina together with a series of other subcolonies founded by oikists summoned from the original mother city, providing a further dimension to this colony's higher status.[39] Camarina, it seems, saw a sharp distinction between itself and Syracuse's other subcolonies.

Syracuse, however, denied this distinction, perceiving Camarina as essentially similar to its other subcolonies: part of the infrastructure of Syracusan control of southeastern Sicily and a dependency subordinated to its mother city, not an independent ally. Herodotus, probably reflecting Syracusan thinking, says that Camarina belonged to Syracuse "of old,"[40] and over the next century, Syracusan armies twice descended on their recalcitrant colony. In 552, following what Thucydides calls a "revolt," Syracuse expelled the Camarinaeans from their city.[41] In 492, Syracuse was forced to cede Camarina to Hippocrates, tyrant of Gela, and he refounded the city as its new oikist.[42] Not long after, in 484, Gelon again expelled the citizens and this time destroyed the city as well;[43] the city was finally resettled by Gela in 461.[44] These traumatic expulsions, I argue, came to be deeply embedded in the collective psyche of the Camarinaean community or, to put it another way, in its identity as a separate *polis*.

---

37. Westermark and Jenkins 1980; Rutter 1997, 118, 137–138; see further below.

38. Dunbabin 1948, 105; Manni 1987, 68–69; De Luna 2009, 78–79.

39. Attested for Epidamnus, Thuc. 1.24.2; Selinus, Thuc. 6.4.2; Zancle, Thuc. 6.4.5. Thucydides calls it a common custom (1.24.2).

40. Hdt. 7.154.3: Συρακοσίων δὲ ἦν Καμάρινα τὸ ἀρχαῖον. Cf. Artemon of Pergamum (*FGrH* 569) F2, a historian of Sicily of the mid-second century BCE, who reports that Camarina had been subject (ὑποτέτακται) to Syracuse.

41. 6.5.3: ἀπόστασις; cf. Ps.-Scymn. 294–296; schol. ad Pind. *Ol.* 5.16. Since Thucydides's source was probably Antiochus of Syracuse (Dover, *HCT* IV.198–210; Hornblower, *CT* III.272–274), this also represents a Syracusan perspective.

42. Hdt. 7.154.3; Thuc. 6.5.3; Philistus (*FGrH* 556) F15.

43. Hdt. 7.156.2. See Demand 1990, 47–49, 54–55; Luraghi 1994, 156–165, 275–276.

44. Thuc. 6.5.3; Diod. 11.76.5.

The war between Camarina and Syracuse in 552 was a substantial one, which saw the Camarinaeans fielding an army and engaging in regional diplomacy. According to the fourth-century Syracusan historian Philistus, they allied with the Sikels and with unspecified others, though Gela refused to join them. Syracuse, meanwhile, sought assistance from Megara Hyblaea and Enna, and a victory near the Hirminus River (modern Irminio) brought Camarina back under Syracusan control.[45] While one literary source claims that Camarina was totally destroyed, Thucydides instead speaks of the expulsion of the population, and there is substantial archaeological evidence for continued occupation of the site in the second half of the sixth century.[46] Moreover, Syracuse continued to control Camarina's territory until 492, when it was ceded to Gela (Hdt. 7.154.3); presumably, the land was settled and worked for the benefit of Syracuse.[47] In other words, Syracuse eliminated the troublemakers and continued its policies of control, merely a step on the way toward domination of southeastern Sicily. But for the people of Camarina, the revolt of 552 may have had a deeper significance as an event in their shared history around which their civic identity began to crystallize. In fact, T. J. Dunbabin described Camarina's *apostasis* from Syracuse as a "war of independence."[48] This formulation underscores the central position this war took in Camarina's civic identity, which came to be predicated on its (failed) war of independence from Syracuse.

Camarina was refounded by Hippocrates, the tyrant of Gela, after the territory had been ceded to him by Syracuse in 492, but its people were expelled again only eight years later. Gelon's destruction of Camarina in 484 was similarly intended to end the existence of Camarina as a separate community that could resist Syracusan control. A somewhat garbled text in the scholia to Aeschines (3.189) suggests that Gelon installed a tyrant, Glaucus of Carystus, in Camarina but that the Camarinaeans killed him rather than accept a foreign

45. Philistus (*FGrH* 556) F5. I reject an emendation of this text by Pais (followed by Di Vita 1956, 200; cf. Di Vita 1987, 82–83) that changes Megara Hyblaea and Enna to Acrae and Casmenae, since there is no reason to alter the text except preconceived notions about the likely political situation in mid-sixth-century Sicily; Jacoby does not even print it in his apparatus. On this war, see Anello 2002a, 68–73; De Luna 2009, 79–83.

46. Ps.-Scymn. 295: αὐτοὶ δὲ ταύτην ἦραν ἐκ βάθρων. According to Thucydides, however, the Camarinaeans were merely uprooted (ἀνάστατος: 6.5.3 *bis*). Continued occupation: Pelagatti 1976, 523–526; cf. Luraghi 1994, 159–160; Cordano 1992, 3–4; De Luna 2009, 83.

47. Cf. Dover, *HCT* IV.219.

48. Dunbabin 1948, 105, followed by Anello 2002a, 72–73.

tyrant.[49] This was an act of rebellion that Gelon could not accept. He destroyed the city and brought its population to Syracuse, where they became citizens (Hdt. 7.156.2). Occupation of the site ceased, as indicated by a gap in the archaeological record in the second quarter of the fifth century.[50] This act, part of a larger program that also saw the destruction or removal of citizens from a number of other cities (see chapter 3), was clearly intended to consolidate power by removing a possible center of resistance. Its legitimacy depended on the idea that Camarina already in essence formed a part of the Syracusan community and that it was legitimate for the ruler of Syracuse to do with them as seemed in the best interests of Syracuse. Camarina, on the other hand, did not consider itself an extension of Syracuse and evidently opposed Gelon in arms; if we can trust Herodotus's phrase Καμαρίνης τὸ ἄστυ κατέσκαψε, Gelon's action was highly destructive.[51] Camarina's separate civic identity was still strong, and Gelon's actions—imposing a tyrant on them and then exiling them from their homeland—only made the Camarinaeans more vehemently opposed to Syracuse.

Despite these reassertions of Syracusan control, Camarinaean identity continued to be relevant, even when the *polis* formally did not exist. In 528, for instance, the Olympic *stadion* race was won by Parmenides of Camarina (Diod. 1.68.6). Perhaps an exile, this otherwise unknown figure considered his status as a citizen of Camarina important enough to proclaim at Olympia. Similarly, in the fifth century, Praxiteles, a Mantinean who became both a Camarinaean and a Syracusan (whom we met in chapter 3), set up a statue with an inscription at Olympia. Despite his new legal status as a Syracusan, he chose to proclaim, in this highly public international venue, his identity as a Camarinaean as well.[52] Like other Sicilian Greek communities under the Deinomenids, discussed in chapter 3, the people of Camarina maintained the memory of their city and its separate identity strongly enough to last through periods of exile and revive it each time the city was re-established.

The two refoundations of Camarina were both led by Gela, once in 492, during the reign of Hippocrates, and once in 461.[53] Although Gela had refused

---

49. Luraghi 1994, 150–151, 275–276; Nicholson 2015, 203–206.

50. Giudice 1988, 56–57.

51. The same verb is also applied to Gelon's destruction of Camarina by Philistus F15, as rendered by the scholiast to Pindar *Ol.* 5.19.

52. *IvO* 266, dating from 480–475; cf. Luraghi 1994, 161–163; Harrell 1998, 183–187.

53. 492: Hdt. 7.154.3, Thuc. 6.5.3, Philistus F15. 461: Diod. 11.76.5; cf. Thuc. 6.5.3. On the history of Camarina in this period, see the useful summary of Cordano 1992, 3–15.

to participate in Camarina's war of independence, its strong support for Camarina in the first half of the fifth century would thus have come as a radical and welcome change and thus may have led to a more favorable opinion of Gela prevailing at Camarina. In 492, Hippocrates of Gela himself was their oikist, which may have led to the institution of an oikist cult.[54] Former citizens of Camarina certainly participated in the refoundations; new settlers from Gela did as well, and so the two groups lived side by side and became a single community.[55] As Sulosky Weaver suggests, this community may have made a deliberate choice to break with their past, by abandoning the Archaic cemetery at Rifriscolaro and opening up a new one at Passo Marinaro (see fig. 5.3).[56] If so, that would suggest a desire to distance themselves from their Syracusan origins; they may even have seen themselves as being essentially Geloan, rather than Syracusan.

In the refounded Camarina after 461, there are additional reasons for thinking that the citizens saw themselves as possessing a unique culture. In many Greek *poleis*, distinctive features of the local landscape—such as the Athenian Acropolis and the rivers Ilissus and Eridanos, or at Syracuse the spring of Arethusa and the island of Ortygia (discussed in chapter 3)—offered important focal points for civic identity.[57] For Camarina, the role of the city's topography is seen most clearly in Pindar's *Olympian* 5 (11–15), written in the 450s for Psaumis, who participated in the refoundation of Camarina in 461.[58]

> ὦ πολιάοχε Παλλάς, ἀείδει μὲν ἄλσος ἁγνόν
> τὸ τεὸν ποταμόν τε Ὤανον ἐγχωρίαν τε λίμναν
> καὶ σεμνοὺς ὀχετούς, Ἵππαρις οἷσιν ἄρδει στρατόν.
> κολλᾷ τε σταδίων θαλάμων ταχέως ὑψίγυιον ἄλσος,
> ὑπ' ἀμαχανίας ἄγων ἐς φάος τόνδε δᾶμον ἀστῶν.   15

Pallas who protects the city, he [Psaumis] sings of your holy grove
and the River Oanos and the nearby lake,

---

54. Thuc. 6.5.3; Luraghi 1994, 164–165, and references in his n. 185. On oikist cult, see Malkin 1987, 189–240.

55. On the composition of the citizen body after 461, see Cordano 2000, 191.

56. Sulosky Weaver 2015, 69.

57. On landscape and identity, see esp. Lewis 2020.

58. The authenticity of *Ol.* 5 has been repeatedly suspected (e.g., Bowra 1964, 414–420). But the alternative, that it was composed by a local Sicilian imitator in the 450s, does not detract from my argument that it reflects Camarinaean civic identity; cf. Rutter 2000a, 80–82; Barrett 2007, 46–53; Nicholson 2011; Lewis 2020, 234–247.

and the august channels with which the Hipparis brings water to
   the people.
Swiftly he builds a lofty grove of sturdy homes,
leading this community of citizens from despair into the light.   15

The newly rebuilt community of Camarina is firmly positioned within its local landscape—a landscape from which the Camarinaeans had been until recently exiled (see fig. 5.3).[59] Together with the nearby marsh, the rivers Hipparis and Oanos, which flow on either side of the urban site, spatially define the Camarinaean community. The Hipparis, recognizable as a river god by his horns, also appears on a series of coins minted by Camarina in the last quarter of the fifth century (fig. 5.4).[60] The reverse of the same coins shows a female figure riding a swan, often identified as the nymph Camarina, who is also addressed by Pindar.[61] The decision to present these two figures to the world as the representatives of their city shows in a second medium how the *polis* emphasized its attachment to its physical environment as a component of its civic ideology. These coins are exactly contemporary with the Peloponnesian War, several decades later than Pindar's description; this lengthy chronological gap suggests that the role of landscape in Camarina's identity—much as we have seen at Croton (chapter 2) and Syracuse (chapter 3)—was a long-term phenomenon.

Moreover, while it is not unusual for Pindar to address the patron deity of the victor's *polis*, Camarina's temple of Athena occupied a particularly prominent and visible location within the city, at its highest elevation and overlooking the sea. These topographical descriptions, juxtaposed with a brief narrative of the reconstruction of the city's built environment, paint a portrait of a deep emotional connection between the citizens of Camarina and the physical site of their *polis*. The emphasis on the community's identity being rooted in a particular place has particular significance for a community so often exiled.

---

59. Mattioli 2002, 24–27, 193–216; Lewis 2020, 239–244. See the historical and topographic description of the site by Sulosky Weaver 2015, 45–63.

60. Westermark and Jenkins 1980, 58–69; Rutter 2000a, 80–82.

61. As a "daughter of Ocean" (2) and by name (4). Cf. Artemon of Pergamum (*FGrH* 569) F2, who in the mid-second century BCE claimed that Pindar's "daughter of Ocean" actually referred to Arethusa, not the nymph Camarina, because "Camarina had been subject [ὑποτέτακται] to Syracuse." If this statement does preserve a much earlier sentiment, then it reflects an attempt by Syracuse to co-opt a celebration of Camarina's civic identity and deny it to Camarina. In any case, it is remarkable that these aspects of identity are still a live issue long afterward, after a century of Roman control in Sicily.

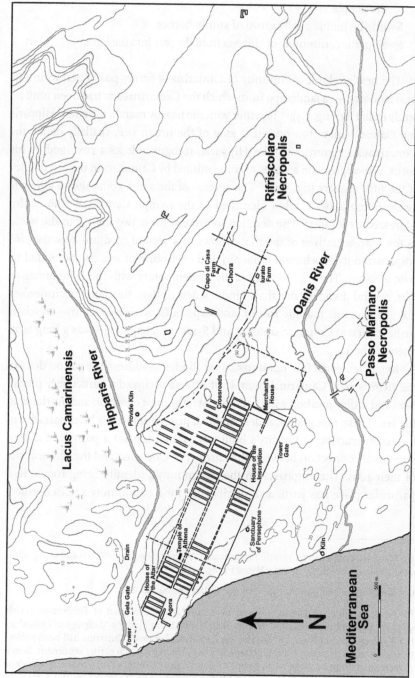

FIG. 5.3 Map of Camarina. Drawing by D. Weiss, after Cerchiai, Jannelli, and Longo 2004, 231.

Lacus Camarinensis

Hipparis River

Oanis River

Rifriscolaro Necropolis

Passo Marinaro Necropolis

Capo di Casa Farm

Chora

Iurato Farm

Provide Kiln

Crossroads

Merchant's House

Tower Gate

House of the Inscription

Sanctuary of Persephone

Temple of Athena

Drain

Kiln

House of the Altar

Agora

Gela Gate

Tower

Mediterranean Sea

N

500 m

FIG. 5.4 Didrachm of Camarina, c. 415. Obverse: River Hipparis. Reverse: Nymph Camarina on a swan. © Trustees of the British Museum.

As in many other cities, it appears that Camarina's topography contributed to its sense of distinctiveness.

Camarinaean identity continued to be relevant through various periods of turmoil, destruction, and exile. Since the history shared by a community conditions that community's view of itself (essentially, its identity), I argue that Camarina's bloody history with Syracuse became one of the dominant factors in Camarinaean identity. Fear and hatred of Syracuse represented a prominent similarity that bound the Camarinaeans together, defined their community, and, of course, marked them off as separate from the Syracusans. So did the sense of belonging to an independent *polis*, rooted in their home territory—precisely what Syracuse had rejected. Civic identity thus helps explain Camarina's unusual policies in 427. While the other Sicilian *poleis* viewed their decision to join one alliance or the other through the lens of ethnicity, the Camarinaeans were guided instead by their *polis* identity, choosing to fight against Syracuse rather than with their fellow Dorians.

It is, of course, crucial to keep in mind what Thucydides may have left out. Camarina's policies play alarmingly well into both Thucydides's interest in kinship diplomacy and colonial relationships and the literary architecture of his work. His report of the war of 427–424 is notoriously sketchy and incomplete,[62] and he may have omitted other factors—conceivably, ones that were more historically important than civic identity—that contributed to Camarina's decisions. These might have included preexisting alliances with the Chalcidians, desire to secure their help in the future, or territorial ambitions;

---

62. Westlake 1960, 387–388.

after all, at the end of the war, Morgantina was ceded to Camarina by Syracuse, the only territorial change Thucydides mentions.[63] However, there is no real evidence that any of these considerations played an important role in determining Camarina's initial adherence to the Chalcidian side. Furthermore, any of these speculative scenarios would apply just as well to any other city. Why did Gela or Akragas, for example, not go over to the Chalcidians as well? What separated Camarina from the rest of the Dorian cities was its history with Syracuse, now embedded in Camarina's civic identity.

Even if some unknown strategic factor was, in fact, decisive, however, a further question remains. How did they create legitimacy for this decision? How did they convince themselves that what they were doing was not only strategically sound but morally right? If most Camarinaeans believed that they were fighting their fellow Dorians and that this fact was truly important and *wrong*, they surely would not have done it. In order to get around this issue, they did not deny their Dorian status. Rather, they denied that it was important. They valued their *polis* identity, which was predicated on opposition to the Syracusans, above their ethnic affiliation with them.

Undoubtedly, not all citizens of Camarina shared this same sense of civic identity and opposition to Syracuse. A second poem of Pindar, *Olympian 4*, which (like *Ol. 5*) was also commissioned by Psaumis in the 450s, presents a rather different view. Although the Deinomenids had been out of power for a decade or more, Pindar included for his honorand, a former Deinomenid mercenary, familiar elements of Hieron's ideology (*Ol.* 4.6–9):

> ἀλλὰ Κρόνου παῖ, ὃς Αἴτναν ἔχεις
> ἶπον ἀνεμόεσσαν ἑκατογκεφάλα Τυφῶνος ὀβρίμου,
> Οὐλυμπιονίκαν
> δέξαι Χαρίτων θ' ἕκατι τόνδε κῶμον.

> Son of Cronus, you who hold Etna,
> the windy weight on mighty hundred-headed Typhos,
> receive, with the aid of the Graces,
> this revel procession of an Olympic victor.

The reference to Zeus Aetnaeus, one of Hieron's most favored deities, as well as Typhos (who famously appeared in *Pyth.* 1), suggests strong links

63. 4.65.1. Territorial ambitions are emphasized by Bell 2000; cf. Pace 1927, 47–48; Westlake 1958, 179–180; Mattioli 2002, 151–152.

back to the glorious Syracusan past.[64] Reading *Olympian* 4 and 5 together suggests a rather complex view of identities at Camarina, in which pro- and anti-Syracusan views both have a place.

Similarly, at the end of the century, alongside the Hipparis coins discussed above, many others suggest close numismatic ties to Syracuse. Several of the so-called Signing Masters who revolutionized coinage at Syracuse also worked for Camarina; their Camarinaean coins closely imitate their Syracusan ones, including the choice of a tetradrachm, rather than a didrachm, as the primary denomination. They also put a quadriga on the reverse, much as at Syracuse, though the driver is not a generic charioteer but rather Athena, Camarina's chief deity.[65] This, too, suggests a complex combination of Syracusan culture and Camarinaean distinctiveness. Finally, Thucydides (4.25.7) records one instance of a faction that was ready to betray the city to Syracuse in 425. This group was led by Archias, evidently a pro-Syracusan politician whose name (the same as that of Syracuse's founder) may indicate that his family had strong Syracusan connections. What is clear, however, is that Camarina had little ability to articulate a *polis* identity that did not reference Syracuse in one way or another. The small *polis* dominated by its larger neighbor was never able to escape its shadow.

Thus, while the articulation of Camarinaean identity emphasized here was contested and not universal, it was a common one. Moreover, even for citizens who did feel that opposition to Syracuse was a key part of what it meant to be Camarinaean, they certainly did not view discussions about going to war through that lens alone. Nevertheless, identity undoubtedly contributed to shaping how they viewed the decision. Although Camarina sometimes made different choices from other Sicilian communities, on a deeper level, the role played by identity in its political decision-making was entirely typical. This should be conceptualized in terms of a general consensus, built up among a majority of citizens, that shaped discussions and framed deliberations under a democratic constitution.[66] In this way, civic identity would lead the *polis* as a whole toward one decision while still accommodating a great variety of viewpoints.

---

64. Nicholson 2011; Lewis 2020, 237–239.

65. Rutter 1997, 148–149; but cf. the cautionary remarks of Fischer-Bossert 2018.

66. That Camarina was a democracy is the conclusion of Robinson (2011, 96–100). However, even if the constitution was oligarchic, the same conclusions about the political role of identity would still hold, albeit applied to the decision-making body rather than to all citizens.

Rhetoric and Identity

Of course, Camarina's civic identity did not guide its political decision-making permanently and exclusively. The subsequent decades were turbulent times in Sicily, and many of Camarina's multiple identities became relevant to its debates over war and peace in the fifteen years after 427. The mechanisms by which various identities—especially Sicilian and Dorian identities—came into focus are particularly interesting. Over such a short time frame, ethnogenesis and the creation of new identities are not significant processes. Instead, the crucial concept is salience, the extent to which a particular form of identity is perceived as relevant or important in a given situation. As circumstances changed, so, too, did the levels of salience, determined in a purely subjective way through a process of consensus-building, associated with Camarina's various identities; the citizens of Camarina would then view the decision through a different lens. Moreover, Camarina's decisions were influenced at critical moments by two speeches of the Syracusan politician Hermocrates, which (at least as rewritten by Thucydides) used arguments based on identity to persuade his audiences to adopt certain decisions. Analysis of these speeches, together with audience responses to them, can provide meaningful insights into the identities perceived by Sicilian communities and the role of political rhetoric in shaping their decisions.

Hermocrates at Gela and Sicilian Identity

By 424, the war in Sicily had dragged on for a further three years after Athens's intervention, with little result.[67] Exhausted, the Sicilian *poleis* sent representatives to a peace conference at Gela.[68] In his speech there, Hermocrates invoked a pan-Sicilian community, the Sikeliotai (4.64.3), that transcended ethnic and civic divisions and in particular asked his audience to ignore the difference between Dorians and Chalcidians, since both sides were equally in danger from Athens (4.61.2). Thucydides tells us that many speakers spoke at Gela, but he chooses only one to report at length. The historian's selectivity is already at work here, and there is much that we will never know about this meeting.

---

67. On the course of the war, see Westlake 1960; Kagan 1974, 187–193, 265–270; Bosworth 1992.

68. 4.58–65. Thucydides refers to πρέσβεις (4.58), and Timaeus (F22) explicitly states that Hermocrates's audience consisted of plenipotentiary representatives, rather than citizens at large. On the speech generally, see Hammond 1973; Cogan 1981, 77–81; Hornblower, *CT* II.220–228; Fauber 2001; Vanotti 2003.

Still, the speech Thucydides provides for Hermocrates offers important insight into the possibilities available to a politician who could successfully manipulate the identities of his audience.

Any interpretation of Thucydidean speeches must take into account both the literary and the historical goals of the text.[69] In his methodological passage (1.22), Thucydides pairs the speeches (*logoi*) with the narrative of deeds (*erga*) that together make up the history. Both are subject to the distorting processes of writing history. The choice to include certain speeches and exclude others is already an act of distortion; within each speech, in all likelihood, Thucydides condensed some arguments, expanded others, and perhaps even imported some that he thought were relevant. All of this would be consistent with his claim that he has characters say *ta deonta* (1.22.1, a much-discussed phrase).[70] Yet the speeches, like the narrative, are designed to further Thucydides's primary goal of historical analysis and interpretation.[71] They do have serious research behind them, since he tells us that he did have informants for many, if not all, of the speeches, though "they had difficulty remembering the precise words used." While his procedure certainly varied from one speech to another, he most likely combined that data with other information about a speech's context and applied his own historical analysis to produce the texts we have. A speech that bore little relationship to the historical circumstances, contexts, and processes that Thucydides thought were important would be pointless. Thus, we should assume that the historian had a good idea of what the speaker's goals were for each particular speech, and of his audience, and of what arguments might have succeeded in that situation. Moreover, we can evaluate Thucydides's opinions, to some extent, by placing the speeches in the context of all that we know about identity in Sicily. Speeches therefore can represent a reality that is worth investigating.

On this model, it appears that Thucydides, a well-informed contemporary observer of Greek Sicily, thought that arguments based on Sicilian identity would have convinced a late-fifth-century Sicilian audience. Of course, other arguments were almost certainly deployed at the Conference of Gela, if not by Hermocrates, then perhaps by other speakers. For instance, Timaeus's version of Hermocrates's speech, as transmitted (and distorted) by Polybius,

---

69. What follows is essentially the approach of Pelling 2000, 112–122; for various approaches to the speeches, see Stadter 1973; Wilson 1982, 95–103; Macleod 1983, 68–87; Hornblower 1987, 45–72; Rood 1998, 46–48; Marincola 2001, 77–85.

70. See esp. Hornblower 1987, 45–47; Marincola 2001, 77–78; Pelling 2000, 114–118.

71. Pelling 2000, 112–122.

apparently included arguments about the benefits of peace that are absent from Thucydides.[72] However, it is the arguments from identity that are central to Thucydides's analysis of Sicilian history in this period. The very selectivity of Thucydides here suggests that the historian thought these particular arguments were the most important.[73]

Hermocrates's speech at Gela dominates Thucydides's account of the first Athenian expedition, and it introduces a number of important themes that recur later.[74] In particular, the question of Sicilian unity—or lack thereof—will be critical to the narrative of the subsequent expedition, providing a backdrop against which to evaluate the role of Alcibiades in particular. Alcibiades's entire strategy is based around the idea that Sicily will be unable to unite against Athens (esp. 6.17.2–4), and his expectation that the Sicilians would στασιάζουσιν (6.17.4) finds its parallel in Hermocrates's admonition that *stasis* would destroy Sicily (4.61.1). However, the success, albeit temporary, of Hermocrates at uniting the Sicilians around their common identity as Sikeliotai should give the reader pause in assuming that Alcibiades's self-confidence will be anything other than disastrous.[75] Alcibiades believes that in Sicily, "no one feels that he is fighting for his fatherland [οἰκείας πατρίδος]" (6.17.3), yet in Hermocrates's vision, the Sikeliotai do have a fatherland: Sicily as a whole. Alcibiades has hopelessly misunderstood the role identity will play in leading the Sicilians to resist the Athenian invasion.

These considerations open up the possibility that Thucydides may have anachronistically overemphasized in this passage themes that are actually more important in the subsequent narrative or perhaps focused on concepts that are more important for understanding Athens than Sicily.[76] If Thucydides did so, however, he did so precisely because the ideas contained in the speech are important. He includes the speech because, in his estimation, it led directly to the withdrawal of Athenian forces when the Sicilians adopted Hermocrates's proposals, showing how the rhetoric of identity contributed to this historical event. Regardless of whether a speaker like Hermocrates actually used these

---

72. On Timaeus's version of the speech, see Bearzot 2006; Baron 2013, 180–191.

73. Cf. Rood 1998, 137n16.

74. Connor 1984, 124–125; Fragoulaki 2013, 96–99.

75. Hunter 1973, 138; Macleod 1983, 78; cf. Stahl 1973; Bloedow 1996. It is often thought that the "young men" attacked by Athenagoras at 6.38.5 (in 415) include Hermocrates; they could equally well be his supporters.

76. Grosso 1966, 106–107; Hammond 1973, 53, 57–59; Hunter 1977, 283–285; Hornblower 1987, 56; Vanotti 2003; *contra*, Westlake 1958, 176–181; Fauber 2001.

precise arguments or not, the ideas attributed to him represent a reality that is worth investigating.

I have already discussed (in chapter 4) the nature of the Sikeliotai. To recap briefly, I argue that they are not an ethnic group, since they are not defined by kinship, but rather that they are a geographically defined regional collectivity.[77] Moreover, this regional identity was not new: the Deinomenid tyrants, half a century earlier, had encouraged a common sense of Sicilian identity as a way of unifying their domains and solidifying their power. What I emphasize here, however, is the political use to which Hermocrates put them. Up to this point, the Sicilians had made their decisions on the basis of ethnicity or, in one case, *polis* identity. Hermocrates argued instead that they should consider Sicilian identity more important and make their political decisions on this basis. This rhetoric had a real political impact; since the cities did make peace and turn against Athens, it seems that the various ambassadors were persuaded by his arguments.

The exact nature of this process of persuasion can be further delimited. Such rhetoric could only be successful if his audience was already receptive and already familiar with the identity to which he was appealing. Only then could an appeal to Sicilian identity strike a chord with his audience. Therefore, Hermocrates's achievement should not be understood as the creation of a new identity; while new identities certainly did emerge from time to time, this process typically took longer than the duration of a speech. Sicilian identity was not new or unfamiliar in 424; rather, it was one of many options available for the self-identification of Sicilian Greeks in the fifth century, but it had faded into the background. Hermocrates, then, called it back into the foreground, by persuading his listeners to view their political choices through the lens of Sicilian identity, rather than the ethnic or civic identities that had previously conditioned their thinking. He was able to identify some useful criteria that were already latent in people's minds and encouraged them to consider those similarities and differences, associated with Sikeliote identity, more important than the ethnic criteria they had been using before.[78] This kind of rapid cognitive switching from one type of identity to another is characteristic of the role of identity in Greek political decision-making, and it is enabled by shifting levels of salience, the degree to which a particular identity is felt to be relevant in a given context. While Hermocrates could not realistically convince

---

77. *Contra*, Antonaccio 2001, 118–121; Fragoulaki 2013, 98–99.

78. Fauber (2001, 43–44) agrees that Hermocrates "attempted to suppress shared descent in an effort to unite the entire island, so that 'Sikeliote' identity would take rhetorical priority."

204   POLITICS OF IDENTITY IN SICILY & SOUTHERN ITALY

his listeners to adopt an identity that was far from their prior self-conceptions, he could easily persuade them to consider one familiar identity more salient than others.

Several important elements of the speech seem designed to ease the transition from one mode of identification to another. Specifically, Hermocrates tries to link aspects of Sikeliote identity to more familiar types such as ethnicity and *polis* identity. He refers to wars between the Sicilian cities as *stasis* (4.61.1). This word normally denotes civil war within a *polis*, not war between independent cities. By likening Sicily as a whole to a single city, Hermocrates is encouraging his listeners to think of Sicily as a single unit.[79] The parallel between the *polis*, within which war is not normally socially acceptable, and the island of Sicily suggests that war should not occur between Sicilian cities as well. By drawing this comparison, Hermocrates is helping people to recognize the implications of his arguments and making it easier for his audience to accept them, since the conceptual underpinnings are made familiar. He continues this line of thought by comparing cities to individuals; each city should not try to increase *ta idia* but act for the common good (4.59.4, 4.60.1, 4.63.1). This encourages people to think in terms of joining a larger community composed of cities; the frequent use of forms of *koinos* (which appear six times) reinforces this thought.[80] The orator also compares the Sikeliotai to the two main ethnic groups, saying that just as it is not shameful for members of an ethnic group to give way to one another, so, too, the Sikeliotai may yield to one another (4.64.3). This passage does not suggest that the Sikeliotai actually are an ethnic group.[81] Rather, Hermocrates is saying that the Sikeliotai are *like* an ethnic group; he is using a comparison to help people understand what he wants them to think. These comparisons to more familiar conceptions of identity help people understand and categorize the less familiar one and encouraged them to reconsider which type of identity would guide their decisions at the moment.

The outcome of the Conference of Gela—the Sikeliotai did make peace, albeit temporarily—suggests that this encouragement was successful. Hermocrates's speech did alter the way most Sicilians viewed their identities and demonstrates

79. Cf. Thuc. 3.62.5, 4.92.6, where Theban speakers (hardly disinterested, of course) attribute Athenian successes in Boeotia to *stasis* among the Boeotians; cf. Price 2001, 116–123.

80. Connor (1984, 121–122) treats these issues as a question of identity, though not systematically.

81. So Antonaccio 2001, 118–119; cf. Gomme, *HCT* III.520.

clearly how identity, when deployed in political rhetoric, can have a real impact on political events.

Ethnicity in the Camarina Debate

A decade later, in 415, the Athenians returned with a much larger armada, and the idea that the Sicilians had more to fear from Athens than from Syracuse was even easier to believe. This time, Camarina hesitated between the two sides, and Hermocrates spoke again to encourage them to ally with Syracuse.[82] One would think this would be a prime opportunity for a renewal of the geographic basis of Sikeliote identity of the previous decade, and, in fact, such rhetoric is not entirely absent: Hermocrates does ask the Camarinaeans to "guard the common interests of Sicily" against Athens.[83] Far more prominent in this speech, however, is a vicious ethnic screed urging the Camarinaeans to support Syracuse as fellow Dorians against Ionian invaders. It is particularly surprising that Hermocrates would think this argument likely to succeed, since little more than a decade earlier, Camarina had refused to join the alliance of its Dorian kinsmen. How can we understand this shifting rhetoric of identity?

In comparison to the Gela speech, in which Hermocrates asked the Sicilians to ignore ethnicity altogether, the change in rhetoric is substantial. The language of kinship pervades the speech. A decade earlier, Athens was an "enemy by nature" (4.60.1: φύσει πολέμιον) but not because of ethnicity. Rather, the sea that divides Athens from the Sikeliotai was enough, for Hermocrates, to constitute a natural boundary that should not be crossed. In his Camarina speech, however, it is the Ionians as a whole who are "enemies by nature" (6.79.2: φύσει πολεμίους; cf. 6.80.3). The ethnic divide is strongly felt, and presented as permanent, inherent, and unsurpassable, since "we are plotted against by the Ionians, who are always our enemies, while we Dorians are betrayed by Dorians."[84] On the only occasion when he does refer to "the common interests of Sicily," he does so in the same breath as an argument from kinship: for

---

82. The Camarinaeans contributed twenty cavalrymen and fifty archers to oppose the initial Athenian landing at Syracuse in 415 (Thuc. 6.67.2), but after the Athenian victory at Dascon (6.66–70), they evidently appeared persuadable to both sides. On the Camarina Debate (6.75–88) generally, see Cogan 1981, 106–112; Hornblower, CT III.489–508; Fauber 2001.

83. 6.80.2: τήν τε κοινὴν ὠφελίαν τῇ Σικελίᾳ φυλάξαι; cf. 77.2 (τοῦ ἄπωθεν ξυνοίκου); Fragoulaki 2013, 99.

84. 6.80.3: δεόμεθα δὲ καὶ μαρτυρόμεθα ἅμα, εἰ μὴ πείσομεν, ὅτι ἐπιβουλευόμεθα μὲν ὑπὸ Ἰώνων αἰεὶ πολεμίων, προδιδόμεθα δὲ ὑπὸ ὑμῶν Δωριῆς Δωριῶν.

Camarina to help Syracuse would be the "nobler" (*kallion*) course of action (among other reasons) precisely because they are *syngeneis*.[85] Mention of *syngeneia* as the Athenians' pretext for the invasion (6.76.2, 77.1) only strengthens the moral value attached to the idea of protecting one's kinsmen. Arguments rooted in ethnicity, placed near the beginning of the speech and again at the end, thus receive the most emphasis.

Other prominent arguments in the speech are closely intertwined with the themes of ethnic kinship and ethnic divisions. For instance, Thucydides places Camarina's existing alliance with Athens at the center of a sophisticated ring composition, indicating its importance.[86] Hermocrates argues, naturally, that Camarina should not abide by this alliance, but, crucially, he makes his argument in terms of ethnicity: if the people of Rhegium, who are not only Athenian allies but also their *syngeneis*, did not uphold the alliance, then the Camarinaeans, who are not bound by kinship ties, should feel even less bound by its terms (6.79.2). Similarly, the contrast between freedom and slavery, a common rhetorical *topos*,[87] is here closely associated not only with the Athenian Empire but also with the gulf between Dorians and Ionians. Hermocrates asks the Camarinaeans to make it clear to the Athenians that they are not dealing with "Ionians, Hellespontines or islanders, who, though changing masters, are always slaves either to the Mede or to someone else, but free Dorians from the autonomous Peloponnese, inhabiting Sicily."[88]

Hermocrates here compliments the Camarinaeans by inviting them to take pride in their Dorian culture and origins and contrasting them with slavish Ionians. It is worth noting, too, that Euphemus, the Athenian speaker who answers Hermocrates, does not reject the fundamental hostility between Dorians and Ionians but rather accepts it and tries to turn it to his advantage.

---

85. 6.80.2; cf. 79.2. Other reasons helping Syracuse is *kallion* include that Syracuse is the injured party and not allowing their Athenian friends to make a serious mistake.

86. Hornblower (*CT* III.491–494, 499–500) emphasizes Camarina's "interestingly conflicted symmachical obligations" in explaining why Thucydides chose to highlight this debate.

87. It is especially noticeable in rhetoric surrounding the Persian Wars (see Raaflaub 2004, 58–89), which is noteworthy given the heavy intertextual presence of Herodotus's account throughout Books 6 and 7: Rood 1999, 152–164.

88. 6.77.1: οὐ ξυστραφέντες βουλόμεθα προθυμότερον δεῖξαι αὐτοῖς ὅτι οὐκ Ἴωνες τάδε εἰσὶν οὐδ᾽ Ἑλλησπόντιοι καὶ νησιῶται, οἳ δεσπότην ἢ Μῆδον ἢ ἕνα γέ τινα αἰεὶ μεταβάλλοντες δουλοῦνται, ἀλλὰ Δωριῆς ἐλεύθεροι ἀπ᾽ αὐτονόμου τῆς Πελοποννήσου τὴν Σικελίαν οἰκοῦντες.

In this debate, ethnicity is taken for granted as a reason for action, and other arguments are made to align with ethnic concerns.

As a result of Hermocrates's speech, Camarina decided to support Syracuse but in a moderate way, in case Athens's success continued (6.88.1); the city sent no troops immediately but eventually provided 1,100 men (7.33.1). That represented a substantial contribution for a small *polis*; by comparison, Gela, a larger city, sent five ships but only 400 foot soldiers. Thucydides gives no further indication of Camarina's reasons for sending troops, suggesting that, despite the delay, Hermocrates's message of Dorian unity played an important role in persuading the city to help Syracuse, though it was probably not the only factor in the decision. Moreover, even in the short term, Hermocrates was able to persuade the Camarinaeans to abandon their alliance with Athens, indicating that his rhetoric was at least partially successful.

For Thucydides, the Camarina Debate is a crucial exploration both of Athenian imperialism and of the role of small states in a world dominated by large ones. In particular, the reasons small states might choose to align with one side or the other come under the microscope, and ethnicity is one such reason. This goal of analyzing small states more broadly opens up the possibility that this debate might bear rather little relationship to what was actually said and that Thucydides might have brought together many possible arguments relevant to small states of all kinds, rather than those relevant to Camarina specifically.[89] At the same time, however, numerous references specific to Camarina and to Sicily in 414 demonstrate that Thucydides has taken care to tailor such broadly relevant arguments to the specific situation under consideration.[90] Much as I argued above for the Gela speech, the prominence of ethnicity in the speech only makes sense if Thucydides (and his audience) thought that the ethnic argument was a reasonable one to deploy in this situation. Why is this, and what does it tell us about the role of ethnicity in political decision-making?

Political Speeches and the Making of Identity

The success of Hermocrates's two speeches in persuading first the Sicilian ambassadors and then the assembly of Camarina to adopt his proposals has

---

89. In fact, the historical Hermocrates may have done something similar, speaking implicitly to all the Greeks of Sicily: Westlake 1958, 187.

90. Hermocrates's appeal to "the common benefit of Sicily" (6.80.2) would not make sense in mainland Greece, and he is particularly careful to address Camarina's concerns about Syracusan imperialism (6.78).

enormous significance for the role of identity in Greek politics. The historical Hermocrates—and, by extension, the character Hermocrates through whom Thucydides analyzes Sicilian history—hoped to achieve concrete political results through his rhetorical deployment first of Sicilian identity and then of ethnicity. As a seasoned politician and orator, Hermocrates was well aware of his listeners and what strategies might persuade them to follow his advice. A strategy that attempts to persuade through appeals to identity could only be successful if his audience was already receptive and familiar with the identities to which he was appealing. As recent approaches to Greek oratory have emphasized, the rhetoric of identity is a reciprocal process, where the audience actively chooses to accept the speaker's arguments and make decisions on that basis.[91] If, through listening to Hermocrates, the listeners (or at least a significant proportion of them) came to agree with the arguments presented, then he had, at least temporarily, had a genuine impact on how they viewed their identities. This new sense of identity among the decision-making audience was no less real than any other.

Speech-making was an important part of the decision-making process in virtually every Greek community, even in oligarchic polities such as Sparta, and citizens throughout the Greek world were accustomed to developing their opinions through listening to oratory. Where we have sufficient evidence, such as Athens, it is clear that rhetoric involving identity was an important aspect of the political process. Politicians invoked identity as a way of manipulating their audience toward a desired endpoint, an eminently practical goal that could not succeed unless the audience was receptive. The flexible and discursive nature of identity suggests that an individual's sense of identity can be affected by persuasive speaking, with no diminution of the genuineness of that feeling of being Dorian, Sicilian, or whatever. Thus, speeches can provide a window into the shared assumptions of the speaker and his audience, and a successful speech can indicate the framework of identity within which a majority of the audience made its decision.

This approach largely removes from the equation the opinions of Hermocrates himself. Some scholars have argued that Hermocrates was not so much a genuine Sicilian patriot as a cynical politician whose propaganda of Sicilian and Dorian unity was merely a self-serving front for his own tyrannical ambitions.[92] This view would take his speeches out of the realm of identity

---

91. Pelling 2000, 37–43; Steinbock 2013, 30–43.

92. Hermocrates's later career saw him fighting the Athenians in the Aegean and the Carthaginians in Sicily, with the possible aim of making himself tyrant of Syracuse; Dionysius

entirely, substituting an interpretive framework centered around propaganda. Even if this were the case, however, the role of the audience would still be crucial, since a successful speech, regardless of the motives of the speaker, cannot stray too far from mainstream public opinion. The identities actually perceived and adopted by Hermocrates himself—whether Sicilian, Dorian, or anything else—are not only unrecoverable but also irrelevant.

It is instead audience responses to rhetoric that can reveal much about how considerations of identity affect decisions. After listening to a speech about the value of a common Sicilian identity, numerous ambassadors voted to unite against an outsider, an invader from overseas. Hermocrates's words led them to consider the geographic criterion, which united all Sicilians and separated them from Athens, more important than the ethnic differences that had previously kept them apart. The assembly of Camarina, after hearing about the difference between Dorians and Ionians, decided by majority vote not to actively support Athens and, eventually, to send troops to Syracuse. Whereas previously Camarina had acted on the basis of its *polis* or regional identities, now the ethnic criterion became much more prominent. In both situations, rhetoric affected the lens through which decision makers viewed their choices, by encouraging them to prioritize one type of identity over another in the present situation.

This "prioritization" is another way of describing salience, the relative importance of different identities, as perceived by community members, in a given situation. While new identities are built up and articulated over time, through a process of consensus-building among the members of a community, salience often changes quickly and is easily susceptible to rhetorical persuasion. Politicians can address the salience of various criteria of identity, persuading their audience that one criterion is more important than another. Such rhetoric is no less valid a way for community members to come to a new consensus about the relative importance of each of their multiple identities than any other.

The increased salience of one type of identity would only be temporary, however, a conclusion supported by several assumptions made in the speeches. When arguing in favor of one identity, Hermocrates does not assume that other identities will cease to exist or will never again play a role in decision-making. On the contrary, in the Gela speech, he admits that the Dorian and Chalcidian ethnic groups will continue to exist and may even go to war against each other at some future date (4.64.3). Temporarily, however, those ethnic differences will become less important than what they share as Sicilians. At Camarina, Hermocrates does briefly argue for "the common benefit of Sicily," which would make no sense if Sicilian identity was not also important (6.80.2). He even attempts to turn Camarina's *polis* identity to his advantage, by pointing out how the city's concern for its political independence is now threatened more by Athens than by Syracuse. Ultimately, Camarina's other identities are merely temporarily submerged underneath other considerations, including (but not limited to) its Dorian ethnicity. Kinship ties to Syracuse thereby help override, on a temporary basis and at least in the opinions of enough people to constitute a majority in a democratic assembly, the framework of *polis* identity through which it more commonly viewed its decisions.

Conclusion

In the end, Thucydides's analysis of Greek international politics encompasses far more than the factors of power, necessity, and self-interest for which he is best known. In fact, Thucydides is interested in all of the considerations that impact foreign policy and state decision-making, and the various episodes discussed above show that identity is prominent among them. At Gela, for instance, Hermocrates was still asking people to act on the basis of self-interest, but whose self-interest? In other words, what is the extent of the "self" part of self-interest? Up to this point, cities or at most ethnic groups were the largest entities whose self-interest his audience was willing to consider; Hermocrates asks his listeners merely to broaden their vision and act in the best interests of Sicily as a whole.[93] In his Camarina speech, meanwhile, Hermocrates sets the argument from self-interest alongside that from justice, arguing that it is nobler (*kallion*) to help one's kinsmen than to fight them.[94]

For Thucydides, too, this kind of kinship diplomacy is normal: it is eminently natural for members of the same ethnic group to ally with one another. In fact, the prevalence of ethnic alliances may help explain Hermocrates's choice in the Camarina Debate to appeal to Dorian ethnicity rather than Sicilian identity. If kinship ties were stronger than the criterion of geographical proximity,

---

93. 4.59.1: ἐς κοινὸν δὲ τὴν δοκοῦσάν μοι βελτίστην γνώμην εἶναι ἀποφαινόμενος τῇ Σικελίᾳ πάσῃ.

94. 6.80.2: καίτοι κάλλιον τοῖς ἀδικουμένοις καὶ ἅμα ξυγγενέσι προσθεμένους τήν τε κοινὴν ὠφελίαν τῇ Σικελίᾳ φυλάξαι καὶ τοὺς Ἀθηναίους φίλους δὴ ὄντας μὴ ἐᾶσαι ἁμαρτεῖν.

he may therefore have anticipated that he would be more likely to persuade them by this argument than by any other. While identities do shift freely, not all identities have an equal claim to salience. Only in rare situations—such as the topsy-turvy world of the Peloponnesian War or the uniquely bad blood between Camarina and Syracuse—does this general practice not hold.

Beyond the pages of Thucydides, too, identity had a measurable impact on Greek history, shaping and conditioning the political events, decisions, and rhetorical strategies of numerous *poleis* and politicians. Identities form and change through a subjective process of consensus-building among community members, and here we see important examples of this process in action. The use by politicians of rhetoric involving identity should not be dismissed as mere propaganda.[95] Instead, political oratory formed an important component of Greek decision-making processes. By focusing on audience responses, we can see how speeches contribute to a community's consensus. The exact composition of the audience is less crucial. Of the two speeches analyzed above, one addresses an audience of international elites, while the other appeals to the assembly of a democratic *polis*; both groups, however, were the decision makers at the time, and this aspect is what matters.

Each of the Greek communities of Sicily perceived its set of alternative identities differently, and those perceptions shifted as circumstances changed. Camarina offers a good model for this phenomenon. The manner in which Camarina switched from emphasizing one of these identities to another differs substantially from the processes (discussed in previous chapters) by which new identities are created and existing ones altered. All three of these different identities—as Camarinaeans, as Sicilians, and as Dorians—already existed long before 427, when that *polis* first enters Thucydides's *History*. Differing situations and political oratory led the citizens of Camarina to reassess how they valued their various identities, and within fifteen years, they made momentous political decisions on the basis of each of those identities.

---

95. Jowett and O'Donnell 2015, 1–57; cf. Beetham 1991, esp. 19.

6

Continuity and Change in the Third Century

THE THIRD CENTURY BCE was a turbulent time for the Greeks of Sicily and southern Italy. While the conquests of Alexander the Great and the wars of the Successors had not touched the West significantly, the western Greeks were nonetheless embedded in the new world of the Hellenistic Mediterranean, and they needed to find their place within it. Meanwhile, closer to home, the sociopolitical landscape of these regions was changing rapidly, as non-Greeks—Lucanians and Bruttians in Italy, Carthaginians and Mamertines in Sicily—began to play an increasingly important role in politics and society. How did Greeks respond to these changing historical circumstances? How did they adapt their self-perceptions and self-representations to new realities? In this final chapter, two case studies will demonstrate both significant continuities and change over time in the identities of the Greeks of the Hellenistic West.

First, the discourse of Hellenism gained increasing prominence in southern Italy. The growing presence of non-Greeks in the region was perceived by some as a barbarian invasion and a threat to Greek civilization. Greek identity, constructed in opposition to these barbarians, became widely salient once again. Nevertheless, this discourse was not universal; each *polis* responded differently, and for some, local concerns and local identities were more important than any notion of a shared panhellenic identity. Such a fractured set of identities, each relevant for different communities in different circumstances, is, of course, nothing new, and when the Romans initially arrived on the political scene in the late fourth century, they were slotted into this paradigm. For some cities, such as Taras, the Romans were just another barbarian tribe to be defeated, while others, such as Thurii, saw them as potential allies. The place of Greekness—sometimes prominent, sometimes ignored—in the discourse

The Politics of Identity in Greek Sicily and Southern Italy. Mark R. Thatcher, Oxford University Press. © Oxford University Press 2021. DOI: 10.1093/oso/9780197586440.003.0006

of this period and in early Italiote perceptions of Rome can shed important light on the role of identity in politics.

A second case study will more closely examine civic identity in Hellenistic Syracuse. The city remained an independent *polis* down to its capture by Marcellus in 212, and yet it became the capital of a Hellenistic kingdom and a small Sicilian empire, interconnected with the Hellenistic Mediterranean yet fiercely independent. What did it mean to be Syracusan in the third century? Under Hieron II especially, Syracuse focused in part on its Greekness, while also distinguishing itself through pride in its Dorian, Corinthian, and Peloponnesian origins as well as the memory of the city's past greatness. Comparing this body of material to that available in earlier periods shows both the long-term durability of many aspects of Syracusan identity and its evolution in historical time.

This period and region—southern Italy and Sicily in the third century—have often fallen through the cracks, central to neither Greek nor Roman history. The sources (and indeed much scholarship) no longer approach the material from a Greek perspective, as in earlier centuries, but now start from a Roman perspective and interpret events through the lens of Roman biases. Nevertheless, this study attempts to recenter the experience of the western Greeks in this period and to reconstruct their neglected perspective and their perceptions of themselves and others.

Greeks and Barbarians in Southern Italy

In a fragment from a work entitled the *Sympotic Miscellany* (F124 Wehrli = Athenaeus 14.632a–b), the late-fourth-century philosopher, music theorist, and polymath Aristoxenus of Taras lamented the "barbarization" of Poseidonia:[1]

Ἀριστόξενος ἐν τοῖς Συμμίκτοις Συμποτικοῖς ὅμοιον, φησί, ποιοῦμεν Ποσειδωνιάταις τοῖς ἐν τῷ Τυρσηνικῷ κόλπῳ κατοικοῦσιν. οἷς συνέβη τὰ μὲν ἐξ ἀρχῆς Ἕλλησιν οὖσιν ἐκβεβαρβαρῶσθαι Τυρρηνοῖς ἢ Ῥωμαίοις γεγονόσι, καὶ τήν τε φωνὴν μεταβεβληκέναι τά τε λοιπὰ τῶν ἐπιτηδευμάτων, ἄγειν δὲ μίαν τινὰ αὐτοὺς τῶν ἑορτῶν τῶν Ἑλληνικῶν ἔτι καὶ νῦν, ἐν ᾗ συνιόντες ἀναμιμνήσκονται τῶν ἀρχαίων ἐκείνων

---

1. A large bibliography has developed on this passage; see Fraschetti 1981; Asheri 1999; Meriani 2000; Wonder 2002; Crawford 2006a; Russo 2008; Simon 2012, 381–383; Humm 2018. On Aristoxenus more broadly, see Gibson 2005, esp. 1–4.

ὀνομάτων τε καὶ νομίμων καὶ ἀπολοφυράμενοι πρὸς ἀλλήλους καὶ ἀποδακρύσαντες ἀπέρχονται.

Aristoxenus says in his *Sympotic Miscellany* that we are acting like the people of Poseidonia who live on the Tyrrhenian Sea. What happened to them is that, although they were originally Greeks, they have turned into barbarians and become Etruscans or Romans, and they have changed their language and the rest of their customs. Even still now, they celebrate only one of the Greek festivals, in which they come together and remember their old words and customs; after lamenting them to each other and weeping, they depart.

Aristoxenus then draws a comparison with contemporary musical performances, which in his opinion have also been "barbarized" and do not meet the standards of the past. This is clearly a tendentious and one-sided report, from an author not directly concerned with relations between Greeks and others—after all, the anecdote about Poseidonia merely serves the needs of Aristoxenus's real interest, the decline of music—and need not be taken at face value as historically accurate. Nevertheless, the passage contains some rich reflections on concepts of Greekness in the late fourth century, and its attitude toward the cultural status of Poseidonia represents the opinion of at least some contemporary Greeks.

The Achaean *polis* of Poseidonia had been taken over in the late fifth century by the Lucanians, a large non-Greek people in south-central Italy.[2] The exact identity of the city's new rulers matters little to Aristoxenus, however, since he misidentifies them as either Tyrrhenians (i.e., Etruscans) or Romans.[3] He focuses instead on the idea that Greeks no longer dominate their own community. Their culture has vanished, as we see from two key indicia of Hellenic identity: the people of Poseidonia no longer speak Greek but (presumably) speak Oscan, the language broadly shared by most peoples of southern Italy, and their daily customs have changed as well. From Aristoxenus's vantage point, nearly a century later, the cultural shifts wrought by this event were

---

2. Strabo 5.4.13 identifies the Lucanians as the aggressors; the date is estimated from archaeological sources, especially the destruction layer at the Foce del Sele sanctuary: Frederiksen 1984, 137, 150n28; Pedley 1990, 74–75.

3. The reference to Romans in particular is surprising, since the Roman colony of Paestum was not established until 273. Some emend the reference out of the text, while others push Aristoxenus's dates into the mid-third century. Yet the Romans were heavily involved in Campania in the late fourth century, and it is unlikely that Aristoxenus was concerned about the precise status of the city under Roman law; it is better to accept the transmitted text.

hugely significant. Moreover, he imputes to the people of Poseidonia a sense of loss; they meet to celebrate briefly their past Greekness and lament their fate and then return to their un-Hellenic ways.

This is not a neutral description of cultural change but a strong condemnation of what has happened. The highly charged language—especially *ekbarbarōsthai*, "to become barbarized"—shows Aristoxenus's concern with the maintenance of Greek identity and with the dichotomy between Greeks and barbarians. In fact, this precisely underlies his lack of concern for the difference between Etruscans, Romans, and Lucanians; he is writing within a model where those distinct cultures are all flattened into a single concept of "barbarians." This way of thinking had a long pedigree, going back to the Persian Wars. For Aristoxenus in the late fourth century, Greek civilization in southern Italy was under threat, and this has made Hellenic identity enormously salient for him.

Conflict between the Greek cities of Italy and their non-Greek neighbors was not new, of course. In the fifth century, Taras, Thurii, and Rhegium all fought non-Greek neighbors, with mixed success.[4] But the frequency of conflict escalated in the fourth century, especially following the emergence of first the Lucanians and then the Bruttians as formidable new opponents who drastically increased the pressure on Greek communities.[5] This led to a qualitative change as well. Until the end of the fifth century, no Greek *polis* in Italy had been captured and held by non-Greeks.[6] But from that point forward, Poseidonia was not alone in suffering this fate; most of Campania, including Cumae, soon followed. Farther down the Tyrrhenian coast, the small *poleis* of Laus, Terina, Temesa, and Hipponion all fell during the fourth century; so did the final incarnation of Sybaris, which had been refounded on the Traeis River. The larger cities of Thurii and Heraclea were both captured but later regained their independence, while Croton and Metapontion were

4. Hdt. 7.170.3; Diod. 11.52; Arist. *Pol.* 5.1303a3; Paus. 10.10.6, 13.10; Polyaenus, *Strat.* 2.10; Frontin. *Str.* 2.3.12; with Wuilleumier 1939, 53–59; Nenci 1976; Brauer 1986, 27–29; Malkin 1994, 115–127; De Juliis 2000, 21–24; Cappelletti 2002, 1–4.

5. On the ethnogenesis of the Lucanians (late fifth century) and the Bruttians (mid-fourth), see Lombardo 1987; Herring 2000; Horsnaes 2002, 125–128; Yntema 2013, 165–170; Cappelletti 2018; Wonder 2018. Their work attributes their emergence to long-term processes of urbanization and growing social complexity, rather than an "Italic Migration" from the highlands to the coast (for which see Cornell 1974; Cornell 1995, 304–305; Frederiksen 1984, 136–140; Salmon 1988, 699–711; Pedley 1990, 97). Cf. the historiographical analysis of Simon 2012, 342–356.

6. For the political-military history of this period, see above all Lombardo 1987 (with full sources); cf. Brauer 1986, 43–86; Lomas 1993, 33–50; Purcell 1994, 386–389.

repeatedly threatened. By the late fourth century, wide swaths of formerly Greek southern Italy were in non-Greek hands. Strabo later summarized this situation with the same word, *ekbarbarōsthai*, used by Aristoxenus: "Today all parts of [Magna Graecia], except Taras, Rhegium, and Neapolis, have become completely barbarized."[7] For those Greek cities that remained independent, these developments were deeply alarming; they seemed to be facing an existential threat.

However, this perception differed from the reality on the ground. Recent scholarship has emphasized that war was not constant; treaties and even cooperation between Greeks and non-Greeks were also possible.[8] While Greeks fought non-Greeks repeatedly, they also fought each other; for instance, both Dionysius I and Agathocles campaigned in Italy, mainly against Greeks. Moreover, while the Italiote League sometimes acted as a forum for unified Greek action against barbarians, it equally served as a vehicle for Tarantine hegemony, and they were willing to attack other Greeks to keep it.[9] The idea of a unified Greek front against a barbarian menace is therefore revealed as a convenient fiction designed to support Tarantine imperialism. These considerations led Kathryn Lomas to describe fourth-century Italy instead as the site of opportunistically shifting alliances, in which a model of civilized Greeks versus barbarian Italians is not valid.[10]

Equally important, many communities flourished in their new incarnations under non-Greek rule; in fact, the fourth century was a time of great prosperity, visible above all archaeologically, for both Greek and non-Greek communities.[11] Peaceful relations between the two led to fruitful cultural exchange and innovation. Neapolis, for instance, allowed Oscan speakers to gain citizenship and developed a mixed culture but maintained its Hellenic identity into the Roman imperial period.[12] Throughout southern Italy, religious, linguistic, and cultural influences flowed in both directions, and Nicholas Purcell has argued

7. Strabo 6.1.2: νυνὶ δὲ πλὴν Τάραντος καὶ Ῥηγίου καὶ Νεαπόλεως ἐκβεβαρβαρῶσθαι συμβέβηκεν; cf. Simon 2012, 380–390.

8. E.g., Diod. 14.102.3; 19.10.3–4; 20.104; App. *Sam.* 7.1; Strabo 6.3.4; with Lomas 1993, 42–48.

9. See Diod. 14.101.1 for a rule mandating league members to send help to anyone under Lucanian attack, a strong statement of the need for unity under pressure. On the Italiote League, see Lombardo 1996; Wonder 2012; Fronda 2015. Tarantine hegemony: Wuilleumier 1939, 67–75; Brauer 1986, 43–59; Lomas 1993, 35–42; Huffman 2005, 8–18; Simon 2012, 208–212, 260–268.

10. Lomas 1993, 44; cf. Lombardo 1987, 76.

11. See esp. the work of the University of Texas project at Metapontion: Carter 2006, 218–232.

12. Lomas 2015. Oscan names also appear in the epigraphic record of several other "Greek" communities: Lomas 1995, 351–352.

forcefully that to accept the simplistic Greek-versus-barbarian dichotomy is "not just to distort the truth, but also to miss the opportunity to examine one of the most fascinatingly complicated patterns of cultural interchange which we can perceive from antiquity."[13] As a description of a historical moment, these statements capture an important and interesting reality.

Nevertheless, they fail to consider the attitudes held by Greeks at the time. A sense of Greekness was particularly strong among Tarantines, who took the lead in resisting the barbarians and even summoned a series of generals from Greece, the so-called *condottieri*, to assist.[14] The last and best-known of these was Pyrrhus, to whom I will return. Yet it is the first, King Archidamus III of Sparta, who shows most clearly the sense among the Greeks of Italy that their struggle against the barbarians mattered greatly. His death in battle against either the Messapians or the Lucanians in 338 was said to have occurred on the same day and at the same hour as the Battle of Chaeronea in Greece.[15] Synchronisms of this sort are usually reserved for the most important events, such as the one repeated in several forms synchronizing the Battle of Himera in 480 with either Salamis or Thermopylae.[16] Thus, some observers evidently considered Archidamus's war against the barbarians just as important for western history as Chaeronea was for mainland Greeks.

Purcell calls the idea of Taras as a bulwark against barbarians "a *mythos*, an explanatory narrative, that is informed by another powerful antithesis, that between the pure Hellenism of Laconian Taras and the native hordes growling at the borders."[17] It is this *mythos* on which I focus here. This is a study not of historical facts and trends but of the perceptions of those trends that Greeks held at the time. The constructed nature of identity allowed the Greeks to define themselves based on subjective factors, not objective reality. According to many at the time, communities such as Poseidonia may have gained prosperity but had lost something crucial: their identity as Hellenes.

---

13. Purcell 1994, 393–394; cf. Guzzo 1984; Lomas 1995, 349–353; Wonder 2002; Dench 2003; Yntema 2013, 234–235.

14. Wuilleumier 1939, 77–98; Giannelli 1969; Giannelli 1974; Brauer 1986, 61–86; Lombardo 1987, 76–84; Lomas 1993, 41–44; De Juliis 2000, 27–30; Cappelletti 2002, 48–90; Cabanes 2005; Simon 2012, 205–278; and the articles in *Alessandro il Molosso* 2004.

15. Diod. 16.88.3; Plut. *Cam.* 19.5; cf. Diod. 16.63.1; Plut. *Agis* 3.2; Paus. 3.10.5; Theopompus (*FGrH* 115) F232 (= Ath. 12.536c–d).

16. Hdt. 7.166; Diod. 11.24.1; cf. Asheri 1992a and chapter 3.

17. Purcell 1994, 393.

In fact, many Tarantines in the fourth and third centuries came to believe that their civilization was threatened by barbarian invasion. This resulted from a reciprocal cycle in which identity conditioned how the Tarantines viewed events and trends as they occurred, and those events in turn helped make Greek identity ever more salient. As a result, the discourse of Hellenism became predominant at Taras. Still, as we will see, this discourse of Hellenism was always in tension with the *polis* identities of the various communities concerned, and each city responded differently to the situation. Shared Greekness mattered much to some but little to others. By the early third century, Taras's failure to achieve a lasting victory had soured many other communities on its vision of Greek identity, and they began looking for other protectors. Thus, the multiple identities of Greek communities—both Hellenic and local—played an important role in conditioning responses to changing circumstances. The flexibility of identity and the availability of different choices are critical to properly understanding these developments. This sets the stage for the arrival of Rome.

Taras and Thurii

By the 280s, then, Taras had developed a policy of resisting barbarians, based on a fundamental perception of themselves as Greeks leading the resistance against a barbarian onslaught and defending Hellenic civilization in Italy. When the Romans first appeared on the stage, the Tarantines understood them according to their existing paradigm: they were another barbarian people to be resisted. This can be observed in a few scattered examples from the late fourth century[18] but appears most strongly in the context of the so-called Pyrrhic War. Yet the actions of Thurii, which sought help from Rome, rather than Taras, against the nearby Lucanians, show that not all Greek cities saw the situation in the same way. The Greeks of Italy, therefore, articulated a range of identities, based on their particular situation and conditioned by their own histories. Yet for all Greeks, identity played an important role in conditioning their responses to the arrival of Rome.

---

18. Conflict over Neapolis in 327 (Liv. 8.22–23; Dion. Hal. *Ant. Rom.* 15.5–6); Taras attempts to arbitrate between Rome and the Samnites in 320 (Liv. 9.14.1–8); Cleonymus summoned to fight "the Lucanians and the Romans" in 303 (Diod. 20.104–105). On early Roman–Tarantine relations, see Wuilleumier 1939, 89–96; Brauer 1986, 73–81; Raaflaub, Richards, and Samons 1992, 19–20; Lomas 1993, 44–50; for Roman contact with Magna Graecia more broadly, see Simon 2012, 193–278, 319–335.

The crisis that led to Taras's appeal to Pyrrhus began at Thurii. In 284, Thurii, again under attack by the Lucanians, called for help not to Taras but to Rome.[19] Although Rome's response was initially minimal, when the invitation was renewed two years later, Roman troops arrived in force under C. Fabricius and left a garrison in the city; it appears that other Greek cities, including Rhegium, Locri, and Croton, received garrisons at the same time. In the same year, ten Roman ships appeared at Taras, in contravention of an earlier treaty barring Rome from the Gulf of Taranto, and the Tarantines immediately sailed out and sank five of them.[20] What is more, they immediately marched to Thurii and expelled both the Roman garrison and the pro-Roman party, thus reasserting their hegemony over the city. Rome then sent an embassy led by L. Postumius to demand reparations.[21] He spoke Greek, in an unusual effort for a Roman on official business, and yet the Tarantines jeered at his imperfect command of the language and also at his clothing. After their overture was rejected, a Roman army invaded Tarantine territory, and the Tarantines, foreseeing a substantial war, sought assistance from overseas.

Taras's motivations throughout this period are difficult to discern, since they come down to us filtered through layers of historiographical thinking. Yet two references suggest that the Tarantines were thinking specifically in terms of Greek unity and identity. First, Appian reports that the Tarantines were particularly incensed at the Thurians for preferring Rome "although they were Greeks."[22] If this accurately reflects contemporary thinking at Taras, they were operating under the assumption that all Greeks rightly ought to be united against a common enemy. Their sense of betrayal at Thurian actions, therefore, reflects a privileging of Hellenic identity above all others.

Second, the Tarantine response to the embassy of L. Postumius repays closer examination. According to both Dionysius of Halicarnassus and Appian, Postumius made a special and unusual effort to speak Greek to the assembly at Taras, yet the Tarantines jeered at his imperfect command of the language.[23]

---

19. App. *Sam.* 7.1–2; Liv. *Per.* 11; Plin. *N.H.* 34.32; Dion. Hal. *Ant. Rom.* 19.13, 20.4; Val. Max. 1.8.6. For the following events, see Wuilleumier 1939, 100–104; Brauer 1986, 121–124; Franke 1989, 456–458; Raaflaub, Richards, and Samons 1992, 20–23; Rosenstein 2012, 38–41; De Sensi Sestito 2016, 290–297; Kent 2020, 28–35.

20. App. *Sam.* 7.2; Cass. Dio 9.39.5.

21. App. *Sam.* 7.3–6; Dion. Hal. *Ant. Rom.* 19.5.

22. App. *Sam.* 7.2: ἔς τε Θουρίους ἐγκλήματα ποιούμενοι, ὅτι Ἕλληνες ὄντες ἐπὶ Ῥωμαίους κατέφυγον ἀντὶ σφῶν; cf. Kent 2020, 29.

23. App. *Sam.* 7.4; Dion. Hal. *Ant. Rom.* 19.5.1. The locus classicus for the idea that Roman officials should speak Latin while conducting official business occurs more than a century

Moreover, they ridiculed his *toga praetexta*, and, ultimately, a particularly un-
ruly Tarantine attacked him physically and befouled his clothing. This story is
clearly derived from a virulently anti-Tarantine and pro-Roman tradition, and
much of this coloring should be rejected in historical reconstructions. Yet it
still seems likely that the ambassador actually was mistreated,[24] and so the precise criteria on which the Tarantines criticized Postumius are worth noting.
First, language had long been one of the factors distinguishing Greeks from
barbarians, suggesting that the Tarantines' implication was that Postumius
himself was a barbarian.[25] As we saw above, the Tarantines perceived themselves as a pure bastion of Hellenic culture, and a pure form of the Greek
language was likely part of this. Second, clothing sometimes played a similar
role. For Romans, the toga was a key symbol of Roman citizen identity (cf. *Aen.*
1.282, the *gens togata*) and helped distinguish Romans from others.[26] The texts
of our sources clearly reflect this Roman perspective, yet if the Tarantines were
aware of the significance that Romans placed on the toga, they might have
known that this would be a particular insult. In any case, it shows that they
were concerned to highlight the cultural differences between the Romans and
themselves. Hellenic identity was prominent in their minds.

In a more general sense, too, the Tarantines understood the Romans
through a set of perceptions and categories that had been developing over the
previous century. They understood the Romans as barbarians, no different
from the Lucanians, Messapians, and others whom they had fought in the
past. Meanwhile, they saw themselves as the defenders of Greekness, with a
duty to lead the other Greeks in safeguarding Greek civilization in Italy. This
leadership role resulted in a loose Tarantine hegemony over other Greek cities,
exercised partly through the Italiote League, and Thurii's turn toward Rome
represented a defection from Tarantine control. Taras's sudden and violent
response to Rome's actions must represent a sudden outburst of pent-up

---

later (Aemilius Paullus after Pydna in 168: Liv. 45.29.3; cf. 45.8.6); cf. Cato's jab at the historian Postumius Albinus, who apologized in his proem for his poor Greek (Plut. *Cat.
Mai.* 12.5).

24. Accepted by Brauer 1986, 124; Eckstein 2006, 155–156; Rosenstein 2012, 40; cf. Polyb.
1.6.5, which is not based on the embroideries of the annalistic tradition (on which see the
detailed analysis of Barnes 2005).

25. Brauer 1986, 124. Language is one of Herodotus's four criteria of Greekness (8.144.2), and
cf. Aristoxenus F124 (quoted above), who focused on the change of language at Poseidonia as
a key indicator of its barbarization.

26. See now Rothe 2020.

hostility based on what they perceived as Roman encroachment on their sphere of influence at Thurii and in southern Italy in general.[27]

In Thurii, of course, thinking was completely different, yet identity of a different sort still played an important role. The Thurians were not interested in projecting their own power or vying for leadership of the Greeks; instead, they were merely trying to protect their own independence. As a result, they did not see themselves primarily as members of a larger Hellenic community. In fact, such claims were downright dangerous for Thurii, when made by a neighbor with dreams of hegemony; they were just as concerned about being ruled by other Greeks as by anyone else. When Thurii asked for help from Rome, therefore, the fact that the Romans were not Greek was simply not important to them.[28] Instead, they were concerned with a more local problem, the Lucanians who were attacking them and how to defend themselves. And, in fact, they were delighted by the help Rome also provided, going so far as to set up a statue of C. Aelius, a tribune of the plebs who was instrumental in securing aid.[29]

Rhegium, it seems, was thinking along similar lines. According to one report, it asked for and received a Roman garrison because it feared barbarian aggression and also because it was suspicious of Taras.[30] Rhegium was fully aware that Taras expected it to fall into line, but instead it chose its own path. Croton and Locri in all probability also received garrisons.[31] All of these Greek communities sought Roman instead of Tarantine assistance, in part due to tensions with their fellow Greek city. This attitude partakes of a long tradition of Greeks finding local identities more salient than a larger conflict with non-Greeks; we may compare the behavior of Aristagoras, the early-fifth-century tyrant of Miletus, who employed Persian help in a conflict with Naxos, unconcerned by their status as non-Greeks (Hdt. 5.30–34). Locri, in fact, switched to Pyrrhus's side when he arrived and was a sufficiently trustworthy ally for

27. Brauer 1986, 122–124; Hoffmann 1936, 15.

28. Cf. Brauer 1986, 122; Kent 2020, 29. Lévêque (1957, 246) unfairly chastises Thurii for ignoring the need for Hellenic unity.

29. Pliny *N.H.* 34.32.

30. Dion. Hal. *Ant. Rom.* 20.4.2: τὴν Ταραντίνων πόλιν ἐν ὑποψίαις ἔχοντες. Diod. 22.1.2 states instead that the garrison was stationed "to guard Rhegium against King Pyrrhus," but this fragmentary section is badly garbled; a parallel passage, which is printed as 22.1.3 and does not mention Pyrrhus, likely more closely represents what Diodorus wrote.

31. Locri: Just. 18.1.9. Cf. Lévêque 1957, 246; Wuilleumier 1939, 101–102; Frederiksen 1984, 222–223.

him to locate his mint there. Yet after his eventual defeat, Locri became a loyal Roman ally, even minting coins with the legend ΠΙΣΤΙΣ to highlight its loyalty.[32] For these small cities caught between more powerful antagonists, Greek identity did not govern their actions.

Thus, comparing the responses of Taras to those of Thurii and others shows the complex role of identities in southern Italy. Greekness was prominent in some communities, leading to policies of resistance; in others, local *polis* identities overrode this, since they were just as concerned about the danger from Taras. The arrival of Rome did not change these factors. For Taras, the Romans were another barbarian tribe to be defeated, who threatened their independence and their empire. For Thurii, they were a potential ally, who could help defend it against its Greek neighbor. Only by considering multiple identities can the complex politics of this period be understood.

Pyrrhus

In 280, the entrance of a powerful new player—Pyrrhus, king of Epirus— temporarily swept away some of these complexities. Invited by the Tarantines to assist them against Rome, Pyrrhus led a coalition that included not only the Tarantines, other Italiotes, and his own mercenary troops but also several Italic peoples: the Lucanians, Messapians, and Samnites.[33] Despite this mixed set of allies, Pyrrhus carefully deployed the ideology of panhellenism to create legitimacy for his campaigns both in Italy and later in Sicily. His choice to do so highlights the artificial and constructed nature of identity but also suggests the ideological power it wielded. In a variety of media, Pyrrhus presented himself as the champion of Hellenic identity, leading the forces of the Greek world against a barbarian threat. He may actually have believed this at first, on the basis of information provided by the Tarantines. His famous statement preserved by Plutarch—while on a reconnaissance mission, he observed the Roman encampment and remarked that "the discipline of the barbarians is not barbarous"—implies, of course, that prior to that point, he had thought of the Romans unequivocally as barbarians.[34] The story, if historical, shows that he quickly revised his assessment, yet what is more important

---

32. Kraay and Hirmer 1966, 313; Lomas 1993, 52; Rutter 1997, 98–99.

33. E.g., Plut. *Pyrrh.* 13.6, 15.5, 17.5, 21.4; cf. De Sensi Sestito 2016, 300–302.

34. Plut. *Pyrrh.* 16.4–5: τάξις . . . αὕτη τῶν βαρβάρων οὐ βάρβαρος. On this passage in its literary context, see Mossman 2005.

for my purposes is the way Pyrrhus represented himself and his campaign to the public.

The portrait he promoted was first and foremost for local consumption, by the Tarantines and other allied Italiotes, and was designed to present his goals in line with theirs. In fact, as we have seen in earlier chapters, such an ideological campaign could not have succeeded without substantial local buy-in. The Tarantines, in fact, were initially enthusiastic about the prospect of participating in a panhellenic campaign. The success of Pyrrhus's ideology of Greek identity, therefore, sheds much light on Tarantine perceptions of what it meant to be Greek in southern Italy at this time. By referencing his claims of descent from Achilles and from Heracles and by deploying a series of coin types such as the well-known figure of Athena Promachos, Pyrrhus signaled to them that he was an appropriate leader for them and that he and they were part of a single community working together against Rome.

The Molossian royal house claimed to be descended from Achilles and his son Neoptolemus, who, happily, was also known as Pyrrhus.[35] The Hellenistic monarch frequently emphasized this claim throughout his career, including on coins minted during the Italian campaigns. For instance, a series of didrachms shows on the obverse a helmeted head of Achilles and on the reverse Thetis seated on a hippocamp bringing Achilles his new shield. Another ten-nummi bronze coin shows a head of Phthia, the homeland of Achilles.[36] Both of these draw attention to Pyrrhus's descent from the greatest hero of the panhellenic epics and even suggest that Pyrrhus himself is playing the role of a new Achilles. For Tarantines who saw themselves in a struggle for the survival of Greek civilization, Pyrrhus thus appeared to be the right man to lead them.

And the campaign may have been imbued with an even deeper meaning, if it was conceptualized by contemporaries as a new Trojan War, fought by a descendant of Achilles against a city with Trojan origins. Pausanias's account of the Tarantine embassy sent to invite Pyrrhus to Italy attributes this thought to him explicitly (1.12.1). Unfortunately, it is unclear how trustworthy this is, particularly since the story implies that Pyrrhus already knew of Rome's Trojan origins (a relatively unlikely scenario at this early date) and spontaneously made the connection with his own expedition. Andrew Erskine has forcefully

---

35. This claim dates back at least to Pindar (*Nem.* 7.38–9) and Euripides (*And.* 1248); cf. esp. Plut. *Pyrrh.* 1.2., with Garoufalias 1979, 165–170.

36. Kraay and Hirmer 1966, 339; Garoufalias 1979, 208; Franke 1989, 463–465; Borba Florenzano 1992, 208; Rutter 1997, 98.

argued that Trojan origins were unimportant to Romans until the time of Augustus; instead, such stories were told primarily by Greeks in order to conceptually locate Rome in relation to themselves.[37] Yet this argument assumes that such stories were circulating among Greeks by the early third century, and it is precisely Greek views of Rome that are at issue here. As Erskine himself and others have shown, conceptualizing Trojans as barbarians had been possible since the fifth century.[38] Particularly in an environment highly charged with tension between Greeks and barbarians, the Trojan War may well have been perceived as a relevant model in a south Italian context. If so, Pyrrhus's arrival would have invited the Tarantines to perceive themselves as the successors to the great panhellenic achievements of the past, enacting their identity as Greeks. Even if we reject the Trojan War as a model in the early third century, however, Pyrrhus's emphasis on the figure of Achilles still places a strong emphasis on the panhellenic valence of his expedition.

Two further ideological themes also invited Pyrrhus's allies to emphasize their Greekness. First, the king also claimed Heracles as an ancestor, and according to Plutarch, he recalled this lineage explicitly during the Sicilian phase of his campaign when he celebrated games in honor of Heracles following his victory at Eryx.[39] A series of bronze coins also showed a head of Heracles wearing the lion skin. Heracles was a particularly useful ancestor for Pyrrhus because this hero enjoyed such widespread acclaim throughout the region; he had been everywhere in the West. Moreover, as we saw in chapter 2, myths of Heracles often presented him as a civilizing force who overcomes barbarians, very much like what Pyrrhus was trying to accomplish.[40] The figure of Athena Promachos, too, had long symbolized the struggle against barbarians. She appears frequently on Pyrrhus's silver coinage and also as the reverse type on the bronze coins with Heracles mentioned above. An octobol from the Sicilian campaign also combines her with a head of Persephone crowned with wheat.[41] This coin combines the barbarian theme with a local touch, since

---

37. Erskine 2001, esp. 157–161 on Pyrrhus, but cf. the important critiques of Rose 2003; for a different reconstruction, see Gruen 1992, 6–51. Pyrrhus's Trojan War ideology is accepted by, e.g., Galinsky 1969, 170–172; Franke 1989, 465; Gruen 1992, 26–27; Lomas 1993, 53; doubted by Lévêque 1957, 251–258; Brauer 1986, 129–130.

38. Hall 1989; Erskine 2001, 61–92.

39. This line of descent runs through Neoptolemus's wife, Lanassa, granddaughter of Heracles: Just. 17.3.1–8, with Garoufalias 1979, 169–170. Games: Plut. *Pyrrh.* 22.5–6.

40. Borba Florenzano 1992, 210–212; Zambon 2008, 123–124; Franke 1989, 463–465.

41. Lévêque 1957, 466; Kraay and Hirmer 1966, 339–340; Garoufalias 1979, 206; Borba Florenzano 1992, 208–209; Zambon 2008, 123–124.

Persephone was particularly worshipped in Sicily (see chapter 4). Moreover, Athena Promachos was popular among the Tarantines, since she appears on one of their gold issues from this period.[42] The adoption of Pyrrhus's iconography suggests that its message resonated strongly with the Tarantines and that they, too, put great weight on their identities as Greeks.

Of course, these coin types were not limited to Pyrrhus or to the period of his western adventures. Rather, they were part of a common pool of motifs often deployed by a variety of Hellenistic monarchs. A generation earlier, for instance, both Ptolemy I and Agathocles had used Athena Promachos, while Alexander the Great had regularly used Heracles.[43] Similarly, Hellenic identity was only one of many parts of Pyrrhus's ideological program; he was equally concerned to link himself with Alexander, to extol his own personal valor in combat, and to center himself within his Epirote kingdom. Within those limits, however, Pyrrhus does seem to have emphasized Greekness as part of an ideological program. These coin types take on added meaning in a south Italian context in this period, where they would be interpreted by Tarantines through the lens of their own history and experiences. The Tarantines were primed to place their Greekness at the forefront of their identities, and Pyrrhus was ready to take advantage of that.

Yet Pyrrhus's quest to establish a kingdom in the West on long-lasting foundations was ultimately a failure. With heavy-handed policies, such as conscripting troops and garrisoning friendly cities, he alienated his local allies until they turned against him.[44] After six years of constant warfare, he retreated across the Adriatic in 275, having achieved little, and three years later, he was killed in battle at Argos against the forces of Antigonus Gonatas. The failure of Pyrrhus's ideological program offers a sharp demonstration of the limits of identity politics and how identity works in conjunction with other factors to produce political outcomes.

Initially, by presenting himself as a champion of Greeks against the barbarian Romans, Pyrrhus persuaded the Tarantines and his other allies to unify on the basis of their Hellenic identity. This was possible because Pyrrhus's goals aligned with the Tarantines' long-standing interest in defending themselves against barbarians. Significant policy differences later

---

42. Brauer 1986, 160–163; Rutter 2001, 102.

43. Havelock 1980; Borba Florenzano 1992, 209–210.

44. Plut. *Pyrrh.* 22–23; App. *Sam.* 8.1–3; with Wuilleumier 1939, 136–137; Brauer 1986, 158–159; Franke 1989, 483; cf. the different account of Garoufalias 1979, 121–122.

arose between them, however, and identity could not overcome this. When, in 278, envoys from Syracuse invited him to come to Sicily to fight Carthage, Pyrrhus abandoned Taras to its fate but attempted to retain the city within his kingdom by leaving behind a garrison. According to Plutarch's account, "the Tarantines were very annoyed at this and demanded that he either apply himself to the task for which he had come—assisting in the war against the Romans—or abandon their territory and leave their city as he had found it."[45] The Tarantines thus showed what really mattered to them: the fight against Rome for their own independence. When Pyrrhus's actions revealed that he was not sufficiently committed to their defense, this proved that he and they were no longer one community with a common purpose. In this situation, Greek identity was not a strong enough force to bind the Tarantines to him, and their coalition splintered.

In third-century Italy, much had changed since the Achaean world discussed in chapter 2. The intra-Hellenic ethnic boundaries that had been so important in the sixth and fifth centuries had mostly faded. Taras's Dorian ethnicity was not especially relevant in this period, for instance, and neither was the Achaean identity of Croton and Metapontion. Meanwhile, Hellenic identity had become much more prominent, especially during Taras's confrontation with Rome. Although in later times, Romans could be viewed as "honorary Greeks," civilized people who partook in the values and cultural attitudes that sometimes defined Greekness and who could be understood within a Greek framework, this was not always the case.[46] For the Tarantines, their long history of conflict with non-Greeks led to a perception of the Romans as barbarians and a desire to resist them at all costs. This desire remained strong even during the Second Punic War, when, after more than half a century of Roman rule, Taras revolted and joined the Carthaginian cause. Nevertheless, despite these changes, much in Hellenistic Italy remained the same. Identities continued to be multiple and contested—after all, Thurii took a very different view of Rome—and the interplay between various types of identities gives much insight into the politics and culture of Magna Graecia.

---

45. Plut. *Pyrrh.* 22.3: Ταραντίνοις . . . δυσανασχετοῦσι καὶ ἀξιοῦσιν ἢ παρέχειν ἐφ' οἷς ἧκε συμπολεμοῦντα Ῥωμαίοις, ἢ τὴν χώραν προέμενον αὐτῶν ἀπολιπεῖν τὴν πόλιν οἵαν παρέλαβε. Cf. Garoufalias 1979, 101–102; Brauer 1986, 152–153.

46. On the complexities of these attitudes, see Champion 2000.

Being Syracusan in the Third Century

In Alexandria, sometime in the 270s BCE, two women—Syracusans who had settled there—set out across the city. They are bound for the royal palace, where Queen Arsinoe, wife of Ptolemy II, is holding a festival of Adonis. As these women, Gorgo and Praxinoa, make their way across town, a bustling urban metropolis is on display: the streets are crowded; the king's horses and chariots pass by; the women speak of petty crime committed by the native Egyptians and how Ptolemy has put a stop to it. At the palace, they hear a song sung by the daughter of a woman from Argos, as part of a ritual for Adonis that combines elements drawn from both Greek and Egyptian traditions. So far, this looks like a typical picture of the globalized Hellenistic world, full of the pageants of kings and cosmopolitan cities where diverse cultures meet.

Then an unexpected twist. A stranger in the crowd complains about the women chattering, and one of them responds vigorously: "Ah! Where's this fellow from? What's it to you if we chatter? Give your orders where you're master. We're Syracusan women that you're giving your orders to. And just so you know, we're Corinthians from way back, just like Bellerophon. We speak Peloponnesian, and Dorians are allowed to speak in Doric, I believe." In the midst of a wide-open world, Praxinoa expresses her local pride and insists on her right to adhere to her local customs and local identities. This scene is, of course, fictional, drawn from the fifteenth *Idyll* of the Syracusan poet Theocritus,[47] and its poetics represent a methodological challenge, which I deal with below. Nevertheless, it represents a crucial piece of contemporary evidence for how Syracusans perceived themselves and their place in the world in the early Hellenistic period.

Sicily in the third century faced a different set of challenges from those of southern Italy. In the middle of the century, the island became a battleground between Carthage, which had ruled western Sicily for 150 years, and the growing power of Rome. While parts of Sicily became a Roman province, the remainder consisted of an independent kingdom of Syracuse until the Second Punic War. Meanwhile, Syracuse maintained close relations with the Hellenistic kingdoms to the east, especially under Agathocles (317–289) and Hieron II (c. 276–215). Caught between Rome, Carthage, and the kingdoms to the east, Syracuse in the third century carved out a separate place for itself in the Hellenistic world. It had a long and glorious past (unlike many newly founded cities in the East), and yet, unlike many of the older cities of mainland

---

47. The quote is Theoc. 15.89-93 (tr. Hopkinson).

Greece, it also served as an imperial center. It was ruled by a *basileus*, who nonetheless governed carefully within a *polis* framework.[48] Syracuse does not quite fit any model for a Hellenistic city, and its strong sense of local identity— both as a separate *polis* and as part of the larger region of Sicily—must be taken on its own terms.

How did this unique situation shape Syracusan identity? What factors defined it? In short, what did it mean to be Syracusan in the third century? How had these factors changed over the two centuries since the Deinomenid period, and what had stayed the same? What can this case study tell us about the ways identity changes over time and about the role of *polis* identities in the Hellenistic world? A variety of sources give us a clear picture of how Syracusans constructed their identities in the third century. Two poems of Theocritus, *Idylls* 15 and 16, loom large in this discussion, since as a Syracusan himself, Theocritus's articulations of Syracusan identity offer some of the best inside evidence we have. They must, however, be read sensitively and in conversation with other evidence. I will argue that three factors played particularly important roles in articulating Syracusan identity: first, its sense of Greekness, emphasizing its role as defender of the Sicilian Greeks against barbarian enemies; second, the memory of the city's past greatness, especially under the Deinomenids; and third, pride in its Dorian, Corinthian, and Peloponnesian origins. None of these factors was entirely new in the third century, but some were reshaped to fit new circumstances, showing how both tradition and innovation shaped identities in the Hellenistic West.

Defending Hellenism

Carthage, as we have seen, had been a frequent enemy of Syracuse for centuries. After years of alternating between success and disaster, Dionysius I agreed to divide the island between himself and the Carthaginians, who remained the major power in western Sicily for some 150 years. Yet during this time, many Greeks, primarily under Syracusan leadership, renewed the struggle against the barbarian. In the 340s, the Syracusans invited the Corinthian Timoleon to Sicily to free them from the tyrant Dionysius II and to fight Carthage; his victory over Carthage at the Crimisus River temporarily won back much territory for Syracuse. Three decades later, Agathocles defended the city from another Carthaginian siege and even invaded Africa in 310.[49] Pyrrhus continued the

---

48. See esp. Lewis 2006a; Lewis 2009, 117–121.

49. On this theme in Sicilian history, see esp. Prag 2010; cf. also Hans 1985.

campaign in the 270s, and soon after his departure, one of his lieutenants, Hieron, embarked on yet another Carthaginian War, this one also involving the Romans. All of these rulers derived much of their legitimacy from fighting Carthage.

Meanwhile, a second barbarian threat arose closer to home. In the 280s, a group of Campanian mercenaries—once in the service of Agathocles but unemployed after his death—seized the city of Messina. Calling themselves the Mamertines (after the god Mamers, the Oscan equivalent of Mars), they quickly carved out a state for themselves in northeast Sicily.[50] Non-Greek mercenaries had been a growing presence on the island since the early days of Dionysius I, and their occupation of cities had a precedent: in 404, Campanian mercenaries fresh from Dionysius's service had seized Entella, in western Sicily.[51] Messina became an Oscan-speaking city under the Mamertines,[52] who spent much of the next twenty years raiding other parts of Sicily. Their predatory behavior, combined with long experience of the danger posed by Campanian mercenaries, led the Syracusans to perceive them as barbarians.

This historical experience, which unfolded over more than two centuries, deeply impacted how Sicilian Greeks, especially Syracusans, understood their own identities and their place in the world. In particular, they came to place great emphasis on their Greekness. While this kind of panhellenic thinking had long been available to all Greeks, it was not always prominent or important everywhere.[53] For Syracusans, though, identifying themselves as Greeks and others as barbarians developed an even deeper meaning, which was unique to this community; it became a key part of what it meant to be Syracusan, a sense of identity that was encouraged by a series of rulers.

The man who came to be called King Hieron II was able to parlay this component of Syracusan identity into a long-lasting kingship. Like many previous rulers of Syracuse, he found that the best way to unite the Sicilians under his

---

50. Tagliamonte 1994, 191–198; Herring 2000, 69–71; Orioles 2001; Prestianni Giallombardo 2006, 115–118; Zambon 2008, 33–53.

51. Diod. 14.9.8–9. The Oscan occupation of Entella (originally an Elymian community) is also attested via Oscan inscriptions found there and on its coins, while the appearance of Oscan magistracies such as the *meddix* side by side with Greek ones suggests a mixed culture; cf. Orioles 2001, 285; Prestianni Giallombardo 2006, 111–112.

52. Crawford 2006b; Clackson 2012.

53. Similar phenomena were seen in Asia Minor and elsewhere, however, in response to the Celtic invasions of the early third century: see Nelson forthcoming. I thank Thomas Nelson for allowing me to see his work in advance of publication.

rule was to focus their attention on a crusade against a barbarian enemy.[54] Hieron conducted a rapid and successful series of campaigns against the Mamertines, recovering substantial territory, and his victory at the Longanus River, probably in 269, confined the Mamertines to the northeast corner of Sicily near Messina. Five years later, still under pressure from Syracuse, the Mamertines appealed to Rome for help. A consular army under Appius Claudius crossed the Straits and occupied the citadel of Messina. After a brief standoff, Appius defeated first the Syracusans and then the Carthaginians, and the First Punic War was under way.[55]

Two narratives of Hieron's campaigns, those of Polybius and Diodorus, highlight the barbarism of the Mamertines. Polybius (1.9.7–8) describes the Longanus campaign in this way:

> θεωρῶν δὲ τοὺς βαρβάρους ἐκ τοῦ προτερήματος θρασέως καὶ προπετῶς ἀναστρεφομένους, καθοπλίσας καὶ γυμνάσας ἐνεργῶς τὰς πολιτικὰς δυνάμεις ἐξῆγεν καὶ συμβάλλει τοῖς πολεμίοις ἐν τῷ Μυλαίῳ πεδίῳ περὶ τὸν Λογγανὸν καλούμενον ποταμόν. τροπὴν δὲ ποιήσας αὐτῶν ἰσχυρὰν καὶ τῶν ἡγεμόνων ἐγκρατὴς γενόμενος ζωγρίᾳ τὴν μὲν τῶν βαρβάρων κατέπαυσε τόλμαν, αὐτὸς δὲ παραγενόμενος εἰς τὰς Συρακούσας βασιλεὺς ὑπὸ πάντων προσηγορεύθη τῶν συμμάχων.

> Observing that the barbarians, because of their success, were behaving boldly and recklessly, he efficiently armed and trained the citizen troops, led them out, and attacked the enemy in the plain of Mylae near the river Longanus. He inflicted a severe defeat on them, capturing their leaders alive, and put an end to the audacity of the barbarians. When he returned to Syracuse, he was proclaimed king by all the allies.

Polybius twice calls the Mamertines "barbarians," and their actions characteristically live up to this description: they are "bold and reckless," and they behave with "audacity." Elsewhere, he claims that they "broke truces" (paraspondein: 1.7.3), calls their actions "lawlessness" (paranomias: 1.7.4), and calls them barbaroi twice more (1.9.3, 4). Diodorus (23.1.4) takes this description

54. On Hieron's rise to power, see Berve 1959, 7–19; De Sensi Sestito 1977, 9–40; Hoyos 1985; Zambon 2008, 179–200.

55. Polyb. 1.8–12; for recent surveys of the outbreak of the First Punic War, with further sources, see Lazenby 1996, 43–53; Hoyos 1998; Zambon 2008, 200–207; Rosenstein 2012, 53–61; Vacanti 2012, 14–28.

even further. During a brief negotiation with Appius Claudius, Hieron gives his reasons for refusing to withdraw:

ὁ δὲ Ἱέρων ἀπεκρίνατο διότι Μαμερτῖνοι Καμάριναν καὶ Γέλαν ἀναστάτους πεποιηκότες, Μεσσήνην δὲ ἀσεβέστατα κατειληφότες, δικαίως πολιορκοῦνται, Ῥωμαῖοι δέ, θρυλλοῦντες τὸ τῆς πίστεως ὄνομα, παντελῶς οὐκ ὀφείλουσι τοὺς μιαιφόνους, μάλιστα πίστεως καταφρονήσαντας, ὑπερασπίζειν.

Hieron responded [to Appius] that the Mamertines, who had laid waste to Camarina and Gela and had so impiously seized Messina, were besieged justly, and the Romans, who kept chattering about the word *fides*, certainly should not protect bloodthirsty men who above all despised good faith.

Hieron ascribes further traits of barbarians to the Mamertines: they have done terrible deeds and committed great impieties, they are murderers, and they despise good faith.[56] Of course, these are later historiographical accounts, but Polybius, in particular, does not usually draw a sharp distinction between Greeks and barbarians.[57] It is therefore unlikely that this language originates with Polybius putting his own spin on events; more likely, this characterization of the Mamertines goes back ultimately to the contemporary situation of c. 269 BCE. These characterizations strongly suggest that Hellenic identity was highly salient in these circumstances, shaping Hieron's strategic thinking as well as popular responses.

The Syracusans were delighted at these successes. According to Polybius, the campaign was fought with citizen troops, not mercenaries. Sicilian tyrants had hired mercenaries regularly for more than two centuries, but in this case, Hieron chose otherwise. His ability to mobilize the citizen manpower of Syracuse indicates that he had already built a strong relationship with them and had proposed a rationale for the campaign—namely, defeating the barbarians—that they backed eagerly. Fighting the barbarians to safeguard the Greeks of Sicily was a task they enthusiastically took on. What this shows is that Hieron's focus on Greekness was not merely his own idiosyncratic

---

56. Vacanti 2012, 42–43.

57. Gruen 2020, 56–71 (and cf. 18 on the Mamertines, reaching different conclusions from mine); though see Eckstein 1995, 119–125; Champion 2004. Walbank (1957, 53–54) ascribes the entire passage on Hieron's rise (1.8.3–9.8) to Timaeus, which would still place the words in a third-century Sicilian context.

propaganda but part of a much larger trend. Most Syracusans felt the same way. He had accomplished exactly what they, too, wanted to see happen—the defeat of the barbarians and the defense of Greekness—and this is what gained him their support.

Over the next several years, Hieron maintained his focus on Greekness through turbulent times. In 264, after the Mamertines summoned Roman assistance, four armies—those of Syracuse, Carthage, Rome, and the Mamertines—confronted one another at Messina. Polybius reports that Hieron thought that "present circumstances were favorable for expelling from Sicily entirely the barbarians who were occupying Messina."[58] He therefore took a remarkable step: making an alliance with Carthage against the Mamertines. In this instance, Hieron's goal of crushing the Mamertines forever overrode a centuries-long tradition of hostility toward Carthage, indicating the importance of the anti-Mamertine crusade in his articulation of Hellenic identity. Yet this alliance with Carthage was temporary. The Romans were victorious outside Messina, and the next year, they swept through Sicily and began to besiege Syracuse. Hieron quickly saw that by switching sides and fighting with the Romans against Carthage, he could inscribe himself into that age-old identity predicated on hostility to Carthage. In terms of identity, this was actually a very small switch; Hieron was still basing his legitimacy on Hellenic identity, changing only from one barbarian enemy (the Mamertines) to another. Although the danger from the Mamertines had been more immediate, it was now overshadowed by the threat of Carthage, which had existed for much longer and was more deeply rooted in the consciousness of the Sicilian Greeks.[59]

A key piece of contemporary evidence, Theocritus's sixteenth *Idyll*, adds to this picture of the pervasive role of Hellenic identity and of the Carthaginian enemy at Syracuse in the third century. This poem, an encomium of Hieron II, probably came out of this same context, early in the king's reign.[60] At lines 73–89, Theocritus focuses on Hieron's great deeds:

---

58. Polyb. 1.11.7: Ἱέρων νομίσας εὐφυῶς ἔχειν τὰ παρόντα πρὸς τὸ τοὺς βαρβάρους τοὺς τὴν Μεσσήνην κατέχοντας ὁλοσχερῶς ἐκβαλεῖν ἐκ τῆς Σικελίας.

59. On this move, see Prag 2010, 67–71; cf. Zambon 2008, 211–215; Péré-Noguès 2006.

60. For the date, see Gow 1950, 306–307; Hunter 1996, 83. Of course, the poem is also several other things, including a "meditation on the relation between poet and patron" (Hunter 1996, 77), a manifesto in defense of poetry, and a claim that Theocritus is the equal of past poets: see Gow 1950, 305–324; Griffiths 1979, 9–50; Gutzwiller 1983; Dover 1985, 216–229; Hunter 1996, 77–109. Stephens (2018, 79–82) argues that the poem shows Hieron as a bad king, contrasted with Ptolemy II in *Id.* 17.

ἔσσεται οὗτος ἀνὴρ ὃς ἐμεῦ κεχρήσετ' ἀοιδοῦ,
ῥέξας ἢ Ἀχιλεὺς ὅσσον μέγας ἢ βαρὺς Αἴας
ἐν πεδίῳ Σιμόεντος, ὅθι Φρυγὸς ἠρίον Ἴλου.   75
ἤδη νῦν Φοίνικες ὑπ' ἠελίῳ δύνοντι
οἰκεῦντες Λιβύας ἄκρον σφυρὸν ἐρρίγασιν·
ἤδη βαστάζουσι Συρακόσιοι μέσα δοῦρα,
ἀχθόμενοι σακέεσσι βραχίονας ἰτεΐνοισιν·
ἐν δ' αὐτοῖς Ἱέρων προτέροις ἴσος ἡρώεσσι   80
ζώννυται, ἵππειαι δὲ κόρυν σκιάουσιν ἔθειραι.
αἲ γάρ, Ζεῦ κύδιστε πάτερ καὶ πότνι' Ἀθάνα
κούρη θ' ἣ σὺν μητρὶ πολυκλήρων Ἐφυραίων
εἴληχας μέγα ἄστυ παρ' ὕδασι Λυσιμελείας,
ἐχθροὺς ἐκ νάσοιο κακαὶ πέμψειαν ἀνάγκαι   85
Σαρδόνιον κατὰ κῦμα φίλων μόρον ἀγγέλλοντας
τέκνοις ἠδ' ἀλόχοισιν, ἀριθμητοὺς ἀπὸ πολλῶν.
ἄστεα δὲ προτέροισι πάλιν ναίοιτο πολίταις,
δυσμενέων ὅσα χεῖρες ἐλωβήσαντο κατ' ἄκρας.

There will be a man who will need me as his poet,
when he has done as much as great Achilles or stern Ajax
on the plain of the Simois where the tomb of Phrygian Ilus stands. 75
Already now the Phoenicians who live beneath the setting sun,
at the farthest edge of Libya, tremble with fear;
already the Syracusans raise their spears by the middle
burdening their arms with their wicker shields;
and among them Hieron girds himself, the equal of earlier heroes, 80
and a horsehair crest covers his helmet.
Most glorious father Zeus, and Lady Athena,
and Kore, you who with your mother were allotted
the great city of the land-rich Ephyraeans by the waters of Lysimelea,
may harsh necessity send away the enemy from this island 85
across the Sardinian Sea, announcing to wives and children the fates
of their loved ones, a small number surviving out of many.
May cities which the hands of the enemy had utterly ruined
be inhabited once again by their former citizens.

Theocritus emphasizes the struggle against the western barbarians and
the role of both the Syracusans and their king in fighting it. The poet names
Phoenicians—that is, Carthaginians—as the foe and highlights their fear of

Syracusan military might. While he does not use the word "barbarian," he does focus heavily on ethnic and cultural difference. The enemies live in the far west, "beneath the setting sun," and dwell on the edges of the known world. They have arrived in Sicily from overseas, crossing a maritime boundary that had long been a marker of identity in Sicily. Their numbers are given as "many," which might recall the massive size of the barbarian armies that invaded both Greece and Sicily in 480. Yet, due to the prowess of Hieron and the Syracusans, "a small number" will return. The Syracusans, by contrast, are presented as traditional Greek hoplites, wielding shield and spear as they march into battle.[61] This image, combined with their description as *politai* in line 88, presents them as a citizen army defending their homeland, much as Polybius emphasized, setting up a stark contrast between the Syracusans and mercenary soldiers. Among the latter can be counted not only the Mamertines but also the Carthaginians, who primarily employed mercenaries rather than their own citizens.

Meanwhile, their captain, Hieron, stands among them, leading his fellow citizens from the front while earning glory for himself. He is later described as a "spearman with his people" (103). Comparing him to the Homeric heroes is not at all unusual for encomiastic poetry but is noteworthy in this context for its activation of a sense of shared panhellenic purpose in the Trojan War. Hieron's war against Carthage is made equivalent to past wars against barbarians. Moreover, Troy's namesake, Ilus, is described as "Phrygian." This activates a strand of thought in which Troy itself stands as an eastern barbarian, emphasizing even further the importance of Greek identity in the ideology of Hieronian Syracuse.[62] By placing himself in the role of protector of the Greeks of Sicily from the barbarians, Hieron succeeded in solidifying a legitimate position for himself.

Memory and Identity

Another aspect of Theocritus 16 brings out a different facet of Syracusan identity: the memory of the city's past greatness, especially under the Deinomenids. As a number of commentators have pointed out, the section of the poem quoted above draws heavily on Pindar's *Pythian* 1, which similarly honors

---

61. These hoplites carry "wicker shields" (σακέεσσι . . . ἰτεΐνοισιν, 79), which is a poetic expression, used several times by Euripides (*Heraclid.* 376; *Troad.* 1193; *Suppl.* 695; *Cycl.* 7; cf. Gow 1950, 320); applying it to hoplites underscores their heroism.

62. Erskine 2001, 61–92; cf. Hall 1989.

Hieron I.[63] Beyond the shared focus on battles against a barbarian enemy, both poets place their honorand at the center of the action (Theocritus's Hieron by name [80]; Pindar's by the periphrasis "commander of the Syracusans" [73]), yet both also in different ways give the Syracusans an important role. Both refer to Phoenicians as the enemies (*Pyth.* 1.72, Theoc. 16.76). Both include a prayer to Zeus (*Pyth.* 1.71, Theoc. 16.82) that, finally, expresses a wish about the barbarians: Pindar that their war cry would stay away (71–72), Theocritus that their defeat would be announced in their homeland (82–87).

This redeployment of Pindaric themes heightens the poem's focus on Greekness, which is a key element of *Pythian* 1, but it also gives Hieron's campaign a history, locating him within a centuries-long struggle that spans Syracusan history. By associating him with the most glorious earlier victories, those of the Deinomenids at Himera and Cumae (see chapter 3), Theocritus places Hieron on a continuum with past rulers, with achievements to match theirs, and their memory encourages Hieron to imitate them.[64] By contrast, newer communities like Alexandria did not have this kind of shared history to draw on for self-definition, and while the cities of mainland Greece did have glorious pasts, their history still differed from that of Syracuse. For Syracusans, remembering the Deinomenids in particular was a way of distinguishing themselves from others who did not share that history. Moreover, this was a history that impacted the present, since Hieron was looking back to the Deinomenids to see what a king ought to be. Thus, Syracusan identity in the age of Hieron II was also articulated by remembering the city's past greatness and striving to recreate it.

The Deinomenids, and Hieron I in particular, were also remembered for their patronage of poetry, the arts, and culture more broadly. Theocritus, too, urges his addressee to become a patron of poetry and make Syracuse once again a center of Greek culture and poetry. The comparison to Hieron I and the poets who wrote for him is nowhere made explicit. Instead, Theocritus cites Simonides's praise for the Aleuad dynasty of Thessaly as a model for encomiastic poetry (esp. 34–47). Yet Simonides also wrote for Hieron, along with Pindar and Bacchylides, and it is clear from the imitation of *Pythian* 1 that Theocritus intends this body of poetry to be very near the surface. For Syracusans, the Deinomenid model would immediately spring to mind.[65] In

---

63. E.g., Griffiths 1979, 37–38; Gutzwiller 1983, 231–233; Hunter 1996, 82–90; Prag 2010, 66.

64. Cf. Hunter 1996, 86–87.

65. Gow 1950, 312–313; Hunter 1996, 83–87. The court of Dionysius I was also a hotbed of literary (especially dramatic) production, although hardly any of this work survives.

fact, Hieron II was much less interested in literature than his predecessors. There is no evidence that Theocritus received the patronage he desired, and Syracuse did not become home to a thriving poetic community. Other arts and sciences flourished, however, including the most famous intellectual of Hieron's Syracuse, the scientist, mathematician, and engineer Archimedes.[66] But the king did rebuild Syracuse's large theater in the Neapolis district, providing a popular venue for cultural performance that is still used today.[67] In this way, he followed the example of his namesake, who sponsored performances of Aeschylus.

Hieron himself most explicitly laid claim to the memory of the Deinomenids through the names of his family members. Two of his children were named Gelon and Damarata, both extremely resonant names in Syracusan history (after the former tyrant and his wife). Together with the king's own name, these children suggest the Deinomenid dynasty reborn, and they link the entire ruling family to the memory of Syracusan history.[68] This link was designed to endure, moreover, since the younger Gelon was Hieron's designated successor until his death just a year before his father's, in 216.[69] Meanwhile, the name and family of Hieron's wife, Philistis, daughter of Leptines, evoke characters from the story of Dionysius: Leptines, brother of Dionysius I, and Philistus the historian, one of his closest advisers. Hieron did not choose Philistis's name, of course, and according to Polybius (1.9.2), he contracted the marriage during his rise to power in order to take advantage of Leptines's wealth and political connections, not because she had a convenient name. Still, it is clear that he recognized the power of names and made use of them. While the age of Dionysius was remembered by many authors mainly for the excesses and cruelty of his rule, it was also a time of great Syracusan power; clearly, at home, it could be remembered positively.[70]

---

66. De Sensi Sestito 1977, 191–193; Wilson 2013, 83–98; Veit 2013. On Archimedes, see Knorr 1978, 235–238; Netz 2013.

67. On the theater, see Campagna 2004, 171–183; Marconi 2012, 179–180, 203–206. Hieron's building program also included the massive altar, a full stade in length, that bears his name.

68. De Sensi Sestito 1977, 183–184; see Haake 2013, 110–111, for sources. Hieron also had other children, whose names are not recorded, except one daughter, Heraclea.

69. De Sensi Sestito 1977, 125–135; Haake 2013.

70. A further example may be the mythicized stories of Hieron's birth and upbringing, which mirror stories told about Gelon and Dionysius: Just. 23.4.3–11, with Lewis 2000, 105–106.

FIG. 6.1 Stater of Syracuse, c. 274–216. Obverse: Philistis. Reverse: Quadriga. © Trustees of the British Museum.

The king ensured that the names of the royal family were well known in third-century Syracuse. For example, they appear on an inscription in the *cavea* of the theater, which names the various seating sections; some of the names can still be seen today. Along with at least two deities (Zeus and Heracles), four of the sections are named after members of the royal family: Gelon; his wife, Nereis; Philistis; and Hieron.[71] The king may not have sponsored poets, but he carefully linked his name to theatrical productions; it would be seen by all the spectators, every time they entered the theater. Moreover, for the first time in Syracusan history, the city's coinage displayed portraits of the royal family: occasionally Hieron himself, sometimes Gelon, and, most commonly and most remarkably, Philistis, with the inscription *Basilissas Philistidos* (fig. 6.1). Her portrait is frequently combined with a quadriga, a traditionally Syracusan image that had appeared on coins since the beginning of the fifth century.[72] Hieron's coinage thus combined a reverence for Syracusan traditions with a radical innovation much in line with other contemporary Hellenistic monarchs. In fact, the closest parallel for the Philistis coins are those of Ptolemaic Egypt with portraits of Queen Arsinoe.[73] In Syracuse, however, they were designed to associate the ruling house with past Syracusan greatness.

---

71. *IG* XIV.3 = *ISic.* 824; cf. Bell 1999, 270–272; Campagna 2004, 173–183; Dimartino 2006, 704–705; Lehmler 2005, 122–127; Veit 2009, 368–369.

72. Head 1911, 183–185; Kraay and Hirmer 1966, 293; Rutter 1997, 177–179; Caccamo Caltabiano, Carroccio, and Oteri 1997; Lehmler 2005, 89–95.

73. Head 1911, 184–185; Rutter 1997, 123, 178–179; cf. Kraay and Hirmer 1966, 382.

In these ways, the memory of past greatness was inscribed into the landscape of Syracuse and into the daily lives of its residents and even its visitors,
making it a part of what it meant to be Syracusan. Such an attitude was not
unusual in the Hellenistic world. The "pride of Halicarnassus" inscription,
for instance, constructs a local identity by celebrating the community's past
achievements, ranging from mythical to historical to literary. The Lindian
Chronicle similarly highlights above all Rhodes's long and glorious history.[74]
While all of these cities used the same technique to construct their identities, the content naturally varied, since their histories differed. Syracuse's past
greatness mattered little to the people of Halicarnassus, but for Syracusans, it
was essential.

We Speak Peloponnesian

Finally, we return to the palace at Alexandria, where we left Gorgo and
Praxinoa. As we saw above, at Theoc. 15.89–93, Praxinoa expresses a third
aspect of her Syracusan identity: pride in the Dorian, Peloponnesian, and
Corinthian origins of the city.

μᾶ, πόθεν ὤνθρωπος; τί δὲ τίν, εἰ κωτίλαι εἰμές;
πασάμενος ἐπίτασσε· Συρακοσίαις ἐπιτάσσεις.   90
ὡς εἰδῇς καὶ τοῦτο, Κορίνθιαι εἰμὲς ἄνωθεν,
ὡς καὶ ὁ Βελλεροφῶν. Πελοποννασιστὶ λαλεῦμες,
Δωρίσδειν δ' ἔξεστι, δοκῶ, τοῖς Δωριέεσσι.

Ah! Where's this fellow from? What's it to you if we chatter?
Give your orders where you're master. We're Syracusan women   90
that you're giving your orders to. And just so you know, we're
Corinthians from way back, just like Bellerophon. We speak
Peloponnesian, and Dorians are allowed to speak in Doric, I believe.
  (tr. Hopkinson)

With a strong defense of her Doric dialect and Corinthian origins, Praxinoa
prioritizes a Syracusan interpretation of these facts over external frameworks
that devalue such characteristics. In fact, Theocritus dramatizes the clash between these two sources of meaning, as the unnamed interlocutor takes a

---

74. On these two inscriptions, see Higbie 2003; Isager and Pedersen 2004; Stevens
2016, 78–82.

cosmopolitan attitude toward the Doric dialect while Praxinoa values it. The poem highlights the complexities that are typical of identity in an imperial center: the Syracusan women embody the diversity of the capital and participate in the royal festival, but they also maintain their sense of local distinctiveness, without being subsumed into a larger Ptolemaic imperial identity.[75] Although scholars have recently begun to recognize Egyptian elements within Ptolemaic culture, showing that expressions of identity in Alexandria were much more complex than previously understood,[76] Praxinoa herself rejects all this in favor of defending her Syracusan identity.

Much work on this passage has focused either on the role of dialect or on what it can tell us about Alexandria under the Ptolemies, but there is far more to it than that.[77] Praxinoa is asserting a claim to Dorian, Peloponnesian, and Corinthian origins, all tightly interwoven but each worth considering. She claims continuity with past Syracusans who made similar claims going all the way back to the foundation of the city, and she maintains a unique *polis* identity that contrasts with the sophisticated setting of Alexandria. Travel has not weakened her adherence to her ancestral identity; if anything, travel has strengthened it, as it is challenged by the unnamed interlocutor.[78]

Of course, this scene, and the ideas about identity expressed in it, cannot simply be taken as face value. It is a highly wrought piece of Hellenistic poetry, and I am drawing attention to only one out of many facets of a complex poem.[79] A number of scholars have drawn attention to a thick layer of irony in Theocritus's presentation of Praxinoa and Gorgo. Much of the poem showcases the cosmopolitan setting and cultural mixture of Alexandria, a far cry from Praxinoa's emphasis on pure Dorian Greekness. Should the Syracusan women be understood as so provincial and so foolish that they do not realize the cultural mixing and lack of ethnic purity that characterizes their world? Jay Reed argues that their "naive pride in being Greek points up

---

75. Cf. Stevens 2016.

76. See esp. Reed 2000; Stephens 2003; Moyer 2011b; cf. Thompson 2001; Burstein 2008; Moyer 2011a.

77. Dialect: see esp. Willi 2012; cf. Gow 1950, 290–291; Zanker 1987, 164–165; Hunter 1996, 119–123. Alexandria: e.g., Zanker 1987, 9–24; Burton 1995, 9–19; Hunter 1996, 131–138; Reed 2000.

78. In this way, she takes an even stronger position than the mercenaries and other "new citizens" discussed in chapter 3, who added a new Syracusan identity while retaining their prior ones.

79. For other angles on the poem, see Gow 1950, 262–304; Dover 1985, 188–216; Zanker 1987, 9–24; Goldhill 1991; Burton 1995; Hunter 1996, 110–138; Reed 2000.

their obliviousness to the larger ethnic view that enfolds theirs," especially the Egyptianizing elements that he sees in the poem. Simon Goldhill similarly asks, "Does the need to emphasize descent in this way highlight a fiction of Hellenization?"[80] Perhaps Theocritus does not intend readers to take seriously Praxinoa's statements of identity and is instead showing that they are both incorrect and irrelevant.

Still, while this external scholarly perspective is a valuable one, it neglects the experience of identity from the inside.[81] Despite, or perhaps even because of, the diversity and change happening in her world, Praxinoa deeply believes in her Dorian and Corinthian identity, and that, too, creates a certain kind of reality. While she is a fictional character, she does, I suggest, represent something real. The irony that Theocritus is creating gains much point from the contrast between the global and the local if the local identity she expresses is one that was deeply felt by many in Syracuse.

Moreover, each element in her claim can be traced in other sources, both in Hellenistic Syracuse and farther back. Theocritus may indeed be layering his picture with irony, but he is using building blocks with real meaning. Peloponnesian and Corinthian origins had been part of Syracusan *polis* identity for centuries. Thucydides's account of Hermocrates's speech at Camarina, for instance, has him declare that "we are free Dorians from the autonomous Peloponnese, inhabiting Sicily."[82] That strong statement of identity brings together geographical origins and Dorian ethnicity. Syracusans also regularly remembered their origins in the Peloponnese in the myth of Arethusa, a nymph who was pursued by the River Alpheus as she fled to Sicily; the river followed her, flowing underwater until it emerged on the island of Ortygia, in Syracuse, to become the spring known as Arethusa.[83] This story asserts a mythically justified relationship between Syracuse and the Peloponnese, and an ongoing one, since the spring still provides the water of Alpheus every day. Asserting identity by reference to distant regions of mainland Greece had always been a key technique in the articulation of Syracuse identity.[84]

---

80. Reed 2000, 345–346; Goldhill 1991, 275–276; cf. Griffiths 1979, 84–86; Zanker 1987, 10, 164–165. On gendered aspects of this ironic presentation, see Burton 1995.

81. Zanker (1987, 19) recognizes the "fierce pride" in their origins felt by immigrants to Alexandria.

82. 6.77.1: Δωριῆς ἐλεύθεροι ἀπ' αὐτονόμου τῆς Πελοποννήσου τὴν Σικελίαν οἰκοῦντες; see chapters 4 and 5.

83. Known as early as Ibycus (F323 *PMG*) and still relevant in the third century for Timaeus (F41 = Strabo 6.2.4); see chapter 3.

84. Cf. also the Achaeans' references to the Argolid and the northern Peloponnese (chapter 2).

FIG. **6.2** Stater of Syracuse, c. 344–335. Obverse: Athena. Reverse: Pegasus. Courtesy of the American Numismatic Society.

The link to Corinth in particular gained further prominence in the fourth century, when the Syracusans had summoned the Corinthian Timoleon to free them from their tyrants and from the Carthaginian enemy. His success brought tens of thousands of new settlers from the Peloponnese to repopulate Greek Sicily and resulted in a vast influx of Corinthian "Pegasus" coins, a type that Corinth had used for centuries and that was indelibly associated with that city.[85] In Sicily, these types were so popular that local mints, especially at Syracuse, began to include the iconic winged horse on their own coins (fig. 6.2). Throughout the reign of Agathocles and the turbulent periods that preceded and followed him, Pegasus types were prominent on Syracusan coinage; Hieron II occasionally used the type as well.[86] The combination of the name Syracuse with the Pegasus emblem powerfully asserts both the Corinthian origins of the colony and the contemporary relevance of that claim.

For Praxinoa, being Corinthian is a key element of being Syracusan. In an emphatic statement of identity, she says, "We are Corinthians from way back" (*anōthen*). The last word highlights the lengthy history of her claim, which goes back almost half a millennium to the city's foundation by Corinthian colonists in the eighth century—and, in fact, even farther. Praxinoa does not seem interested in contemporary Corinth, which housed a Macedonian garrison in its citadel, the Acrocorinth, and would soon be described as one of the "fetters of Greece."[87] Rather, her point of reference is the mythical Bellerophon,

---

85. Talbert 1974, 161–178; Rutter 1997, 167–174.

86. Head 1911, 179–180; Kraay and Hirmer 1966, 293; Rutter 1997, 167–174.

87. Polyb. 18.11.5, a description attributed to Philip V.

a Corinthian hero who traveled to Lycia, defeated the Chimera with the help of Pegasus, and settled there. Praxinoa strongly identifies with Bellerophon as one of her countrymen; his story was highly relevant to her own sense of identity, perhaps in part because of their shared experience of travel and settling in a foreign land.

Equally important, the linkage from Bellerophon to Corinth to Syracuse give Praxinoa's city a glorious past, especially a mythical past, far beyond what many cities could boast. Similarly, Theocritus elsewhere describes the Syracusans as "land-rich Ephyraeans," referring to Ephyra, an old name for Corinth (16.83). This is more than a mere poetic euphemism; it gives Corinth (and therefore Syracuse) an aura of antiquity, representing it as a place out of the dim mists of time. The same name was also used by Homer in the story told by Glaucus about his ancestry (*Il.* 6.152, 210), where the Lycian hero says that the hometown of his grandfather Bellerophon was Ephyra. So these two names work together to give Syracuse a claim on the epic past. But Theocritus also bridges the gap between myth and history, since his phrase "land-rich Ephyraeans" (*polyklerōn Ephyraiōn*) strongly suggests the *kleroi* allotted to the original settlers of Syracuse and thereby constructs a continuum between myth, early history, and the present.[88] Corinthian origins thus place Syracuse near the conceptual center of the Greek world and give it a prestige and a lineage that newer cities such as Alexandria struggled to match.

Dorian ethnicity was similarly central to Syracusan identity. The Dorians were one of the most prominent ethnic groups in the Peloponnese, and claiming Dorian ethnicity allows Praxinoa to link her city with such famous cities as Sparta, Argos, and, of course, Corinth. In earlier times, Pindar had praised Hieron I for giving his new colony of Aetna Dorian institutions, linking Syracuse and its ruler to a long tradition of Dorian *eunomia*.[89] Even as Koine Greek was developing in other parts of the Mediterranean, Doric was still common in Sicily.[90] In Theocritus, the reference to Dorians is usually understood as referring to the Doric dialect, and perhaps also to the literary genre(s) signaled by that dialect, and not to ethnicity.[91] Certainly, dialect is part of the issue. The stranger has complained that the Syracusans are πλατειάσδοισαι

---

88. Cf. *Id.* 28.17: Syracuse was founded by "Archias from Ephyra," similarly collapsing mythical and historical time.

89. *Pyth.* 1.60–66; see chapter 3.

90. Willi 2008, esp. 45–49; Mimbrera 2012.

91. Gow 1950, 290–291; Zanker 1987, 164–165; Hunter 1996, 119–123; Willi 2012.

(88: speaking with broad vowels, an indication of Doric Greek), and Praxinoa responds with two verbs that describe how she speaks (κωτίλαι, λαλεῦμες).

Still, this is far more than an edict about proper pronunciation. The stranger's dialect is the same literary Doric as the Syracusan women speak, showing that this is not meant to be an accurate *mimesis* of a real-life conversation.[92] Moreover, Praxinoa declares that "we speak Peloponnesian"—but Peloponnesian is not a dialect; several dialects had always been spoken within its boundaries. Instead, this is a claim of identity: we speak like Peloponnesians, because we are Peloponnesians and Dorians. Moreover, her final line— "Dorians are allowed to speak in Doric"—refers not only to a dialect but also to a people, the Dorians. Praxinoa's identity as a Dorian is what enables her to speak Doric, and clearly, she is proud of belonging to this group. Her assertion of a pure Doric identity contrasts particularly strongly with Alexandria, whose population consisted of a mixture of Greeks from everywhere.[93]

Theocritus's scene at Alexandria, together with other evidence, strongly suggests the importance of Dorian, Peloponnesian, and Corinthian origins in Syracuse. This is despite the fact that Syracuse was not and never had been a purely Corinthian community. Recent work on colonial foundations has emphasized that most colonies were only nominally founded by a single mother city, attracting a mixed group of settlers from the beginning.[94] Moreover, Syracuse's population shifted over the next several centuries, as the city received influxes of new settlers throughout the fifth and fourth centuries.[95] Praxinoa's claims of ethnic purity are thus belied by the diversity of contemporary Syracuse, adding a further unnoticed layer to the irony observed by scholars such as Reed and Goldhill. Yet the constructed nature of identities often means that such realities are deemed irrelevant by insiders, who (in this case) prefer to believe in shared origins.

Theocritus's choice of Bellerophon as an emblematically Corinthian hero adds further complications. He was the grandson of Sisyphus, according to Homer (*Il.* 6.153–155), which makes him not a Dorian but a descendant of Aeolus. Since he lived two generations before the Trojan War, he also predates the return of the Heracleidae and so represents a pre-Dorian Corinth.[96] To

---

92. As noted by many commentators: e.g., Gow 1950, 290; Dover 1985, 207; Zanker 1987, 164–165; Hunter 1996, 119–123.

93. Bagnall 1984.

94. E.g., Malkin 2009.

95. See chapter 3.

96. I thank Claudia Antonetti for this point.

a Hellenistic poet and his learned audience, recalling this genealogy might highlight the mutability of ethnic identity, by requiring a moment, sometime after Bellerophon, when Corinth *became* Dorian. At the same time, however, this genealogical datum may not have been prominent in the minds of everyday Syracusans; instead, they would think first of the Dorian ethnicity that had been claimed by Corinth for centuries. In this way, as Praxinoa does, they are likely to have combined different elements of their origins that, while not strictly aligned, overlapped sufficiently that they could be taken together as a key part of their identity. Dorian ethnicity and Peloponnesian origins were not unique to Syracuse, of course. Yet this mattered little to Syracusans like Praxinoa, who took special pride in this status.

Of course, while Hellenistic Syracusans often emphasized their distinctiveness and separateness, they were also eager to build ties with others.[97] Hieron's close alliance with Rome, during and after the First Punic War, is well known, but he also maintained close diplomatic and commercial ties with Ptolemaic Egypt, which can be traced through numismatic links.[98] Hieron even went so far as to build a gigantic warship, called the *Syracosia*, which boasted twenty banks of oars and used enough timber for sixty triremes, too large to berth in any port in Sicily, and then gave it as a gift to one of the Ptolemies.[99] Elsewhere, his son Gelon made a dynastic marriage with Nereis, daughter of Pyrrhus II (king of Epirus 252–234). All of this built on the work of Agathocles, who married Theoxena, a stepdaughter of Ptolemy I, and gave his own daughter Lanassa in marriage to Pyrrhus I.[100] Clearly, these were long-term relationships, built and maintained over many decades, that helped secure Syracuse's place in the world. When Agathocles took the title of king in 305, the first Syracusan to do so, he did so after the Successors had each assumed that title and (in Diodorus's account) precisely because "he thought he was inferior to them neither in power nor in territory nor in deeds" (20.54.1). This motivation, if accurate, suggests that Syracuse perceived itself as the equal of the Hellenistic kingdoms. All of this enabled Syracusans to project to the rest of the world an image of their city as an imperial power.

---

97. De Sensi Sestito 1977, 165–178; De Sensi Sestito 1995; Portale 2004; Wilson 2013, 80–83.

98. Rutter 1997, 178–179.

99. Moschion (*FGrH* 575) F1 (= Ath. 5.206d–9b); cf. Lehmler 2005, 210–232; Castagnino Berlinghieri 2010; Vacanti 2012, 96–102. The ship was also the subject of an epigram by Archimelus: Olson 2017.

100. Theoxena: Just. 23.2.6; Lanassa: Plut. *Pyrrh.* 9.1; cf. De Sensi Sestito 1977, 175–176; Lewis 2009, 106.

Yet Syracuse's *polis* identity remained only part of its story. Syracuse was still an imperial power in the third century. Even as much of the island became Rome's first overseas province, Hieron maintained a small empire in eastern Sicily, encompassing a number of other cities in the region most closely tied to Syracuse.[101] At an important stage in his rise to power, he was proclaimed king not only by the citizens of Syracuse but also by "the allies" (Polyb. 1.9.8), indicating that other Sicilians accepted his power (and that of Syracuse). Polybius also writes that at the outbreak of the First Punic War, Hieron thought that "present circumstances were favorable for expelling from Sicily entirely the barbarians who were occupying Messina."[102] This goal is significant: he intended to continue the fight until there were no barbarians left to threaten the Greeks not merely in Syracuse but anywhere on the island. Similarly, Hieron's list of the Mamertines' crimes, as reported in Diodorus (23.1.4), does not even mention Syracuse but focuses on their depredations against Camarina and Gela as well as their original seizure of Messina. Hieron therefore presents himself as the champion of all the Greeks of Sicily, not just of the Syracusans. And some of the coins with the portrait of Philistis also bear the legend ΣΙΚΕΛΙΩΤΩΝ, indicating that the family's power extends not just over the Syracusans but also over the rest of the Sikeliotai. Sicilian identity still mattered at this time.[103]

Conclusion

The two case studies considered in this chapter both demonstrate the continuing complexities of identity in the Hellenistic West. Identities, both Hellenic and local, deeply mattered to people in the Hellenistic world. The individual histories of specific places and even local mythologies dramatically shaped self-perceptions and self-representations; this also influenced their political choices, which shows that it cannot be ignored as a meaningful factor in political history. Moreover, a nuanced understanding of identity requires considering multiple forms of identity. The politics of southern Italy cannot be boiled down to a simple contrast of Greeks and barbarians, since—although that is exactly how Taras saw it—such a perspective neglects the contrasting

---

101. Berve 1959, 50–56; De Sensi Sestito 1977, 113–123; Bell 1999, 258–269.

102. Polyb. 1.11.7: Ἱέρων νομίσας εὐφυῶς ἔχειν τὰ παρόντα πρὸς τὸ τοὺς βαρβάρους τοὺς τὴν Μεσσήνην κατέχοντας ὁλοσχερῶς ἐκβαλεῖν ἐκ τῆς Σικελίας.

103. For the coins, see Head 1911, 185; cf. more broadly Prag 2013.

experience of Thurii. Similarly, fully unpacking what it means to be Syracusan in the age of Hieron II reveals a rich web of ideas, associations, and meanings that belie the "death of the *polis*" in the Hellenistic period. Five centuries after the first Greeks began to settle in the West, their multiple senses of identity were no less complex and no less meaningful.

Conclusion

IN AROUND 205 BCE, near the end of the Second Punic War, Hannibal dedicated a golden statue of a heifer at the sanctuary of Hera Lacinia near Croton. This statue he placed atop a preexisting gold column, which he had been intending to steal. To that end, he had drilled a hole in the column to ascertain that it was, in fact, made of solid gold. Cicero (*Div.* 1.48) records that Hera appeared to Hannibal in a dream and informed him that his actions were sacrilegious; he promptly realized his mistake, abandoned his plan, and dedicated the heifer, made out of the gold drill shavings, to demonstrate his piety.

This story likely originated in Hannibal's own propaganda, as a way of demonstrating his fealty toward the gods of his local Greek allies, and likely stemmed from a dedication he actually made at the time.[1] Like many leaders we have seen, Hannibal was a master of political messaging, using it to shore up his own image and attract local allies; he presented himself as a new Heracles, for instance, marching from Spain to Italy just as Heracles had done with the cattle of Geryon (Diod. 4.17–24), and he repeatedly claimed to be bringing freedom to the Greeks and other Italians.[2] At this point in the war, Hannibal had been forced out of central Italy and limited to an ever-shrinking portion of Bruttium; Croton and the Lacinion represented his last Italian territories, and he desperately needed their support.

Yet, as a way of concluding this book, the Crotoniate perspective is equally significant. A political leader of enormous importance, who needed Croton's

---

1. Cicero cites both the Roman author Coelius Antipater and Silenus of Caleacte, a pro-Hannibal historian. Silenus likely presented the story positively, while Coelius reoriented the story of the dream to demonstrate instead Hannibal's impiety: Wardle 2006, 228–230; Miles 2011, 273–274; cf. Levene 1993, 68; Jaeger 2006.

2. Erskine 1993; Miles 2011; Intrieri 2011.

The Politics of Identity in Greek Sicily and Southern Italy. Mark R. Thatcher, Oxford University Press. © Oxford University Press 2021. DOI: 10.1093/oso/9780197586440.003.0007

support, was honoring a goddess whose sanctuary was central to Croton's civic self-image, as we saw in chapter 2, and also a meeting point for many other Italiotes.[3] The choice of a heifer, moreover, showed that he understood Hera Lacinia's particular affinity for bovines. By placing his dedication atop the golden column, which had been dedicated by past Crotoniates, he was linking himself to the city's glorious past and to a long-standing tradition of civic dedications at this sanctuary. Thus, Hannibal—following a strategy much like that of the Deinomenids, discussed in chapter 3—was creating legitimacy for himself by inscribing himself within Croton's *polis* identity.

Another episode from a decade earlier shows a second form of identity at work in Croton's politics. In 215, not long after Cannae, the Bruttians (who were allied with Hannibal but acted without his approval) attacked Croton; they succeeded in taking much of the city, but the Crotoniates held on to the citadel.[4] Hanno, one of Hannibal's lieutenants, then tried to mediate between the two sides, suggesting that the Crotoniates surrender and allow Bruttians to settle there as citizens, thereby giving the city's population a much-needed increase.[5] This was unacceptable to the Crotoniates, who (in Livy's account) "declared that they would sooner die than, when mixed with the Bruttians, turn to the rites, customs, laws, and soon even the language of an alien people."[6] Despite the immediate situation of the siege, and despite their long-term problem of depopulation, the Crotoniates were so hostile to the Bruttians that they could not allow this. Multiple identities, both Greek and Crotoniate, contributed to their decision.

The Crotoniates' decision was clearly framed in terms of maintaining their Greekness. The factors cited in 215—language, customs, rituals, and blood (in the phrase *immixti Brutiis*)—are remarkably similar to those cited by Herodotus's Athenians in the face of the Persian invasion: "Next, there is Greekness, which is having the same blood and language, shared temples and ritual, and similar customs."[7] This famous statement is a locus classicus for the factors that go into Greek identity, and while it was never universally

---

3. On the evolution of its role in the fourth and third centuries, see De Sensi Sestito 1984; Fronda 2013.

4. Liv. 24.2–3; Lomas 1993, 68–70; Fronda 2010, 171–178.

5. The population had fallen to about two thousand: Liv. 23.30.6.

6. Liv. 24.3.12: morituros se adfirmabant citius quam immixti Bruttiis in alienos ritus mores legesque ac mox linguam etiam uerterentur.

7. Hdt. 8.144.2: αὖτις δὲ τὸ Ἑλληνικόν, ἐὸν ὅμαιμόν τε καὶ ὁμόγλωσσον, καὶ θεῶν ἱδρύματά τε κοινὰ καὶ θυσίαι ἤθεά τε ὁμότροπα.

agreed upon, it remained one possible interpretation of Greek identity. The Crotoniates expected that admitting Bruttians into the citizen body would result in something quite similar to what had happened centuries earlier to Poseidonia and several other cities (discussed in chapter 6): Croton would no longer be a community of Greeks. Nevertheless, this sense of Greekness was inflected by local concerns; it was a particularly Crotoniate form of Hellenic identity. The Crotoniates expressed no enmity toward either Carthage or Rome, which were equally non-Greek. Instead, their attitudes and decisions were conditioned by their long history of conflict with the Bruttians, much as we saw for Taras in chapter 6. Greek identity at Croton was flexible enough to allow a focus on one non-Greek people while essentially ignoring others.

Croton's experience in the Second Punic War thus bears out the two main arguments I set out in the introduction: first, that the multiple identities held by the western Greeks were deeply intertwined and must be analyzed together, and second, that identity and politics were reciprocally linked. Identity was a key factor that conditioned political decisions and strategies, including Croton's response to the Bruttians and Hannibal's tactics of legitimation. Those identities came in multiple overlapping forms, both Hellenic and Crotoniate, and neither can be fully understood without the other. The Second Punic War gave the Greeks of southern Italy and Sicily one more (and, as it turned out, the final) opportunity to make their own political decisions. In that situation, and despite the vast changes that had come to the region, identity played much the same role as it had for centuries.

The fourfold typology of Greek, sub-Hellenic ethnic, regional, and *polis* identities, developed in the introduction, has proved a productive way to approach the complexities of identity in the Greek world. Hellenic and *polis* identities were not the same thing, nor were regional or ethnic identities, since each of these produced qualitatively different experiences for the communities involved. Distinguishing among them is important, yet it is equally important to analyze them together. We have seen, for example, how both Crotoniate and Metapontine identities were interwoven with Achaean ethnicity but in different ways. Recognizing this interrelationship shifts our analysis of Achaean ethnic identity: it was not a monolithic group so much as a series of separate *poleis* that shared certain elements in articulating their identities. Being Dorian was similarly important for Syracusans but not (or at least, not always) for the people of Camarina. While contrasts (and similarities) between Greeks and non-Greeks are undoubtedly important and interesting, we have also seen that the western Greeks themselves were equally diverse in their self-representations. Each case must therefore be analyzed sensitively and on its own terms, in an attempt to understand how ancient Greeks saw themselves.

The typology of multiple identities also provides a critical framework for understanding political strategies and decision-making. In the Peloponnesian War, many Sicilians chose their alliances on the basis of ethnicity, but the Camarinaeans did not; they were influenced instead by their *polis* identity, predicated on hatred of Syracuse. A few years later, the rhetoric of Hermocrates persuaded all of them (not only Camarina) to reorient their politics on the basis of Sicilian regional identity; later, in another context, he emphasized Dorian solidarity. The changing alliances were surely not determined by these shifting identities alone, but identity was always central to shaping the lenses through which Sicilians viewed these decisions. Similarly, much later, the decisions of Croton, as we have just seen, and Taras's resistance to Rome were conditioned by their various identities. The political history of Sicily and southern Italy throughout this period cannot be understood without full consideration of the impact of identity.

Yet that was only one part of the relationship between identity and politics. We have seen a wide variety of tyrants, kings, and politicians—from Hieron and Gelon to Hermocrates, Timoleon, and Hieron II—using identity as a tool to create legitimacy for themselves and secure their power. For some of these leaders, such as Timoleon, a single type of identity stands out: his use of Demeter and Kore painted him as being essentially Sicilian, protecting his adopted island against Carthage. But the Deinomenids used all four types of identity in different ways for different audiences; they drew attention to the place of landscape in Syracusan identity when speaking to Syracusans, for example, and emphasized their patronage of the two goddesses to make themselves acceptable to a pan-Sicilian audience. Since these strategies depended on a dialogue between rulers and ruled, their success tells us much about the attitudes of a wide range of people in these communities. Identities could not contribute to the legitimacy of rulers unless they already existed, but rulers, in turn, could articulate new identities and reshape existing ones and thereby make a real impact on the identities available to their subjects. Identity was a powerful tool in the arsenal of power in Sicily, used by almost every major figure in various ways, and while it did have limits, it was often extremely successful.

Conflict between (and within) cities was also central to how identities were created in the first place and how existing ones were reshaped. Achaean ethnicity seems to have developed through a series of conflicts between the *poleis* of southern Italy—Croton and Locri, Metapontion and Taras, and several cities against Siris—in the sixth and fifth centuries. Hellenic identity became enormously more salient in the face of Carthaginian invasions, both in 480 and at various times after 409. Although versions of this conclusion have been reached before, placing it alongside the results summarized in the last two paragraphs is new. Taking all of them together, we can see that Greek politics cannot be understood without considering identity, nor can the identities articulated by the Greeks be analyzed apart from their political contexts. Greek historians must take seriously the political role of multiple identities.

Moreover, these identities were not only plural but also dynamic constructs that were flexible and yet remarkably consistent over time. New elements were frequently added to existing *polis* identities—such as, at Syracuse, the city's landscape under the Deinomenids and its glorious past in the Hellenistic age—which, once incorporated, tended to remain in place for centuries. The nature of these identities was often contested. I have argued that the *stasis* in Syracuse after the fall of the Deinomenids ultimately stemmed from disagreements between the new and old citizens over what it meant to be Syracusan. In a somewhat different way, Metapontion's identities were caught between the Metapontines themselves and various outsiders who tried to redefine it for their own purposes. In Hellenistic Italy, by contrast, the biggest disagreements were between *poleis* such as Taras and Thurii, which debated whether shared Greekness or local identities were more important.

Similarly, new identities did develop over time, and others slowly decayed away. Regional identity in Sicily was made drastically more salient by the Deinomenids, although they were working from preexisting elements. In the fourth century, meanwhile, many sub-Hellenic ethnic identities (especially Achaean) gradually lost their salience, due to the increasing importance of Greekness and of the Italiote League, which cut across ethnic boundaries. The full range of available identities thus evolved slowly, but a different form of change—not the creation of a new identity but a change in the salience of an existing one—could happen quickly. Hermocrates's speech at Gela, for instance, combined with the political situation in which it was delivered, drastically increased the salience of regional identity and decreased that of ethnicity. While this was a significant change, the available options remained the same in the short term. In the long run, however, identities changed, but the larger dynamics of identity in the politics of Greek Sicily and southern Italy largely persisted from the Archaic period through the Second Punic War.

We have also traced a series of other threads that shed additional light on the dynamics of identity. Geographical features, such as the local landscapes of Syracuse and Croton or the boundaries of a region, frequently played a central role in articulating specific identities. In other cases, reference to distant lands—such as the Peloponnese for Syracuse or the Argolid for Achaeans—fed into many identities. The movement of people from one place to another also produced varying effects on their identities. New citizens arriving in

Syracuse took on new identities but without giving up their prior ones. More commonly, though, mobility led to a reaffirmation of identities, as suggested by the experiences of Praxinoa in Alexandria and of post-Deinomenid Sicilians refounding their home cities. Finally, full consideration of multiple identities reveals how modern notions of ethnicity and of the nation-state have closed off possibilities. Could the Sikels be counted as Sicilians equally with their Greek neighbors? Perhaps, but only if we discount the paramount importance of Greekness among the various identities held by those Greeks. Similarly, the origins of Achaean ethnicity in conflicts between Greeks have been obscured by heavy focus on relations between Greeks and non-Greeks. Comparing a wide range of material has thus uncovered significant diversity in the dynamics of identity in the Greek West.

The identities discussed in this book were constructed of multiple overlapping strands and articulated in many flexible ways; this means that in seeking to reconstruct the discourses of identity in any given community, we must use all possible evidence. This study has employed historiography, epinician poetry, tragedy, myths, religious practices, coinage, inscriptions, archaeological evidence, and more. These disparate types of evidence must be treated carefully and on their own terms, but they all have much to contribute. Thucydides gives us one picture of the nature of Sicilian regional identity, for example, but myths of Demeter and Kore give us another, while cult practices give yet another; none is complete without the others. In the same way, the full role of Heracles at Croton can only be pieced together from a combination of coins, myths, and bits of historiographical evidence. Although our sources will never be complete and hence conclusions must be provisional, working with all available sources is the best route to the richest possible picture of the western Greeks and their identities.

This picture can and should be expanded in future research. The case studies considered here have by no means exhausted the evidence for the Greek West. I have spoken little of Campania, for instance, a major area of Greek settlement and of contact between Greeks and non-Greeks; in fact, the region's name refers to its non-Greek inhabitants. In Sicily, the *poleis* of Himera (which Thucydides describes as partly Dorian, partly Chalcidian) and Zancle (later Messina, as a result of some striking ethnic reconfigurations) both raise interesting questions.[8] The articulations of Dorian identities at Gela, Akragas, and Selinus might well turn out to be different from the Syracusan ones discussed here. And as I suggested in the introduction, other types of identity beyond

---

8. De Sensi Sestito 1981; Luraghi 2008, 147–172.

the four discussed here—such as *genos* or *phyle* identities or networks of colonies founded by individual mother cities—might broaden the picture further.

Moreover, the method and typology established here could easily be extended to other regions and, in fact, to the entire Greek world. The incredibly complex ethnic and cultural landscape of Asia Minor would present fertile ground for such questions, and sustained analysis would undoubtedly bring out both similarities and differences between the identities of the Greeks of Asia and those of the West. The island of Rhodes is another interesting test case.[9] As a *polis*, Rhodes was only founded in 408/7 BCE, through a synoicism of three preexisting cities of Lindus, Ialysus, and Camirus. Prior to that year, there was no city of Rhodes, but nevertheless, there were Rhodians. Pindar's *Olympian* 7, written in 464, was commissioned by Diagoras of Rhodes. Even earlier, in 688, the city of Gela was founded by Cretans and Rhodians, and the cult of Athena Lindia (notably, named after one of the three cities) served as a unifying force for the whole island. After 408/7, the original three cities maintained a sort of subordinate existence in the new *polis*, indicating that their separate identities still existed. Thus, the island seems a prime candidate for analysis, as an example both of regional identity and of its interaction with *polis* identities. I therefore hope to have established an approach that will bear fruit in a variety of future analyses of these and other regions. This is a beginning, not an end, since I have untangled only a little of the intricate web of identities that the Greeks created for themselves in Sicily and southern Italy. Nearly limitless permutations remain.

---

9. Kowalzig 2007, 224–266; Malkin 2011, 65–95.

Bibliography

Adamesteanu, D., ed. 1999. *Storia della Basilicata*, Vol. 1: *L'Antichità*. Rome: Laterza.

Adorjáni, Z. 2014. *Pindars sechste olympische Siegesode: Text, Einleitung und Kommentar.* Leiden: Brill.

Adornato, G. 2005. "Il tripode di Gelone a Delfi." *RAL* 16: 395–420.

Albanese Procelli, R. M. 1996. "Greeks and Indigenous Peoples in Eastern Sicily: Forms of Interaction and Acculturation." In *Early Societies in Sicily: New Developments in Archaeological Research*, edited by R. Leighton, 167–176. London: Accordia Research Centre.

Albanese Procelli, R. M. 2003. *Sicani, siculi, elimi: Forme di identità, modi di contatto e processi di trasformazione.* Milan: Longanesi.

Alcock, S., and R. Osborne, eds. 1994. *Placing the Gods: Sanctuaries and Sacred Space in Ancient Greece.* Oxford: Clarendon Press.

Alcock, S., and R. Osborne, eds. 2012. *Classical Archaeology.* 2nd ed. Malden, MA: Wiley-Blackwell.

Alessandro il Molosso e i 'condottieri' in Magna Grecia. 2004. Taranto: Istituto per la storia e l'archeologia della Magna Grecia.

Allan, W. 2008. *Euripides: Helen.* Cambridge: Cambridge University Press.

Alle origini della Magna Grecia: Mobilità, migrazioni, fondazioni. 2012. Taranto: Istituto per la storia e l'archeologia della Magna Grecia.

Alty, J. 1982. "Dorians and Ionians." *JHS* 102: 1–14.

Amandry, P. 1987. "Trépieds de Delphes et du Péloponnèse." *BCH* 111: 79–131.

Ameling, W. 2011. "The Rise of Carthage to 264 BC." In Hoyos 2011, 39–57.

Ampolo, C. 2012. "Compresenza di ethne e culture diverse nella Sicilia occidentale: Per una nuova prospettiva storica." *Aristonothos* 7: 15–57.

Anderson, G. 2003. *The Athenian Experiment: Building an Imagined Political Community in Ancient Attica, 508–490 B.C.* Ann Arbor: University of Michigan Press.

Anello, P. 2002a. "L'ambiente greco." In Cordano and Di Salvatore 2002, 59–76.

Anello, P. 2002b. "Siracusa e Cartagine." In Bonacasa, Braccesi, and De Miro 2002, 343–360.

Anello, P. 2008a. "Punici e Greci dal 405/4 a.C. all'età timoleontea." In *Greci e Punici in Sicilia tra 5. e 4. secolo a. C.*, edited by M. Congiu, C. Micciché, S. Modeo, and L. Santagati, 81–100. Caltanisetta: Sciascia.

Anello, P. 2008b. "Sicilia terra amata dalle dee." *Aristonothos* 2: 9–23.

Antonaccio, C. 2001. "Ethnicity and Colonization." In Malkin 2001a, 113–157.

Antonaccio, C. 2003. "Hybridity and the Cultures within Greek Culture." In Dougherty and Kurke 2003, 57–74.

Antonaccio, C. 2004. "Siculo-Geometric and the Sikels: Ceramics and Identity in Eastern Sicily." In Lomas 2004, 55–81.

Antonaccio, C. 2005. "Excavating Colonization." In Hurst and Owen 2005, 97–113.

Antonaccio, C. 2007a. "Colonization: Greece on the Move, 900–480." In *Cambridge Companion to Archaic Greece*, edited by H. A. Shapiro, 201–224. Cambridge: Cambridge University Press.

Antonaccio, C. 2007b. "Elite Mobility in the West." In *Pindar's Poetry, Patrons, and Festivals: From Archaic Greece to the Roman Empire*, edited by S. Hornblower and C. Morgan, 265–285. Oxford: Oxford University Press.

Antonaccio, C. 2010. "(Re)defining Ethnicity: Culture, Material Culture, and Identity." In *Material Culture and Social Identities in the Ancient World*, edited by S. Hales and T. Hodos, 32–53. Cambridge: Cambridge University Press.

Appiah, K. A. 2018. *The Lies That Bind: Rethinking Identity, Creed, Country, Color, Class, Culture.* New York: Liveright.

Arena, E. 2006–2007. "Per una storia dell' 'Acaicità': La definizione identitaria degli achei del Peloponneso." *AION(archeol)* 13–14: 13–80.

Arnold-Biucchi, C., and A. C. Weiss. 2007. "The River God Alpheios on the First Tetradrachm Issue of Gelon at Syracuse." *NAC* 36: 59–74.

Asheri, D. 1980. "Rimpatrio di esuli e ridistribuzione delle terre nelle città siciliote, ca. 466–461 A.C." In *Philias charin: Miscellanea di studi classici in onore di Eugenio Manni*, 141–158. Rome: Bretschneider.

Asheri, D. 1992a. "The Art of Synchronization in Greek Historiography: The Case of Timaeus of Tauromenium." *SCI* 11: 52–89.

Asheri, D. 1992b. "Sicily, 478–431 B.C." In *CAH*² V, 147–170.

Asheri, D. 1997. "Identità greche, identità greca." In *I Greci: Storia cultura arte società*, Vol. 2: *Una storia greca* II: *Definizione*, edited by S. Settis, 5–26. Turin: G. Einaudi.

Asheri, D. 1999. "Processi di 'decolonizzazione' in Magna Grecia: Il caso di Poseidonia Lucana." In *La colonisation grecque* 1999, 361–370.

Ashmore, R. D., K. Deaux, and T. McLaughlin-Volpe. 2004. "An Organizing Framework for Collective Identity: Articulation and Significance of Multidimensionality." *Psychological Bulletin* 130: 80–114.

Asirvatham, S. R. 2008. "The Roots of Macedonian Ambiguity." In *Macedonian Legacies*, edited by T. Howe and J. Reames, 235–255. Claremont, CA: Regina.

Athanassaki, L. 2004. "Deixis, Performance, and Poetics in Pindar's *First Olympian Ode.*" *Arethusa* 37: 317–341.

Aubet, M. E. 2001. *The Phoenicians and the West: Politics, Colonies and Trade.* 2nd ed. Cambridge: Cambridge University Press.

Avery, H. C. 1973. "Themes in Thucydides' Account of the Sicilian Expedition." *Hermes* 101: 1–13.

Bagnall, R. 1984. "The Origins of Ptolemaic Cleruchs." *BASP* 21: 7–20.

Baitinger, H., and T. Hodos. 2016. "Greeks and Indigenous People in Archaic Sicily: Methodological Considerations of Material Culture and Identity." In *Material Culture and Identity between the Mediterranean World and Central Europe,* edited by H. Baitinger, 15–31. Mainz: Verlag des Römish-Germanischen Zentralmuseums.

Bakewell, G. 1999. "Lysias 12 and Lysias 31: Metics and Athenian Citizenship in the Aftermath of the Thirty." *GRBS* 40: 5–22.

Baldassarra, D. 2010. "La saga degli Alfeidi e l'epos messenico." In *Tra panellenismo e tradizioni locali: Generi poetici e storiografia,* edited by E. Cingano, 91–114. Alexandria: Edizioni dell'Orso.

Baldo, G. 1999. "Enna: Un paesaggio del mito tra storia e religio (Cicerone, *Verr.* 2.4.105–115)." In *Sicilia e Magna Grecia: Spazio reale e spazio immaginario nella letteratura greca e latina,* edited by G. Avezzù and E. Pianezzola. Padua: Imprimatur.

Banks, M. 1996. *Ethnicity: Anthropological Constructions.* London: Routledge.

Barceló, P. 1994. "The Perception of Carthage in Classical Greek Historiography." *AClass* 37: 1–14.

Barker, R. S. 1990. *Political Legitimacy and the State.* Oxford: Clarendon Press.

Barnes, C. 2005. *Images and Insults: Ancient Historiography and the Outbreak of the Tarentine War.* Stuttgart: F. Steiner.

Baron, C. A. 2013. *Timaeus of Tauromenium and Hellenistic Historiography.* Cambridge: Cambridge University Press.

Barrett, W. S. 2007. "Pindar and Psaumis: *Olympians* 4 and 5." In W. S. Barrett, *Greek Lyric, Tragedy, and Textual Criticism: Collected Papers,* 38–53. Oxford: Oxford University Press.

Barron, J. 1964. "Religious Propaganda of the Delian League." *JHS* 84: 35–48.

Barth, F. 1969. "Introduction." In *Ethnic Groups and Boundaries: The Social Organization of Cultural Difference,* edited by F. Barth, 9–38. Long Grove, IL: Waveland.

Bearzot, C. 2006. "Ermocrate *dedynasteukos en Sikelia* in Timeo F 22." In *Italo-Tusco-Romana,* edited by P. Amann, M. Pedrazzi, and H. Täuber, 23–30. Vienna: Holzhausen.

Bearzot, C. 2008. "La Sicilia isola 'sacra a Demetra e a Core' (Diod. 16.66.4–5)." *Aristonothos* 2: 141–151.

Beck, H. 2020. *Localism and the Ancient Greek City-State.* Chicago: University of Chicago Press.

Beck, H., and P. Funke, eds. 2015. *Federalism in Greek Antiquity.* Cambridge: Cambridge University Press.

Beetham, D. 1991. *The Legitimation of Power.* Atlantic Highlands, NJ: Humanities Press International.

Bell, M. 1985. "Le terrecotte votive del culto di Persefone a Morgantina." In *Il tempio greco in Sicilia: Architettura e culti,* edited by G. Pugliese Carratelli, 140–147. Catania: Università di Catania Istituto di Archeologia.

Bell, M. 1999. "Centro e periferia nel regno siracusano di Ierone II." In *La colonisation grecque* 1999, 257–277.

Bell, M. 2000. "Morgantina e Camarina al congresso di Gela." In *Un ponte* 2000, 291–297.

Bérard, J. 1963. *La Magna Grecia.* Turin: Einaudi.

Berger, S. 1992. *Revolution and Society in Greek Sicily and Southern Italy.* Stuttgart: F. Steiner.

Berve, H. 1959. *König Hieron II.* Munich: Verlag der Bayerischen Akademie der Wissenschaften.

Bicknell, P. 1966. "The Date of the Battle of the Sagra River." *Phoenix* 20: 294–301.

Bloedow, E. F. 1996. "The Speeches of Hermocrates and Athenagoras at Syracuse in 415 BC: Difficulties in Syracuse and in Thucydides." *Historia* 45: 141–157.

Blok, J. 2017. *Citizenship in Classical Athens.* Cambridge: Cambridge University Press.

Boardman, J. 1999. *The Greeks Overseas: Their Early Colonies and Trade.* 4th ed. New York: Thames and Hudson.

Boardman, J. 2006. "Ethnicity-Shmicity?" *Ancient West and East* 4: 458–459.

Boedeker, D. 1993. "Hero Cult and Politics in Herodotus: The Bones of Orestes." In *Cultural Poetics in Archaic Greece,* edited by C. Dougherty and L. Kurke, 164–177. Cambridge: Cambridge University Press.

Boedeker, D. 2007. "The View from Eleusis: Demeter in the Persian Wars." In *Cultural Responses to the Persian Wars: Antiquity to the Third Millennium,* edited by E. Bridges, E. Hall, and P. J. Rhodes, 65–82. Oxford: Oxford University Press.

Boedeker, D., and K. A. Raaflaub, eds. 1998. *Democracy, Empire, and the Arts in Fifth-Century Athens.* Cambridge, MA: Harvard University Press.

Boehringer, E. 1929. *Die Münzen von Syrakus.* Berlin: De Gruyter.

Bonacasa, N., L. Braccesi, and E. De Miro, eds. 2002. *La Sicilia dei due Dionisî.* Rome: Bretschneider.

Bonanno, D. 2010. *Ierone il dinomenide: Storia e rappresentazione.* Pisa: F. Serra.

Borba Florenzano, M. B. 1992. "The Coinage of Pyrrhus in Sicily: Evidence of a Political Project." In Hackens et al., 207–223.

Borba Florenzano, M. B. 2005. "Coins and Religion: Representations of Demeter and Kore-Persephone on Sicilian Greek Coins." *RBN* 151: 1–29.

Borza, E. N. 1990. *In the Shadow of Olympus: The Emergence of Macedon.* Princeton, NJ: Princeton University Press.

Bosher, K. 2012a. "Hieron's Aeschylus." In Bosher 2012b, 97–111.

Bosher, K., ed. 2012b. *Theater outside Athens: Drama in Greek Sicily and South Italy.* Cambridge: Cambridge University Press.

Bosworth, B. 1992. "Athens' First Intervention in Sicily: Thucydides and the Sicilian Tradition." *CQ* 42: 46–55.

Bowie, A. M. 2007. *Herodotus Histories Book VIII.* Cambridge: Cambridge University Press.

Bowra, C. M. 1964. *Pindar.* Oxford: Clarendon Press.

Bradley, K. R. 1989. *Slavery and Rebellion in the Roman World, 140 B.C.–70 B.C.* Bloomington: Indiana University Press.

Braswell, B. K. 1992. *A Commentary on Pindar Nemean One.* Fribourg: University Press Fribourg Switzerland.

Brauer, G. C. 1986. *Taras: Its History and Coinage.* New Rochelle, NY: Caratzas.

Braund, D. 2018. *Greek Religion and Cults in the Black Sea Region: Goddesses in the Bosporan Kingdom from the Archaic Period to the Byzantine Era.* Cambridge: Cambridge University Press.

Brelich, A. 1965. "La religione greca in Sicilia." *Kokalos* 10–11: 35–54.

Brennan, T. C. 1993. "The Commanders in the First Sicilian Slave War." *Rivista di filologia e istruzione classica* 121: 153–184.

Brock, R., and S. Hodkinson, eds. 2000. *Alternatives to Athens: Varieties of Political Organization and Community in Ancient Greece.* Oxford: Oxford University Press.

Broekaert, W., R. Nadeau, and J. Wilkins, eds. 2016. *Food, Identity and Cross-Cultural Exchange in the Ancient World.* Brussels: Editions Latomus.

Broodbank, C. 2000. *An Island Archaeology of the Early Cyclades.* Cambridge: Cambridge University Press.

Brown, T. 1958. *Timaeus of Tauromenium.* Berkeley: University of California Press.

Brubaker, R., and F. Cooper. 2000. "Beyond 'Identity.'" *Theory and Society* 29: 1–47.

Bundy, E. 1962. *Studia Pindarica.* Berkeley: University of California Press.

Burgers, G. 2004. "Western Greeks in Their Regional Setting: Rethinking Early Greek-Indigenous Encounters in Southern Italy." *Ancient West and East* 3: 252–282.

Burgess, J. S. 2009. *The Death and Afterlife of Achilles.* Baltimore: Johns Hopkins University Press.

Burkert, W. 1983. *Homo Necans: The Anthropology of Ancient Greek Sacrificial Ritual and Myth.* Translated by P. Bing. Berkeley: University of California Press.

Burkert, W. 1985. *Greek Religion.* Cambridge, MA: Harvard University Press.

Burkert, W. 1995. "Greek *Poleis* and Civic Cults: Some Further Thoughts." In *Studies in the Ancient Greek Polis,* edited by K. A. Raaflaub and M. H. Hansen, 201–210. Copenhagen: Royal Danish Academy of Sciences and Letters.

Burnett, A. P. 1985. *The Art of Bacchylides.* Cambridge, MA: Harvard University Press.

Burstein, S. 2008. "Greek Identity in the Hellenistic Period." In Zacharia 2008a, 59–77.

Burton, J. B. 1995. *Theocritus's Urban Mimes: Mobility, Gender, and Patronage.* Berkeley: University of California Press.

Burton, R. W. B. 1962. *Pindar's Pythian Odes: Essays in Interpretation*. Oxford: Oxford University Press.

Bury, J. B., and R. Meiggs. 1975. *A History of Greece to the Death of Alexander the Great*. 4th ed. New York: St. Martin's.

Cabanes, P. 2005. "Les interventions grecques en Grande Grèce et en Sicile aux IVe–IIIe siècle av. J.-C." In *Le canal d'Otrante et la Méditerranée antique et médiévale*, edited by E. Deniaux, 23–30. Bari: Edipuglia.

Caccamo Caltabiano, M., L. Campagna, and A. Pinzone, eds. 2004. *Nuove prospettive della ricerca sulla Sicilia del III sec. a.C.: Archeologia, numisimatica, storia*. Messina: Dipartimento di Scienze dell'Antichità dell'Università degli Studi di Messina.

Caccamo Caltabiano, M., B. Carroccio, and E. Oteri. 1997. *Siracusa ellenistica: Le monete regali di Ierone II, della sua famiglia e dei siracusani*. Messina: Dipartimento di Scienze dell'Antichità dell'Università degli Studi di Messina.

Cagnazzi, S. 1996. "Un atleta di Crotone a Salamina." *Miscellanea Greca e Romana* 20: 11–19.

Cairns, D. L. 2005. "Myth and the Polis in Bacchylides' Eleventh Ode." *JHS* 125: 35–50.

Cairns, D. L. 2010. *Five Epinician Odes (3, 5, 9, 11, 13)*. Cambridge: F. Cairns.

Calame, C. 1990. "Narrating the Foundation of a City: The Symbolic Birth of Cyrene." In *Approaches to Greek Myth*, edited by L. Edmunds, 277–341. Baltimore: Johns Hopkins University Press.

Calciati, R. 1987. *Corpus nummorum Siculorum: La monetazione di bronzo*, Vol. 3. Milan: Ed. I.P.

Caldwell, C. 2020. *The Age of Entitlement: America since the Sixties*. New York: Simon & Schuster.

Calligeri, D. 2002. "The Dorian-Ionian Distinction in Thucydides' Books VI and VII." *Platon* 52: 255–262.

Camassa, G. 1991. "I culti delle *poleis* italiote." In *Storia del Mezzogiorno*, Vol. 1: *Il Mezzogiorno antico*, 422–495. Naples: Edizioni del Sole.

Camassa, G. 1993. "I culti." In *Sibari e la Sibaritide*, 573–594.

Campagna, L. 2004. "Architettura e ideologia della basileia a Siracusa nell'età di Ierone II." In Caccamo Caltabiano, Campagna, and Pinzone 2004, 151–189.

Cappelletti, L. 2002. *Lucani e Brettii: Ricerche sulla storia politica e istituzionale di due popoli dell'Italia antica (V–III sec. a.C.)*. Frankfurt: Peter Lang.

Cappelletti, L. 2018. "The Bruttii." In Farney and Bradley 2018, 321–336.

Carey, C. 1980. "Bacchylides Experiments: Ode 11." *Mnemosyne* 33: 225–243.

Carey, C. 1981. *A Commentary on Five Odes of Pindar*. New York: Arno.

Carpenter, R. 1953. "The Nike of Athena Parthenos." *Archaiologike Ephemeris* 2: 41–55.

Carter, J. C. 1994. "Sanctuaries in the Chora of Metapontum." In Alcock and Osborne 1994, 161–198.

Carter, J. C. 2006. *Discovering the Greek Countryside at Metaponto*. Ann Arbor: University of Michigan Press.

Carter, J. C. 2018. "The Other Sanctuary of Artemis in the Chora." In *The Chora of Metaponto*, Vol. 7: *The Greek Sanctuary at Pantanello*, edited by J. C. Carter and K. Swift, 1517–1524. Austin: University of Texas Press.

Cartledge, P. 2002. *The Greeks: A Portrait of Self and Others*. 2nd ed. Oxford: Oxford University Press.

Caruso, E. 2013. "The Sanctuary at San Francesco Bisconti." In Lyons, Bennett, and Marconi 2013, 52–53.

Casevitz, M., and A. Jacquemin. 2015. *Diodore de Sicile, Bibliothèque Historique: Livre V*. Paris: Les Belles Lettres.

Cassola, F. 1997. "Chi erano i greci?" In *I Greci: Storia cultura arte società*, Vol. 2: *Una storia greca* I: *Formazione*, edited by S. Settis, 5–23. Turin: G. Einaudi.

Castagnino Berlinghieri, E. F. 2010. "Archimede e Ierone II: Dall'idea al progetto della più grande nave del mondo antico, la Syrakosia." *Hesperìa: Studi sulla grecità di occidente* 26: 169–188.

Cataldi, S. 2007. "Atene e l'occidente: Trattate e alleanze dal 433 al 424." In Greco and Lombardo 2007, 421–470.

Caven, B. 1990. *Dionysius I: Warlord of Sicily*. New Haven, CT: Yale University Press.

Cecchet, L., and A. Busetto, eds. 2017. *Citizens in the Graeco-Roman World: Aspects of Citizenship from the Archaic Period to AD 212*. Leiden: Brill.

Cerchiai, L., L. Jannelli, and F. Longo. 2004. *The Greek Cities of Magna Graecia and Sicily*. Los Angeles: J. Paul Getty Museum.

Cerulo, K. A. 1997. "Identity Construction: New Issues, New Directions." *Annual Review of Sociology* 23: 385–409.

Ceserani, G. 2012. *Italy's Lost Greece: Magna Graecia and the Making of Modern Archaeology*. Oxford: Oxford University Press.

Champion, C. 2000. "Romans as BAPBAPOI: Three Polybian Speeches and the Politics of Cultural Indeterminacy." *CPh* 95: 425–444.

Champion, C. 2004. *Cultural Politics in Polybius's Histories*. Berkeley: University of California Press.

Champion, C. 2010. "Timaios (566)." In *BNJ*.

Cipriani, M. 1997. "Il ruolo di Hera nel santuario meridionale di Poseidonia." In De La Genière 1997, 211–225.

Clackson, J. 2012. "Oscan in Sicily." In Tribulato 2012, 132–148.

Clinton, K. 1992. *Myth and Cult: The Iconography of the Eleusinian Mysteries*. Stockholm: Swedish Institute at Athens.

Clinton, K. 1993. "The Sanctuary of Demeter and Kore at Eleusis." In *Greek Sanctuaries: New Approaches*, edited by N. Marinatos and R. Hägg, 110–124. London: Routledge.

Clinton, K. 1994. "The Eleusinian Mysteries and Panhellenism in Democratic Athens." In *The Archaeology of Athens and Attica under the Democracy*, edited by W. D. E. Coulson, 161–172. Oxford: Oxbow.

Cogan, M. 1981. *The Human Thing: The Speeches and Principles of Thucydides' History*. Chicago: University of Chicago Press.

Cohen, A. 1969. *Custom and Politics in Urban Africa: A Study of Hausa Migrants in Yoruba Towns*. Berkeley: University of California Press.

Cohen, E. E. 2000. *The Athenian Nation*. Princeton, NJ: Princeton University Press.

Cole, S. G. 1994. "Demeter in the Ancient Greek City and its Countryside." In Alcock and Osborne 1994, 199–216.

Cole, S. G. 1995. "Civic Cult and Civic Identity." In Hansen 1995, 292–325.

La colonisation grecque en Méditerranée occidentale. 1999. Rome: École française de Rome.

Connor, W. R. 1984. *Thucydides*. Princeton, NJ: Princeton University Press.

Connor, W. R. 1993. "The Ionian Era of Athenian Civic Identity." *PAPhS* 137: 194–206.

Connor, W. R. 1994. "The Problem of Athenian Civic Identity." In Scafuro and Boegehold 1994, 34–44.

Consolo Langher, S. N. 1988. "Tra Falaride e Ducezio: Concezalleione territoriale, forme di contatto, processi di depoliticizzazione e fenomeni di ristrutturazione civico-sociale nella politica espansionistica dei grandi tiranni e in età post-dinomenide." *Kokalos* 34–35: 229–263.

Consolo Langher, S. N. 1997. *Un imperialismo tra democrazia e tirannide: Siracusa nei secoli V e IV a.C.* Rome: Bretschneider.

Constantakopoulou, C. 2005. "Proud to Be an Islander: Island Identity in Multi-Polis Islands in the Classical and Hellenistic Aegean." *MHR* 20: 1–34.

Constantakopoulou, C. 2007. *The Dance of the Islands: Insularity, Networks, the Athenian Empire, and the Aegean World*. Oxford: Oxford University Press.

Copani, F. 2005. "Alle origini di Eloro: L'espansione meridionale di Siracusa arcaica." *Acme* 58: 245–263.

Copani, F. 2009. "Acre e Casmene: L'espansione siracusana sui monti Iblei." In *Argumenta antiquitatis*, edited by G. Zanetto and M. Ornaghi, 11–21. Milan: Cisalpino.

Cordano, F. 1986. *Antiche fondazioni greche: Sicilia e Italia meridionale*. Palermo: Sellerio.

Cordano, F. 1992. *Le tessere pubbliche dal tempio di Atena a Camarina*. Rome: Istituto Italiano per la Storia Antica.

Cordano, F. 2000. "Camarina fra il 461 e il 405 a.C.: Un caso esemplare." In *Un ponte 2000*, 191–193.

Cordano, F., and M. Di Salvatore. 2002. *Il Guerriero di Castiglione di Ragusa: Greci e Siculi nella Sicilia sud-orientale*. Rome: Bretschneider.

Cornell, T. J. 1974. "Notes on the Sources for Campanian History in the Fifth Century B.C." *MH* 31: 193–208.

Cornell, T. J. 1995. *The Beginnings of Rome: Italy and Rome from the Bronze Age to the Punic Wars, c. 1000–263 BC*. New York: Routledge.

Costanzi, M. 2020. "Mobility in the Ancient Greek World: Diversity of Causes, Variety of Vocabularies." In De Angelis 2020a, 11–36.

Coulmas, F. 2019. *Identity: A Very Short Introduction.* Oxford: Oxford University Press.

Crane, G. 1996. *The Blinded Eye: Thucydides and the New Written Word.* Lanham, MD: Rowman & Littlefield.

Crawford, M. 2006a. "From Poseidonia to Paestum via the Lucanians." In *Greek and Roman Colonization: Origins, Ideologies and Interactions,* edited by G. Bradley and J. Wilson, 59–72. Swansea: Classical Press of Wales.

Crawford, M. 2006b. "The Oscan Inscriptions of Messana." In *Guerra e pace 2006,* 521–525.

Crotone. 1984. Taranto: Istituto per la storia e l'archeologia della Magna Grecia.

Currie, B. 2004. "Reperformance Scenarios for Pindar's Odes." In Mackie 2004, 49–69.

Curty, O. 1994. "La notion de la parenté entre cités chez Thucydide." *MH* 51: 193–197.

Cusumano, N. 2009. "Mots pour dire les mots: Interactions, acculturations et relations interculturelles dans la Sicile antique (Ve–Ier siècle avant J.-C.)." *Pallas* 79: 41–63.

Cusumano, N. 2012. "Gérer la haine, fabriquer l'ennemi: Grecs et Carthaginois en Sicile entre les Ve et IVe siècles av. J.-C." *DHA* Supplement 6: 113–135.

Davies, J. K. 1977. "Athenian Citizenship: The Descent Group and Alternatives." *CJ* 73: 105–121.

Davies, M. 2013. "From Rags to Riches: Democedes of Croton and the Credibility of Herodotus." *BICS* 53: 19–44.

De Angelis, F. 1998. "Ancient Past, Imperial Present: The British Empire in T. J. Dunbabin's *The Western Greeks.*" *Antiquity* 72: 539–549.

De Angelis, F. 2003. "Equations of Culture: The Meeting of Natives and Greeks in Sicily (*ca.* 750–450 BC)." *Ancient West and East* 2: 19–50.

De Angelis, F. 2006. "Going against the Grain in Sicilian Greek Economics." *G&R* 53: 29–47.

De Angelis, F. 2016. *Archaic and Classical Greek Sicily: A Social and Economic History.* Oxford: Oxford University Press.

De Angelis, F., ed. 2020a. *A Companion to Greeks across the Ancient World.* Hoboken, NJ: Wiley.

De Angelis, F. 2020b. "Italian-Speaking Traditions and the Study of Ancient Greeks outside Their Homelands." In De Angelis 2020a, 85–100.

De Cesare, M., E. C. Portale, and N. Sojc. 2020. *The Akragas Dialogue: New Investigations on Sanctuaries in Sicily.* Berlin: De Gruyter.

De Juliis, E. M. 2000. *Taranto.* Bari: Edipuglia.

De Juliis, E. M. 2001. *Metaponto.* Bari: Edipuglia.

De La Genière, J. 1991. *Epéios et Philoctète en Italie.* Naples: Centre Jean Bérard.

De La Genière, J. 1997. *Héra: Images, espaces, cultes.* Naples: Centre Jean Bérard.

Delgado, A., and M. Ferrer. 2007. "Cultural Contacts in Colonial Settings: The Construction of New Identities in Phoenician Settlements of the Western Mediterranean." *Stanford Journal of Archaeology* 5: 18–42.

De Luna, M. E. 2009. "Camarina sub-colonia di Siracusa: Dalla fondazione al conflitto." In *Colonie di colonie: Le fondazioni sub-coloniali greche tra colonizzazione e colonialismo*, edited by M. Lombardo and F. Frisone, 75–86. Galatina: Congedo.

Demand, N. H. 1990. *Urban Relocation in Archaic and Classical Greece.* Norman: University of Oklahoma Press.

Demetriou, D. 2012. *Negotiating Identity in the Ancient Mediterranean: The Archaic and Classical Greek Multiethnic Emporia.* Cambridge: Cambridge University Press.

De Miro, E. 2008. "*Thesmophoria di Sicilia.*" In Di Stefano 2008, 47–92.

Dench, E. 2003. "Beyond Greeks and Barbarians: Italy and Sicily in the Hellenistic Age." In *A Companion to the Hellenistic World*, edited by A. Erskine, 294–310. Malden, MA: Blackwell.

De Romilly, J. 1963. *Thucydides and Athenian Imperialism.* Oxford: Blackwell.

De Sensi Sestito, G. 1977. *Gerone II: Un monarca ellenistico in Sicilia.* Palermo: Editrice Sophia.

De Sensi Sestito, G. 1981. "Contrasti etnici e lotte politiche a Zancle-Messina e Reggio alla caduta della tirannide." *Athenaeum* 59: 38–55.

De Sensi Sestito, G. 1984. "La funzione politica dell'Heraion del Lacinio al tempo delle lotte contro i Lucani e Dionisio I." *Contributi dell'Istituto di Storia Antica dell'Università del Sacro Cuore* 10: 41–50.

De Sensi Sestito, G. 1995. "Rapporti tra la Sicilia, Roma e l'Egitto." In *La Sicilia tra l'Egitto e Roma: La monetazione siracusana dell'età di Ierone II*, edited by M. Caccamo Caltabiano, 17–57. Messina: Accademia Peloritana dei Pericolanti.

De Sensi Sestito, G. 2001. "Il paesaggio di Caulonia tra mito, storia, e culti." In *Kaulonía, Caulonia, Stilida (e oltre): Contributi storici, archeologici e topografici*, edited by M. C. Parra, 317–332. Pisa: Scuola Normale di Pisa.

De Sensi Sestito, G. 2016. "Pirro e le città italiote." In *Sulle sponde dello Ionio: Grecia occidentale e Greci d'occidente*, edited by G. De Sensi Sestito and M. Intrieri, 287–335. Pisa: Edizioni ETS.

De Siena, A. 1998. "Metaponto: Problemi urbanistici e scoperte recenti." In *Siritide e Metapontino: Storie di due territori coloniali*, 141–170. Naples: Centre Jean Bérard.

De Siena, A. 1999. "La colonizzazione achea del Metapontino." In Adamesteanu 1999, 211–245.

De Vincenzo, S. 2019. "Sicily." In *The Oxford Handbook of the Phoenician and Punic Mediterranean*, edited by C. López-Ruiz and B. R. Doak, 537–552. Oxford: Oxford University Press.

De Vos, G. A. 1975. "Ethnic Pluralism: Conflict and Accommodation." In *Ethnic Identity: Cultural Continuities and Change*, edited by G. A. De Vos and L. Romanucci-Ross, 5–41. Palo Alto, CA: Mayfield.

De Waele, J. A. 1971. *Acragas graeca: Die historische Topographie des griechischen Akragas auf Sizilien.* The Hague: Staatsuitgsverij.

Dimartino, A. 2006. "Per una revisione dei documenti epigrafici siracusani pertinenti al regno di Ierone II." In *Guerra e pace* 2006, 703–717.

Di Stefano, G. 1987. "Il territorio di Camarina in eta arcaica." *Kokalos* 33: 129–201.

Di Stefano, G. 1988. "Indigeni e greci nell'entroterra di Camarina." *Kokalos* 34–35: 89–105.

Di Stefano, G. 2000. "I recenti scavi di Camarina." In *Un ponte* 2000, 194–212.

Di Stefano, C. A., ed. 2008. *Demetra: La divinità, i santuari, il culto, la leggenda.* Pisa: F. Serra.

Di Vita, A. 1956. "La penetrazione siracusana nella Sicilia sud-orientale alla luce della più recenti scoperte archeologiche." *Kokalos* 2: 177–205.

Di Vita, A. 1987. "Tucidide VI 5 e l'epicrazia siracusana: Acre, Casmene, Camarina." *Kokalos* 33: 77–87.

Dominguez, A. J. 2004. "Greek Identity in the Phocaean Colonies." In Lomas 2004, 429–456.

Dominguez, A. J. 2006a. "Greeks in Sicily." In Tsetskhladze 2006–2008, I: 253–357.

Dominguez, A. J. 2006b. "Hellenic Identity and Greek Colonisation." *Ancient West and East* 4: 446–457.

Donnellan, L. 2012. "Apollo Mediating Identities in Ancient Greek Sicily." *BABesch* 87: 173–186.

Donnellan, L., V. Nizzo, and G. Burgers, eds. 2016. *Conceptualising Early Colonisation.* Brussels: Brepols.

Dougherty, C. 1993. *The Poetics of Colonization: From City to Text in Archaic Greece.* Oxford: Oxford University Press.

Dougherty, C. 1994. "Pindar's Second Paean: Civic Identity on Parade." *CPh* 89: 205–218.

Dougherty, C., and L. Kurke, eds. 2003. *The Cultures within Greek Culture: Contact, Conflict, Collaboration.* Cambridge: Cambridge University Press.

Dover, K. J. 1983. "Thucydides 'As History' and 'As Literature.'" *H&T* 22: 54–63.

Dover, K. J. 1985. *Theocritus: Select Poems.* London: Bristol Classical.

Dowden, K. 1989. *Death and the Maiden: Girls' Initiation Rites in Greek Mythology.* London: Routledge.

Dunbabin, T. J. 1948. *The Western Greeks: The History of Sicily and South Italy from the Foundation of the Greek Colonies to 480 B.C.* Oxford: Clarendon Press.

Eckerman, C. C. 2007. "Panhellenic Places, Spaces, and Landscapes: Pindar and Bacchylides' Manipulations of Greek Sanctuaries." PhD diss., UCLA.

Eckstein, A. M. 1995. *Moral Vision in the Histories of Polybius.* Berkeley: University of California Press.

Eckstein, A. M. 2006. *Mediterranean Anarchy, Interstate War, and the Rise of Rome.* Berkeley: University of California Press.

Eisenfeld, H. Forthcoming. *Pindar and Greek Religion: Images of Mortality in the Victory Odes*. Cambridge: Cambridge University Press.

Eisenstadt, S. N., and B. Giesen. 1995. "The Construction of Collective Identity." *European Journal of Sociology* 36: 72–102.

Emberling, G. 1997. "Ethnicity in Complex Societies: Archaeological Perspectives." *Journal of Archaeological Research*: 295–344.

Enenkel, K. A. E., and I. L. Pfeijffer, eds. 2005. *The Manipulative Mode: Political Propaganda in Antiquity: A Collection of Case Studies*. Leiden: Brill.

Erdas, D. 2006. "Forme di stanziamento militare e organizzazione del territorio nel mondo greco: I casi di Casmene e Brea." In *Guerra e pace 2006*, 45–55.

Eriksen, T. H. 2010. *Ethnicity and Nationalism: Anthropological Perspectives*. 3rd ed. London: Pluto.

Errington, R. M. 2008. *A History of the Hellenistic World*. Malden, MA: Blackwell.

Erskine, A. 1993. "Hannibal and the Freedom of the Italians." *Hermes* 121: 58–62.

Erskine, A. 2001. *Troy between Greece and Rome: Local Tradition and Imperial Power*. Oxford: Oxford University Press.

Evans, R. 2009. *Syracuse in Antiquity: History and Topography*. Pretoria: University of South Africa Press.

Evans, R. 2016. *Ancient Syracuse: From Foundation to Fourth Century Collapse*. London: Routledge.

Farnell, L. R. 1921. *Greek Hero Cults and Ideas of Immortality*. Oxford: Clarendon Press.

Farnell, L. R. 1932. *Critical Commentary to the Works of Pindar*. London: Macmillan.

Farney, G. D. 2007. *Ethnic Identity and Aristocratic Competition in Republican Rome*. Cambridge: Cambridge University Press.

Farney, G. D., and G. Bradley, eds. 2018. *The Peoples of Ancient Italy*. Berlin: De Gruyter.

Fauber, C. M. 2001. "Hermocrates and Thucydides: Rhetoric, Policy, and the Speeches in Thucydides' History." *ICS* 26: 37–51.

Fearn, D. 2003. "Mapping Phleious: Politics and Myth-Making in Bacchylides 9." *CQ* 53: 347–367.

Fearn, D., ed. 2011. *Aegina: Contexts for Choral Lyric Poetry: Myth, History, and Identity in the Fifth Century BC*. Oxford: Oxford University Press.

Fearn, D. 2017. *Pindar's Eyes: Visual and Material Culture in Epinician Poetry*. Oxford: Oxford University Press.

Feeney, D. 2007. *Caesar's Calendar: Ancient Time and the Beginnings of History*. Berkeley: University of California Press.

Fenno, J. B. 1995. "Poets, Athletes and Heroes: Theban and Aeginetan Identity in Pindar's Aeginetan Odes." PhD diss., UCLA.

Ferruzza, M. L. 2013. "*Agalmata ek pelou*: Aspects of Coroplastic Art in Classical and Hellenistic Sicily." In Lyons, Bennett, and Marconi 2013, 186–201.

Figueira, T. J. 2020. "Language as a Marker of Ethnicity in Herodotus and Contemporaries." In *Ethnicity and Identity in Herodotus*, edited by T. J. Figueira and C. Soares, 43–83. New York: Routledge.

Fiorentini, G. 1993–1994. "Attività di indagini archeologiche della Soprintendenza Beni Culturali e Ambientali di Agrigento." *Kokalos* 39–40: 717–733.

Fischer-Bossert, W. 2018. "Imitations and Remodelings of Sicilian Coin Types: Fashion or Politics?" In *TYΠOI: Greek and Roman Coins Seen through Their Images: Noble Issuers, Humble Users?* edited by P. P. Iossif, F. De Callataÿ, and R. Veymiers, 133–141.

Fischer-Hansen, T. 2002. "Reflections on Native Settlements in the Dominions of Gela and Akragas—as Seen from the Perspective of the Copenhagen Polis Centre." In *Even More Studies in the Ancient Greek Polis*, edited by T. H. Nielsen, 125–186. Stuttgart: F. Steiner.

Flower, M. A. 2015. "Religious Expertise." In *The Oxford Handbook of Ancient Greek Religion*, edited by E. Eidinow and J. Kindt, 293–307. Oxford: Oxford University Press.

Foley, H. P. 1994. *The Homeric Hymn to Demeter: Translation, Commentary, and Interpretive Essays*. Princeton, NJ: Princeton University Press.

Fontana, M. J. 1981. "Alcune considerazioni su Ermocrate siracusano." In Gasperini 1981, 151–165.

Forsdyke, S. 2012. "'Born from the Earth': The Political Uses of an Athenian Myth." *Journal of Ancient Near Eastern Religions* 12: 119–141.

Foster, M. 2013. "Hagesias as *Sunoikistêr*: Seercraft and Colonial Ideology in Pindar's Sixth Olympian Ode." *ClAnt* 32: 283–321.

Fowler, R. L. 1998. "Genealogical Thinking, Hesiod's *Catalogue*, and the Creation of the Hellenes." *PCPhS* 44: 1–19.

Fowler, R. L. 2013. *Early Greek Mythography*, Vol. 2: *Commentary*. Oxford: Oxford University Press.

Fragoulaki, M. 2013. *Kinship in Thucydides: Intercommunal Ties and Historical Narrative*. Oxford: Oxford University Press.

Franke, P. R. 1989. "Pyrrhus." In *CAH²* VII.2, 456–485.

Frasca, M. 2015. *Archeologia degli Iblei: Indigeni e Greci nell'altipiano ibleo tra la prima e la seconda età del Ferro*. Scicli: Edizioni di storia e studi sociali.

Fraschetti, A. 1981. "Aristosseno, i Romani e la 'barbarizzazione' di Poseidonia." *AION(archeol)* 3: 97–115.

Frederiksen, M. W. 1984. *Campania*. Rome: British School at Rome.

Freeman, H. A. 1891–1894. *A History of Sicily*. 4 vols. Oxford: Clarendon Press.

Friis Johansen, N. 1973. "Agesias, Hieron, and Pindar's Sixth Olympian Ode." In *Classica et mediaevalia F. Blatt septuagenario dedicata*, edited by O. S. Due, N. F. Johansen, and B. D. Larsen, 1–9. Copenhagen: Gyldendal.

Frisone, F. 2009. "L'isola improbabile: L'insularità' della Sicilia nella concezione greca di età arcaica e classica." In *Immagine e immagini della Sicilia e delle altre isole del Mediterraneo antico*, edited by C. Ampolo, 149–156. Pisa: Edizioni della Normale.

Fronda, M. P. 2010. *Between Rome and Carthage: Southern Italy during the Second Punic War.* Cambridge: Cambridge University Press.

Fronda, M. P. 2013. "Southern Italy: Sanctuary, *Panegyris* and Italiote Identity." In Funke and Haake 2013, 123–138.

Fronda, M. P. 2015. "The Italiote League and Southern Italy." In Beck and Funke 2015, 386–402.

Funke, P., and M. Haake, eds. 2013. *Greek Federal States and Their Sanctuaries: Identity and Integration.* Stuttgart: F. Steiner.

Funke, P., and N. Luraghi, eds. 2009. *The Politics of Ethnicity and the Crisis of the Peloponnesian League.* Washington, DC: Center for Hellenic Studies.

Gaifman, M. 2006. "Statue, Cult and Reproduction." *Art History* 29: 258–279.

Galinsky, K. 1969. *Aeneas, Sicily, and Rome.* Princeton, NJ: Princeton University Press.

Garland, R. 2014. *Wandering Greeks: The Ancient Greek Diaspora from the Age of Homer to the Death of Alexander the Great.* Princeton, NJ: Princeton University Press.

Garoufalias, P. 1979. *Pyrrhus King of Epirus.* London: Stacey International.

Gasperini, L., ed. 1981. *Scritti sul mondo antico in memoria di Fulvio Grosso.* Rome: Bretschneider.

Gauthier, P. 1966. "Le parallèle Himèra-Salamine au Ve et au IVe siécle av. J.-C." *REA* 68: 5–32.

Gehrke, H. 2005. "Heroen als Grenzgänger zwischen Griechen und Barbaren." In Gruen 2005, 50–67.

Gellner, E. 1983. *Nations and Nationalism.* Ithaca, NY: Cornell University Press.

Genovese, C. 2020. "The 'Upper Sanctuary of Demeter' at S. Biago in Akragas: A Review." In de Cesare, Portale, and Sojc 2020, 169–200.

Genovese, G. 2009. *Nostoi: Tradizione eroiche e modelli mitici nel meridione d'Italia.* Rome: Bretschneider.

Genovese, G. 2018. "*Nostoi* as Heroic Foundations in Southern Italy: The Traditions about Epeios and Philoktetes." In Hornblower and Biffis 2018, 105–122.

Gentili, B. 1998. *Le Pitiche.* Milan: Mondadori.

Gentili, B. 2013. *Le Olimpiche.* Milan: Mondadori.

Georges, P. 1994. *Barbarian Asia and the Greek Experience: From the Archaic Period to the Age of Xenophon.* Baltimore: Johns Hopkins University Press.

Gerber, D. E. 1982. *Pindar's Olympian One: A Commentary.* Toronto: University of Toronto Press.

Ghinatti, F. 1974. "Riti e feste della Magna Graecia." *Critica Storica* 11: 533–576.

Giacometti, D. 1990. "Melanippe e i Neleidi a Metaponto: La versione ateniese di Euripide e la quella italiota di Antioco." *Annali della Facoltà di Lettere e Filosofia, Università degli Studi di Perugia* 28: 277–296.

Giacometti, D. 1999. "Il culto di Artemis a Metaponto." *Ostraka* 8: 407–426.

Giacometti, D. 2005. *Metaponto: Gli dei e gli eroi nella storia di una polis di Magna Grecia*. Cosenza: Lionello Diordano.

Giangiulio, M. 1982. "Per la storia dei culti di Crotone antica: Il Santuario di Hera Lacinia: Structure e funzioni cultuali, origini storiche e mitiche." *Archivio storico per la Calabria e la Lucania* 49: 5–69.

Giangiulio, M. 1983. "Locri, Sparta, Crotone e le tradizioni leggendarie intorno alla battaglia della Sagra." *MEFRA* 95: 473–521.

Giangiulio, M. 1989. *Ricerche su Crotone arcaica*. Pisa: Scuola Normale Superiore.

Giangiulio, M. 1991. "Filottete tra Sibari e Crotone: Osservazioni sulla tradizione letteraria." In De La Genière 1991, 37–53.

Giangiulio, M. 1992. "La φιλότης tra Sibariti e Serdaioi (Meiggs-Lewis, 10)." *ZPE* 93: 31–44.

Giangiulio, M. 2001. "Constructing the Past: Colonial Traditions and the Writing of History: The Case of Cyrene." In *The Historian's Craft in the Age of Herodotus*, edited by N. Luraghi, 116–137. Oxford: Oxford University Press.

Giangiulio, M. 2002. "I culti delle colonie achee d'occidente: Stutture religiose e matrici metropolitane." In Greco 2002, 283–313.

Giangiulio, M. 2010. "Deconstructing Ethnicities: Multiple Identities in Archaic and Classical Sicily." *BABesch* 85: 13–23.

Giannelli, G. 1963. *Culti e miti della Magna Grecia: Contributo alla storia più antica delle colonie greche in occidente*. 2nd ed. Florence: Sansoni.

Giannelli, C. A. 1969. "L'intervento di Archidamo e di Alessandro il Molosso in Magna Grecia." *Critica Storica* 8: 1–22.

Giannelli, C. A. 1974. "Gli interventi di Cleonimo e di Agatocle in Magna Grecia." *Critica Storica* 13: 353–380.

Gibson, S. 2005. *Aristoxenus of Tarentum and the Birth of Musicology*. New York: Routledge.

Giudice, F. 1988. "La seconda e terza fondazione di Camarina alla luce dei prodotti del commercio coloniale." *Quaderni dell'Istituto di archeologia della Facoltà di lettere e filosofia della Università di Messina* 3: 29–57.

Giuffrida, M. 2002. "I Dionisî e l'area calcidese." In Bonacasa, Braccesi, and De Miro 2002, 417–426.

Giuliani, A. 1994. "Le migrazioni forzate in Sicilia e in Magna Grecia sotto Dionigi I di Siracusa." In Sordi 1994, 107–124.

Giuliano, A. 1993. "Signum Cereris." *RAL* 4: 49–65.

Glazer, N., and D. P. Moynihan, eds. 1970. *Beyond the Melting Pot*. 2nd ed. Cambridge, MA: MIT Press.

Glazer, N., and D. P. Moynihan, eds. 1975. *Ethnicity: Theory and Experience*. Cambridge, MA: Harvard University Press.

Gleason, P. 1983. "Identifying Identity: A Semantic History." *Journal of American History* 69: 910–931.

Glotz, G., and R. Cohen. 1929. *Histoire grecque*, Vol. 2. Paris: Presses Universitaires de France.

Goegebeur, W. 1990. "Myskellos, Aithra et Phalanthos: Concordance entre les traditions de fondation de Tarente et de Crotone?" In *Studia Varia Bruxellensia*, edited by R. De Smet, H. Melaerts, and C. Saerens, 83–99. Leuven: Peeters.

Goegebeur, W. 1985. "Hérodote et la fondation achéenne de Crotone." *AC* 54: 116–151.

Goff, B. E. 2004. *Citizen Bacchae: Women's Ritual Practice in Ancient Greece*. Berkeley: University of California Press.

Goldhill, S. 1991. *The Poet's Voice: Essays on Poetics and Greek Literature*. Cambridge: Cambridge University Press.

Goodin, R. E. 2011. "The State of the Discipline, the Discipline of the State." In *The Oxford Handbook of Political Science*, edited by R. E. Goodin, 3–57. Oxford: Oxford University Press.

Gorini, G. 1975. *La monetazione incusa della Magna Grecia*. Milan: Edizioni Arte e Moneta.

Gorman, R., and V. B. Gorman. 2014. *Corrupting Luxury in Ancient Greek Literature*. Ann Arbor: University of Michigan Press.

Gouldner, A. W. 1957. "Cosmopolitans and Locals: Toward an Analysis of Latent Social Roles—I." *Administrative Science Quarterly* 2: 281–306.

Gow, A. S. F. 1950. *Theocritus*. Cambridge: Cambridge University Press.

Graf, F. 1982. "Culti e credenze religiose della Magna Graecia." In *Megale Hellas: Nome e immagine*, 157–185. Taranto: Istituto per la storia e l'archeologia della Magna Grecia.

Graf, F. 1985. *Nordionische Kulte: Religionsgeschichtliche und epigraphische Untersuchungen zu den Kulten von Chios, Erythrai, Klazomenai und Phokaia*. Rome: Schweizerisches Institut in Rom.

Graham, A. J. 1964. *Colony and Mother City in Ancient Greece*. Manchester, UK: Manchester University Press.

Gras, M. 1990. "Gélon et les temples de Sicile après la bataille d'Himère." *AION(archeol)* 12: 59–68.

Greaves, A. M. 2010. *The Land of Ionia: Society and Economy in the Archaic Period*. Malden, MA: Blackwell.

Greco, C. 2013. "The Cult of Demeter and Kore between Tradition and Innovation." In Lyons, Bennett, and Marconi 2013, 50–65.

Greco, C. 2015. "Scavi nel santuario tesmoforico di San Francesco Bisconti a Morgantina: Topografia e ritualità." In *Morgantina duemilaquindici: La ricerca archeologica a sessant'anni dall'avvio degli scavi*, edited by L. Maniscalco, 32–43. Palermo: Regione Siciliana.

Greco, E. 1990. "Serdaioi." *AION(archeol)* 12: 39–57.

Greco, E. 1993. "L'impero di Sibari: Bilancio archeologico-topografico." In *Sibari e la Sibaritide* 1993, 458–485.

Greco, E., ed. 2002. *Gli Achei e l'identità etnica degli Achei d'occidente.* Paestum: Pandemos.

Greco, E. 2008. *Archeologia della Grecità occidentale*, Vol. 1: *La Magna Grecia.* Bologna: Monduzzi.

Greco, E., and M. Lombardo, eds. 2007. *Atene e l'occidente: I grandi temi.* Athens: Scuola Archeologica Italiana di Atene.

Greco, G. 1997. "Des étoffes pour Héra." In De La Genière 1997, 185–199.

Greco, G. 1998. "Da Hera argiva ad Hera pestana." In *I culti della Campania antica*, 45–62. Rome: Bretschneider.

Green, P. 2006. *Diodorus Siculus, Books 11–12.37.1: Greek History, 480–431 BC, the Alternative Version.* Austin: University of Texas Press.

Griffith, R. D. 2008. "Alph, the Sacred River, Ran: Geographical Subterfuge in Pindar Olympian 1.20." *Mouseion* 8: 1–8.

Griffiths, A. 1987. "Democedes of Croton: A Greek Doctor at the Court of Darius." In *Achaemenid History II*, edited by H. Sancisi-Weerdenburg and A. Kuhrt, 37–51. Leiden: Netherlands Institute for the Near East.

Griffiths, F. T. 1979. *Theocritus at Court.* Leiden: Brill.

Grosso, F. 1966. "Ermocrate di Siracusa." *Kokalos* 12: 102–143.

Grote, G. 1859. *A History of Greece*, Vol. 7. London: John Murray.

Grote, O. 2016. *Die griechischen Phylen: Funktion, Entstehung, Leistungen.* Stuttgart: Alte Geschichte.

Gruen, E. S. 1992. *Culture and National Identity in Republican Rome.* Ithaca, NY: Cornell University Press.

Gruen, E. S., ed. 2005. *Cultural Borrowings and Ethnic Appropriations in Antiquity.* Stuttgart: F. Steiner.

Gruen, E. S. 2011. *Rethinking the Other in Antiquity.* Princeton, NJ: Princeton University Press.

Gruen, E. S. 2016. "Did Ancient Identity Depend on Ethnicity? A Preliminary Probe." *Phoenix* 67: 1–22.

Gruen, E. S. 2020. *Ethnicity in the Ancient World: Did It Matter?* Berlin: De Gruyter.

Guerra e pace in Sicilia e nel Mediterraneo antico (VIII–III sec. a.C.): Arte, prassi e teoria della pace e della guerra. 2006. Pisa: Edizioni della Normale.

Guildersleeve, B. 1885. *Pindar: The Olympian and Pythian Odes.* New York: Harper.

Gutzwiller, K. 1983. "Charites or Hiero: Theocritus' Idyll 16." *RhM* 126: 212–238.

Guzzo, P. G. 1982. "La Sibaritide e Sibari nell'VIII e VII sec. a.C." *ASAA* 60: 237–250.

Guzzo, P. G. 1984. "Lucanians, Brettians and Italiote Greeks in the Fourth and Third Centuries B.C." In *Crossroads of the Mediterranean*, edited by T. Hackens, N. D. Holloway, and R. R. Holloway. Louvain-la-Neuve: Catholic University of Louvain.

Guzzo, P. G. 1990. "Myths and Archaeology in South Italy." In *Greek Colonists and Native Population*, edited by J. Descoeudres, 131–141. Oxford: Clarendon Press.

Guzzo, P. G. 2011. *Fondazioni greche: L'Italia meridionale e la Sicilia (VIII e VII sec. a.C.).* Rome: Carocci.

Haake, M. 2013. "Agathocles and Hiero II: Two Sole Rulers in the Hellenistic Age and the Question of Succession." In Luraghi 2013b, 99–127.

Hackens, T., N. D. Holloway, R. R. Holloway, and G. Moucharte. 1992. *The Age of Pyrrhus*. Louvain-la-Neuve: Collège Érasme.

Hakenbeck, S. E. 2007. "Situational Ethnicity and Nested Identities: New Approaches to an Old Problem." *Anglo-Saxon Studies in Archaeology and History* 14: 19–27.

Hall, E. 1989. *Inventing the Barbarian: Greek Self-Definition through Tragedy*. Oxford: Oxford University Press.

Hall, J. M. 1995. "The Role of Language in Greek Ethnicities." *Proceedings of the Cambridge Philological Society* 41: 83–100.

Hall, J. M. 1997. *Ethnic Identity in Greek Antiquity*. Cambridge: Cambridge University Press.

Hall, J. M. 2001. "Contested Ethnicities: Perceptions of Macedonia within Evolving Definitions of Greek Ethnicity." In Malkin 2001a, 159–186.

Hall, J. M. 2002. *Hellenicity: Between Ethnicity and Culture*. Chicago: University of Chicago Press.

Hall, J. M. 2004. "How 'Greek' Were the Early Western Greeks?" In Lomas 2004, 35–54.

Hall, J. M. 2008. "Foundation Stories." In Tsetskhladze 2006–2008, II, 383–426.

Hall, J. M. 2012. "The Creation and Expression of Identity: The Greek World." In Alcock and Osborne 2012, 350–367.

Hall, J. M. 2014. *A History of the Archaic Greek World, ca. 1200–479 BC*. 2nd ed. Malden, MA: Blackwell.

Hall, J. M. 2015. "Ancient Greek Ethnicities: Towards a Reassessment." *BICS* 58: 15–29.

Hall, S. 1996. "Introduction: Who Needs 'Identity'?" In *Questions of Cultural Identity*, edited by S. Hall and P. du Gay, 1–17. London: SAGE.

Hammond, M., trans. 2009. *Thucydides: The Peloponnesian War*. Introduction and notes by P. J. Rhodes. Oxford: Oxford University Press.

Hammond, N. G. L. 1973. "The Particular and the Universal in the Speeches in Thucydides with Special Reference to That of Hermocrates at Gela." In Stadter 1973, 49–59.

Hammond, N. G. L. 1986. *A History of Greece to 322 B.C.* 3rd ed. Oxford: Clarendon Press.

Hans, L. 1985. "Theokrits XVI Idylle und die Politik Hierons II von Syrakus." *Historia* 34: 117–125.

Hansen, M. H., ed. 1995. *Sources for the Ancient Greek City-State*. Copenhagen: Royal Danish Academy of Sciences and Letters.

Harrell, S. E. 1998. "Cultural Geography of East and West: Literary Representations of Archaic Sicilian Tyranny and Cult." PhD diss., Princeton University.

Harrell, S. E. 2002. "King or Private Citizen: Fifth-Century Sicilian Tyrants at Olympia and Delphi." *Mnemosyne* 55: 439–464.

Harrell, S. E. 2006. "Synchronicity: The Local and the Panhellenic within Sicilian Tyranny." In Lewis 2006b, 119–134.

Harris, J. 2020. "The Power of Movement: Mercenary Mobility and Empire Building in Sicily during the Classical Period." In Jonasch 2020a, 130–153.

Harrison, T. 2020. "Reinventing the Barbarian." *CP* 115: 139–163.

Havelock, C. M. 1980. "The Archaistic Athena Promachos in Early Hellenistic Coinages." *AJA* 84: 41–50.

Head, B. V. 1911. *Historia Numorum.* 2nd ed. Oxford: Clarendon Press.

Herington, C. J. 1967. "Aeschylus in Sicily." *JHS* 87: 74–85.

Herring, E. 2000. "'To See Ourselves as Others See Us!': The Construction of Native Identities in Southern Italy." In *The Emergence of State Identities in Italy in the First Millennium BC*, edited by E. Herring and K. Lomas, 45–77. London: Accordia Research Institute.

Higbie, C. 1997. "The Bones of a Hero, the Ashes of a Politician: Athens, Salamis, and the Usable Past." *ClAnt* 16: 278–307.

Higbie, C. 2003. *The Lindian Chronicle and the Greek Creation of Their Past.* Oxford: Oxford University Press.

Hinz, V. 1998. *Der Kult von Demeter und Kore auf Sizilien und in der Magna Graecia.* Wiesbaden: Reichert.

Hirata, E. F. V. 1996. "As odes de Pindaro e as tiranias siciliotas." *Classica (Brasil)* 9–10: 61–72.

Hodos, T. 2006. *Local Responses to Colonization in the Iron Age Mediterranean.* London: Routledge.

Hodos, T. 2010. "Globalization and Colonization: A View from Iron Age Sicily." *JMA* 23: 81–106.

Hoffmann, W. 1936. "Der Kampf zwischen Rom und Tarent im Urteil der antiken Überlieferung." *Hermes* 71: 11–24.

Holloway, R. R. 1978. *Art and Coinage in Magna Graecia.* Bellinzona: Edizioni Arte e Moneta.

Holloway, R. R. 1991. *The Archaeology of Ancient Sicily.* New York: Routledge.

Hopkinson, N., trans. 2015. *Theocritus, Moschus, Bion.* Cambridge, MA: Harvard University Press.

Hornblower, S. 1987. *Thucydides.* London: Duckworth.

Hornblower, S. 2008. "Greek Identity in the Archaic and Classical Periods." In Zacharia 2008a, 37–58.

Hornblower, S. 2011. *The Greek World: 479–323 BC.* 4th ed. London: Routledge.

Hornblower, S. 2015. *Lykophron: Alexandra.* Oxford: Oxford University Press.

Hornblower, S., and G. Biffis, eds. 2018. *The Returning Hero: Nostoi and Traditions of Mediterranean Settlement.* Oxford: Oxford University Press.

Horowitz, D. L. 1975. "Ethnic Identity." In Glazer and Moynihan 1975, 111–140.

Horowitz, D. L. 1985. *Ethnic Groups in Conflict.* Berkeley: University of California Press.

Horsnaes, H. W. 2002. *The Cultural Development in North Western Lucania c. 600–273 BC.* Rome: Bretschneider.

Howard, J. A. 2000. "Social Psychology of Identities." *Annual Review of Sociology* 26: 367–393.

Howgego, C. J. 1990. "Why Did Ancient States Strike Coins?" *NC* 150: 1–25.

Hoyos, B. D. 1985. "The Rise of Hiero II: Chronology and Campaigns." *Antichthon* 19: 32–56.

Hoyos, B. D. 1998. *Unplanned Wars: The Origins of the First and Second Punic Wars.* Berlin: De Gruyter.

Hoyos, B. D. 2010. *The Carthaginians.* London: Routledge.

Hoyos, B. D., ed. 2011. *A Companion to the Punic Wars.* Malden, MA: Blackwell.

Hubbard, T. K. 1992. "Remaking Myth and Rewriting History: Cult Tradition in Pindar's Ninth Nemean." *HSPh* 94: 77–111.

Hubbard, T. K. 2004. "The Dissemination of Epinician Lyric: Pan-Hellenism, Reperformance, Written Texts." In Mackie 2004, 71–93.

Huffman, C. A. 2005. *Archytas of Tarentum: Pythagorean, Philosopher and Mathematician King.* Cambridge: Cambridge University Press.

Humm, M. 2018. "La 'barbarisation' de Poséidonia et la fin des cultes grecs à Paestum." *RHR* 235: 353–372.

Hunter, R. 1996. *Theocritus and the Archaeology of Greek Poetry.* Cambridge: Cambridge University Press.

Hunter, V. 1973. *Thucydides the Artful Reporter.* Toronto: Hakkert.

Hunter, V. 1977. "The Composition of Thucydides' *History*: A New Answer to the Problem." *Historia* 26: 269–294.

Hurst, H., and S. Owen, eds. 2005. *Ancient Colonizations: Analogy, Similarity, and Difference.* London: Duckworth.

Hutchinson, J., and A. D. Smith, eds. 1996. *Ethnicity.* Oxford: Oxford University Press.

Huxley, G. L. 1982. "Siris antica nella storiografia greca." In *Siris e l'influenza ionica in occidente,* 27–43. Taranto: Istituto per la storia e l'archeologia della Magna Grecia.

Intrieri, M. 2011. "Fra dialogo e conflitto: Annibale e i Greci d'occidente." In *Fenici e Italici, Cartagine e la Magna Grecia: Popoli a contatto, culture a confronto,* edited by M. Intrieri and S. Ribichini, 53–81. Pisa: Fabrizio Serra Editore.

Isager, S., and P. Pedersen, eds. 2004. *The Salmakis Inscription and Hellenistic Halikarnassos.* Odense: University Press of Southern Denmark.

Ivantchik, A. 2017. "Greeks and the Black Sea: The Earliest Ideas about the Region and the Beginning of Colonization." In Kozlovskaya 2017a, 7–25.

Jacquemin, A. 1992. "Offrandes monumentales italiotes et siciliotes à Delphes." In *La Magna Grecia e i grandi santuari della madrepatria,* 193–204. Taranto: Istituto per la storia e l'archeologia della Magna Grecia.

Jaeger, M. 2006. "Livy, Hannibal's Monument, and the Temple of Juno at Croton." *TAPhA* 136: 389–414.

Jenkins, G. K. 1975. "The Coinages of Enna, Galaria, Piakos, Imachara, Kephaloedion and Longane." In *Le emissioni dei centri siculi fino all'epoca di Timoleonte e i loro rapporti con la monetazione delle colonie greche di Sicilia*, 77–104. Rome: Istituto Italiano di Numismatica.

Jenkins, R. 2008. *Rethinking Ethnicity: Arguments and Explorations*. Thousand Oaks, CA: SAGE.

Jenkins, R. 2014. *Social Identity*. 4th ed. New York: Routledge.

Johnston, H., and B. Klandermans. 1995. *Social Movements and Culture*. Minneapolis: University of Minnesota Press.

Johnston, S. I. 2013. "Demeter, Myths, and the Polyvalence of Festivals." *HR* 52: 370–401.

Jonasch, M., ed. 2020a. *The Fight for Greek Sicily: Society, Politics, and Landscape*. Oxford: Oxbow.

Jonasch, M. 2020b. "The Military Landscape of Greek Sicily." In Jonasch 2020a, 183–212.

Jones, C. P. 1996. "*Ethnos* and *Genos* in Herodotus." *CQ* 46: 315–320.

Jones, C. P. 1999. *Kinship Diplomacy in the Ancient World*. Cambridge, MA: Harvard University Press.

Jones, S. 1997. *The Archaeology of Ethnicity: Constructing Identities in the Past and Present*. New York: Routledge.

Jones, S. 1998. "Ethnic Identity as Discursive Strategy: The Case of the Ancient Greeks." *CArchJ* 8: 271–273.

Jourdain-Annequin, C. 2006. "I greci—les grecs." In *Ethne e religioni nella Sicilia antica*, edited by P. Anello, G. Martorana, and R. Sammartano, 181–203. Rome: Bretschneider.

Jowett, G., and V. O'Donnell. 2015. *Propaganda and Persuasion*. 6th ed. Newbury Park, CA: SAGE.

Just, R. 1998. "The Historicity of Ethnicity." *CArchJ* 8: 277–279.

Kagan, D. 1969. *The Origins of the Peloponnesian War*. Ithaca, NY: Cornell University Press.

Kagan, D. 1974. *The Archidamian War*. Ithaca, NY: Cornell University Press.

Kagan, D. 1981. *The Peace of Nicias and the Sicilian Expedition*. Ithaca, NY: Cornell University Press.

Kallet, L. 2001. *Money and the Corrosion of Power in Thucydides: The Sicilian Expedition and Its Aftermath*. Berkeley: University of California Press.

Kannicht, R. 1991. *Musa tragica: Die griechische Tragödie von Thespis bis Ezechiel*. Göttingen: Vandenhoeck & Ruprecht.

Keesling, C. M. 2005. "Misunderstood Gestures: Iconatrophy and the Reception of Greek Sculpture in the Roman Imperial Period." *ClAnt* 24: 41–80.

Kellogg, D. L. 2013. *Marathon Fighters and Men of Maple: Ancient Acharnai*. Oxford: Oxford University Press.

Kent, P. A. 2020. *A History of the Pyrrhic War*. London: Routledge.

Kim, H. H. 2001. "Archaic Coinage as Evidence for the Use of Money." In *Money and Its Uses in the Ancient Greek World*, edited by A. Meadows and K. Shipton, 7–21. Oxford: Oxford University Press.

Kindt, J. 2012. *Rethinking Greek Religion*. Cambridge: Cambridge University Press.

Kirkwood, G. 1982. *Selections from Pindar*. Chico: Scholars.

Klein, E. 2020. *Why We're Polarized*. New York: Avid Reader.

Knapp, A. B. 2007. "Insularity and Island Identity in the Prehistoric Mediterranean." In *Mediterranean Crossroads*, edited by S. Antoniadou, A. Pace, and H. Pieride, 37–62. Athens: Pierides Foundation.

Knapp, A. B. 2009. *Prehistoric and Protohistoric Cyprus: Identity, Insularity and Connectivity*. Oxford: Oxford University Press.

Knapp, A. B. 2014. "Mediterranean Archaeology and Ethnicity." In McInerney 2014a, 34–49.

Knorr, W. R. 1978. "Archimedes and the Elements: Proposal for a Revised Chronological Ordering of the Archimedean Corpus." *AHES* 19: 211–290.

Konstan, D. 1997. "Defining Ancient Greek Ethnicity." *Diaspora* 6: 97–110.

Konstan, D. 2001. "*To Hēllenikon Ethnos*: Ethnicity and the Construction of Ancient Greek Identity." In Malkin 2001a, 29–50.

Kouremenos, A., ed. 2018. *Insularity and Identity in the Roman Mediterranean*. Oxford: Oxbow.

Kowalzig, B. 2007. *Singing for the Gods: Performances of Myth and Ritual in Archaic and Classical Greece*. Oxford: Oxford University Press.

Kowalzig, B. 2008. "Nothing to Do with Demeter? Something to Do with Sicily!" In *Performance, Iconography, Reception: Studies in Honour of Oliver Taplin*, edited by M. Revermann and P. Wilson, 128–157. Oxford: Oxford University Press.

Kozlovskaya, V. 2017a. "Ancient Harbors of the Northern Black Sea Coast." In Kozlovskaya 2017b, 29–49.

Kozlovskaya, V., ed. 2017b. *The Northern Black Sea in Antiquity: Networks, Connectivity, and Cultural Interactions*. Cambridge: Cambridge University Press.

Kraay, C. M. 1964. "Hoards, Small Change, and the Origin of Coinage." *JHS* 84: 76–91.

Kraay, C. M. 1976. *Archaic and Classical Greek Coins*. Berkeley: University of California Press.

Kraay, C. M., and M. Hirmer. 1966. *Greek Coins*. New York: Harry N. Abrams.

Krings, V. 1998. *Carthage et les Grecs, c. 580–480 av. J.-C: Textes et histoire*. Leiden: Brill.

Kron, U. 1992. "Frauenfeste in Demeterheiligtümern: Das Thesmophorion von Bitalemi: Eine archäologische Fallstudie." *AA*: 611–650.

Krumeich, R. 1991. "Zu den goldenen Dreifüssen der Deinomeniden in Delphi." *JDAI* 105: 37–62.

Kurke, L. 1991. *The Traffic in Praise: Pindar and the Poetics of the Social Economy*. Ithaca, NY: Cornell University Press.

Kurke, L. 1999. *Coins, Bodies, Games, and Gold: The Politics of Meaning in Archaic Greece*. Princeton, NJ: Princeton University Press.

Lacroix, L. 1965. *Monnaies et colonisation dans l'Occident grec*. Brussels: Palais des Académies.

Lane Fox, R. 2009. *Travelling Heroes: In the Epic Age of Homer*. New York: Knopf.

Lape, S. 2010. *Race and Citizen Identity in the Classical Athenian Democracy*. Cambridge: Cambridge University Press.

Larson, S. L. 2007. *Tales of Epic Ancestry: Boiotian Collective Identity in the Late Archaic and Early Classical Periods*. Stuttgart: F. Steiner.

Lasswell, H. D. 1950. *Politics: Who Gets What, When, How*. New York: P. Smith.

La Torre, G. F. 2011. *Sicilia e Magna Grecia: Archeologia della colonizzazione greca d'occidente*. Bari: Editore Laterza.

Lazenby, J. F. 1996. *The First Punic War: A Military History*. Stanford, CA: Stanford University Press.

Lehmler, C. 2005. *Syrakus unter Agathokles und Hieron II: Die Verbindung von Kultur und Macht in einer hellenistischen Metropole*. Frankfurt: Antike.

Leighton, R. 1999. *Sicily before History: An Archaeological Survey from the Palaeolithic to the Iron Age*. Ithaca, NY: Cornell University Press.

Lepore, E. 1974. "Problemi di storia metapontina." In *Metaponto*, 307–326. Taranto: Istituto per la storia e l'archeologia della Magna Grecia.

Levene, D. S. 1993. *Religion in Livy*. Leiden: Brill.

Lévêque, P. 1957. *Pyrrhos*. Paris: De Boccard.

Levine, H. B. 1999. "Reconstructing Ethnicity." *Journal of the Royal Anthropological Institute* 5: 165–180.

Lewis, D. M. 1992. "The Archidamian War." In *CAH²* V, 370–432.

Lewis, D. M. 1994. "Sicily, 413–368 B.C." In *CAH²* VI, 120–155.

Lewis, S. 2000. "The Tyrant's Myth." In Smith and Serrati 2000, 97–106.

Lewis, S. 2006a. "Agathocles: Tyranny and Kingship in Syracuse." *Electrum* 11: 45–69.

Lewis, S., ed. 2006b. *Ancient Tyranny*. Edinburgh: Edinburgh University Press.

Lewis, S. 2009. *Greek Tyranny*. Exeter: Bristol Phoenix.

Lewis, V. M. 2018. "From Resolving Stasis to Ruling Sicily: A Reading of Herodotus 7.153–167 in an Epinician Context." *Mnemosyne*: 1–19.

Lewis, V. M. 2019. "Two Sides of the Same Coin: The Ideology of Gelon's Innovative Syracusan Tetradrachm." *GRBS* 59: 179–201.

Lewis, V. M. 2020. *Myth, Locality, and Identity in Pindar's Sicilian Odes*. Oxford: Oxford University Press.

Lloyd, G. E. R. 1991. "Alcmaeon and the Early History of Dissection." In *Methods and Problems in Greek Science*, edited by G. E. R. Lloyd, 164–193. Cambridge: Cambridge University Press.

Lomas, K. 1993. *Rome and the Western Greeks, 350 BC–AD 200: Conquest and Acculturation in Southern Italy*. London: Routledge.

Lomas, K. 1995. "The Greeks in the West and the Hellenization of Italy." In *The Greek World*, edited by A. Powell, 347–367. London: Routledge.

Lomas, K. 2000. "The Polis in Italy: Ethnicity, Colonization, and Citizenship in the Western Mediterranean." In Brock and Hodkinson 2000, 167–185.

Lomas, K., ed. 2004. *Greek Identity in the Western Mediterranean.* Leiden: Brill.

Lomas, K. 2006. "Tyrants and the Polis: Migration, Identity and Urban Development in Sicily." In Lewis 2006b, 95–118.

Lomas, K. 2015. "Colonizing the Past: Cultural Memory and Civic Identity in Hellenistic and Roman Naples." In *Remembering Parthenope: The Reception of Classical Naples from Antiquity to the Present*, edited by J. Hughes and C. Buongiovanni, 64–84. Oxford: Oxford University Press.

Lomas, K., ed. Forthcoming. *The World of the Western Greeks.* London: Routledge.

Lombardo, M. 1987. "La Magna Grecia dalla fine del V secolo a.C. alla conquista romana." In *Magna Grecia*, Vol. 2: *Lo sviluppo politico, sociale ed economico*, edited by G. Pugliese Carratelli, 55–88. Milan: Electa.

Lombardo, M. 1996. "Greci e 'indigeni' in Italia meridionale nel IV secolo A.C." In *Le IVe siècle av. J.-C.: Approches historiographiques*, edited by P. Carlier, 205–222. Paris: De Boccard.

Lombardo, M. 2002. "Achei, Enotri, Italia." In Greco 2002, 257–270.

Lombardo, M. 2008. "Il trattato fra i Sibariti e i *Serdaioi*: Problemi di cronologia e di inquadramento storico." In *La Calabria tirrenica nell'antichità: Nuovi documenti e problematiche storiche*, edited by G. De Sensi Sestito, 219–232. Soveria Mannelli: Rubbettino.

Lombardo, M. 2012. "Pratiche culturali e rapporti tra colonia e metropoli." In *Alle origini della Magna Grecia* 2012, 399–419.

Longrigg, J. 1993. *Greek Rational Medicine: Philosophy and Medicine from Alcmaeon to the Alexandrians.* London: Routledge.

Loraux, N. 1986. *The Invention of Athens: The Funeral Oration in the Classical City.* Cambridge, MA: Harvard University Press.

Lowe, N. J. 1998. "Thesmophoria and Haloa: Myth, Physics, and Mysteries." In *The Sacred and the Feminine in Ancient Greece*, edited by S. Blundell and M. Williamson, 149–173. London: Routledge.

Lucy, S. 2005. "Ethnic and Cultural Identities." In *The Archaeology of Identity: Approaches to Gender, Age, Status, Ethnicity and Religion*, edited by M. Díaz-Andreu, S. Lucy, S. Babić, and D. N. Edwards, 86–109. London: Routledge.

Luginbill, R. D. 1999. *Thucydides on War and National Character.* Boulder, CO: Westview.

Luraghi, N. 1994. *Tirannidi arcaiche in Sicilia e Magna Grecia.* Florence: Olschki Editore.

Luraghi, N. 2002. "Antioco di Siracusa." In *Storici greci d'occidente*, edited by R. Vattuone, 55–89. Bologna: Il Mulino.

Luraghi, N. 2008. *The Ancient Messenians: Constructions of Ethnicity and Memory.* Cambridge: Cambridge University Press.

Luraghi, N. 2013a. "Antiochos of Syracuse (555)." In *BNJ*.

Luraghi, N., ed. 2013b. *The Splendors and Miseries of Ruling Alone: Encounters with Monarchy from Archaic Greece to the Hellenistic Mediterranean*. Stuttgart: F. Steiner.

Luraghi, N. 2014. "The Study of Greek Ethnic Identities." In McInerney 2014a, 213–227.

Luria, S. 1964. "Zum Problem der griechisch-karthagischen Beziehungen." *AAntHung* 12: 53–75.

Lyons, C. L., M. J. Bennett, and C. Marconi, eds. 2013. *Sicily: Art and Invention between Greece and Rome*. Los Angeles: J. Paul Getty Museum.

Mac Sweeney, N. 2009. "Beyond Ethnicity: The Overlooked Diversity of Group Identities." *JMA* 22: 101–126.

Mackie, C. J., ed. 2004. *Oral Performance and Its Context*. Leiden: Brill.

Mackil, E. M. 2013. *Creating a Common Polity: Religion, Economy, and Politics in the Making of the Greek Koinon*. Berkeley: University of California Press.

Mackil, E. M., and P. G. Van Alfen. 2006. "Cooperative Coinage." In *Agoranomia: Studies in Money and Exchange Presented to John H. Kroll*, edited by P. G. Van Alfen, 201–246. New York: American Numismatic Society.

Macleod, C. 1983. *Collected Essays*. Oxford: Clarendon Press.

Mac Sweeney, N. 2011. *Community Identity and Archaeology: Dynamic Communities at Aphrodisias and Beycesultan*. Ann Arbor: University of Michigan Press.

Mac Sweeney, N. 2013. *Foundation Myths and Politics in Ancient Ionia*. Cambridge: Cambridge University Press.

Maddoli, G. 1980. "Filottete in Italia." In *L'epos greco in occidente*, 133–167. Taranto: Istituto per la storia e l'archeologia della Magna Grecia.

Maddoli, G. 1984. "I culti di Crotone." In *Crotone 1984*, 313–343.

Maddoli, G. 1988. "I culti delle *poleis* italiote." In *Magna Grecia*, Vol. 3: *Vita religiosa e cultura letteraria, filosofica e scientifica*, edited by G. Pugliese Carratelli, 115–148. Milan: Electa.

Maddoli, G. 1996. "La dedica degli Ipponiati a Olimpia (*SEG* XI 1211) e il suo contesto storico." In *L'incidenza dell'antico*, Vol. 2, edited by A. S. Marino, 193–202. Naples: Luciano.

Maddoli, G. 2000. "Dal tempio di Hera alla genesi del pantheon posidoniate." In *Paestum: Scavi, studi, ricerche*, edited by E. Greco and F. Longo, 45–52. Paestum: Pandemos.

Maehler, H. 2004. *Bacchylides: A Selection*. Cambridge: Cambridge University Press.

Mafodda, G. 1990. "La politica di Gelone dal 485 al 483 a.C." *Messana* 1: 53–69.

Mafodda, G. 1996. *La monarchia di Gelone tra pragmatismo ideologia e propaganda*. Messina: Società Messinese di Storia Patria.

Magrath, W. T. 1974. "Pindar's First Nemean Ode: The Herakles Myth as Political Symbol." PhD diss., Stanford University.

Malešević, S. 2006. *Identity as Ideology: Understanding Ethnicity and Nationalism*. Basingstoke, UK: Palgrave Macmillan.

Malkin, I. 1986. "Apollo Archegetes and Sicily." *ASNP* 16: 959–972.

Malkin, I. 1987. *Religion and Colonization in Ancient Greece*. Leiden: Brill.

Malkin, I. 1994. *Myth and Territory in the Spartan Mediterranean*. Cambridge: Cambridge University Press.

Malkin, I. 1998. *The Returns of Odysseus: Colonization and Ethnicity*. Berkeley: University of California Press.

Malkin, I., ed. 2001a. *Ancient Perceptions of Greek Ethnicity*. Cambridge, MA: Harvard University Press.

Malkin, I. 2001b. "Greek Ambiguities: Between 'Ancient Hellas' and 'Barbarian Epirus.'" In Malkin 2001a, 187–212.

Malkin, I. 2001c. "Introduction." In Malkin 2001a, 1–28.

Malkin, I. 2002. "Exploring the Validity of the Concept of 'Foundation': A Visit to Megara Hyblaia." In *Oikistes: Studies in Constitutions, Colonies, and Military Power in the Ancient World*, edited by V. B. Gorman and E. W. Robinson, 195–224. Leiden: Brill.

Malkin, I. 2005a. "Herakles and Melqart: Greeks and Phoenicians in the Middle Ground." In Gruen 2005, 238–258.

Malkin, I. 2005b. "Networks and the Emergence of Greek Identity." In *Mediterranean Paradigms and Classical Antiquity*, edited by I. Malkin, 56–74. London: Routledge.

Malkin, I. 2009. "Foundations." In *A Companion to Archaic Greece*, edited by K. A. Raaflaub and H. van Wees, 373–394. Malden, MA: Blackwell.

Malkin, I. 2011. *A Small Greek World: Networks in the Ancient Mediterranean*. Oxford: Oxford University Press.

Malkin, I. 2014. "Between Collective and Ethnic Identities: A Conclusion." *DHA* Supplement 10: 283–292.

Malkin, I. 2017. "Hybridity and Mixture." In *Ibridazione e integrazione in Magna Grecia*, 11–27. Taranto: Istituto per la storia e l'archeologia della Magna Grecia.

Manganaro, G. 1974. "La caduta dei Dinomenidi e il politikon nomisma in Sicilia nella prima metà del V sec. a.C." *AIIN* 21/22: 9–40.

Manganaro, G. 1982. "Monete e ghiande inscritte degli schiavi ribelli in Sicilia." *Chiron* 12: 237–244.

Manganaro, G. 2003. "Demeter degli Ennaioi." *Epigraphica* 65: 9–18.

Manganaro Perrone, G. 2007. "La prima (metà V sec. a.C.) e l'ultima (44–36 a.C.) emissione degli Hennaioi in gloria di Demetra." *Sicilia Antiqua* 4: 33–43.

Mann, C. 2001. *Athlet und Polis im archaischen und frühklassischen Griechenland*. Göttingen: Vandenhoeck & Ruprecht.

Manni, E. 1963. *Sicilia pagana*. Palermo: S. F. Flaccovio.

Manni, E. 1987. "Brani di storia di Camarina arcaica." *Kokalos* 33: 67–76.

Mansfeld, J. 1975. "Physikos or Physician." In *Kephalaion: Studies in Greek Philosophy and Its Continuation Offered to Professor C. J. de Vogel*, edited by J. Mansfeld and L. M. de Rijk, 26–38. Assen: Van Gorcum.

Manville, P. B. 1990. *The Origins of Citizenship in Ancient Athens.* Princeton, NJ: Princeton University Press.

Manville, P. B. 1994. "Toward a New Paradigm of Athenian Citizenship." In Scafuro and Boegehold 1994, 21–33.

Marconi, C. 2008. "Gli acroliti da Morgantina." *Prospettiva* 130–131: 2–21.

Marconi, C. 2012. "Between Performance and Identity: The Social Context of Stone Theaters in Late Classical and Hellenistic Sicily." In Bosher 2012b, 175–207.

Marconi, C. 2013. "The Goddess from Morgantina." In Lyons, Bennett, and Marconi 2013, 60–61.

Marconi, P. 1933. *Agrigento arcaica: Il santuario delle divinità ctonie e il tempio detto di Vulcano.* Rome: Società Magna Grecia.

Marincola, J. 2001. *Greek Historians.* Oxford: Oxford University Press.

Martin, T. R. 1995. "Coins, Mints, and the Polis." In Hansen 1995, 257–291.

Martin, T. R. 1996. "Why Did the Greek 'Polis' Originally Need Coins?" *Historia* 45: 257–283.

Martorana, G. 1982. "Kore ed il prato sempre fiorito di Enna." *Kokalos* 28–29: 105–112.

Matheson, S. B. 1994. "The Mission of Triptolemus and the Politics of Athens." *GRBS* 35: 345–372.

Mattaliano, F. 2010. "Guerra e diplomazia tra Atene e Siracusa nel V secolo a.C." *Hormos: Ricerche di Storia Antica* 1: 140–147.

Mattioli, M. 2002. *Camarina città greca.* Milan: Edizioni Universitarie di Lettere Economia Diritto.

Maurizio, L. 1998. "The Panathenaic Procession: Athens' Participatory Democracy on Display?" In Boedeker and Raaflaub 1998, 297–317.

McCoskey, D. 2003. "By Any Other Name? Ethnicity and the Study of Ancient Identity." *CB* 79: 93–109.

McInerney, J. 1999. *The Folds of Parnassos: Land and Ethnicity in Ancient Phokis.* Austin: University of Texas Press.

McInerney, J. 2001. "Ethnos and Ethnicity in Early Greece." In Malkin 2001a, 51–73.

McInerney, J. 2013. "Making Phokian Space: Sanctuary and Community in the Definition of Phokis." In Funke and Haake 2013, 185–203.

McInerney, J., ed. 2014a. *A Companion to Ethnicity in the Ancient Mediterranean.* Malden, MA: Blackwell.

McInerney, J. 2014b. "Ethnicity: An Introduction." In McInerney 2014a, 1–16.

McNelis, C., and A. Sens. 2016. *The Alexandra of Lycophron: A Literary Study.* Oxford: Oxford University Press.

Meister, K. 1984. "Agathocles." In *CAH²* VII.1, 384–411.

Mele, A. 1984. "Crotone e la sua storia." In *Crotone* 1984, 9–87.

Mele, A. 1995. "Tradizioni eroiche e colonizzazione greca: Le colonie achee." In *L'incidenza dell'antico*, Vol. 1, edited by A. S. Marino, 427–450. Naples: Luciano.

Mele, A. 1998. "Culti e miti nella storia di Metaponto." In *Siritide e Metapontino: Storie di due territori coloniali*, 9–32. Naples: Centre Jean Bérard.

Mele, A. 2007. "Atene e la Magna Grecia." In Greco and Lombardo 2007, 239–268.

Melfi, M. 2000. "Alcune osservazioni sul cosidetto Tempio di Ares a Monte Casale-Kasmenai." *Geo-archeologia* 2: 39–48.

Melita Pappalardo, M. R. 1996. "Caratteri della propaganda timoleontea." *Kokalos* 42: 263–273.

Melucci, A. 1996. *Challenging Codes: Collective Action in the Information Age.* Cambridge: Cambridge University Press.

Merante, V. 1967. "Pentatlo e la fondazione di Lipari." *Kokalos* 13: 88–104.

Meriani, A. 2000. "La festa greca dei Poseidoniati e la nuova musica (Aristox. fr. 124 Wehrli)." *SemRom* 3: 143–163.

Mertens, D. 1999. "Metaponto: L'evoluzione del centro urbano." In Adamesteanu 1999, 247–294.

Mertens, D. 2006. *Città e monumenti dei greci d'occidente: Dalla colonizzazione alla crisi di fine V secolo a.C.* Translated by M. Papini. Rome: Bretschneider.

Mertens, D., and A. De Siena. 1982. "Metaponto: Il teatro-ekklesiasterion." *BA* 16: 1–60.

Micciché, R. 2020. "Sometimes Pigs Fly." In de Cesare, Portale, and Sojc 2020, 253–268.

Miles, M. 1998. *The City Eleusinion.* Princeton, NJ: American School of Classical Studies.

Miles, R. 2010. *Carthage Must Be Destroyed: The Rise and Fall of an Ancient Mediterranean Civilization.* London: Allen Lane.

Miles, R. 2011. "Hannibal and Propaganda." In Hoyos 2011, 260–279.

Mili, M. 2015. *Religion and Society in Ancient Thessaly.* Oxford: Oxford University Press.

Miller, S. G. 2004. *Ancient Greek Athletics.* New Haven, CT: Yale University Press.

Mimbrera, S. 2012. "The Sicilian Doric Koina." In Tribulato 2012, 223–250.

Mitchell, L. G. 2006. "Ethnic Identity and the Community of the Hellenes: A Review." *Ancient West and East* 4: 409–420.

Mitchell, L. G. 2007. *Panhellenism and the Barbarian in Archaic and Classical Greece.* Swansea: Classical Press of Wales.

Mitchell, L. G. 2013. *The Heroic Rulers of Archaic and Classical Greece.* London: Bloomsbury.

Mitchell, L. G. 2015. "The Community of the Hellenes." In Beck and Funke 2015, 49–65.

Mitford, W. 1835. *The History of Greece,* Vol. 3. London: Thomas Tegg.

Molyneux, J. H. 1992. *Simonides: A Historical Study.* Wauconda, IL: Bolchazy-Carducci.

Montiglio, S. 2005. *Wandering in Ancient Greek Culture.* Chicago: University of Chicago Press.

Morel, J. 2002. "Grecs et indigènes en Grande Grèce: 'Coexistence' et rapports de force." In *Autour de la mer Noire: Hommage à Otar Lordkipanidzé,* edited by D. D. Kacharava, M. Faudot, and E. Geny, 95–110. Besançon: Presses universitaires franc-comtoises.

Morgan, C. 1999a. "The Archaeology of Ethnicity in the Colonial World of the Eighth to Sixth Centuries BC: Approaches and Prospects." In *Confini e frontiera nella grecità d'occidente*, 85–145. Taranto: Istituto per la storia e l'archeologia della Magna Grecia.

Morgan, C. 1999b. "Cultural Subzones in Early Iron Age and Archaic Arkadia." In Nielsen and Roy 1999, 382–456.

Morgan, C. 2002. "Ethnicity: The Example of Achaia." In Greco 2002, 95–116.

Morgan, C. 2003. *Early Greek States beyond the Polis*. London: Routledge.

Morgan, C. 2009. "Ethnic Expression on the Early Iron Age and Early Archaic Greek Mainland: Where Should We Be Looking?" In *Ethnic Constructs in Antiquity: The Role and Power of Tradition*, edited by T. Derks and N. Roymans, 11–36. Amsterdam: Amsterdam University Press.

Morgan, C., and J. M. Hall. 1996. "Achaian Poleis and Achaian Colonisation." In *Introduction to an Inventory of Poleis*, edited by M. H. Hansen, 164–231. Copenhagen: Munskgaard.

Morgan, K. A. 2015. *Pindar and the Construction of Syracusan Monarchy in the Fifth Century B.C.* Oxford: Oxford University Press.

Morris, I. 1998. "Words and Things." *CArchJ* 8: 269–270.

Morris, S. P. 2012. "Greeks and 'Barbarians.'" In Alcock and Osborne 2012, 396–414.

Morrison, A. D. 2007. *Performances and Audiences in Pindar's Sicilian Victory Odes*. London: Institute of Classical Studies.

Morton, P. 2012. "Refiguring the Sicilian Slave Wars: From Servile Unrest to Civil Disquet and Social Disorder." PhD diss., University of Edinburgh.

Moscati Castelnuovo, L. 1989. *Siris: Tradizione storiografica e momenti della storia di una città della Magna Graecia*. Brussels: Latomus.

Mossman, J. 2005. "*Taxis ou Barbaros*: Greek and Roman in Plutarch's *Pyrrhus*." *CQ* 55: 498–517.

Moyer, I. S. 2011a. *Egypt and the Limits of Hellenism*. Cambridge: Cambridge University Press.

Moyer, I. S. 2011b. "Finding a Middle Ground: Culture and Politics in the Ptolemaic Thebaid." In *Perspectives on Ptolemaic Thebes*, edited by P. F. Dorman and B. M. Bryan, 115–145. Chicago: Oriental Institute of the University of Chicago.

Murray, O. 2014. "Thucydides and the Altar of Apollo Archegetes." *ASNP* 5: 447–474.

Musti, D. 1983. "Metaponto: Note sulla tradizione storica." *Rivista di filologia e di istruzione classica* 111: 267–291.

Musti, D. 1988. *Strabone e la Magna Grecia: Città e popoli dell'Italia antica*. Padua: Programma.

Musti, D. 1991. "Lo sviluppo del mito di Filottete, da Crotone a Sibari: Tradizioni achee e troiane in Magna Graecia." In De La Genière 1991, 21–36.

Musti, D. 2005. *Magna Grecia: Il quadro storico*. Rome: GLF Editori Laterza.

Nafissi, M. 1985. "Le genti indigine: Enotri, Coni, Siculi, e Morgeti, Ausoni, Iapigi, Sanniti." In *Magna Grecia*, Vol. 1: *Il Mediterraneo, le metropoleis e la fondazione delle colonie*, edited by G. Pugliese Carratelli, 189–208. Milan: Electa.

Nafissi, M. 1997. "Atene e Metaponto: Ancora sulla *Melanippe Desmotis* e i Neleidi." *Ostraka* 6: 337–357.

Nafissi, M. 1999. "From Sparta to Taras: *Nomima, Ktiseis*, and Relationships between Colony and Mother City." In *Sparta: New Perspectives*, edited by S. Hodkinson and A. Powell, 245–272. London: Duckworth.

Nagy, G. 1990. *Pindar's Homer: The Lyric Possession of an Epic Past*. Baltimore: Johns Hopkins University Press.

Nash, M. 1989. *The Cauldron of Ethnicity in the Modern World*. Chicago: University of Chicago Press.

Neer, R. 2003. "Framing the Gift: The Sikyonian Treasury at Delphi and the Politics of Architectural Sculpture." In Dougherty and Kurke 2003, 129–149.

Nelson, T. J. Forthcoming. "Beating the Galatians: Ideologies, Analogies, and Allegories in Hellenistic Literature and Art." In *Towards a New History of Ancient Galatia*, edited by A. Coskun.

Nenci, G. 1966. "L'Heraion di Metaponto (Plinio, N. H. xiv,2,9)." *PP* 21: 128–131.

Nenci, G. 1976. "Il *barbaros polemos* fra Taranto e gli Iapigi e gli anathemata Tarentini a Delfi." *ASNP* 6: 719–738.

Netz, R. 2013. "Science in Syracuse: Archimedes in Place." In Lyons, Bennett, and Marconi 2013, 124–133.

Nicholson, N. J. 2011. "Pindar's Olympian 4: Psaumis and Camarina after the Deinomenids." *CPh* 106: 93–114.

Nicholson, N. J. 2015. *The Poetics of Victory in the Greek West: Epinician, Oral Tradition, and the Deinomenid Empire*. Oxford: Oxford University Press.

Nielsen, T. H. 1997. "Triphylia: An Experiment in Ethnic Construction and Political Organization." In *Yet More Studies in the Ancient Greek Polis*, edited by T. H. Nielsen. Stuttgart: F. Steiner.

Nielsen, T. H. 1999. "The Concept of Arkadia: The People, Their Land, and Their Organization." In Nielsen and Roy 1999, 16–79.

Nielsen, T. H. 2002. *Arkadia and Its Poleis in the Archaic and Classical Periods*. Göttingen: Vandenhoeck & Ruprecht.

Nielsen, T. H. 2005. "A Polis as a Part of a Larger Identity Group: Glimpses from the History of Lepreon." *C&M* 56: 57–89.

Nielsen, T. H., and J. Roy. 1999. *Defining Ancient Arkadia*. Copenhagen: Royal Danish Academy of Sciences and Letters.

Noe, S. P., and A. Johnston. 1984. *The Coinage of Metapontum*. New York: American Numismatic Society.

Öhlinger, B. 2015. *Ritual und Religion im archaischen Sizilien: Formations- und Transformationsprozesse binnenländischer Kultorte im Kontext kultureller Kontakte*. Wiesbaden: Reichert.

Olson, S. D. 2017. "Archimelus: On the Great Ship of Hieron II." In *Hellenistic Poetry: A Selection*, edited by D. Sider, 149–152. Ann Arbor: University of Michigan Press.

Orioles, V. 2001. "I Mamertini a Messana fra dominanza greca e identità italica." In *Norma e variazione nel diasistema greca*, edited by C. Consani and L. Mucciante, 279–288. Alexandria: Edizioni dell'Orso.

Orlandini, P. 1968. "Lo scavo di del Thesmophorion di Bitalemi e il culto delle divinità ctonie a Gela." *Kokalos* 12: 8–35.

Orlandini, P. 2008. "Demetra a Gela." In Di Stefano 2008, 173–186.

Ormand, K. 2014. *The Hesiodic Catalogue of Women and Archaic Greece.* Cambridge: Cambridge University Press.

Osanna, M. 1992. *Chorai coloniali da Taranto a Locri: Documentazione archeologica a ricostruzione storica.* Rome: Istituto Polografica a Zecco dello Stato, Libreria dello Stato.

Osanna, M. 1996. *Santuari e culti dell'Acaia antica.* Naples: Edizioni Scientifiche Italiane.

Osanna, M. 2002. "Da Aigialos ad Achaia: Sui culti più antichi della madrepatria delle colonie achee di occidente." In Greco 2002, 271–281.

Osborne, R. 1985. *Demos: The Discovery of Classical Attika.* Cambridge: Cambridge University Press.

Osborne, R. 1998. "Early Greek Colonization? The Nature of Greek Settlement in the West." In *Archaic Greece: New Approaches and New Evidence*, edited by N. Fisher and H. van Wees, 251–269. London: Duckworth and the Classical Press of Wales.

Osborne, R. 2009. *Greece in the Making, 1200–479 B.C.* 2nd ed. London: Routledge.

Pace, B. 1927. *Camarina: Topografia, storia, archeologia.* Catania: F. Guaitolini.

Pace, B. 1935–1949. *Arte e civiltà nella Sicilia antica.* 4 vols. Milan: Dante Alighieri.

Panvini, R., and L. Sole, eds. 2009. *La Sicilia in età arcaica: Dalle apoikiai al 480 A.C.* Palermo: Centro Regionale per l'Inventario, la Catalogazione e la Documentazione.

Papadopoulos, J. K. 2001. "Magna Achaea: Akhaian Late Geometric and Archaic Pottery in South Italy and Sicily." *Hesperia* 70: 373–460.

Papadopoulos, J. K. 2002. "Minting Identity: Coinage, Ideology and the Economics of Colonization in Akhaian Magna Graecia." *CArchJ* 12: 21–55.

Parker, R. 1998. *Cleomenes on the Acropolis.* Oxford: Clarendon Press.

Parker, R. 2005. *Polytheism and Society at Athens.* Oxford: Oxford University Press.

Parker, R. 2011. *On Greek Religion.* Ithaca, NY: Cornell University Press.

Patanè, A. 2009. "Grammichele." In Panvini and Sole 2009, 115–116.

Patanè, R. P. A. 2008. "Demetra a Centuripe." In Di Stefano 2008, 255–260.

Patera, I. 2020. "Identifier Déméter *Thesmophoros* et son culte en Sicile à partir des données matérielles." In de Cesare, Portale, and Sojc 2020, 27–57.

Patterson, L. 2010. *Kinship Myth in Ancient Greece.* Austin: University of Texas Press.

Patterson, O. 1975. "Context and Choice in Ethnic Allegiance: A Theoretical Framework and Caribbean Case Study." In Glazer and Moynihan 1975, 305–349.

Pautasso, A. 2009. "La stipe votiva di piazza San Francesco." In Panvini and Sole 2009, 103–105.

Pearson, L. 1987. *The Greek Historians of the West: Timaeus and His Predecessors.* Atlanta: Scholars.

Pedley, J. G. 1990. *Paestum: Greeks and Romans in Southern Italy.* London: Thames and Hudson.

Pelagatti, P. 1976. "L'attività della Soprintendenza alle Antichità della Sicilia Orientale." *Kokalos* 22–23: 519–550.

Pelagatti, P. 1980. "L'attività della Soprintendenza alle Antichità della Sicilia Orientale." *Kokalos* 26–27: 694–730.

Pelliccia, H. 1999. "Simonides, Pindar, and Bacchylides." In *The Cambridge Companion to Greek Lyric*, edited by F. Budelmann, 240–262. Cambridge: Cambridge University Press.

Pelling, C. 2000. *Literary Texts and the Greek Historian.* London: Routledge.

Pelling, C. 2009. "Bringing Autochthony Up-to-Date: Herodotus and Thucydides." *CW* 102: 471–483.

Péré-Noguès, S. 2004. "Citoyenneté et mercenariat en Sicile à l'époque classique." *Pallas* 66: 145–155.

Péré-Noguès, S. 2006. "Les 'identités' siciliennes durant les guerres puniques: Entre culture et politique." *Pallas* 70: 57–70.

Péré-Noguès, S. 2016. "Les symmachies en Sicile des expéditions d'Athènes à la stratégie de Timoléon." *DHA* Supplement 16: 97–112.

Petruzzella, M. 1999. "La stasis a Gela in età arcaica e la figura dello ierofante Telines." *Kokalos* 45: 501–507.

Pettinato, M. 2000. "Pausania, la Tirannide e i Dinomenidi." *Kokalos* 46: 127–156.

Philipp, H. 1994. "Olympia, die Peloponnes und die Westgriechen." *JDAI* 109: 77–92.

Picard, G. C. 1994. "Carthage, from the Battle of Himera to Agathocles' Invasion (480–308 B.C.)." In *CAH²* VI, 361–380.

Polacco, L. 1986. "I culti di Demetra e Kore a Siracusa." *NAC* 15: 21–37.

Pomeroy, S. B., S. M. Burstein, W. Donlan, J. T. Roberts, D. W. Tandy, and G. Tsouvala. 2018. *Ancient Greece: A Political, Social, and Cultural History.* 4th ed. New York: Oxford University Press.

Porciani, L. 2015. "Early Greek Colonies and Greek Cultural Identity: Megara Hyblaea and the Phaeacians." *DHA* 41: 9–18.

Portale, E. C. 2004. "*Euergetikotatos . . . kai philodoxotatos eis tous Hellenas*: Riflessioni sui rapporti fra Ierone II e il mondo greco." In Caccamo Caltabiano, Campagna, and Pinzone 2004, 229–264.

Portale, E. C. 2008. "Coroplastica votiva nella Sicilia di V–III secolo a.C.: La stipe di Fontana Calda a Butera." *Sicilia Antiqua* 5: 9–58.

Pownall, F. 2013. "Philistos (556)." In *BNJ*.

Prag, J. R. W. 2010. "Tyrannizing Sicily: The Despots Who Cried 'Carthage!'" In *Private and Public Lies: The Discourse of Despotism and Deceit in the Graeco-Roman*

World, edited by A. J. Turner, K. O. Chong-Gossard, and F. J. Vervaet, 51–71. Leiden: Brill.

Prag, J. R. W. 2013. "Sicilian Identity in the Hellenistic and Roman Periods: Epigraphic Considerations." In *Epigraphical Approaches to the Postclassical Polis: Fourth Century BC to Second Century AD*, edited by P. Martzavou and N. Papazarkadas, 37–53. Oxford: Oxford University Press.

Prestianni Giallombardo, A. M. 2006. "Il ruolo dei mercenari nelle dinamiche di guerra e di pace in Sicilia tra fine V e metà del III sec. A.C." In *Guerra e pace* 2006, 107–129.

Pretzler, M. 1999. "Myth and History at Tegea: Local Tradition and Community Identity." In Nielsen and Roy 1999, 89–129.

Pretzler, M. 2003. "City Devices and City Identities: The Development of Symbols to Represent Community Identity." In *Inhabiting Symbols: Symbol and Image in the Ancient Mediterranean*, edited by J. Wilkins and E. Herring, 148–174. London: Accordia Research Institute.

Price, J. J. 2001. *Thucydides and Internal War*. Cambridge: Cambridge University Press.

Privitera, G. A. 1980. "Politica religiosa dei Dinomenidi e ideologia dell'optimus rex." In *Perennitas: Studi in onore di Angelo Brelich*, 393–411. Rome: Ateneo.

Privitera, S. 2003. "I tripodi dei Dinomenidi e la decima dei Siracusani." *ASAA* 81: 391–424.

Privitera, S. 2014. "L'oro dopo la vittoria: Il donario delfico dei Dinomenidi tra battaglie e vittorie agonistiche." In *Guerra e memoria nel mondo antico*, edited by E. Franchi and G. Proietti, 177–187. Trento: Tipografia Editrice TEMI.

Prontera, F. 1992. "Antioco di Siracusa e la preistoria dell'idea etnico-geografica di Italia." *GeogrAnt* 1: 109–135.

Pugliese Carratelli, G., ed. 1983. *Megale Hellas: Storia e civiltà della Magna Grecia*. Milan: Libri Scheiwiller.

Purcell, N. 1994. "South Italy in the Fourth Century B.C." In *CAH²* VI, 381–403.

Purcell, N. 2005. "Colonization and Mediterranean History." In Hurst and Owen 2005, 115–139.

Pyrcz, G. E. 2011. *The Study of Politics: A Short Survey of Core Approaches*. Toronto: University of Toronto Press.

Quinn, J. C. 2018. *In Search of the Phoenicians*. Princeton, NJ: Princeton University Press.

Quinn, J. C., and N. C. Vella, eds. 2014. *The Punic Mediterranean: Identities and Identification from Phoenician Settlement to Roman Rule*. Cambridge: Cambridge University Press.

Raaflaub, K. A. 2004. *The Discovery of Freedom in Ancient Greece*. Chicago: University of Chicago Press.

Raaflaub, K. A., J. D. Richards, and L. J. Samons. 1992. "Rome, Italy and Appius Claudius Caecus before the Pyrrhic Wars." In Hackens et al. 1992, 13–50.

Raffiotta, S. 2007. *Terrecotte figurate dal santuario di San Francesco Bisconti a Morgantina*. Assoro: Editopera.

Raffiotta, S. 2008. "Nuove testimonianze del culto di Demetra e Persefone a Morgantina." In *Morgantina: A cinquant'anni dall'inizio delle ricerche sistematiche*, edited by G. Guzzetta, 105–131. Caltanissetta: S. Sciascia.

Raubitschek, A. E., and I. Raubitschek. 1982. "The Mission of Triptolemus." In *Studies in Athenian Architecture, Sculpture, and Topography: Presented to Homer A. Thompson*, 109–117. Princeton, NJ: American School of Classical Studies at Athens.

Raviola, F. 1986. "Temistocle e la Magna Grecia." In *Tre studi su Temistocle*, edited by L. Braccesi, 13–112. Padua: Editoriale Programma.

Redfield, J. M. 2003. *The Locrian Maidens: Love and Death in Greek Italy*. Princeton, NJ: Princeton University Press.

Reed, J. D. 2000. "Arsinoe's Adonis and the Poetics of Ptolemaic Imperialism." *TAPhA* 130: 319–351.

Reger, G. 1997. "Islands with One *Polis* versus Islands with Several *Poleis*." In *The Polis as an Urban Centre and as a Political Community*, edited by M. H. Hansen, 450–492. Copenhagen: Royal Danish Academy of Sciences and Letters.

Renfrew, C. 1998. "From Here to Ethnicity." *CArchJ* 8: 275–277.

Rhodes, P. J. 2010. *A History of the Classical Greek World, 478–323 BC*. 2nd ed. Malden, MA: Wiley-Blackwell.

Richardson, N. J. 1974. *The Homeric Hymn to Demeter*. Oxford: Clarendon Press.

Rizza, G. 1960. "Stipe votiva di un santuario di Demetra a Catania." *BA* 45: 247–262.

Rizza, G. 2008. "Demetra a Catania." In Di Stefano 2008, 187–191.

Rizzo, F. P. 1970. *La repubblica di Siracusa nel momento di Ducezio*. Palermo: Manfredi Editore.

Robbins, E. 1997. "Pindar." In *A Companion to the Greek Lyric Poets*, edited by D. E. Gerber, 253–277. Leiden: Brill.

Robert, R. 2012. "Diodore e le patrimoine mythico-historique de la Sicile." *DHA* Supplement 6: 43–68.

Robertson, N. 2002. "The Religious Criterion in Greek Ethnicity: The Dorians and the Festival Carneia." *AJAH* 1: 5–74.

Robinson, E. W. 2011. *Democracy beyond Athens: Popular Government in Classical Greece*. Cambridge: Cambridge University Press.

Roller, D. W. 2018. *A Historical and Topographical Guide to the Geography of Strabo*. Cambridge: Cambridge University Press.

Romano, C. 2000. "Ermocrate tra Sicilia e Ionia." *Kokalos* 46: 345–363.

Romano, D. 1980. "Cicero e il ratto di Proserpina." *Ciceroniana* 4: 191–201.

Rood, T. 1998. *Thucydides: Narrative and Explanation*. Oxford: Oxford University Committee for Archaeology.

Rood, T. 1999. "Thucydides' Persian Wars." In *The Limits of Historiography: Genre and Narrative in Ancient Historical Texts*, edited by C. S. Kraus, 141–168. Leiden: Brill.

Roosens, E. 1989. *Creating Ethnicity: The Process of Ethnogenesis*. Newbury Park, CA: SAGE.

Rose, C. B. 2003. "Re-Evaluating Troy's Links to Rome." *JRA* 16: 379–381.

Rosenstein, N. S. 2012. *Rome and the Mediterranean, 290 to 146 BC: The Imperial Republic*. Edinburgh: Edinburgh University Press.

Rosivach, V. J. 1987. "Autochthony and the Athenians." *CQ* 37: 294–306.

Roskin, M., R. L. Cord, J. A. Medeiros, and W. S. Jones. 2014. *Political Science: An Introduction*. 12th ed. Harlow, UK: Pearson.

Rothe, U. 2020. *The Toga and Roman Identity*. London: Bloomsbury.

Roy, J. 2014. "Autochthony in Ancient Greece." In McInerney 2014a, 241–255.

Ruby, P. 2006. "Peuples, fictions? Ethnicité, identité ethnique et sociétés anciennes." *REA* 108: 25–60.

Russo, F. 2008. "Ancora sulla barbarizzazione di Poseidonia." *Aevum* 82: 25–39.

Rutter, N. K. 1997. *The Greek Coinages of Southern Italy and Sicily*. London: Spink.

Rutter, N. K. 2000a. "Coin Types and Identity: Greek Cities in Sicily." In Smith and Serrati 2000, 73–83.

Rutter, N. K. 2000b. "Syracusan Democracy: 'Most Like the Athenian'?" In Brock and Hodkinson 2000, 137–151.

Rutter, N. K. 2001. *Historia Numorum: Italy*. London: British Museum.

Sabbione, C. 1982. "Le aree di colonizzazione di Crotone e Locri Epizefiri nell'viii e vii sec. a. C." *ASAA* 44: 251–299.

Said, S. 2001. "The Discourse of Identity in Greek Rhetoric from Isocrates to Aristides." In Malkin 2001a, 275–299.

Salmon, E. T. 1988. "The Iron Age: The Peoples of Italy." In *CAH²* IV, 676–718.

Sammartano, R. 2015. "Da Teocle ad Ermocrate: Quale identità per i Greci di Sicilia?" *Kokalos* 52: 231–272.

Sanders, L. J. 1987. *Dionysius I of Syracuse and Greek Tyranny*. London: Croom Helm.

Scafuro, A. C., and A. L. Boegehold, eds. 1994. *Athenian Identity and Civic Ideology*. Baltimore: Johns Hopkins University Press.

Schaps, D. M. 2004. *The Invention of Coinage and the Monetization of Ancient Greece*. Ann Arbor: University of Michigan Press.

Scheer, T. S. 2018. "Women and *Nostoi*." In Hornblower and Biffis 2018, 123–145.

Schepens, G. 1994. "Politics and Belief in Timaeus of Tauromenium." *AncSoc* 25: 249–278.

Schipporeit, S. 2008. "Enna and Eleusis." In Di Stefano 2008, 41–46.

Schuller, W. 1974. *Die Herrschaft der Athener im ersten attischen Seebund*. Berlin: De Gruyter.

Schwarz, G. 1987. *Triptolemos: Ikonographie einer Agrar- und Mysteriengottheit*. Graz: F. Berger.

Scibona, C. G. 2003. "I Dinomenidi e la funzionalizzazione politica del culto di Demetra in Sicilia." In *Potere e religione nel mondo indo-mediterraneo tra ellenismo e tarda-antichità*, edited by G. Gnoli and G. Sfameni Gasparro, 137–150. Rome: ISIAO.

Scibona, C. G. 2012. "Demeter and Athena at Gela: Personal Features of Sicilian Goddesses." In *Demeter, Isis, Vesta, and Cybele*, edited by G. Sfameni Gasparro, A. Mastrocinque, and C. G. Scibona, 59–90. Stuttgart: F. Steiner.

Scott, M. 2010. *Delphi and Olympia: The Spatial Politics of Panhellenism in the Archaic and Classical Periods*. Cambridge: Cambridge University Press.

Seaford, R. 1988. "The Eleventh Ode of Bacchylides: Hera, Artemis, and the Absence of Dionysos." *JHS* 108: 118–136.

Sealey, R. 1976. *A History of the Greek City States, ca. 700–338 B.C.* Berkeley: University of California Press.

Segal, C. 1976. "Bacchylides Reconsidered: Epithets and the Dynamics of Lyric Narrative." *QUCC* 22: 99–130.

Sen, A. 2006. *Identity and Violence: The Illusion of Destiny*. New York: W. W. Norton.

Sevieri, R. 2000. "Cantare la città: Tempo mitico e spazio urbano nell'Istmica 7 di Pindaro per Strepsiade di Tebe." In *Presenza e funzione della città di Tebe nella cultura greca*, edited by P. A. Bernardini, 179–192. Pisa: Istituti Editoriali e Poligrafici Internazionali.

Sfameni Gasparro, G. 2008. "Demetra in Sicilia: Tra identità panellenica e connotazioni locali." In Di Stefano 2008, 25–40.

Shapiro, H. A. 1989. *Art and Cult under the Tyrants in Athens*. Mainz: P. von Zabern.

Shapiro, H. A. 1996. "Democracy and Imperialism: The Panathenaia in the Age of Perikles." In *Worshipping Athena: Panathenaia and Parthenon*, edited by J. Neils, 215–228. Madison: University of Wisconsin Press.

Shapiro, H. A. 1998. "Autochthony and the Visual Arts in Fifth-Century Athens." In Boedeker and Raaflaub 1998, 127–151.

Shapiro, H. A. 2002. "Demeter and Persphone in Western Greece: Migrations of Myth and Cult." In *Magna Graecia: Greek Art from South Italy and Sicily*, edited by M. J. Bennett and A. J. Paul, 82–97. New York: Cleveland Museum of Art.

Shepherd, G. 1995. "The Pride of Most Colonials: Burial and Religion in the Sicilian Greek Colonies." *Acta Hyperborea* 6: 51–82.

Shepherd, G. 2005. "Dead Men Tell No Tales: Ethnic Diversity in Sicilian Colonies and the Evidence of the Cemeteries." *OJA* 24: 115–136.

Shepherd, G. 2006. "Hellenicity: More Views from the Margins." *Ancient West and East* 4: 437–445.

Shepherd, G. 2011. "Hybridity and Hierarchy: Cultural Identity and Social Mobility in Archaic Sicily." In *Communicating Identity in Italic Iron Age Communities*, edited by M. Gleba and H. W. Horsnaes, 113–129. Oxford: Oxbow Books.

Shepherd, G. 2014. "Archaeology and Ethnicity: Untangling Identities in Western Greece." *DHA* Supplement 10: 115–143.

Shipley, G. 2000. *The Greek World after Alexander, 323–30 B.C.* London: Routledge.

Siapkas, J. 2003. *Heterological Ethnicity: Conceptualizing Identities in Ancient Greece.* Uppsala: Uppsala University Press.

Sibari e la Sibaritide. 1993. Taranto: Istituto per la storia e l'archeologia della Magna Grecia.

Sicking, C. M. J. 1983. "Pindar's First Olympian: An Interpretation." *Mnemosyne* 36: 60–70.

Simon, M. 2012. *Le rivage grec de l'Italie romaine: La Grande Grèce dans l'historiographie augustéenne.* Rome: Ecole Française de Rome.

Sinatra, D. 1992. "*Xenoi, misthophoroi, idioi oikétores*: Lotte interne ed equilibri politici a Siracusa dal 466 al 461." *Kokalos* 38: 347–363.

Siracusano, A. 1983. *Il santuario rupestre di Agrigento in località S. Biagio.* Rome: Bretschneider.

Sjöqvist, E. 1958. "Timoleonte e Morgantina." *Kokalos* 4: 107–118.

Sjöqvist, E. 1973. *Sicily and the Greeks: Studies in the Interrelationship between the Indigenous Populations and the Greek Colonists.* Ann Arbor: University of Michigan Press.

Skinner, J. 2010. "Fish Heads and Mussel-Shells: Visualizing Greek Identity." In *Intentional History: Spinning Time in Ancient Greece*, edited by L. Foxhall, H. Gehrke, and N. Luraghi, 137–160. Stuttgart: F. Steiner.

Skinner, J. 2012. *The Invention of Greek Ethnography: From Homer to Herodotus.* Oxford: Oxford University Press.

Smart, J. D. 1972. "Athens and Egesta." *JHS* 92: 128–146.

Smith, A. D. 1986. *The Ethnic Origins of Nations.* Oxford: Blackwell.

Smith, C., and J. Serrati, eds. 2000. *Sicily from Aeneas to Augustus: New Approaches in Archaeology and History.* Edinburgh: Edinburgh University Press.

Smith, D. G. 2003. "How the West Was One: The Formation of Greek Cultural Identity in Italy and Sicily." PhD diss., Stanford University.

Smith, D. G. 2004. "Thucydides' Ignorant Athenians and the Drama of the Sicilian Expedition." *SyllClass* 15: 33–70.

Smith, D. G. 2011. "Colonisation in Sicily and North America." *Ancient West and East* 10: 309–328.

Snodgrass, A. M. 1987. *An Archaeology of Greece: The Present State and Future Scope of a Discipline.* Berkeley: University of California Press.

Snodgrass, A. M. 1994. "The Nature and Standing of the Early Western Colonies." In *The Archaeology of Greek Colonization*, edited by G. R. Tsetskhladze and F. De Angelis, 1–10. Oxford: Oxford University Committee for Archaeology.

Snodgrass, A. M. 2006. "Sanctuary, Shared Cult and Hellenicity: An Archaeological Angle." *Ancient West and East* 4: 432–436.

Sojc, N. 2020. "Depositions of Sacrificial Material and Feasting Remains from the Extra-Urban Sanctuary of S. Anna (Agrigento). Appendix: A Note on Characteristic Finds by Linda Adorno." In de Cesare, Portale, and Sojc 2020, 221–252.

Sordi, M. 1981. "Ermocrate di Siracusa: Demagogo e tiranno mancato." In Gasperini 1981, 595–600.

Sordi, M. 1994. *Emigrazione e immigrazione nel mondo antico.* Milan: Vita e Pensiero.

Sourvinou-Inwood, C. 1988. "Further Aspects of *Polis* Religion." *AION(archeol)* 10: 259–274.

Sourvinou-Inwood, C. 1990. "What Is *Polis* Religion?" In *The Greek City: From Homer to Alexander,* edited by O. Murray and S. Price, 295–322. Oxford: Oxford University Press.

Sourvinou-Inwood, C. 2005. *Hylas, the Nymphs, Dionysos and Others: Myth, Ritual, Ethnicity.* Stockholm: Paul Aaström.

Souza, R. 2020. "Enslavement and Redemption in Classical Sicily." In Jonasch 2020a, 57–72.

Spadea, R., ed. 1996. *Il tesoro di Hera: Scoperte nel santuario di Hera Lacinia a Capo Colonna di Crotone.* Milan: Edizioni ET.

Spadea, R. 1997. "Santuari di Hera a Crotone." In De La Genière 1997, 235–259.

Spadea, R., ed. 2006. *Ricerche nel santuario di Hera Lacinia a Capo Colonna di Crotone: Risultati e prospettive.* Rome: Gangemi.

Spadea, R. 2012. "Crotone e Crotoniatide: Primi documenti archeologici (fine VIII–inizio VII secolo a.C.)." In *Alle origini della Magna Grecia* 2012, 721–740.

Spatafora, F. 2008. "Entella: Il *thesmophorion* di Contrada Petraro." In Di Stefano 2008, 273–284.

Spatafora, F. 2013. "Ethnic Identity in Sicily: Greeks and Non-Greeks." In Lyons, Bennett, and Marconi 2013, 37–47.

Spigo, U. 2009. "Francavilla di Sicilia: L'abitato ed il santuario." In Panvini and Sole 2009, 67–72.

Sposito, A. 2008. "Architettura e rito nel santuario delle divinità ctonie a Morgantina." In Di Stefano 2008, 221–233.

Stadter, P. A., ed. 1973. *The Speeches in Thucydides.* Chapel Hill: University of North Carolina Press.

Stahl, H. 1973. "Speeches and Course of Events in Books Six and Seven of Thucydides." In Stadter 1973, 60–77.

Stazio, A. 1998. "Qualche osservazione su origine e funzioni della più antica monetazione delle colonie achee in occidente." In *Helike II: Ancient Helike and Aigialeia,* edited by D. Katsonopoulou, S. Soter, and D. Schilardi, 371–380. Athens: Chatziyiannis.

Stehle, E. 2007. "Thesmophoria and Eleusinian Mysteries: The Fascination of Women's Secret Ritual." In *Finding Persephone: Women's Rituals in the Ancient Mediterranean,* edited by M. G. Parca and A. Tzanetou, 165–185. Bloomington: Indiana University Press.

Steinbock, B. 2013. *Social Memory in Athenian Public Discourse: Uses and Meanings of the Past.* Ann Arbor: University of Michigan Press.

Stephens, S. A. 2003. *Seeing Double: Intercultural Poetics in Ptolemaic Alexandria.* Berkeley: University of California Press.

Stephens, S. A. 2018. *The Poets of Alexandria.* London: I.B. Tauris.

Stevens, K. 2016. "Empire Begins at Home: Local Elites and Imperial Ideologies in Hellenistic Greece and Babylonia." In *Cosmopolitanism and Empire: Universal Rulers, Local Elites, and Cultural Integration in the Ancient Near East and Mediterranean,* edited by M. Lavan, R. E. Payne, and J. Weisweiler, 65–88. Oxford: Oxford University Press.

Stewart, E. 2017. *Greek Tragedy on the Move: The Birth of a Panhellenic Art Form, c. 500–300 BC.* Oxford: Oxford University Press.

Stroheker, K. F. 1958. *Dionysios I: Gestalt und Geschichte des Tyrannen von Syrakus.* Wiesbaden: F. Steiner.

Stryker, S. 1968. "Identity Salience and Role Performance: The Relevance of Symbolic Interaction Theory for Family Research." *Journal of Marriage and Family* 30: 558–564.

Stryker, S. 1980. *Symbolic Interactionism: A Social Structural Version.* Menlo Park, CA: Benjamin/Cummings.

Stryker, S., T. J. Owens, and R. W. White, eds. 2000. *Self, Identity, and Social Movements.* Minneapolis: University of Minnesota Press.

Sulosky Weaver, C. L. 2015. *The Bioarchaeology of Classical Kamarina: Life and Death in Greek Sicily.* Gainesville: University Press of Florida.

Tagliamonte, G. L. 1994. *I figli di Marte: Mobilità, mercenari e mercenariato italici in Magna Grecia e Sicilia.* Rome: Bretschneider.

Talbert, R. J. A. 1974. *Timoleon and the Revival of Greek Sicily, 344–317 B.C.* Cambridge: Cambridge University Press.

Taylor, M. C. 2010. *Thucydides, Pericles, and the Idea of Athens in the Peloponnesian War.* Cambridge: Cambridge University Press.

Thatcher, M. 2012. "Syracusan Identity between Tyranny and Democracy." *BICS* 55: 73–90.

Thatcher, M. 2019. "Aeschylus' *Aetnaeans,* the Palici and Cultural Politics in Deinomenid Sicily." *JHS* 139: 67–82.

Thomas, R. 1989. *Oral Tradition and Written Record in Classical Athens.* Cambridge: Cambridge University Press.

Thomas, R. 2001. "Ethnicity, Genealogy, and Hellenism in Herodotus." In Malkin 2001a, 213–233.

Thompson, D. J. 2001. "Hellenistic Hellenes: The Case of Ptolemaic Egypt." In Malkin 2001a, 301–322.

Tilly, C. 2003. "Political Identities in Changing Polities." *Social Research* 70: 605–620.

Tribulato, O., ed. 2012. *Language and Linguistic Contact in Ancient Sicily.* Cambridge: Cambridge University Press.

Tsetskhladze, G. R., ed. 2006–2008. *Greek Colonisation: An Account of Greek Colonies and Other Settlements Overseas*. 2 vols. Leiden: Brill.

Uhlenbrock, J. P. 2016. "Research Perspectives in Greek Coroplastic Studies: The Demeter Paradigm and the Goddess Bias." *Les Carnets de l'ACoSt* 14. doi: 10.4000/acost.866.

Uhlenbrock, J. P. 2019. "The Study of Figurative Terracottas: A Cautionary Tale from a Personal Perspective." *Les Carnets de l'ACoSt* 19. doi: 10.4000/acost.1703.

Un ponte fra l'Italia e la Grecia. 2000. Padua: Bottega d'Erasmo–Aldo Ausilio.

Urquhart, L. M. 2014a. "Competing Traditions in the Historiography of Ancient Greek Colonization in Italy." *Journal of the History of Ideas* 75: 23–44.

Urquhart, L. M. 2014b. "Graves, Gods, and Extratextual Ritual in Archaic Colonial Sicily." In *Gods, Objects, and Ritual Practice*, edited by S. Blakely, 305–327. Atlanta: Lockwood.

Urquhart, L. M. 2020. "English-Speaking Traditions and the Study of Ancient Greeks outside Their Homelands." In De Angelis 2020a, 37–51.

Vacanti, C. 2012. *Guerra per la Sicilia e guerra della Sicilia: Il ruolo delle città siciliane nel primo conflitto romano-punico*. Naples: Jovene.

Vanotti, G. 1979. "Sofocle e l'occidente." In *I tragici greci e l'occidente*, edited by L. Burelli Bergese, E. Culasso Gastaldi, and G. Vanotti, 93–125. Bologna: Pàtron.

Vanotti, G. 2003. "Quale Sicilia per Ermocrate?" In *Gli stati territoriali nel mondo antico*, edited by C. Bearzot, F. Landucci, and G. Zecchini, 179–197. Milan: Vita e Pensiero.

Vanotti, G. 2005. "L'Ermocrate di Diodoro: Un leader 'dimezzato.'" In *Diodoro e l'altra Grecia: Macedonia, occidente, ellenismo nella Biblioteca Storica*, edited by C. Bearzot and F. Landucci, 257–281. Milan: Vita e Pensiero.

Vattuone, R. 1991. *Sapienza d'occidente: Il pensiero storico di Timeo di Tauromenio*. Bologna: Pàtron.

Vattuone, R. 1994. "'Metoikesis': Trapianti di popolazioni nella Sicilia greca fra VI e IV sec. A.C." In Sordi 1994, 81–113.

Vattuone, R., ed. 2002. *Storici greci d'occidente*. Bologna: Il Mulino.

Veit, C. 2009. "Zur Kulturpolitik Hierons II in Syrakus." In *Stadtbilder im Hellenismus*, edited by A. Matthaei and M. Zimmermann, 365–379. Berlin: Antike.

Veit, C. 2013. "Hellenistic Kingship in Sicily: Patronage and Politics under Agathocles and Hieron II." In Lyons, Bennett, and Marconi 2013, 27–36.

Verdenius, W. J. 1987. *Commentaries on Pindar*. Leiden: Brill.

Verity, A., trans. 2008. *Pindar: The Complete Odes*. Introduction and notes by Stephen Instone. Oxford: Oxford University Press.

Vermeulen, H., and C. Govers, eds. 2000. *The Anthropology of Ethnicity: Beyond "Ethnic Groups and Boundaries."* Amsterdam: Het Spinhuis.

Veronese, F. 2006. *Lo spazio e la dimensione del sacro: Santuari greci e territorio nella Sicilia arcaica*. Padua: Esedra.

Vickers, M. 1995. "Heracles Lacedaemonius: The Political Dimensions of Sophocles *Trachiniae* and Euripides *Heracles.*" *DHA* 21: 41–69.

Villard, F. 1994. "Les sièges de Syracuse et leurs pestilences." In *L'eau, la santé et la maladie dans le monde grec*, edited by R. Ginouvès, A. Guimier-Sorbets, J. Jouanna, and L. Villard, 337–344. Paris: De Boccard.

Vlassopoulos, K. 2007. "The Regional Identity of the Peloponnese." In *Being Peloponnesian*, chap. 5. Nottingham, UK: Center for Spartan and Peloponnesian Studies. http://www.nottingham.ac.uk/csps/documents/beingpeloponnesian/kostas.pdf.

Vlassopoulos, K. 2013. *Greeks and Barbarians.* Cambridge: Cambridge University Press.

Vlassopoulos, K. 2015. "Ethnicity and Greek History: Re-Examining Our Assumptions." *BICS* 58: 1–13.

Von Reden, S. 2010. *Money in Classical Antiquity.* Cambridge: Cambridge University Press.

Von Reden, S. 1995. *Exchange in Ancient Greece.* London: Duckworth.

Voza, G. 1976–1977. "L'attività della Soprintendenza alle Antichità della Sicilia orientale." *Kokalos* 22–23: 551–586.

Voza, G. 1980–1981. "L'attività della Soprintendenza alle Antichità della Sicilia orientale." *Kokalos* 26–27: 674–693.

Voza, G. 1999. *Nel segno dell'antico: Archeologia nel territorio di Siracusa.* Palermo: A. Lombardi.

Walbank, F. W. 1957. *A Historical Commentary on Polybius*, Vol. 1. Oxford: Oxford University Press.

Walbank, F. W. 2000. "Hellenes and Achaians: 'Greek Nationality' Revisited." In *Further Studies in the Ancient Greek Polis*, edited by P. Flensted-Jensen, 19–33. Stuttgart: F. Steiner.

Wallace, R. W. 1987. "The Origins of Electrum Coinage." *AJA* 91: 385–397.

Walthall, D. A. 2020. "Agriculture in Magna Graecia (Iron Age to Hellenistic Period)." In *A Companion to Ancient Agriculture*, edited by D. B. Hollander and T. Howe, 317–341. Medford, MA: Wiley-Blackwell.

Wardle, D. 2006. *Cicero on Divination: De Divinatione, Book 1, Translated with Introduction and Historical Commentary.* Oxford: Oxford University Press.

West, M. L. 1985. *The Hesiodic Catalogue of Women: Its Nature, Structure, and Origins.* Oxford: Oxford University Press.

Westermark, U., and G. K. Jenkins. 1980. *The Coinage of Kamarina.* London: Royal Numismatic Society.

Westlake, H. D. 1958. "Hermocrates the Syracusan." *BRL* 41: 239–268.

Westlake, H. D. 1960. "Athenian Aims in Sicily, 427–424 B.C." *Historia* 9: 385–402.

White, D. 1964. "Demeter's Sicilian Cult as a Political Instrument." *GRBS* 5: 261–279.

Whitehead, D. 1986. *The Demes of Attica, 508/7–ca. 250 B.C.: A Political and Social Study*. Princeton, NJ: Princeton University Press.

Whittaker, C. R. 1974. "The Western Phoenicians: Colonisation and Assimilation." *PCPhS* 20: 58–79.

Wijma, S. M. 2014. *Embracing the Immigrant: The Participation of Metics in Athenian Polis Religion (5th–4th Century BC)*. Stuttgart: F. Steiner.

Will, E. 1956. *Doriens et Ioniens: Essai sur la valeur du critère ethnique appliqué à l'étude de l'histoire et de la civilisation grecques*. Paris: Belles-Lettres.

Willi, A. 2008. *Sikelismos: Sprache, Literatur und Gesellschaft im griechischen Sizilien (8.–5. Jh. v. Chr.)*. Basel: Schwabe.

Willi, A. 2012. "'We Speak Peloponnesian': Tradition and Linguistic Identity in Post-Classical Sicilian Literature." In Tribulato 2012, 265–288.

Wilson, J. 1982. "What Does Thucydides Claim for His Speeches?" *Phoenix* 26: 95–103.

Wilson, R. J. A. 2013. "Hellenistic Sicily, c. 270–100 BC." In *The Hellenistic West: Rethinking the Ancient Mediterranean*, edited by J. R. W. Prag and J. C. Quinn, 79–119. Cambridge: Cambridge University Press.

Winkler, J. J. 1990. *The Constraints of Desire: The Anthropology of Sex and Gender in Ancient Greece*. New York: Routledge.

Wohl, V. 2015. *Euripides and the Politics of Form*. Princeton, NJ: Princeton University Press.

Wonder, J. W. 2002. "What Happened to the Greeks in Lucanian-Occupied Paestum? Multiculturalism in Southern Italy." *Phoenix* 56: 40–55.

Wonder, J. W. 2012. "The Italiote League: South Italian Alliances of the Fifth and Fourth Centuries BC." *ClAnt* 31: 128–151.

Wonder, J. W. 2018. "The Lucanians." In Farney and Bradley 2018, 369–384.

Woodman, A. J. 1988. *Rhetoric in Classical Historiography*. Portland, OR: Areopagitica.

Wuilleumier, P. 1939. *Tarente des origines à la conquête romaine*. Paris: De Boccard.

Xanthakis-Karamanos, G. 1980. *Studies in Fourth-Century Tragedy*. Athens: Akademia Athenon.

Xella, P. 1969. "Sull'introduzione del culto di Demetra e Kore a Cartagine." *SMSR* 40: 215–228.

Yates, D. C. 2019. *States of Memory: The Polis, Panhellenism, and the Persian War*. Oxford: Oxford University Press.

Yntema, D. 2000. "Mental Landscapes of Colonization: The Ancient Written Sources and the Archaeology of Early Colonial Greek Southeastern Italy." *BABesch* 75: 1–49.

Yntema, D. 2011. "Archaeology and the *Origo* Myths of the Greek *Apoikiai*." *Ancient West and East* 10: 243–266.

Yntema, D. 2013. *The Archaeology of South-East Italy in the First Millennium BC: Greek and Native Societies of Apulia and Lucania between the 10th and the 1st Century BC.* Amsterdam: Amsterdam University Press.

Zacharia, K. 2001. "'The Rock of the Nightingale': Kinship Diplomacy and Sophocles' *Tereus*." In *Homer, Tragedy and Beyond*, edited by F. Budelmann and P. Michelakis, 91–112. London: Society for the Promotion of Hellenic Studies.

Zacharia, K. 2003a. *Converging Truths: Euripides' Ion and the Athenian Quest for Self-Definition.* Leiden: Brill.

Zacharia, K. 2003b. "Sophocles and the West: The Evidence of the Fragments." In *Shards from Kolonos: Studies in Sophoclean Fragments*, edited by A. H. Sommerstein, 57–76. Bari: Levante.

Zacharia, K., ed. 2008a. *Hellenisms: Culture, Identity and Ethnicity from Antiquity to Modernity.* Aldershot, UK: Ashgate.

Zacharia, K. 2008b. "Herodotus' Four Markers of Greek Identity." In Zacharia 2008a, 21–36.

Zahrnt, M. 1993. "Die Schlacht bei Himera und die sizilische Historiographie." *Chiron* 23: 353–390.

Zahrnt, M. 2006. "Sicily and Southern Italy in Thucydides." In *Brill's Companion to Thucydides*, edited by A. Rengakos and A. Tsamakis, 629–655. Leiden: Brill.

Zambon, E. 2008. *Tradition and Innovation: Sicily between Hellenism and Rome.* Stuttgart: F. Steiner.

Zancani Montuoro, P., and U. Zanotti-Bianco. 1937. "Heraion alla Foce del Sele: Relazione preliminare." *NSA* 13: 206–354.

Zanker, G. 1987. *Realism in Alexandrian Poetry: A Literature and Its Audience.* London: Croom Helm.

Index